D0984678

Commodity Market Money Management

COMMODITY MARKET MONEY MANAGEMENT

F. GEHM
F. Gehm & Associates
Money Management Consultants
Palo Alto and Sunnyvale, California

A Ronald Press Publication
JOHN WILEY & SONS
New York · Chichester · Brisbane · Toronto · Singapore

This publication is designed to provide accurate and authoritative information in regard to the subject matter covered. It is sold with the understanding that the publisher is not engaged in rendering legal, accounting, or other professional service. If legal advice or other expert assistance is required, the services of a competent professional person should be sought. *From a Declaration of Principles jointly adopted by a Committee of the American Bar Association and a Committee of Publishers.*

Library of Congress Cataloging in Publication Data:

Gehm, F. (Fred S.)
Commodity market money management.

"A Ronald Press publication."
Includes index.
1. Commodity exchanges. I. Title. II. Title: Money management.

HG6046.G44 1982 332.64'4 82-10844
ISBN 0-471-09908-2

Printed in the United States of America
10 9 8 7 6 5 4 3

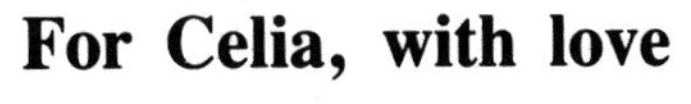

For Celia, with love

The race is not to the swift, nor the battle to the strong, nor bread to the wise, nor riches to the intelligent, nor favor to the men of skill; but time and chance happen to them all.

Ecclesiastes 9:11

The race is not always to the swift, nor the battle to the strong—but that's the way to bet.

Damon Runyon

Foreword

Throughout this comprehensive work, the author continually stresses how important it is that the commodity trader adopt a professional attitude and be prepared to incorporate modern management techniques into his trading strategy. While utilizing theory, the text downplays its mathematical derivation and concentrates on straightforward "how-to" rules and formulas which are easily understood and have a practical payoff.

It should be pointed out that this book is not another of the many which outline various "trading systems" guaranteed to "beat the market." The author assumes that the reader has already developed or is using some adequate forecasting technique or trading system. This book supplements such techniques by providing an examination of the underlying concepts of money management procedures and risk/reward analysis. While the mathematics involved in these concepts can be formidable, the author has taken great pains to present abbreviated, simple-to-use, and "not too dirty" shortcut techniques which are easily understood yet readily applicable to the commodity markets. In addition, the many charts and diagrams interspersed throughout the book provide an extra dimension of explanation. For those readers who would prefer to more fully explore and understand the underlying mathematical concepts for certain topics, an extensive mathematical primer and appropriate statistical tables have conveniently been provided at the back of the book. Yet, make no mistake. The emphasis of this book is on the practical application of money management and risk/reward techniques, not on their mathematical derivation.

While a list of all topics covered in the book would be impractical at this point, some of the more important include: efficient market hypothesis, avoidable and unavoidable risk; risk management by diversification, dominance, and the efficient frontier; mathematical portfolio theory; Sharpe ratio and portfolio construction; elementary probability and statistical theory; and the vital importance of planning in the development of a consistent trading strategy.

I personally was particularly interested in the sections of portfolio theory and construction. The author not only conveys the significance of current developments in mathematical portfolio research, but has also successfully translated these theoretical results into practical rules for effective application to today's commodity markets. And these techniques can be readily applied by the individual trader who has no access to extensive computer capability.

At one point in this book, the author distinguishes between a "wise" decision and a "correct" one. A "wise" decision is one that effectively uses the available data. The wise decision may or may not be the "correct" one, that is, the decision which in retrospect would have been the best. It is my contention that the reader's decision to invest in Fred Gehm's book is not only "wise" but undoubtedly will turn out to be "correct" as well. No commodity trader, if he or she is to be successful, can afford to ignore the results of current research into risk management and portfolio theory. With this book Fred Gehm has provided not only a clear description of current research in these areas, but also a detailed prescription for its effective implementation in today's commodity markets. This book constitutes a valuable and timely addition to the reference library of all commodity traders, novice as well as experienced.

DENNIS D. DUNN
President
Dunn and Hargitt, Inc.

Lafayette, Indiana
October 1982

Preface

I wrote this book to help commodity traders make better, more professional, more profitable trading decisions. This is a "how to" book.

This is not an introductory textbook. I have assumed that the reader has some familiarity with trading, that he or she is willing to dedicate time and money to trading, and that he or she is seriously interested in winning. The amount of money the reader is willing to dedicate to trading is not overly important, the amount of time and energy is.

In this book I have presented the money management approach to commodity trading. As the words are usually used, "money management" has little real meaning. Although many traders claim to practice money management, virtually none of them does; at least none or virtually none uses any of the available techniques. This is unfortunate. Over the past 20 years or so, traders, economists, statisticians, mathematicians, and financial theorists have created many useful and practical techniques for managing trading funds. Unfortunately, virtually all of this material is buried in technical journals that few, if any, traders will ever read. My intention is to present traders with the most practical and useful of this material, including techniques such as statistics, probability theory, marginal analysis, and portfolio theory.

These techniques can definitely improve a trader's performance. A detailed written trading plan, for example, can definitely reduce a trader's uncertainty. If the trader can forecast the market with some accuracy, diversification can definitely increase a trader's return, reduce his or her risk, or both. Efficient cash management can definitely improve any trader's return on investment.

This is not a matter of opinion: Money management techniques are more than common sense, they are tools and techniques that allow the trader to solve difficult and important problems in valid but sometimes unobvious ways.

There is no magic involved. Few traders use all of the available information, and fewer still use the available information correctly. Many trading decisions are therefore *necessarily* bad. In all cases, the trader who uses the techniques in this book will make decisions that are at least as profitable as those who do not. In most cases, the trader will make *much* better decisions. The rewards are real and obtainable.

The rewards are not easily obtained, however. The money management approach is a business approach, and that means work.

The money management approach is also a technical approach, that is, it involves the use of highly sophisticated and technical tools. It is as difficult to trade profitably without using these tools as it is to pour steel successfully without using metallurgy.

Some of the tools are conceptual, some are mathematical. The conceptual tools are the most difficult and important. Conceptual tools involve thinking about the market in new and different ways, asking new questions. Asking new questions is no assurance that the right questions will be asked, but there is no other place to start. Moreover, asking the right question is no assurance of getting the right answer, but then there is no "right" answer to a wrong question.

An understanding of the concepts in this book is critical; the mathematics, on the other hand, is merely useful. Clearly, the trader must understand the revenues and costs of trading; their difference, of course, is profit or loss. But the relationships between revenues and costs are not always obvious. Fortunately, both are represented by numbers, and the relationships can be clarified and manipulated mathematically.

Most of the mathematics in this book makes use of techniques that produce the best or nearly the best possible solution for a given problem, such as determining the proportion of trading capital that should be committed to the market at any given time. It is possible to guess, of course, but when a mathematical solution is available, guessing is invariably costly.

Fortunately, although the mathematics is sometimes tedious, it is not difficult. Moreover, there is a mathematical appendix that should put the techniques within the range of all or almost all readers. The reader need not know even high school algebra.

Unfortunately, even the use of managerial techniques such as marginal analysis and portfolio theory cannot guarantee market success. Nothing can. The most these techniques can do is increase a trader's probability of success, or increase the trader's average return. But these are advantages of no small importance.

Can money management techniques really be of use?

As Richard Epstein might say, "You can bet on it."

F. GEHM

Palo Alto, California
November 1982

Acknowledgments

A writer must give credit to those who influence him. But I will not relegate to text or footnote those who have helped me most; I would like to thank them here.

I would like to thank Celia Wolf, who typed and critiqued many versions of this book. Without Celia's help and support, this book would never have been written.

My thanks are also due to my mother, who not only did a great deal of typing, but made my life easier while I wrote.

The first person to impress on me the importance of statistical research was Dr. David Mirza. I would like to thank David for his help and advice, and for influencing my thinking about the market in many ways.

The theoretical and practical difficulties statistics present are considerable, and I would like to thank Dr. Jerry Funk and Dr. Norman Johnson for helping me with the problems involved.

I would like to thank Jim Alphier—one of the market's great minds! Had I not met Jim early in my career, this book might never have been written.

Finally, I would like to thank Paul Pekin, who taught me how to write.

F. G.

Contents

Commodity Market Money Management

Chapter One

Introduction: What Is Money Management?

If the articles and advertisements in the trade press are any indication, "money management" is currently a popular approach to trading commodities. Among the claims made for the money management approach is that it can guarantee, or almost guarantee, trading success. Are such claims valid?

To some extent, the money management approach is merely the attitude that commodity trading should be taken seriously, that is, professionally. Risks, for example, should only be taken when the potential reward justifies them. Trading, in other words, is a business venture, and the trader is a business manager or an entrepreneur.

Clearly, the money management approach is essential to successful trading. But just as clearly, the money management approach will *not* guarantee success. Both business managers and entrepreneurs fail on occasion.

One reason that the money management approach cannot guarantee success is that the approach is managerial rather than entrepreneurial. The money management approach focuses on those tasks where proper management will produce certain or nearly certain benefits. Unfortunately, entrepreneurial tasks cannot really be managed, they can only be accepted and acted upon; they demand not so much analysis as creativity; they demand not so much tools and techniques as ideas and action. Managerial tasks are important, but not critical; entrepreneurial tasks are critical.

The trader's only necessary entrepreneurial task is to produce trading ideas, that is, forecasts. Without forecasts, trading profits are impossible.

Indeed, without entrepreneurship profits are impossible.[1] Entrepreneurship, and therefore profits, depends both upon the imperfections of the market and upon innovation, that is, ideas. If innovation were impossible and competition were perfect, there would be no profits at all. There would be no profits because no rational individual would loan to, sell to, or work for another if they could earn more themselves. Competition would therefore quickly drive prices down to costs, including, of course, the costs of the owner's own money, goods, and work.

"Profits" would still be reported, of course. But the reported "profits" would not contain a single cent of real profit; rather, the reported profits would just equal the implicit interests, rents, and wages.

The fact that competition is imperfect does not mean that profits are guaranteed, only that they are possible. Profits are made by innovation, that is, by ideas. But innovation is pointless if profits are impossible.

---

[1] This is simply a restatement of the work of Joseph A. Schumpeter, *The Theory of Economic Development*, Oxford University Press, New York, 1961.

The fact that competition is imperfect insures that profits will not be immediately competed away, that is, that profits will last some period of time. Nevertheless, profits are remarkably ephemeral. Profits are only possible as long as the ideas upon which they are based are uncommon. For that reason profits dissipate as the ideas upon which they are based disperse (see Exhibit 1).

The available evidence suggests that the commodity market is remarkably efficient in disseminating information. In other words, profits are competed away remarkably quickly. For that reason, if a trader knows a way of beating the market, he would be well advised to keep it to himself.

In another sense, the money management approach is a group of tools and techniques for managing the rewards and costs of trading. These techniques allow the trader to make decisions at least as good, and in many cases much better, than he or she could otherwise. Oddly enough, these tools are hardly used at all, even among those who advocate the money management approach.

The reasons for this involve both form and content. Commodity trading can generally be understood better in terms of form than content. Commodity trading forms, or rather styles, change as frequently and as frantically as fashion does, and for much the same reasons. Adopting a money management attitude is easy and fashionable, and many traders have done so for no other reason than that.

Money management techniques, on the other hand, are not easy. As a matter of fact, until recently many money management techniques have been hideously difficult. For example, calculating the optimum diversified portfolio has traditionally involved quadratic programming with constraints. If the trader wished to construct a portfolio of ten commodities, for example, he would have to solve one or more equations involving one hundred or more terms. Few traders would be willing to bother, even if they understood the techniques. Moreover, few traders are likely to know about such techniques, as they have been published only in academic journals. Naturally, only academicians read about them there,

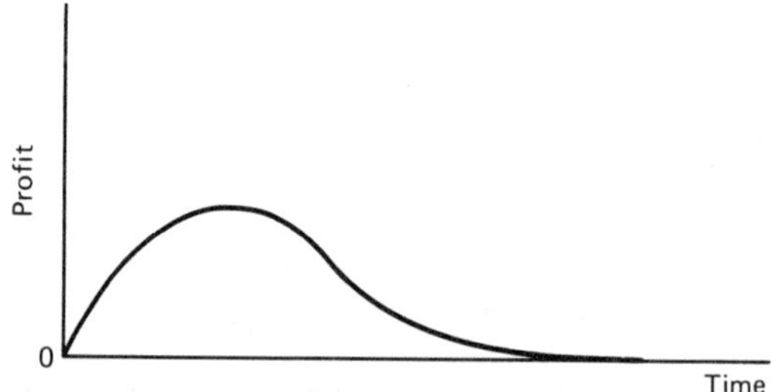

Exhibit 1. All profits are based on uncommon ideas. As time passes the ideas disperse, competition increases, and profits diminish.

which is perhaps appropriate, as such techniques are much too difficult to be useful.

This book was not written for academicians–it was written for speculators. It was my intention to provide commodity traders with practical tools, tools that can improve their trading performance. Admittedly, some of the tools provided are difficult to use, but then some of the problems facing the commodity trader are difficult to solve. Worse, almost any error the trader makes will be costly.

In many cases, there are more sophisticated techniques available than those I have presented here. In all cases, however, these more sophisticated techniques are more difficult to use, in most cases *much* more difficult to use. Academicians often stress the theoretical elegance and power of their techniques. Elegance is not important in the "real world," on the other hand, power, which, roughly, is the effectiveness or the usefulness of a technique, is. However, I believe that practical power is an even more important concept. Practical power is the theoretical power of a technique times the probability of its being used.

Naturally, I selected techniques from which I felt relatively certain speculators could benefit. It is for this reason that there are no discussions of forecasting techniques in this book. Whereas I can guarantee that a trader who follows a trading plan will be at least as well off as one who does not, I cannot guarantee that any trading methods will ever be profitable. Tomorrow is forever unknown.

This book presupposes that the reader has some forecasting ability. For some readers, this will be a reasonable assumption, for others not. However, this assumption need not remain an assumption. The discussion in Chapter 4 and the techniques in Chapter 5 can help the reader decide which group he is in. Chapter 4 discusses the efficient market hypothesis. If this hypothesis is true, as is believed by many academic economists, the market is unbeatable and trading is pointless. Chapter 5 discusses statistical techniques. These techniques allow the trader to judge how likely it is that he or she can really beat the market. If the reader decides to abandon trading after reading these chapters, his money will have been well spent.

However, Chapters 4 and 5 may be difficult to understand if the trader has not read the preceding chapters. Chapter 2 discusses the inevitability of risk. Chapter 3 discusses the nature of the risks the trader must manage and the means by which this can be done. Chapter 4 and 5 discuss the risk that the trader may not be able to forecast the market. If the trader can forecast the market, however, the forecasts must be turned into trades. Chapter 6 discusses the tradeoffs and choices the trader must make to do so. The actual process of transforming a forecast into a trade is discussed in Chapter 7. Finally, in Chapter 11, a particular method of doing so is discussed.

The last few chapters can be read in any order. Chapter 8 discusses diversification, a risk reduction technique. Chapter 9 discusses how to minimize a particular type of risk, the risk of very large losses. Finally, Chapter 10 discusses a method of increasing the trader's return at little or no risk by prudently investing the trader's cash reserves.

This book presupposes that the reader is familiar with the commodity market. Ideally, the reader should have traded for a year or more. Failing that, the reader should put this book down and read an introductory book or two on commodity trading.[2]

This book cannot be read like a novel. (Only novels can be.) If this book is to be of any use to the reader, he must understand the techniques and adapt them to his own use. Clearly, the experienced trader has an advantage here that the inexperienced trader can only overcome by thinking long and hard about the problems involved.

On the other hand, the inexperienced trader may have an advantage over the experienced trader. If my experiences are typical, many experienced traders are not open to new ideas.[3] Such traders are likely to reject this book as being too theoretical, too academic, and too mathematical.

Although I have tried to minimize the amount of mathematics in this book, I simply cannot eliminate it. Profit is a numbers game, and there is no way to avoid mathematics. Hopefully the mathematical appendix will make this book accessible even to readers with the most modest mathematical skills.

On the other hand, many businessmen find academic work irrelevant. Academicians often seem unaware of what is happening in the real world. For example, many academicians do not seem to realize that *every* business decision must be cost-justified. Needless to say, I do not think these criticisms can be applied fairly to my book.

Many businessmen have the attitude that "no one ever made a dime from theory." To the extent that a theory is wrong or unapplied, this attitude is clearly correct. But nothing is as practical or as profitable as good theory.

Consider, as an example, Thales of Miletus (640?–546 BC). Thales was one of the first philosophers and, apparently, out of touch with the real world on occasion. For example, one night while he was gazing at the stars, he fell or walked into a pit. At other times, he was very much in touch with the real world. According to Aristotle (*Politics* 1259a):

---

[2] For a review of a number of introductory trading books, see Gehm, F., How to Get a Trader Started, *Commodities*, September 1981, pp. 44–46.

[3] I am, of course aware of the irony here.

> He was reproached for his poverty, which was supposed to show that philosophy is of no use. According to the story, he knew by his skill in the stars while it was yet winter that there would be a great harvest of olives in the coming year; so, having a little money, he gave deposits for the use of all the olive presses in Chios and Miletus, which he hired at a low price because no one bid against him. When the harvest time came, and many were wanted all at once and of a sudden, he let them at any rate which he pleased, and made a quantity of money. Thus he showed the world that philosophers can easily be rich if they like. . .

What was then philosophy would now be a great many things, including, no doubt, business administration. In a certain sense, philosophy is nothing more than thinking as hard as you can about something. Although I do not believe any amount of thinking can guarantee that a trader will make money, I do believe that those who trade without thinking are certain or almost certain to lose.

What follows is some of the best thinking of which I am capable. I hope it makes you money.

Unfortunately, I cannot assure you that it will. The techniques I have presented will insure that good decisions, even in some cases the best possible decisions, are made with the information and resources available. Unfortunately, the techniques presented here cannot insure profitable trading. Nothing can. The best possible decision may be not to trade.

Chapter Two

Risk-Free Trading Is Risky Stuff

Currently, a number of financial advisers are selling "conservative" and even "risk-free" commodity trading methods or advice. Are such things possible?

Risk-free trading is a very quick road to bankruptcy and suicide. It is not difficult to see why. If there were really no possibility of losing on a given trade, the proper procedure would be to borrow as much money as possible and invest it all in the next such trade. Only a half dozen trades should be sufficient for you to retire if you pyramid your winnings. But assume the odds of success are really a mere 0.9, where one indicates winning is certain and zero that it is impossible; then the chance of not losing at least one trade in six (and only one losing trade is necessary to send you to bankruptcy court rather than Bermuda) is $0.9^6 = 0.53$, and if the odds of success are 0.6 on a given trade, the odds of a six-trade profitable run are $0.6^6 = 0.05$.

So long as the future cannot be known with complete certainty, there can be no such thing as risk-free trading. What is marketed as risk-free trading is simply trading with the risk understated or ignored. For example, one trading method recently advertised allegedly will enable you ". . .to trade on the commodity market without fear of loss of your working capital. . . ." In fact it will do no such thing. What the author is selling is the same three-zone system that Pugh sold three decades ago. With this system, you identify three zones on the basis of the past several years' price action, and buy when the price is in the lowest of the three zones. The author assumes that the price cannot go lower than the lowest zone, which is nonsense unless the lowest limit is zero. The first bear market will wipe out anyone using this method. Worse, the price doesn't even have to drop below the bottom of the lowest zone for you to lose; all that is necessary is that the price drop below your purchase point and stay there.

A better example is that of the Mexican peso fiasco. Buying distant peso contracts and "riding them in" was the short and riskless path to wealth. One adviser even put his clients' short-term funds into peso contracts. But there is no such thing as a free lunch. The risk-free profits were in fact insurance premiums that in many sad cases were insufficient to cover the losses when the Mexican government devalued the peso.

But while risk-free trading is not possible, conservative trading is not only possible, in one sense it is necessary. In *Playboy's Investment Guide* (the best introductory book on investing and speculating I know of) Michael Laurence writes, "Too often we tend to think that millionaires are conservative because

---

This chapter was originally published in slightly different form: Gehm, F., Risky "Risk Free" Trading, *Commodities Magazine*, 250 South Wacker Drive, Chicago, IL 60606, April 1979, p. 70.

they are rich, without considering the equally plausible converse: that they are rich because they are conservative."[1]

"Conservative" here has no political connotation. It refers solely to risk management. Inadequate or nonexistent risk management is probably the reason that most traders lose their trading capital. It is necessary that most traders lose, of course, but it is not necessary for a trader to lose if he can forecast the market with some accuracy.

The primary tool of risk management is diversification over time and over investments. Consider an investment that has a 0.50 probability of gaining 0.50 in value and a 0.50 probability of losing the same over a year. Over a period of years, you would expect to lose about 0.13 a year on this investment. But if you diversified by buying a portfolio of two such investments that never moved up or down together, you would raise your return to zero. It is for this reason that a properly diversified commodity portfolio is both more profitable and less risky than trading a single contract at a time.

Obviously, diversification depends on investments moving independently of each other. In *this* sense commodity trading can be much more conservative than buying and holding blue chip stocks, for corn and copper, say, are much more likely to move independently than, for example, Chrysler and Kodak. In addition, as there is little dependency between stock price movements and commodity price movements, the effect on a stock portfolio of trading commodities would be to reduce the total risk.[2] If trading can be done profitably, all portfolios, especially the most conservative ones, might be profitably supplemented by trading commodities.

Diversification must be over income sources rather than just investments.[3,4] For most individuals, there is little relationship between business or salary income and trading profits, so commodity trading can reduce income fluctuations. But some individuals should not speculate and they are, oddly enough, just those individuals who are most inclined to—trading advisers, fund managers, brokers, and hedgers. No doubt, this is one reason for the huge turnover of advisers, managers, and brokers. Even the best advisers or managers can expect to have losing periods, and if their own portfolios are eroding at the same time that their

---

[1] Laurence, Michael, *Playboy's Investment Guide*, Playboy Press, 1971.

[2] Dusak, Katherine, Futures Trading & Investor Returns: An Investigation of Commodity Market Risk Premiums, *Journal of Political Economy*, November/December 1973.

[3] Miller, Edward M., Portfolio Selection in a Fluctuating Economy, *Financial Analysts Journal*, May/June 1978.

[4] Coxon, Terry, How Borrowing Can *Reduce* Your Risk, *Inflation Survival Letter*, November 30, 1977.

incentive fees or subscriptions are drying up, they can be financially ruined. Of course, they could have their own commodity portfolio traded by someone with a completely different approach than their own, but it would be safer to invest in stocks or real estate or, better yet, bonds. For brokers, the situation is similar to the extent their clients do not make their own decisions. Again, for similar reasons, hedgers should not speculate and hedge in the same or related commodities. However, there is no reason that a farmer, for example, cannot hedge corn and speculate in copper and deutsche marks.

There is a profound difference between investing in the stock market and trading in the commodity market. There is no need to forecast the stock market. According to a University of Chicago study, an individual can expect to make an average 9 percent a year in dividends and capital gains by buying and selling common stocks at random.[5] What studies of the commodity market exist show that the odds of any given trader making money in any given year is one in four. It is in this essential context that there can be no conservative commodity trading. It does not matter that you think your chance of success is considerably better—so do the others.

Profitable trading depends on building and validating a forecasting system, and that's a *lot* harder than most traders seem to realize. Almost no traders show an understanding of the formidable statistical (and in some cases accounting) barriers to validation.[6] This is not to say that commodity trading cannot be profitable. It can be gloriously profitable. But these profits, if any, are not so much a return on the investment of money as a return on the investment of brains, self-discipline, and work. The commodity trader is not an investor. The commodity trader is a speculator and businessman. The successful ones know it.

---

[5] Fisher, Lawrence, Outcomes for "Random" Investments in Common Stocks Listed on the New York Stock Exchange, *Journal of Business,* Volume XXXVII, June 1964.

[6] Gehm, F., "Crooks, Cranks and Honest Citizens: Buying a Technical Trading System is Harder Than It Seems" (unpublished).

Chapter Three

The Nature of Risk and Risk Management

If a trader indifferent to risk must choose among a group of investments or speculations, he (or she) obviously should choose the single investment or speculation that promises the highest return. On the other hand, if the investor is not indifferent to risk and if he must choose among investments and speculations with varying risks and returns, the best decision is much less obvious.

Theoretically, there is a "best" portfolio for each trader. The procedure, again theoretically, is to first locate all of the portfolios the trader might obtain.

Exhibit 2 is a chart of all the possible investment choices a trader might make. Each point on the chart represents a portfolio of investments and speculations with a different potential combination of risk and return. Each portfolio may contain many investments and speculations or only one.

Unfortunately, no investor or speculator can obtain every potential portfolio; for example, curve α-α' in Exhibit 2 represents all the portfolios obtainable by investor A. In other words, investor $\ddot{A}$ has no possibility of obtaining any portfolio to the left of α-α'.

Second, the best portfolios of those available are identified. The best portfolios, those that dominate the others, are clearly on line α-α'. In Exhibit 2, for example, portfolio $\ddot{Z}$ is dominated by portfolios $\ddot{W}$, $\ddot{X}$, and $\ddot{Y}$. Portfolio $\ddot{W}$ has the same return as $\ddot{Z}$ but lower risk, portfolio $\ddot{Y}$ has a higher return for the same risk, and portfolio $\ddot{X}$ has both a higher return and a lower risk. Portfolios $\ddot{W}$, $\ddot{X}$, and $\ddot{Y}$ are clearly better than $\ddot{Z}$. Furthermore, there are no available portfolios that dominate or are "better" than $\ddot{W}$, $\ddot{X}$, and $\ddot{Y}$. (An umlaut over a letter indicates that the letter represents an arbitrary value. Such values are *not* constant from example to example.)

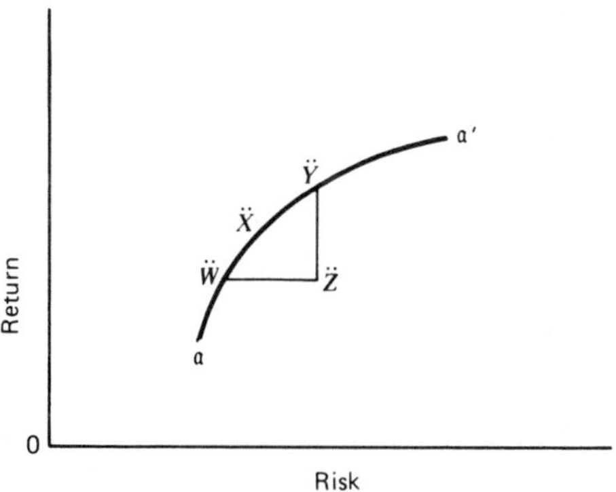

Exhibit 2. Of all conceivable combinations of risk and return, only those on or to the right of line α-α' are obtainable by investor $\ddot{A}$. If investor $\ddot{A}$ holds portfolio $\ddot{Z}$ he can acquire a portfolio with a higher return, a lower risk, or both.

Finally, from the best portfolios available, the trader selects the single portfolio whose combinations of return and risk he likes best. Though this can be an interesting and complex process, ultimately it is a question of taste.

In the real world, it is a waste of time to try to locate the best portfolio. For one thing, exchanging portfolios is costly. The better the portfolio the trader possesses, the more costly it will be for him to find a better one; at some point, a better portfolio won't be worth the cost of finding it. Second, risk has more than one dimension. Theoretically, risk and reward should not be represented on a plane but on a multidimensional hypercube (see Exhibit 3). The amount of information needed to locate the best portfolio in such a case greatly exceeds the amount of information a trader really possesses.

If the trader cannot find the best portfolio, he might be able to find a good one. A reasonable approach would be for the trader to upgrade his portfolio in whatever areas he can and hope the cumulative effect will be a good portfolio.

Unless upgrading in one area has a detrimental effect on other areas, the cumulative effect should at least be a better portfolio than the trader would have had otherwise. Sometimes, unfortunately, upgrading one area does detrimentally affect others; judgment is needed in using the techniques presented.

Over the past twenty years or so, traders, economists, statisticians, mathematicians, and financial theorists have created a number of techniques for selecting and managing portfolios. I have tried to present those techniques commodity traders might find most useful in this book. Some of the techniques may be difficult, but so is making money in the market. All of the techniques presented can be mastered by the average trader–if he takes the time to work through the examples.

Without doubt, the trader who learns and uses the techniques presented here

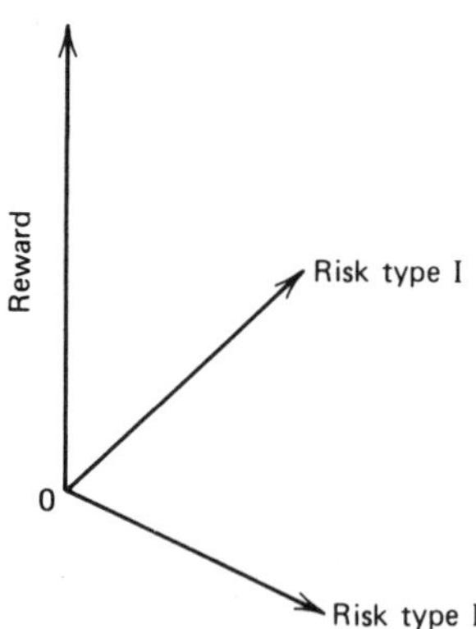

Exhibit 3. Risk has more than one dimension, perhaps an infinite number.

will find himself better off than the trader who does not. Unless, perchance, he is already using more sophisticated techniques than those presented here, the trader is, in effect, investor $\ddot{A}$ and he will, in effect acquire portfolio $\ddot{Z}$.

Clearly, if one portfolio dominates another, the investor can raise his return or lower his risk, or both, by switching. In other words, *use of the techniques presented here will enable the reader to increase his return without increasing his risk, reduce his risk without reducing his return, or even increase his return while reducing his risk.*

The commodity trader must cope with both avoidable and unavoidable risks. Risk is the primary cost of trading. As such, some risk is unavoidable. Money management techniques can only insure, or attempt to insure, that the trader accepts little or no avoidable risk, and accepts only the unavoidable risk that he wants to accept.

If a trader does not understand what risks he is accepting, he can scarcely make a reasonable judgment about them. Yet in my experience, few traders have any idea what kind of risks they are accepting when they accept a trade.

For example, in my opinion, the biggest risk a trader must accept is that he may not understand what is going on.[1] Each of us has a psychological map of the real world. All of our maps differ, each corresponding to the real world in some ways but not in others. Whenever our maps differ from the real world *and* we act as if they did not, we get into trouble. An old mathematical joke may make this clearer:

Teacher: "Let X equal the number of sheep in this problem. . ."
Student: "But, sir, what if X is not equal to the number of sheep in the problem?"

What if, indeed! Of course, one can tell how many sheep there are by looking

---

[1] Three additional points along similar lines must be made. First, the trader who uses the techniques in this book must also accept the risk that *I* do not understand what is going on. Naturally, I believe this risk is slight but, then, I would believe the same thing if I were deluded. Second, in a certain sense much of this book is almost certainly wrong or at least dated. Very little is known, or, at least, very little has been published about many important areas of money management. It would be remarkable if techniques were not eventually developed that were superior to many of those presented in this book. But the trader must manage his money now. He cannot wait while academicians debate. Third, to the best of my knowledge and belief, there are no errors of fact or logic in this book. Still, such errors are possible and the trader uses this book at his or her own risk. I would greatly appreciate being informed of any errors the reader finds. I can be reached through F. Gehm & Associates and through John Wiley & Sons.

at them, by *really* looking at them. But this is much harder than it seems; we tend to see our maps of the world rather than the world itself (see Exhibits 4, 7, 9, and 11).

Ironically, the less seriously a trader takes this problem, the more serious the problem is for him. Conversely, the more fully the trader understands the problem, the less risk of this type he will have to accept. In other words, to the extent that the trader's thinking is influenced by evidence rather than ideology, he will have to accept less of this type of risk.

One way of quantifying this type of risk might be to audit past analyses and forecasts. However, if such an audit is not to be an exercise in self-delusion, detailed records must be kept. Chapter 7 describes these records in detail.

Another unavoidable risk is the risk of loss the trader must accept every time he initiates a trade. To some extent, the size of this loss is under the trader's control. By manipulating stops, profit objectives, and other parts of the trading plan, the trader can make some values more likely and others less.

But notice that changing the potential loss will also change the potential profit, and vice versa. Because of this, many rules of thumb suggested in market folklore are irrelevant or, even worse, wrong. Chapter 6 provides more reliable rules, rules derived from probability theory and other management techniques.

Two other unavoidable risks are the risk of ruin and the risk of catastrophic loss. The risk of ruin is the risk that the trader will lose his trading capital, or a large enough portion of it that he will quit trading. By using money management techniques, this risk can be made arbitrarily small, but it can *never* be eliminated. The risk of catastrophic loss is the risk that the trader might lose much more than he planned. This loss, which is small to begin with, can be made even smaller by proper money management. Again, however, it cannot be eliminated. Traders who cannot cope with this fact should not trade.

Another type of risk that is unavoidable, at least to some extent, is the risk that the trader may not be able to forecast the market. This type of risk can also be minimized, though not eliminated, yet virtually no traders attempt to do so. Clearly, unless the trader can forecast the market correctly, on average, it makes no sense for him to trade. Yet virtually no traders attempt to validate their trading methods. In other words, virtually all traders are trading with methods that are untested, with methods that may or may not have forecasting power. Chapters 4 and 5 present a number of techniques for dealing with this type of risk.

Although much risk is unavoidable, some risk can definitely be avoided. Because some unavoidable risk can be minimized—which is to say, avoided—and some avoidable risks are too expensive to avoid, the distinction may seem arbitrary. It is not. The distinguishing criteria is this: A skillful market forecaster will

Exhibit 4. It is quite easy to connect the nine dots above with five continuous straight lines. Nine dots can also be connected with *four* continuous straight lines, but only by those who see the world as it is. The solution is displayed in Exhibit 7.

generally be rewarded for accepting unavoidable risk, but *there is no reward for accepting avoidable risk.*

Avoidable risk can be avoided by diversifying over investments and over time. For example, a prudent investor might invest in both common stocks and gold. As stock prices and gold prices rarely move up and down together, the investor should find his portfolio eroding less often and less severely than investors holding only one asset (see Exhibit 5).

Indeed, if the trader is holding a fully diversified portfolio, he is holding one of the best portfolios available. In other words, he is holding a portfolio somewhere on line $\alpha - \alpha'$ in Exhibit 2. This is not a matter of debate, but can be mathematically proven.

Besides diversifying over investments, the trader can also diversify over time.

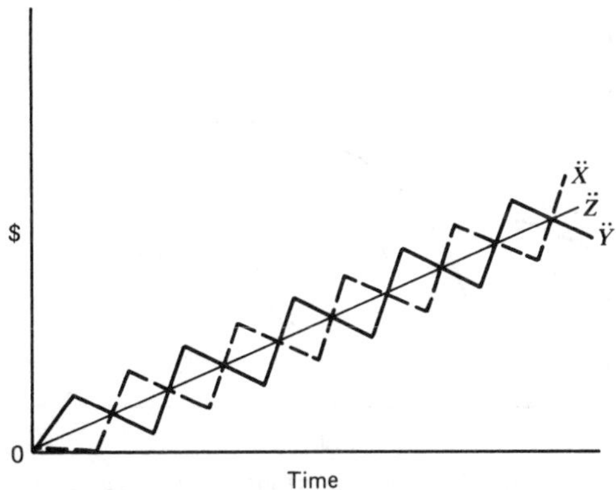

Exhibit 5. Portfolio $\ddot{Z}$, which is composed of independent investments $\ddot{X}$ and $\ddot{Y}$, should erode less often and less severely than either.

For example, as both stocks and gold will occasionally decline together, the investor should consider keeping some of his funds in cash or cash equivalents.

It can also be mathematically proven that keeping of some assets in cash equivalents can improve even the best portfolio. Consider, for example, Exhibit 6. Let us assume that investor $\ddot{A}$ has acquired portfolio $\ddot{X}$. Because $\ddot{X}$ is on line a-a', $\ddot{X}$ is obviously one of the best portfiolos $\ddot{A}$ can acquire. Let us also assume that given $\ddot{A}$'s taste in risk and reward, $\ddot{X}$ is the single best portfolio currently available. Nevertheless, investor $\ddot{A}$ can do still better.

Portfolio $\ddot{V}$ consists solely of cash equivalents such as T-bills and money market funds. These assets are generally considered to be risk-free. In fact, they are not, but U.S. government debt has so little risk that it is reasonable to use it as a surrogate.

Portfolio $\ddot{Z}$ is also one of the best portfolios available; it is, after all, on line a-a'. But because it has both higher risk and higher returns, it is less desirable for investor $\ddot{A}$ by itself. However, when combined with portfolio $\ddot{V}$, it may be more desirable than portfolio $\ddot{X}$. Line $\ddot{V}$–$\ddot{Z}$ represents the portfolios that could be created by combining portfolios $\ddot{V}$ and $\ddot{Z}$. Notice that portfolios $\ddot{W}$–$\ddot{Y}$ dominate portfolio $\ddot{X}$. Clearly, investing in cash equivalents can improve any portfolio.

While money management techniques are valuable, they are not infinitely so. A certain amount of time spent managing money is essential to successful trading. More time may be even more useful. At some point, however, it becomes useless or even harmful to indulge more.

Ultimately, each trader will have to decide how much effort he should devote

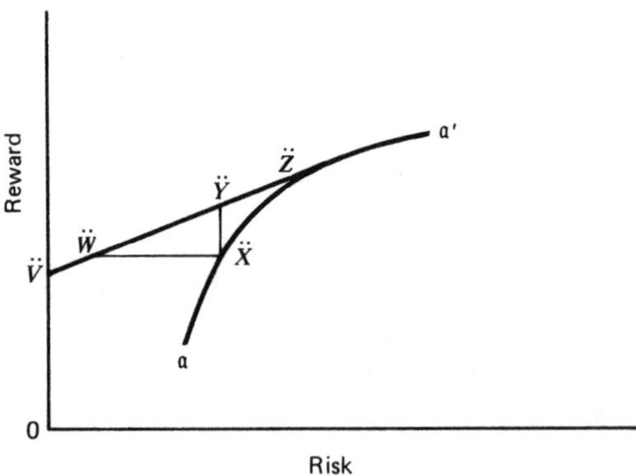

Exhibit 6. Portfolio $\ddot{X}$ is one of the best portfolios investor $\ddot{A}$ can acquire. Nevertheless, investor $\ddot{A}$ can do better by investing some assets in riskless investment $\ddot{V}$ and some assets in risky portfolio $\ddot{Z}$.

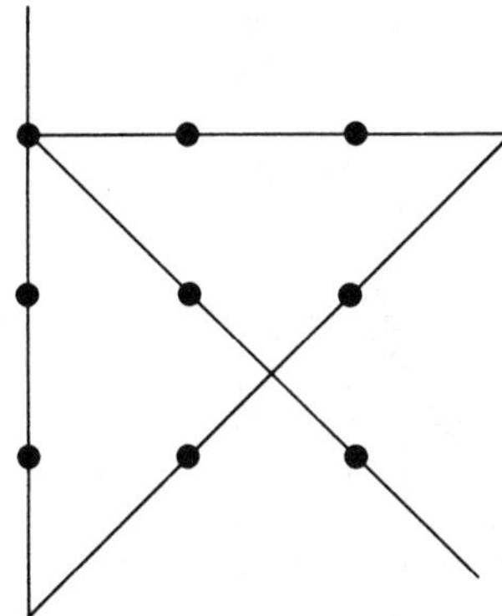

Exhibit 7. The nine dots above can be connected by four continuous straight lines only by extending several of the lines outside the area bounded by the dots. Most people fail to solve this problem because they assume that the lines cannot go beyond this area. This prohibition is not given in the problem itself, however. Solving problems demands seeing the problem itself, not an image or map of the problem. Understand? Then connect the dots above with *three* continuous straight lines. The solution is displayed in Exhibit 9.

to money management. But economic theory can at least insure that the trader is estimating, or guessing, if you will, the right quantities.

A critical distinction must be made between marginal and total analysis. Let's consider the law of diminishing returns in this context. The law of diminishing returns refers to the relationship between the marginal input of any one production factor, such as capital or labor, and the marginal output of the resulting good or service, such as profitable trades. The marginal input is the smallest extra input that can be added. The marginal output is the extra output that the marginal input generates. Often the marginal input or output will be infinitesimal, but here we will assume that it is some reasonably large amount.

Exhibit 8 shows what happens to the output when an input is marginally increased. Notice that while the total output continues to increase, the marginal output first increases, then remains constant, then decreases. The law of diminishing returns holds that although the marginal output may at first increase, eventually it must decrease.

The law of diminishing returns implies that production will be the most cost efficient when the proper mix of production factors is used. When more than two or three factors are involved, the proper mix can hardly be selected intuitively. In such cases, the only way to maximize the return from the resources employed is to analyze the data on a marginal basis.

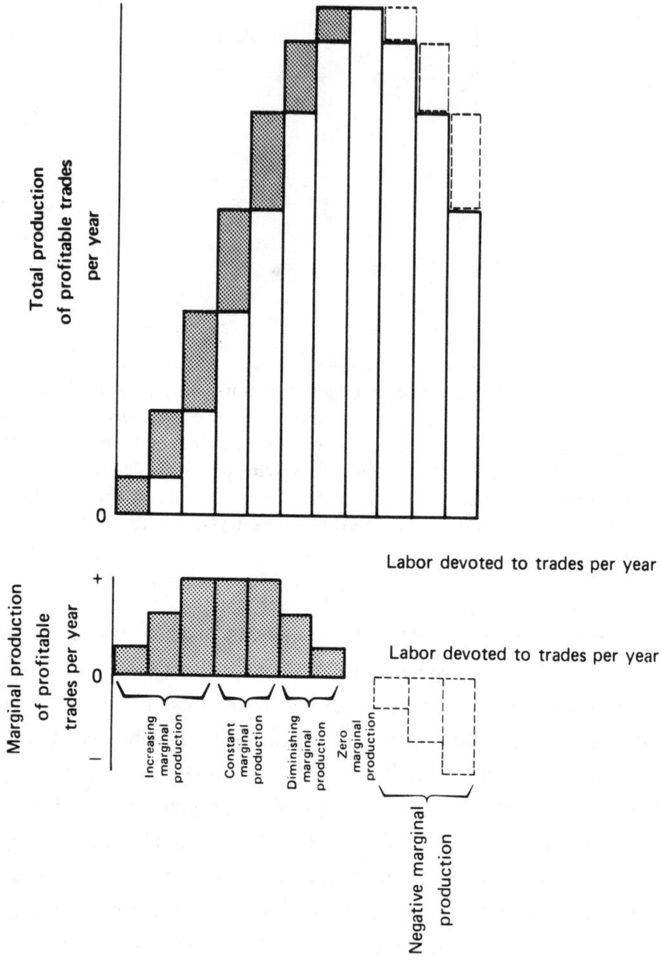

Exhibit 8. Although the marginal output may increase at first, eventually it must diminish.

Indeed, much economic analysis is the use of marginal analysis in an attempt to maximize or minimize some value. For example, the economic theory of the firm demonstrates that profits will be their greatest when the firm produces until its marginal cost equals its marginal revenue. The marginal revenue, of course, is the extra revenue produced by the last unit sold of good or service $\ddot{A}$. Marginal cost is the cost of producing that unit. All other things being equal, the marginal revenue of one unit will always be less than or equal to the marginal revenue of

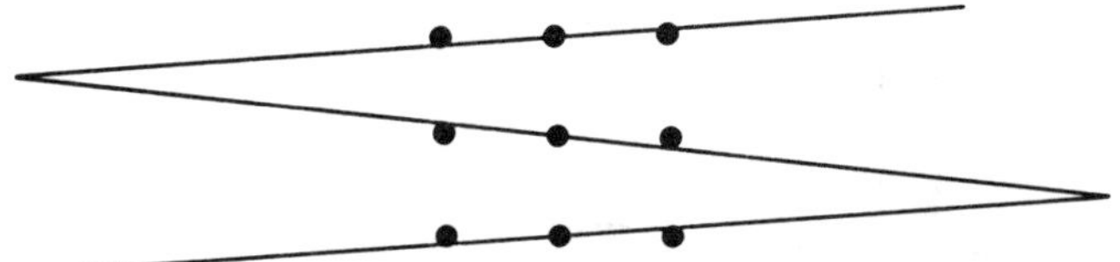

Exhibit 9. The nine dots above are not really dots at all; that is, they are not mathematical points, but have height and width, thus allowing three straight, continuous, intersecting lines to be drawn through them. Solving the problem demands realizing that our map of the world is not the world itself. Understand? Then connect the nine dots above with *one* continuous straight line. The solution is displayed in Exhibit 11.

the preceding unit. In the real world, in fact, the trader will amost certainly find marginal revenue continually dropping. On the other hand, marginal costs will continually rise, although they may drop somewhat in the beginning as economies of scale come into play.

As long as the marginal cost is less than the marginal revenue, the firm can still produce units profitably. On the other hand, when the marginal costs become larger than the marginal revenues, as they eventually will, the firm is producing some units at a loss. As Exhibit 10 demonstrates, the single place where earnings are greatest is where the marginal costs just equal the marginal revenue.

The implications of the analysis above should be fairly obvious. The trader should, ideally, continue to diversify and devote effort to money management until the marginal reward of the effort in the form of lowered risk and increased return (revenue is, perhaps, not the proper term) just equals the marginal cost of the effort.

Unfortunately, if the trader does not know his marginal costs and marginal rewards, which is generally the case, the technique above is difficult to use. A more usable technique would be to break the rewards and costs of money management into a number of factors and to estimate, separately, the marginal rewards and marginal costs of each factor. Estimates, of course, are unavoidable, but these at least are easier and more reasonable. The trader can then upgrade each factor in turn until the marginal costs equal the marginal reward.

Factors should not be upgraded at random, of course. Factors with high marginal reward/cost ratios should be upgraded before those with lower ratios. Specifically the factor with the highest marginal reward/cost ratio is located first and upgraded; then the factor with the next highest marginal reward/cost ratio, which may or may not be the same factor, is located and upgraded, until the trader reaches a factor with a marginal reward/cost ratio equal to or less than one. The trader then stops. Exhibit 12 may make this clearer.

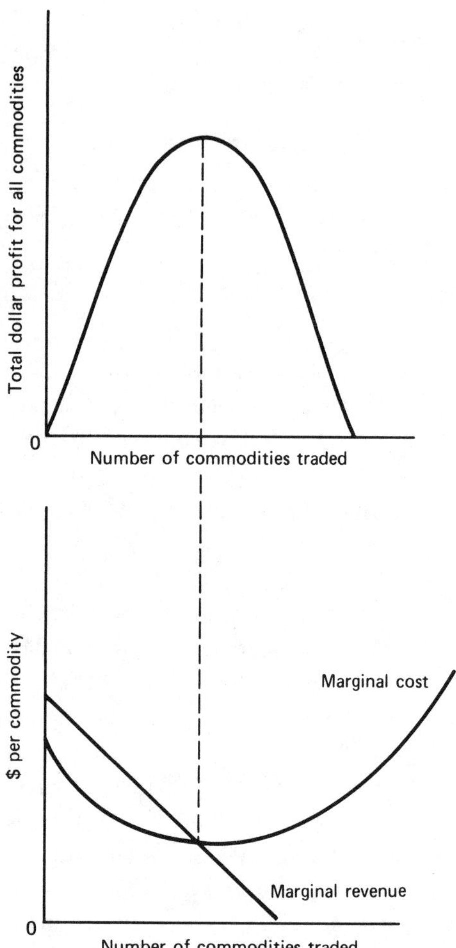

Exhibit 10. Profits will be their greatest when marginal costs just equal marginal benefits.

Under certain conditions, the above technique will allow the trader to make the best possible use of his resources. Unfortunately, a formal analysis consumes resources itself, and its costs may exceed its benefits. In this case, the trader may have to settle for a less formal or even an intuitive approach.

However, even if the trader guesses, he should guess in the right way. The above technique will generally be valid, and the trader can generally use it as a guide to decision making, but the technique also has limitations and the trader should be able to recognize them.

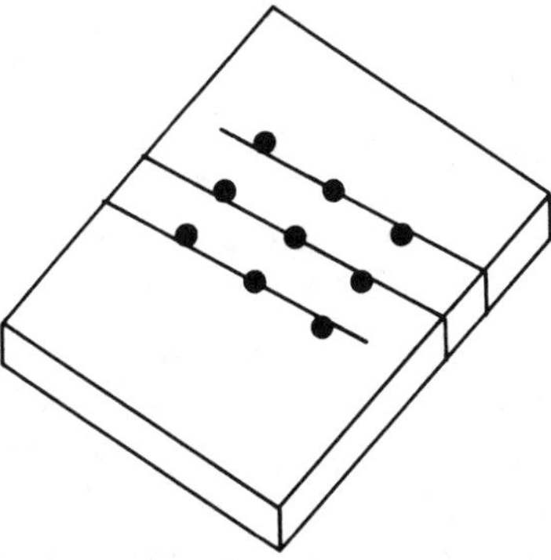

Exhibit 11. Nine dots can be connected with one straight line either by wrapping the line around the page the dots are drawn on or by drawing a very thick line. Understand? Then. . . .

The technique assumes that rewards and costs come in some reasonably sized unit, that they are not infinitely divisible. In the real world, this is often the case: Live cows, for example, cannot be divided. On the other hand, milk is almost infinitely divisible.

If the rewards and costs are infinitely divisible, an optimal solution demands calculus. Fortunately, an optimal solution is unnecessary. A good solution is to create units or packages of rewards and costs of some reasonable size, and use the above technique. Milk, for example, comes in quarts.

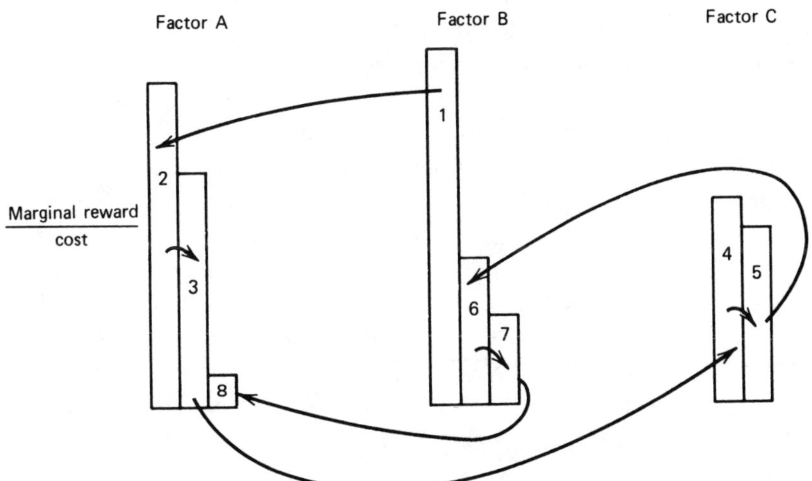

Exhibit 12. Factors should be upgraded in order of their marginal reward/cost ratios.

Another assumption this technique makes is that the rewards and costs of the various factors are independent. This will probably be true more often than not. When it is not true, however, an optimal solution cannot be found by examining the reward/cost ratios of the various factors individually.

If two or more factors are not useful independently, they must be either complementary or competing. For example, sugar and honey are competing commodities. The more sugar an individual consumes, the less honey he will consume and vice versa. On the other hand, for some people, peanuts and beer are complementary commodities. The more peanuts such a person consumes, the more beer he will want to consume and vice versa.

If two or more factors are conflicting or complementary, the optimal solution demands that the trader construct indifference maps. A good solution would be to analyze the complementary or conflicting factors in groups. The marginal utility (utility theory is explained in Chapter 9) of the "optimal" mix of conflicting or competing factors can be used as the reward. The cost of that mix can be used as the cost of the group.

Theoretically, selecting the optimum mix of several competing or conflicting factors also demands an indifference map. In practice a good, if not an optimal, mix can be selected by deciding what mixes are possible for a given amount of money and then deciding which of the mixes is the most desirable (see Exhibits 13 and 14). The benefit that would be derived from this mix of factors must then be estimated or guessed. Theoretically, the benefit estimated should be the marginal utility of the optional mix, but the value of the mix on a 1–100 scale, or simply the dollar benefit, might be estimated.

Another set of assumptions the above techniques make is that the factors do not vary greatly in cost and that the trader possesses enough resources to acquire all of them with marginal reward/cost ratios larger than or equal to one. If the trader cannot acquire all of the desirable factors and if the costs are reasonably equivalent, the trader should purchase those factors with the highest marginal reward/cost ratios; this will be the best possible set of factors he could acquire.

However, if prices do vary greatly, it is possible that another set of factors may be better. Unfortunately, if this is the case, that set may be difficult to locate. There are $N!$ possible rankings of N factor units. The ! in $N!$, which reads "N factorial," indicates that all of the integers from one to N are to be multiplied together. (For example, if $N = 5$, then $N! = 1 \cdot 2 \cdot 3 \cdot 4 \cdot 5 = 120$.) Clearly, if N is even moderately large, there will be too many possible rankings to consider all of them without a computer.

On the other hand, it is not necessary to consider every possible permutation to get a good ranking. First, ranking according to the marginal reward/cost ratio

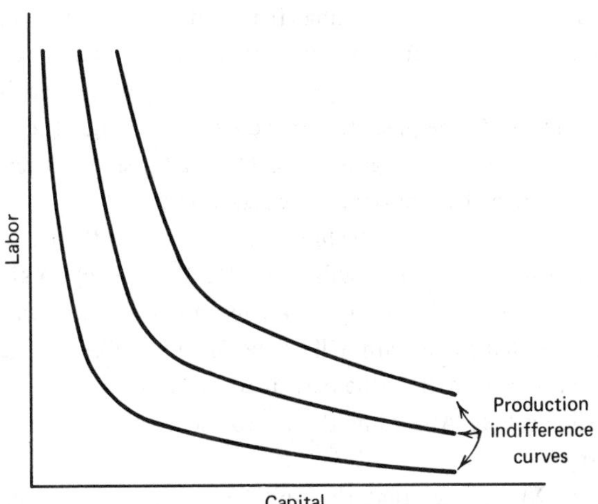

Exhibit 13. A production indifference map or an equal product map represents the ways various production factors can be combined. In this case the capital and labor that might be devoted to trading are represented. Each point on each curve represents a different combination of capital and labor. Moreover, each curve is constructed so that each point on the curve represents a combination of capital and labor that will produce the same return on investment.

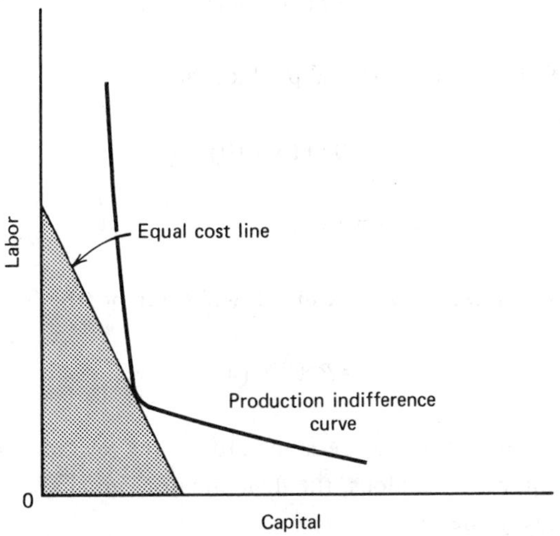

Exhibit 14. The shaded area represents all possible combinations of labor and capital that a particular trader can afford. Economic theory shows that the optimal combination of labor and capital is at the point where the highest indifference curve just touches the shaded area. Actually, almost the same thing can be accomplished by just looking for the most desirable point on the shaded area.

may still produce the optimal ranking. If not, it will probably produce a good ranking. Second, if the ranking is not optimal, the trader may be able to tell which ranking is optimal by looking and considering where the factors with the largest costs might better be placed. If this does not produce the optimal ranking it will, at least, produce a very good one. The trader should then acquire those factor units with the highest rankings (see Exhibit 15).

A final assumption the above techniques make is that the trader really knows what reward a given factor unit will produce. More likely, a given factor unit might produce any of several rewards. One method of dealing with this problem is simply to assume that the reward will be the one most likely. A second method, and the one that is theoretically the best, is to use a probability-weighted average of all the possible values. A third method is to use a relatively simple probability-weighted average.

This average (λ) assumes that the unit factor can only produce one of two possible results, a minimum reward ($\mathfrak{m}$) and the most likely reward ($\mathfrak{M}$). Also needed is the probability of the unit factor producing the most likely reward (P). A probability is a number from zero to one inclusive, where zero indicates that there is no probability of success and one indicates that success is certain. The formula, then, is:

$$\lambda = P(\mathfrak{M} - \mathfrak{m}) + \mathfrak{m}$$

For example, if $\mathfrak{M} = 15, \mathfrak{m} = 10$, and $p = 0.6$, then:

$$\lambda = 0.6(15 - 10) + 10$$

$$= 13$$

If the minimum reward is zero, which it will often be, the formula reduces to:

$$\lambda = P\,\mathfrak{M} \qquad (\mathfrak{m} = 0)$$

The λ values can be used as the numerator in the reward/cost ratio. Whereas the numerator may be nebulous, the denominator can almost always be easily determined or easily guessed.

These techniques may seem difficult. Indeed, for many traders they will be difficult, but they are well worth any effort spent to master them. The rule of working until the marginal costs equal the marginal reward is a law of logic itself, not just a law of economics. The trader, therefore, should find the above tech-

Marginal factors	Benefits	Costs	Benefits/costs
A	125	100	1.25
B	320	200	1.60
C	525	300	1.75
D	800	400	2.00
E	750	500	1.50
F	780	600	1.30

The marginal factors above are rearranged in order of benefits/costs below.

Marginal factors	Benefits/costs	Benefits	Cumulative benefits	Costs	Cumulative costs
D	2.00	800	800	400	400
C	1.75	525	1325	300	700
B	1.60	320	1645	200	900
E	1.50	750	2395	500	1400
F	1.30	780	3175	600	2000
A	1.25	125	3300	100	2100

Exhibit 15. Ranking marginal factors by benefit/cost ratios and acquiring the marginal factors with the highest ratios first will produce the best or almost the best results possible. When there is a better ranking, it can often be found by inspecting the ranked data.

niques and tools not only useful in maximizing the value of his portfolio of factors, but useful in many situations outside of trading.

The portfolio of factors a trader might manipulate are a function of the trader's managerial sophistication, his forecasting style, and his trading funds. Helping to develop managerial sophistication is one of the functions of this book. Changing the reader's forecasting style is not.

It is emphatically not one of the functions of this book to encourage or discourage trading, nor to encourage the trader to commit more or less funds to the market. However, the trader should know that both his return on investment and his optimal strategy will depend on his trading capital.

A popular managerial tool for analyzing problems of scale is the break-even chart. Traditionally, the vertical axis measures the dollar profits or losses. However, profits and losses must be risk adjusted if the technique is to be useful. One technique is to convert dollars into certainty equivalents, another is to use the geometric rather than the arithmetic mean of returns on investment. Which technique is used is probably not important. Both techniques are explained later (Chapter 9 and Appendix 5, respectively), but it is not important that the trader understand them at this point.

Traditionally, the horizontal axis represents the quantity of some good or service, produced and sold over some period of time. A more reasonable measure for the commodity trader is the amount of money dedicated to trading. As explained later in the book (see Chapter 6), profitable trading is more dependent on profitable trades than on frequent trades. However, the number of profitable trades that can be accepted is a function of the amount of trading capital available.

Break-even analysis generally divides costs into two types: fixed and variable. Fixed costs are those that do not vary with the amount of trading, the cost of a chart service would be an example. In turn, variable costs are those that do depend on the amount of trading, commissions would be an example.

Clearly, if trading is profitable, it is because trading revenues are larger than trading costs. If revenues and costs are linear functions of the amount of funds dedicated to trading, then the amount that must be dedicated to trading can easily be calculated as follows:

$$\mathrm{BK} = \mathrm{FC}/(\mathrm{TR} - \mathrm{VC})$$

where

BK = breakeven point

FC = fixed costs

TR = total revenue

VC = variable costs

(When several letters constitute one symbol, the letters are placed closely together and printed in roman type.)

For example, if, over the next year, the trader's fixed costs are \$750, and he expects to gross 0.3 on his dedicated capital, but to pay out about 0.1 in commissions and execution costs, then:

$$\mathrm{BK} = \$750/(0.3 - 0.1)$$

$$= \$3750$$

In other words, if the trader cannot afford to dedicate at least $3750 to trading, he should not trade.

The break-even chart (see Exhibit 16) illustrates this relationship. Notice that the traditional break-even chart implies that the more money that is dedicated to trading, the more profitable trading will be. Unfortunately, this is simply not true.

Consider costs, for example. Costs rarely increase in the simple fashion that the above analysis assumes. In fact, some trading costs will increase and others will decrease with the amount of trading.

Technically, trading involves economies of scale when costs decrease as trading is done on a larger basis; for example, when large funds are dedicated to trading, it may be cost effective to employ extremely sophisticated cash management techniques and to employ an accountant to handle the paperwork. The proportional costs of cash management and accounting will be smaller for the large trader than the small trader because the large trader will be able to afford specialists that the small trader cannot.

On the other hand, as more funds are dedicated to trading it will become increasingly difficult to coordinate activities and to react to changing conditions. These are diseconomies of scale.

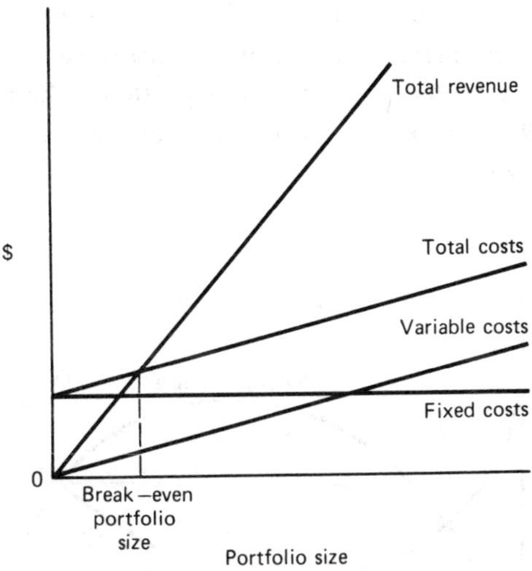

Exhibit 16. Traditional break-even analysis implies that trading is pointless if the amount dedicated to trading is too small and that profits will grow without limit as trading funds grow. The latter conclusion is wrong.

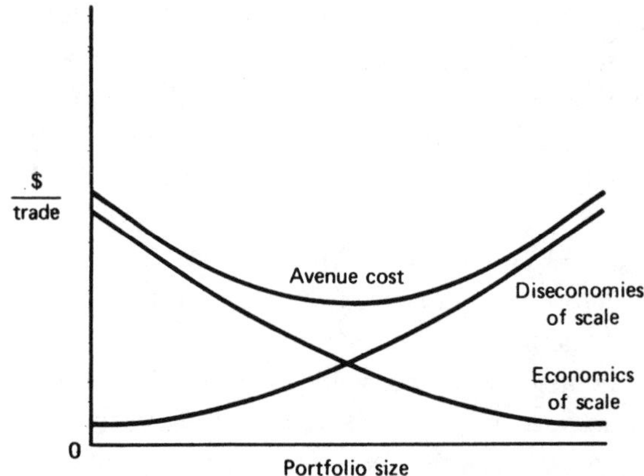

Exhibit 17. Average cost is the sum of both economies and diseconomies of scale.

The result is that the average cost curve first declines and then rises (see Exhibit 17). The curve declines because at first the economics involved more than offset the diseconomies; thus the average cost curve, which is the net result of both, declines. Eventually, however, the diseconomies offset the economies and the curve turns up.

Trading revenue for similar reasons will first rise and then fall as the amount of money dedicated to trading increases. It will first rise as money management techniques allow the trader to locate better portfolios. Eventually, however, trading revenue will fall as execution costs consume increasing portions of the profit (see Exhibit 18).

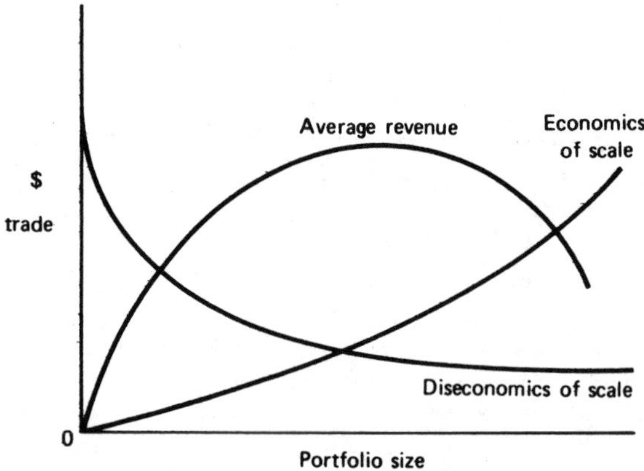

Exhibit 18. Average revenue is the result of both economies and diseconomies of scale.

The net effect of this analysis can be seen in Exhibit 19. If not enough money is dedicated to trading, trading will not be successful. On the other hand, trading will not succeed if too much money is dedicated to it, either.

One implication of the above analysis is that there is, theoretically, an optimum amount that should be dedicated to trading. However, that amount may be larger than the trader can afford, either financially or psychologically. In practice, therefore, the amount that is dedicated to trading should be a function of the trader's capital and his taste for risk.

Still, the trader should realize, other things being equal, that economic theory suggests that the return from an investment will be a function of the investment's size (see Exhibit 20).

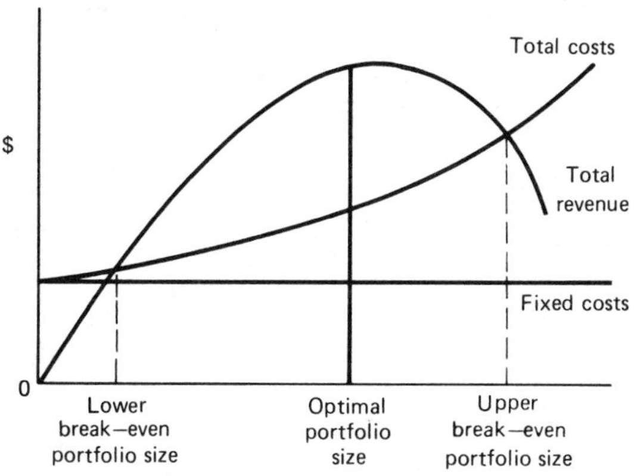

Exhibit 19. Trading is pointless if the portfolio is either too large or too small.

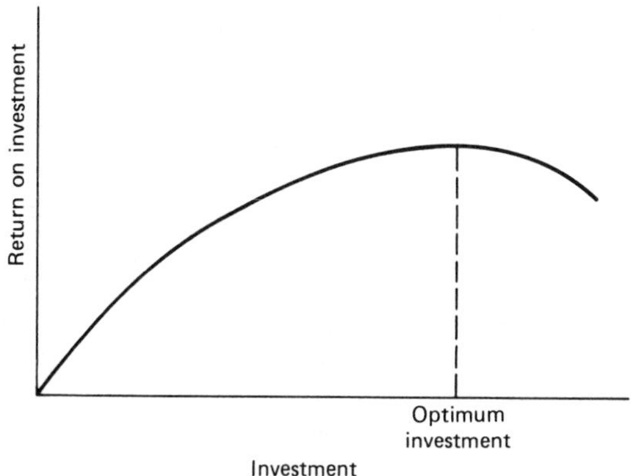

Exhibit 20. Economic theory suggests that there is a "right" portfolio size.

Economic theory also assumes, however, that among the things "being equal" are brains, discipline, and the capacity for hard work. And there's not the slightest evidence that that is true.

Chapter Four

Forecasting Theory: Insight and Irony

Successful commodity trading demands successful forecasting. Indeed, *if the trader cannot successfully forecast the market, on average, all of his other trading skills are useless.* Unfortunately, because the future is forever unknown, the trader can *never* be certain that he can really forecast the market.

On the other hand, if it seems reasonable or likely that the trader can, on average, forecast the market accurately, trading is still a reasonable business venture. How reasonable or likely it is that the trader can successfully forecast the market is a question of probabilities and statistics, of course. Although both topics are discussed in this book, the trader should be aware that many individuals who understand these topics best believe that the probability is zero or almost zero that the trader can beat the market.

Many academicians argue, in effect, that no one can make money in the market *precisely* because anyone can make money in the market. An account can be opened for a few thousand dollars. Fortunes can be made on hardly any investment at all.

Precisely because of this, much *is* invested in beating the market. Hundreds of millions of dollars have been invested in commodity funds. Decades of computer time have been dedicated to price analysis. Tens of thousands of man hours a year are invested in collecting and analyzing commodity data. More important, some of the finest minds in the world are working full time trying to beat the market. Possibly, the net result of this effort is that all potential profits have been beaten out of the market.

If all potential profit has been beaten out of the market, the market is "efficient." When the market is efficient, the current price will always, or nearly always, be the most reasonable one possible, in terms of all currently available information.

This theory is known as the efficient market hypothesis. One form of this theory that is particularly well known is the random walk theory. A market that follows a random walk will be an efficient market but an efficient market will not necessarily follow a random walk.

"Random" has a special meaning here. It does not mean irrational. Rather, it means that there is no pattern or structure to the data. Consider, for example, the following price series:

6 9 0 1 4 8 4 5 8 3 0 7 6 7 2 5 2 5 6 4

1 1 1 1 1 1 1 1 1 1 1 1 1 1 1 1 1 1 1 1

The first series is clearly random; the second series clearly is not. The first series is random because it does not have a pattern or structure; the second series does. Because the first series lacks any pattern, it can be communicated only by repeating each digit in order. The second series can be communicated the same way, of course, but it can also be communicated as follows: "Construct a number 20 digits long consisting solely of ones."

The sentence above is a simple verbal algorithm. The algorithm, which is an explicit and exhaustive set of instructions, generates the number series; that is, it contains all the information in the original data but in a more economical form.

Randomness and nonrandomness involve the presence and absence of patterns. More explicitly, a number series is random if and only if there is no algorithm to generate the series that can be transmitted more economically than the series itself (see Exhibit 21).

If prices follow a random walk, they cannot be dependent upon or coorelated with past price changes. Curiously enough, the efficient market hypothesis allows prices to be dependent upon past price behavior as long as such dependence is not of a form that allows trading profits; for example, the efficient market hypothesis would allow the size, but not the sign, of today's price change to be dependent upon yesterday's price change. The random walk theory would allow neither.

A distinction between the random walk theory and the efficient market hypothesis is necessary only if the theory or hypothesis is to be tested. Evidence that will contradict the random walk theory will not necessarily contradict the efficient market hypothesis. Indeed, although there is evidence that the market is not a random walk, there is little evidence that the market is not efficient. Fortunately, in terms of trading implications the theories are almost identical.

The most important trading implications[1] are:

1. **The Value of Price Analysis.** When the market is efficient, prices are appropriate, at least in terms of the available information. When this is the case there is no profit potential to exploit and, therefore, no value to price analysis.

2. **The Value of Commodity Speculation.** On a gross basis, the commodity futures market is a zero sum game: every dollar won by one player must be lost by another. Worse, on a net basis, the market is a negative sum game. In other words, not every dollar lost will be won, the difference of course going to the commodity industry. The commodity industry—that is, the brokerage companies, the money managers, and the trading advisers—are playing a positive sum game. On average, the industry makes money. On average, traders do not.

---

[1]See Loris, James H., and Hamilton, Mary, *The Stock Market—Theories and Evidence*, Richard D. Irwin, Homewood, Il., 1973.

```
1   REM PROGRAM NUMBER 1
2   READ A1
3   PRINT A1
4   GO TO 2
5   DATA 6, 9, 0, 1, 4
6   DATA 8, 4, 5, 8, 3
7   DATA 0, 7, 6, 7, 2
8   DATA 5, 2, 5, 6, 4
9   END
```

```
1   REM PROGRAM NUMBER 2
2   FOR N=1 TO 20
3   PRINT "1"
4   NEXT N
5   END
```

Exhibit 21. Both of the above programs are written in the programming language BASIC. The first program prints out a list of twenty random numbers. The second program prints out the number "1" twenty times. The fact that the second program is shorter and more efficient than the first indicates that the second number series is less random than the first.

Commodity trading cannot be a valid business venture for the average trader, but it can be a valid business venture for those who can forecast the market successfully on average. If this cannot be done, commodity trading is clearly valueless.

3. The Value of Large Portfolios. The importance of this concept depends on how large the fixed costs of trading are; that is, how large those costs of trading are that are independent of the size of the trading portfolio. Much of the trading literature assumes that fixed costs are small or nonexistent. But surely this cannot be the case. If the market can be beaten at all, surely it cannot be beaten by obvious and unsophisticated means. Unfortunately, obscure and sophisticated techniques are likely to be expensive. Moreover, their expense is almost certain to be independent of the number of contracts traded. For example, an advisory service that charged $1000 a year could as easily be used to trade one contract as a hundred, but the average cost—that is, the cost per contract—will drop as the number of contracts traded rises. If the gross profit per contract is constant, it clearly makes more sense to trade a large portfolio than a small one.

4. The Relative Value of Technical and Fundamental Analysis. If the market is efficient, the current price will be the most reasonable one possible in terms of all currently available information. What trading implications the theory has depends on what information is considered available. Currently, the theory takes three forms: the weak, the semistrong, and the strong.

The weak form of the theory alleges that the present price of a futures contract reflects all past price, volume, and open interest trends. If this is true, such data cannot be used to forecast the market and technical analysis is, therefore, of no use.

The semistrong form of the theory alleges that the current price reflects all publicly known information. If this form of the theory is true, neither technical analysis nor any method of fundamental analysis based on public data, such as news or government crop reports, is of any value.

The strong form of the theory alleges that the price of a futures contract reflects everything that is knowable about the commodity. If this form of the theory is true, even a private survey of supply and demand would not give the trader an edge. If this form of the theory is true, there is no rational reason for trading.

A fourth alternative, of course, is that the current prices may not even reflect past price trends, much less other data. If this is the case, both technical and fundamental analysis could be used to forecast the market.

Given these alternatives, it is clear that whereas both types of analysis may be of value, neither type need be. It is also clear that if technical analysis is of value, then fundamental analysis must be also, but that the converse is not necessarily true.

The overwhelming academic opinion is that the above theory is almost certainly true in its weak form and true to at least some extent even in its strongest form. The overwhelming opinion of the investment community is that regardless of form, the theory is a piece of trash.

In recent years the investment community has heaped considerable scorn on the efficient market hypothesis. This is understandable, because if the theory is true, or almost true, then almost all the products and services the community provides are completely without value. Nevertheless, this scorn is misplaced. The theory is perfectly reasonable, though it may not be true.

Over the last few years a large number of articles and books have attempted to discredit the efficient market hypothesis. Unfortunately, none of the writers seem to understand the theory. This is, of course, understandable. Few individuals are willing to invest the considerable effort necessary to understand a theory they believe is wrong. Although this may be good time management, it is rotten science. A theory must be refuted, if at all, in its own terms. For example, I myself believe that numerology is worthless, but I would never commit myself to that in print without attempting to understand numerology in its own terms, that is, in terms numerologists themselves understand and use.

The most common misunderstanding of the efficient market hypothesis is probably the belief or intuition that the market must provide at least some valid trading opportunities if only because it provides so many opportunities to trade. Actually, *none* of the numerous opportunities the market provides need favor the trader.

Consider, by way of analogy, a wager on three fair but bizarrely numbered dice.[2] None of the dice are numbered from one to six, but for each of the dice, the probability of the die landing on any one of its six faces is one in six. You will be allowed to examine the dice and select one. Your opponent will then select one of the two remaining dice. You will both then roll your dice and the player with the higher number wins.

The wager certainly seems fair. Surely, at worst the dice are equally likely to win, in which case it does not matter which die you choose. At best, one of the dice may be more likely to win than the others, in which case you can surely determine which die is favorable by examining them. Since you select the first die, you should find the bet at least fair and possibly favorable. Right?

Wrong. This analysis assumes that the relationship among the dice is transitive; this is, if the first die beats the second die on average and the second die beats the third die on average, then the first die will beat the third die on average. It seems reasonable to assume that the relationship among the dice will be transitive because most betting situations are transitive. If, to give an example from poker, four of a kind beats a full house and a full house beats two pair, then four of a kind beats two pair. Unfortunately, not all bets are transitive.

For example, consider three dice with the following faces:

1, 1, 4, 4, 4, 4
3, 3, 3, 3, 3, 3
2, 2, 2, 2, 6, 6

No matter which die the trader selects, there is another that will beat it on

[2] Gambling involves the creation of risk, speculation does not. Economically, legally, and morally, speculation and gambling differ. Nevertheless, from the gambler's or speculator's point of view, the economic characteristics are identical. Therefore, because gambling examples are often simpler, they will be used when possible.

average. On average, the first die will beat the second die, the second die will beat the third die, and the third die will beat the first die.

It is not clear whether the market resembles the above example. What is clear is that the fact that the market provides many trading opportunities does not necessarily imply that any of them are desirable.

A second common misunderstanding of the efficient market hypothesis is the belief that price behavior should be lawful, that unlawful price behavior is somehow unnatural or irrational. In a sense unintended by its advocates, this belief is certainly true. Prices may or may not obey causal laws; that is, they may or may not be forecastable, but they certainly obey the laws of probability.

A third common misunderstanding is the belief that obvious market "trends" are somehow prima facie evidence of market inefficiency. For example, one trader[3] writes, ". . . can anyone deny that the silver move that started late in December, 1973 and ended in March, 1974 showed a well-defined trend? If that was a random walk it was one up the side of a mountain!" (See Exhibit 22.)

There is nothing whatsoever unnatural or illogical about a random walk over mountainous terrain, however. Indeed, some random walks look exactly like this (see Exhibit 23.)

In other words, a trend may be nothing more than a drift. A price series has a drift if, *in retrospect,* the price changes are positive or negative on average. But a drifting series can only be said to have a trend or trends if the drifts could have been successfully forecasted, on average. Silver may have indeed trended from December 1973 to March 1974, but if so, it is far from obvious.

A fourth misunderstanding is the belief that the theory is somehow self-contradictory. Actually, the theory does allow a number of delightful ironies and paradoxes. For example, the theory has the curious property that it can be true only to the extent that it is not believed; that is, to the extent that traders continue to trade. But this does not imply that the theory is false, as some writers believe or wish to believe. A paradox is not a contradiction. The paradox only implies that *if* the efficient market hypothesis is true, then traders cannot really understand the nature of the market, at least not to the extent that academic economists do. No doubt economists find this flattering, but the theory is not necessarily false for this reason. The theory is quite capable of being true.

A theory that is capable of being true must be accepted or rejected on the basis of how well it describes the real world; that is, on the basis of evidence.[4]

---

[3] Jones, Don. The *Mis*behavior of Commodity Prices, *Commodities,* August 1975, p. 20.

[4] Although a review of the evidence would seem appropriate, it would shift the subject from money management to trading methods, and it is emphatically not one of the functions of this book to recommend individual trading methods. Moreover, it seems unnecessary, as 50 to 90 percent of the professional literature concerns trading methods.

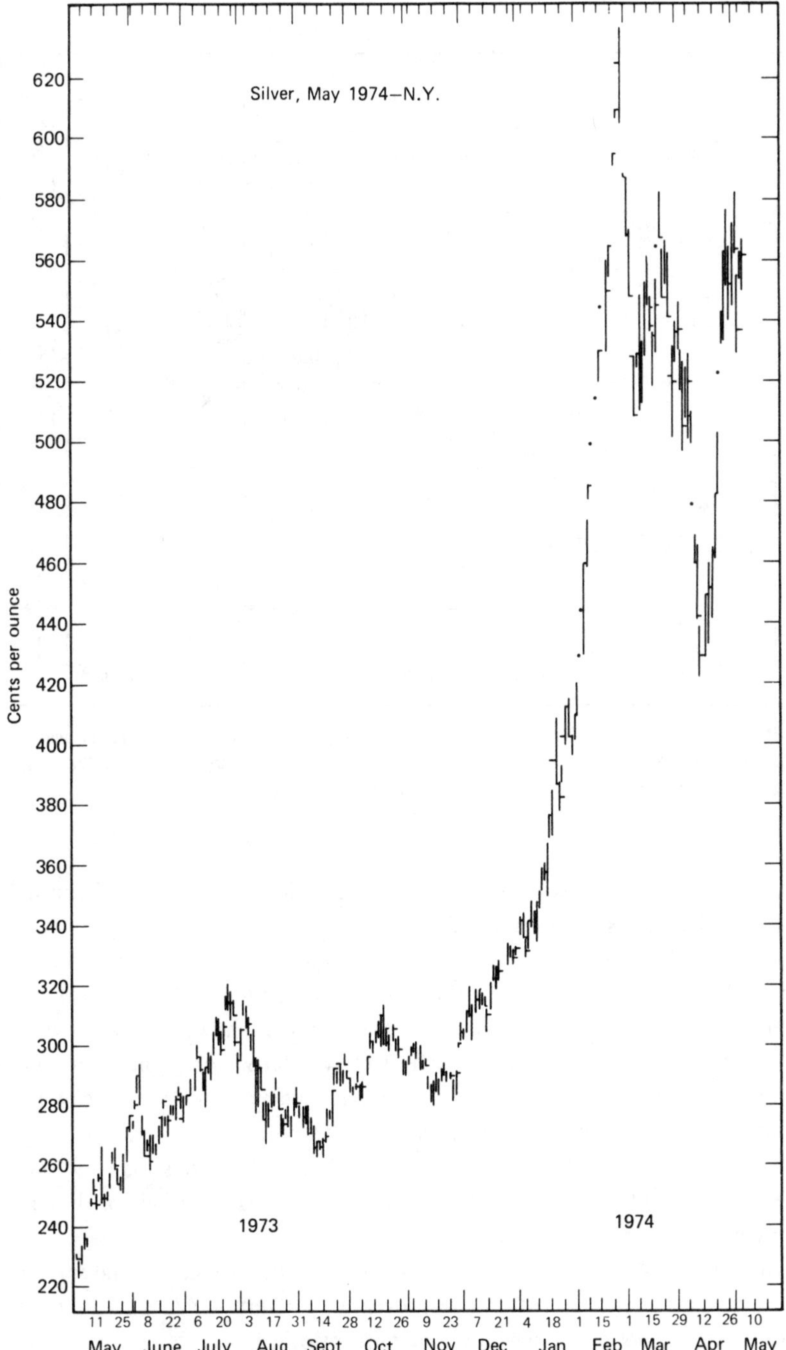

Exhibit 22. Silver prices in May 1974. A counterexample to the random walk? From Commodity Chart Service.

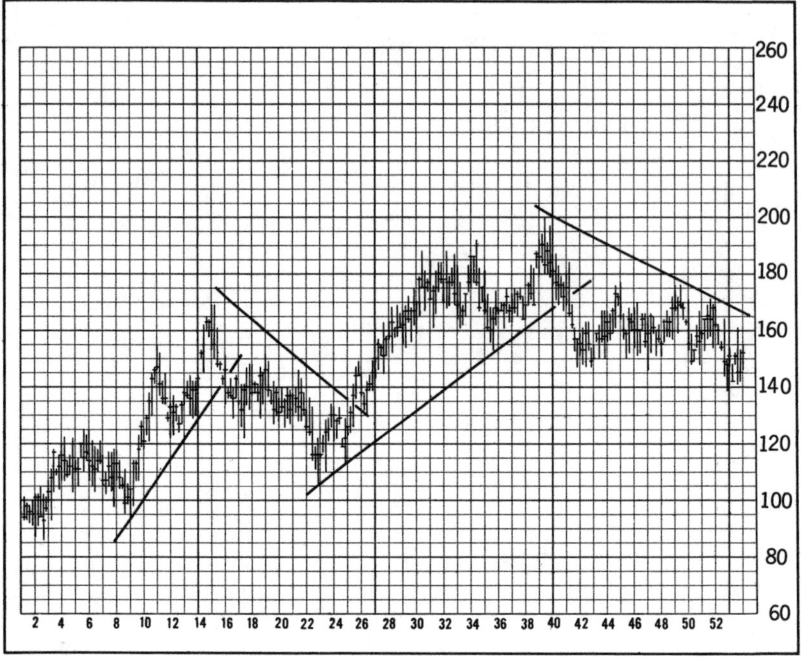

Exhibit 23. Notice the chart patterns and trend-like behavior, yet the chart was constructed from randomly generated data. From Sklarew, A., *Techniques of a Professional Commodity Chart Analysis*, Commodity Research Bureau Inc., 1980, p. 12.

For example, to the best of my knowledge, astrology has no internal contradictions but there is also no evidence that it works.

Oddly enough, traders and academicians produce the same type of evidence; that is, historical studies showing that a given method did or did not work over a given period. Traders have presented so many studies showing so many ways of beating the market that the reader may well wonder why anyone loses. On the other hand, academicians have presented many studies showing that many popular trading methods have not beaten the market after all.

Since the academic literature is considerably more rigorous than the trading literature, it would seem prudent that the trader acquaint himself with the academic literature or give up trading.

Academicians, of course, have *not* proven that the market is random. Moreover, they never will. All they have proven is that certain types of nonrandom price behavior do not appear over certain historical periods. If these periods are representative, that is, if they have been randomly selected, these types of nonrandom price behavior are unlikely to appear in the future. Other types of nonrandom behavior may well appear, however.

The academician is in the same position that an ornithologist would be who tried to prove that all ducks are black. Clearly, one nonblack duck, say a white or a tan one, would disprove his theory. But although each black duck he observes strengthens his theory, no amount of black ducks can prove it. Even if he examined every living duck, he could not prove his theory because it is always possible that ducks had been or might be born some other color than black.

Clearly, if science demanded absolute proof there would be no science. Scientifically, statistically significant results, that is, results that are reasonably unlikely or improbable, are sufficient. For example, the ornithologist's belief that all or almost all ducks are black would seem justified if each of a thousand randomly selected ducks were found to be black. Similarly, the academician's belief that the market is random would seem justified if each of a large number of randomly selected trading methods were found to be useless.

In recent years, so many forecasting and trading methods have been found useless that most academicians no longer consider the efficient market hypothesis an interesting area of inquiry. But that, of course, does not prove that the market is random. The methods selected for testing have never been selected randomly. They have, of course, been selected in order of their obviousness and testability. It is not reasonable to conclude that the market cannot be beaten when a less obvious or more expensive method might do so.

Indeed, it seems not only possible but probable that the market can be beaten. As one observer[5] noted:

> . . . commodity price developments are watched by relatively few traders, most of them quite set in their ways; even in the most active futures markets, the volume of serious research by participants seems to be quite small. It is therefore possible that systematic patterns will remain largely unknown for a very long time.

In a certain sense, therefore, the market is almost certainly not random. Surely at any given moment there are numerous obscure facts that could be exploited profitably. No doubt methods could be found to eke profits from even the most available and analyzed data. But such methods should not be easy to find. *If the cost of finding a method of beating the market exceeds the potential profit, as it does for many, perhaps most, traders, the market is in effect random.*

[5] Honthaker, Hendrick, Systematic and Random Elements in Short Term Price Movements, *American Economic Review*, May 1961, p. 164.

The question, therefore, is not whether or not the efficient market hypothesis is true, but to what extent it is true. The evidence in favor of the hypothesis is considerable—but it is not overwhelming. There is almost certainly some truth to the weakest form of the theory. Certainly, the most obvious and naive forms of technical analysis are barren. On the other hand, it seems unlikely that the theory is true in its strongest form. Surely, at any given moment there are numerous obscure facts that could be exploited profitably—if only one knew how.

The extent to which the efficient market hypothesis is true depends upon the logic of the hypothesis and the validity of the assumptions. When the logic is flawless, which in this case is almost certainly true, the truth of the hypothesis depends on the validity of the underlying assumptions. If the assumptions are true, the hypothesis must be true.

The consensus among academicians is that the efficient market hypothesis depends upon five assumptions.[6] These assumptions are sufficient but not necessary; that is, the market must be efficient if these assumptions are true, but the market can be efficient without these assumptions being completely true. On the other hand, if the market is not efficient, then one or more of the following assumptions must be false.

1. **Low Transaction Costs.** This means that commissions, execution costs, and taxes must be low enough so that potential traders and hedgers are not prevented or inhibited from acting. This seems to be the case. Commissions and execution costs are quite low for most commodities. Commodity profits are taxed at moderate rates, of course, but moderate or even high rates do not seem to excessively inhibit trading, at least if the market's growth in recent years is any indication.

2. **High Liquidity.** This means that individual trades must not excessively affect the market price. For many commodities, this also seems to be the case; in wheat, for example, the trading volume is high enough that even large buy and sell orders cause little more than ripples.

3. **Effective Information Flow.** This means that news must flow quickly and freely to all real and potential traders and hedgers. This is not quite the case. News is available at a relatively low cost but it is not available free. News is available to anyone willing to pay for it, but not all traders are willing.

More important, there is no "inside information," other than the actions of our own and other governments. The most important government influence is

[6] cf. Fama, Eugene F., Efficient Capital Markets: A Review of Theory and Empirical Work, *Journal of Finance*, May 1970, pp. 387–388.

the U.S. Department of Agriculture, which takes considerable pains to insure that the information they procure is released simultaneously, after the market's close, to all concerned. Other agencies may not be so scrupulous.

There is no other inside information because there is no inside. Commodities can scarcely be produced or consumed in secret. Individual producers and consumers may act in secret, of course, but there are so many producers and consumers of most commodities that this scarcely matters. Thus, while it is possible for a trader to consistently get market news before others, in fact it rarely appears to happen.

4. Rapid Price Adjustments. This means that the price must change rapidly when new information indicates that a change is appropriate. This seems to be the case.

5. Rational Traders and Hedgers. This means that traders and hedgers must recognize prices that are too high or low in terms of the available information. The assumption here is that all or almost all traders and hedgers will not make the same errors. Clearly, whenever traders and hedgers with the same information disagree, at least some of them must be in error. If all or almost all of them are in error, the assumption is violated.

Without doubt, this assumption is the most dubious of the lot. Indeed, in the past, traders and investors have been frequently and unanimously wrong; that is, they have frequently and unanimously been stupid and irrational.

Irrationality is the substitution, in whole or in part, of greed or fear for reason. For example, during the 17th century, tulip bulbs became a major focus of the Dutch economy. Tulips were attractive, exotic, and potentially profitable as an export item. They were valuable and had the potential of becoming even more so.

The profit potential was large, but it was not infinite. Yet in many people's minds, the profit potential quickly became infinite, or nearly so. More and more money was paid for tulip bulbs, until fortunes were paid for individual bulbs. In one sad case, a farmer traded all of his worldly goods, including[7] "a farm of 38 acres, cattle and sheep, hundreds of pounds of cheese, lard and butter, all of the furnishings of the farmhouse, and a gold drinking cup. . ." for a single tulip.

Eventually, there was no more money for tulips. The tulip boom crested and shattered, leaving the Dutch economy in ruins. Bulbs that had once sold for fortunes now sold for pennies.

Unfortunately, the Dutch tulip boom was not unique. It was followed by the Mississippi land frauds and the South Seas bubble, which almost bankrupted

[7]Shapiro, M., Trading In Tulips?, *Barron's,* August 26, 1968, p. 1.

18th century France and England, respectively. The South Seas bubble was a stock fraud large enough to retire the English national debt. During the boom, stock was sold in ventures to supply England with sea coal, to rebuild every home in England, to build a perpetual motion machine, and most fascinating of all, to develop "a company for carrying on an undertaking of great advantage, but nobody to know what it is." Apparently, speculators could buy shares at 100 pounds each, each of which would produce an annual return of 100 pounds and each share of which could be purchased with only a 2-pound deposit. Within five hours the issue was oversubscribed. Naturally, the promoter left England that evening and was never heard of again.

The Mississippi land fraud and the South Seas bubble were followed by the Florida land boom, the 1929 stock market collapse, and scores of other booms and busts (see Exhibit 24). Historically, mass irrationality has been so prevalent that it is sometimes difficult to believe that the market is basically rational. Indeed, irrationality has been so frequent that it is sometimes difficult to believe that the market price is ever appropriate.

The market price during a boom or bust is virtually never appropriate. Indeed, the market price could only be appropriate if the millenium or the apocalypse were approaching.

Sometimes, of course, the millenium or the apocalypse is approaching. For example, holders of Czarists bonds should have sold when they saw the Russian revolution coming, regardless of price. Since the revolution, the bonds have been worthless or virtually worthless. Only hope or delusion gives the bonds value.

More often, the millenium or the apocalypse does not arrive. Jensen[8] describes the nonarrival like this:

> When the pressure to sell is the greatest, that is when I start shaking my head and state, "It should hold here." When I rush to the brokerage office a half hour before opening time to be sure I am there to watch the crash, when I feel my stomach turn and food doesn't appeal to me, when the blood is rushing to my head and my breathing is a little short because I know I must make a decision, possibly to salvage what is left, when my broker's voice is trembling, when the faces in the board room are full of fear, then, I have learned this is not the time to sell. THIS IS THE TIME TO BUY.

It generally becomes clear sooner or later that the millenium or the apocalypse will not arrive during the near future and prices return to normal. Clearly, any-

---

[8] Jensen, Edward S., *Mass Psychology,* quoted in Dines, James, *How The Average Investor Can Use Technical Analysis for Stock Profits,* Dines Chart Company, New York, 1972, p. 83–84.

The number of objects that have been used for speculation is far too large to be catalogued here. The following list is partial and suggestive:

British Government debt: Amsterdam, 1763.

Selected companies: South Sea Company, Compagnie d'Occident, Sword Blade Bank, Banque Generale, Banque Royale, 1720; British Eash India Company, 1772; Dutch East India Company, 1772, 1783.

Import commodities: sugar, coffee, 1799; 1857 in Hamburg; cotton in Britain and France, 1836, 1861; wheat in 1847.

Country banks: England, 1750s, 1793, 1824.

Canals: 1793, 1820s in Britain; 1823 in France.

Export goods: 1810, 1816, 1836 for Britain.

Foreign bonds: 1825 in London; 1888 in Paris; 1924 in New York.

Foreign mines: Latin American in Britain, 1825; German in Britain and France, 1850.

Foreign direct investment: by U.S. companies, 1960s.

Building sites: 1825 in France; 1857 in the United States; 1873 in Austria and Germany; 1925 in Florida; 1970s in Florida, Arizona, and New Mexico.

Agricultural land: <u>biens nationaux</u> (noble land confiscated during the Revolution in France), speculated in from 1815 to 1830s.

Public lands: United States, 1836, 1857; Argentina, 1888-90.

Railroad shares: 1836, 1847 in Britain; 1847, 1857 in France; 1857, 1873 in the United States.

Joint-stock banks: Germany, 1850s and early 1870s.

Joint-stock discount houses: Britain in the 1860s.

Private companies going public: 1888 in Britain; 1928 in the United States.

Existing and merged companies: 1920 in Britain; 1928 in the United States; conglomerates in the United States, 1960s.

Copper: 1888 in France; 1907 in the United States.

Foreign exchange: the mark in 1921-23; the franc in 1924-26; sterling in 1931, 1964, etc.; the dollar in 1973.

Gold: 1960s, 1970s.

New industries: the United States in 1920s, 1960s.

Buildings: hotels, condominiums, office buildings, nursing homes, retirement villages.

Commodity futures.

Stock puts and calls (options).

Exhibit 24. From Kindleberger, Charles P., *Manias, Panics and Crashes: A History of Financial Crisis*, Basic Books, New York, 1978, pp. 45–46.

one with the foresight to buy during a crash or sell during a boom will earn extraordinary returns. But this is not easy to do. It not only demands considerable foresight, it demands courage.

Stupidity is the misunderstanding of market economics. In a sense, stupidity is unavoidable. Understanding is a map, and no map completely describes its territory. Still, some maps are better, that is, more accurate or more useful, than others.

Consider, for example, the slot machine. The slot machine is one of the most popular forms of gambling. In Las Vegas, according to Richard Epstein, ". . .they outnumber all other forms of gambling by more than 10 to 1." This popularity is remarkable, considering that the slots are one of Las Vegas' least favorable games. If we disregard the entertainment these machines provide, the slot machine players clearly are acting irrationally.

The slot machine player has only two obvious alternatives: to bet or not to bet. If the player bets, he or she can choose the size of the bet but nothing else. As all bets have the same apparently negative expected value, there seems to be little point in betting. Indeed, it can be proven that there is no betting system or strategy that will allow the trader, on average, to beat the machine.

Yet slot machines have been beaten. They have been beaten because the map or description above was, and perhaps still is, wrong.

All bets on the slot machine are not necessarily equal and negative. The manufacturers, of course, attempt to insure that this is the case, but they are not necessarily successful. Profits are possible if the machines have[9]

> . . . mechanical imperfections. One example is the celebrated "rhythm method." Discovered in 1949 by an Idaho farmer who had aided a friend in repairing slot machines, this method rested on the fact that certain symbols would reappear after a certain number of seconds if they had previously stopped near the pay line. A player could insert a coin, pull the handle, pause for the correct time interval, and pull the handle a second time. The concomitant payoff was approximately 120 percent of the funds invested. By 1951 the slot machine manufacturers had installed a "variator," which caused the symbols to appear at varying intervals, thereby destroying the effectiveness of the "rhythm method."

Slot machines have been beaten only by individuals who understand their workings better than their manufacturers. Similarly, the market can be beaten only by those who understand market economics better than the market itself, that is, better than average.

[9]Epstein, Richard A., *The Theory of Gambling and Statistical Logic,* Academic Press, New York, 1977, p. 118.

This can be done in only three ways. Profitable trading must be based either upon exploiting information that other traders do not possess or upon exploiting their irrationality or stupidity.

Unfortunately, theory provides little help in constructing profitable trading systems; that is, there are no other obvious attributes that *every* successful trading system must have, although there are certainly attributes that any given trading system must have. Therefore, if a trading system is to be constructed rationally, the underlying theory must be analyzed in terms of criteria intrinsic to the theory itself. Trading implications must be developed in the same way.

For psychological reasons, this is difficult to do. Psychologically, most people tend to apply one set of criteria to most situations. Sometimes this is exactly the right thing to do, but sometimes it is not.

Perhaps the distinction between intrinsic and extrinsic criteria can be clarified by the dog show metaphor. In a dog show, awards are given to the best of each of several breeds and a second award, the best of show, is given to one of those winners. Each breed is judged by different extrinsic criteria. Dachshunds, for example, are judged by the blackness or brownness of their coats and the shortness of their legs. Irish Setters are judged by the redness of their coats and the length of their legs. But the dog awarded the best of show may have black hair or red, long legs or short, it doesn't matter. What does matter is whether the best Dachshund is more like what a Dachshund should be than the best Irish Setter is like what an Irish Setter should be. The best of show is judged by intrinsic criteria.

Trading methods must be analyzed in terms of intrinsic criteria. The goal, of course, is always the same—a valid set of buy and sell signals—but the way the theory is developed and the trading signals derived will necessarily vary from theory to theory. A trend-following method must be analyzed in a different manner than an econometric method, which must be analyzed in a different manner than the Elliott wave method.

Any or all of these techniques may be of value; at least, there is no reason to believe that if the market can be beaten at all, it can be beaten in only one way. If the market can be beaten at all, surely there are numerous valid approaches, numerous valid points of view (see Exhibit 25).

Because theory provides little help, profitable trading methods are difficult to construct. There is and can be no logical method of constructing a trading method. If one can be constructed at all, it can only be constructed by someone who is intelligent, disciplined, and knowledgeable about market economics, by someone who watches for the market's stupidities and irrationalities and then acts.

Exhibit 25. Is the figure above a leftward looking bird or a rightward looking rabbit? Actually, both views and perhaps others are equally valid. From Hanson, N.P., *Patterns of Discovery*, Cambridge University Press, London, 1961.

Interestingly enough, an individual who has spent that last 10 years studying the market does not necessarily have an advantage over a beginner, for much of his or her knowledge was rotting as it was acquired. The way wheat is grown and consumed, for example, is hardly the same now as it was a decade ago.

It is not simply that the nature of the game changes over time; rather, the act of playing the game changes its nature. When slot machines are beaten, they will be redesigned and rebuilt. When some traders beat the market, others will anticipate them. Ultimately, the profit will dissipate.

Ultimately, the market cannot be beaten, but money can be taken before the market's nature changes. At least, money can be taken by those who understand market economics best.

Market knowledge is therefore relative. The market is a zero sum game, a game that can be won only by those with superior knowledge. Market knowledge is therefore a zero sum game. It is for this reason that traders with average or below average knowledge are doomed. In effect, they know nothing or less than nothing about the market.

The average or below average trader is doomed. Yet we may be that trader. Unfortunately, we cannot know.

Consider the slot machine example above. The slot machine is a relatively simple game and yet there are at least three levels of insight or understanding possible, each of which implies its own tactics. On the first or simplest level, the player plays because he or she does not understand that the slot machine offers only bad or unfavorable bets. On the second level, the player refuses to play precisely because he does understand that. On the third level, the player plays because he understands that if played in a certain way, the machine really does offer good bets.

The third level is the correct level, of course, at least if there are no higher levels. This seems to be the case, but then, individuals on the first two levels also seem to believe that they are on the top level. The market allows both insight and irony.

For that reason, ultimately, we cannot know whether the bets the market offers are good ones. Things are not always as they seem. Damon Runyon[10] puts it this way:

> Son, no matter how far you travel or how smart you get, always remember this: Someday, somewhere, a guy is going to come to you and show you a nice brand-new deck of cards on which the seal is not yet broken, and this guy is going to offer to bet you that the Jack of Spades will jump out of this deck and squirt cider in your ear. But, son, do not bet this man, for as sure as you do, you are going to get an earful of cider.

In many ways the commodity market is a confidence game. In most confidence games, the victim plays the game only as long as he (or she) believes that he understands the game better than the other players do. For example, the victim may be allowed to cheat another player who is, of course, one of the confidence men. Sadly, ironically, justly, the victim is cheated as he attempts to cheat someone else.

The commodity market is not a confidence game because of a conspiracy of hedgers and floor traders; the truth is worse: the con is in the nature of the game.

The only rational people to play the market are those who expect to win. Yet the nature of the game demands that some of them lose. A zero sum game demands losers, and anything that prevents losers from entering the game must necessarily stop the game or turn potential winners into losers. As long as there is a market, there can be no way of knowing who will win and who will lose.

Yet fortunes can be made *precisely because* no one knows and no one ever will know how the market can be beaten. *All profitable trading methods are dependent upon some bias among market participants; this bias both creates profit opportunities and inhibits their discovery.* This is the principle of contrary opinion, a principle necessarily more subtle than most market participants realize. A curious corollary to this principle is that most traders are likely to select just those trading methods least likely to be profitable.[11] Indeed, if you've discovered a strong enough bias among traders, you could publish your discovery in *The Wall Street Journal* and still trade it profitably forever, for it will be disregarded by all, or almost all, other traders.[12]

---

[10] Runyon, Damon, *The Idyll of Miss Sarah Brown.*

[11] This is not completely theory. According to Dennis Dunn of *Dunn & Hargit* (personal communication, no date), few of the purchasers of their $500 pork belly trading systems were still using the system a year after purchase. Yet according to *Dunn & Hargitt* the system had been profitable, on average, in the interim. Presumably for different reasons, *Dunn & Hargit* no longer uses the system itself.

[12] Another curious corollary to this theory is that if the theory is true, it should be difficult to believe and therefore difficult to publish. Unsympathetic editors and reviewers should keep this in mind.

Chapter Five

Statistics and Certainty

THEORY

Statistics is a body of methods for making wise decisions in the face of uncertainty.[1] Given this definition, statistics is clearly an important trading tool. After all, there are few areas outside of trading where uncertainty is as prevalent or where wise decisions are as profitable.

A wise decision is one that effectively uses the available data; it will not necessarily be the "correct" decision, that is, the decision that in retrospect would have been best. For example, if you are interested in acquiring money and if you accept 1 to 100 odds on a flip of a fair coin, you have accepted a bad bet and made a bad decision; it will not become a wise decision if, by chance, you win.[2]

Chance is an important concept. Indeed, it is another word for probability, and probability theory is the basis of statistics. A probability is a number be-

---

This chapter deviates from statistical tradition in several ways. First, much more attention is given to nonparametric techniques than is usually the case. Most introductory texts spend most of their space on parametric techniques, which make all the same assumptions as nonparametric techniques and others, in addition. Although nonparametric techniques are never as powerful as parametric techniques (when the assumptions of the parametric techniques are satisfied), they frequently are almost as powerful and almost invariably simpler and safer.

Second, this chapter teaches a group of esoteric techniques. The first is a low-arithmetic method based on the sample range. This technique is less powerful than a similar and much more popular technique based on the standard deviation. Indeed, it cannot reasonably be used when the sample is of even moderate size. However, small-sample problems are more frequent and frequently more important than large-sample problems. I believe quick but not-too-dirty techniques have a place in the practitioner's repertoire.

A second esoteric technique is based on sample mean absolute deviation. This technique is also similar to one based on the sample standard deviation. However the mean absolute deviation is both safer to use and easier to understand than the standard deviation, and, lacking a preprogrammed calculator, it is easier to calculate.

Finally, the symbols taught here frequently violate convention. This will be an inconvenience for those readers who already have a knowledge of the conventions and those readers who hope to acquire a knowledge of the conventions. My apologies. However, I believe few of my readers will have either a background in statistics or the desire to learn more than the minimum that would be useful. My hope is that the symbols presented here will make the techniques presented as easy to learn as possible.

[1] Wallis, W. Allen, and Roberts, Harry V., *Statistics: A New Approach.* The Free Press, New York 1956, p. 3. (This, incidentally, is the best introductory book on statistics I know of.)

[2] Actually, there are situations where accepting a 1 to 100 bet is rational. Such a bet is rational, for example, for an individual who owned only $100.00 and who had no prospect of obtaining more but who needed a minimum of $101.00 for a project of life and death importance. Such situations are rare, of course. The example given is not a counterexample to the idea that making wise decisions is important. It only shows that utility values (see Chapter 9) rather than dollar values must be used. Unfortunately, giving an example in terms of utility values, rather than in dollars, would obscure rather than clarify the point.

tween zero and one inclusive, where zero indicates that a given event has no possibility of occurring and one indicates that the event is certain.

The trader will find that most of the most interesting events do *not* have probabilities of zero or one. On the other hand, in most of the most interesting cases, the trader will have to act *as if* an event had a probability of one or zero. For example, no reasonable individual would trade commodities if they did not believe they could forecast the market accurately, on average. Yet that probability will never be one, for no matter how much evidence the trader accumulates, there is *always* the possibility that the results are a fluke. However, if it is unlikely that the results are a fluke, that is, if the probability is, say, 0.99999999, the trader may well be willing to act as if the probability were one.

In many cases, the evidence is so extensive that the trader may confidently act as if the probability was one or zero. On the other hand, many times the evidence is less persuasive than it seems. For example, Edson Gould's Seasonal Stock market price change data are presented in Exhibit 26. Presumably, he believed the data to be of value or he wouldn't have published them. Unfortunately, he was wrong. A statistical test of the data shows no evidence of seasonal patterns.

Statistical techniques are useful in just those cases where the trader is not willing to depend on his intuition. In other words, statistical techniques are most useful when it is costly to be wrong and when the data are meager or ambiguous or expensive to collect. Under even the most impoverished conditions, statistical techniques will allow the trader to estimate how likely or unlikely an event is, so he can make a decision and take action.

The two most important classes of statistical techniques are estimators and tests. An estimator is a rule or strategy that estimates the value of a carefully defined population on the basis of a carefully defined sample; for example, an estimate of the number of hogs currently being raised in the United States is 5,000,000. A test is a rule or strategy that accepts or rejects a hypothesis about a carefully defined population on the basis of a carefully defined sample; for example, a hypothesis is that the number of hogs currently being raised in the United States is 5,000,000. A test of that hypothesis could determine if the number of hogs currently being raised in the United States is likely to be significantly larger than 5,000,000, if it is significantly smaller than 5,000,000, or if it is significantly larger or smaller than 5,000,000.

Notice the distinction between sample and population and between statistic and parameter. Assume, for example, that we would like to know the average yield per acre for corn grown in the United States. The population, in this case, consists of all the land in the United States devoted to growing corn. The value

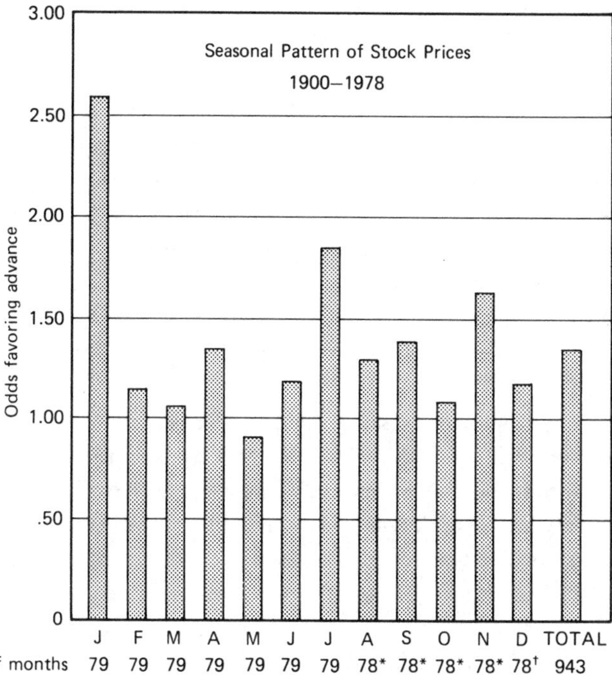

	J	F	M	A	M	J	J	A	S	O	N	D	TOTAL
Total number of months	79	79	79	79	79	79	79	78*	78*	78*	78*	78†	943
Total plus months‡	57	41	40	46	37	43	51	44	45	40	48	42†	534
Total minus months‡	22	38	39	33	42	36	28	34	33	38	30	36†	409
Odds favoring advance (plus months ÷ minus months)	2.59	1.08	1.03	1.39	0.88	1.19	1.82	1.29	1.36	1.05	1.60	1.17	1.31

†Figures as of 1977.

*One fewer month; New York Stock Exchange closed July 31 to December 12, 1914.

‡Plus months are those showing advance from previous month; minus months are those showing decline from previous month.

NOTE: Figures based on monthly mean of Dow Jones Industrial Average.

Exhibit 26. These data look important, but are not; the results are statistically insignificant. From Gould, E., *Edson Gould's 1979 Forecast*, Anametrics, New York, 1978.

that we desire, the parameter, is the average yield per acre of corn. Unfortunately, to acquire this information we would have to know exactly how many bushels of corn are growing on each and every acre in the United States dedicated to growing corn.

Although theoretically it might be possible to get this information, the costs surely outweigh the benefits. A more reasonable approach is to estimate the parameter value. This is done by taking a sample from the population and calculating a statistic. For example, the yield on each of 1000 randomly selected acres of U.S. corn could be counted and an average of the yields calculated. The 1000 acres would constitute the sample and the average the statistic.

It is clearly unreasonable to expect the statistic and parameter to be identical. However, if the sample is selected correctly, that is, randomly, and if the sample is large enough, the statistic should be reasonably close to the parameter. How close, on average, the statistic will be to the parameter will depend on the sample size, the statistic used, and the population's size and distribution.

A distribution is a description of a variable that relates the probability of the variable, taking a given value, to each value the variable might take. If the variable is discrete, that is, if it can take on only certain specific values, the distribution can be pictured by a histogram. A histogram is a graph of vertical bars where the areas are proportional to the probabilities represented. If the bars are equally wide, the heights alone can be used to represent the probabilities (see Exhibit 27).

If the variable is not discrete, that is, if it is continuous, the distribution can be fairly represented only by a frequency curve. In a sense, a curve is a histogram with an infinite number of infinitely thin bars (see Exhibit 28).

If a variable is continuous, the probability of the variable taking on any given value is zero. For that reason a frequency curve cannot be used in the same way a histogram can. However, a curve can be used to represent the probability of a variable taking on a *range* of values. For example, a kruggerrand is supposed to contain a troy ounce of gold. But no kruggerrand ever contains *exactly* an ounce of gold. In other words, the probability of a given krugerrand containing exactly one troy ounce is zero. However, the probability of an unseen coin containing between, say, 1.000 troy ounces and 1.010 troy ounces might be, say, .95.

Histograms are useful, but statistics are even more useful. The two most popular and useful groups of statistics are measures of location and dispersion.

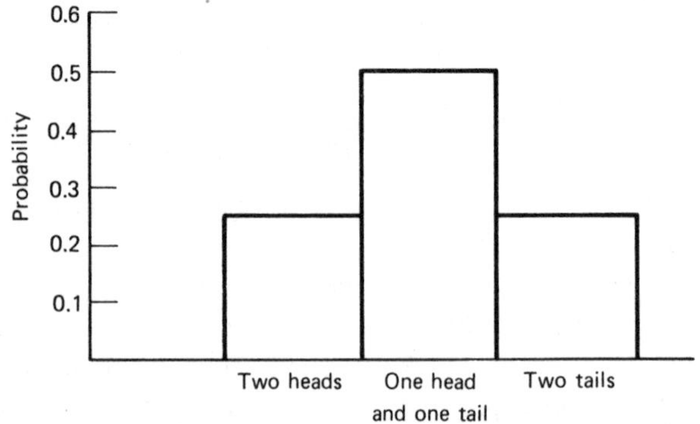

Exhibit 27. A histogram represents frequencies or probabilities by the area of vertical bars. The probability of two fair coins landing in various ways is represented above.

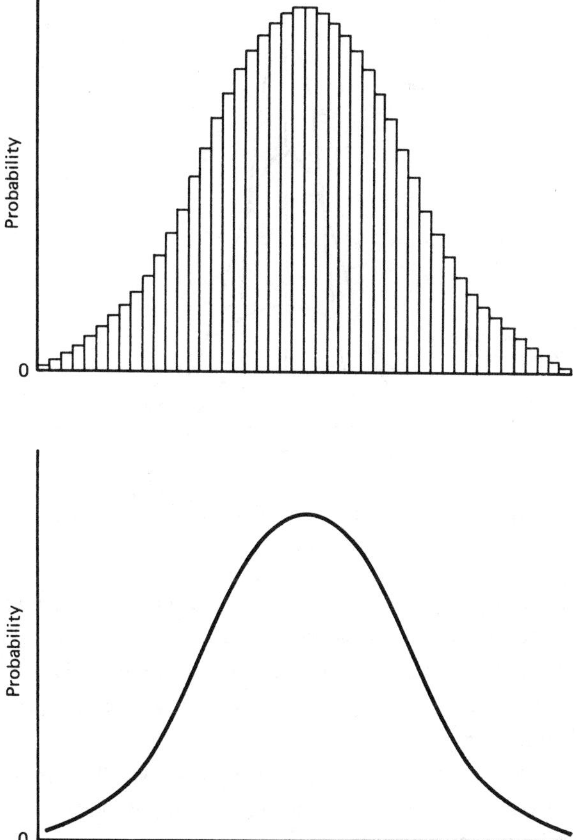

Exhibit 28. A frequency curve is a histogram with an infinite number of infinitely thin bars.

The most obvious and popular measure of location is the arithmetic mean. It is calculated by adding up all the sample values and dividing by the sample size.

The most popular measure of the dispersion or width of a distribution is the range. The second most popular measure, and a measure that is technically superior, is the standard deviation. In Exhibit 29 the various curves all have the same mean and area but they have different widths. The narrower curves have the smaller standard deviations.

In the same way a population has a distribution, a statistic has a distribution. In the same way a population can have a mean and a standard deviation, a statistic can have a mean and a standard deviation, although the standard deviation of a statistic is called a standard error.

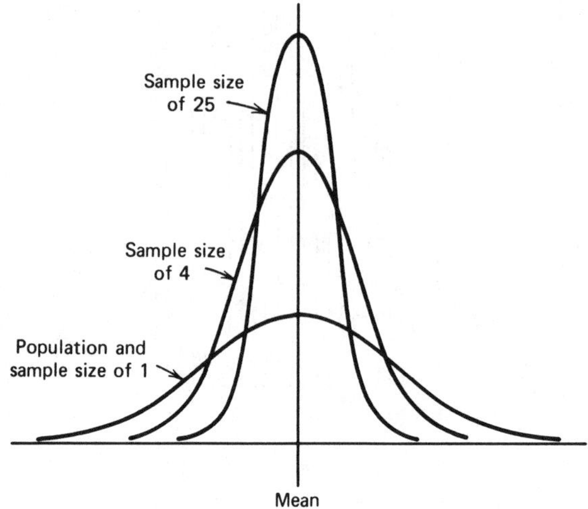

Exhibit 29. The larger the sample size, the more closely the sampling distribution clusters about the mean.

Any given sample mean may or may not equal the population mean, of course. On average, however, the sample mean will equal the population mean as long as the population has a mean and the sample is randomly selected (populations without means and standard deviations are discussed in Chapter 9). However, only when the sample size is one will the standard error of the sample mean equal the standard deviation of the population. Whenever the sample size is larger than one, the standard error will be smaller than the standard deviation. Notice in Exhibit 29 how the distributions of the sample means cluster progressively tighter about the population mean as the sample sizes increase.

It is generally easier to think in terms of confidence intervals, which are multiples or fractions of the standard error, than in terms of the standard error itself.[3] A confidence interval is a range of values within which the parameter has a known probability of appearing. This probability is called the confidence coefficient and it is known because it is chosen. A confidence coefficient can be chosen between zero and one exclusive, where numbers approaching one indicate virtual certainty and numbers approaching zero indicate almost no probability. For example, if a confidence coefficient of .5 is chosen, on average only half of the confidence intervals calculated will have the parameter within them (see Exhibit 30).

[3] The logic of confidence intervals can be more obscure than the logic of standard errors, as, for example, when confidence intervals for the standard deviation are being constructed. In my opinion, however, it is unlikely that the trader will need such tools.

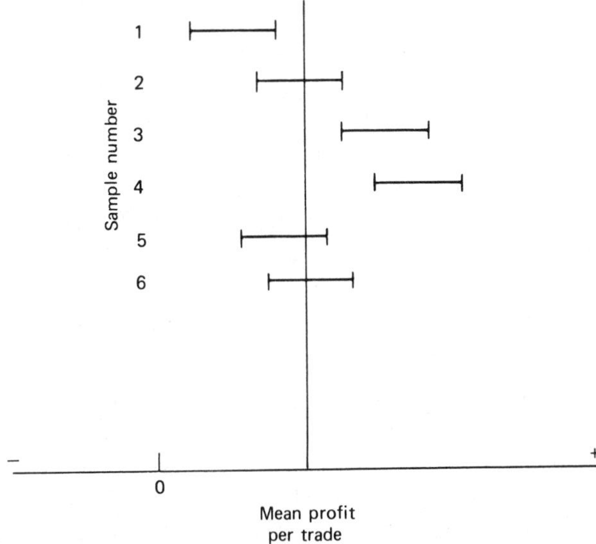

Exhibit 30. On average, half the 0.50 confidence intervals contain the parameter.

In a sense, the confidence intervals of a statistic are a measure of how useful the statistic is. If for a given confidence coefficient the confidence limits are relatively narrow, the statistic will be a relatively good estimate of the parameter. On the other hand, if for a given confidence coefficient the confidence limits are relatively wide, the statistic will be a relatively poor estimate.

Tests are another method of measuring the usefulness of a statistic. A test is a procedure for deciding which of two mutually exclusive hypotheses are true. Two hypotheses are mutually exclusive if and only if one of the hypotheses must be true and the other false (e.g., a given trading method is either profitable on average or it is not).

By convention one of the hypotheses, called the null hypothesis, is assumed to be true until it is proven false. A legal analogy may make this clearer. The null hypothesis is put on trial, in a sense, where the trial consists of obtaining a sample and calculating a statistic. The null hypothesis is assumed to be innocent, that is, true, until it is proven guilty or false.

Guilt need not be proven beyond any possible doubt but only beyond a reasonable doubt. A reasonable doubt is a chosen probability value, a chosen level of significance [i.e., $(1 - \alpha)$] [0.1, 0.05, 0.01 and 0.001 are popular values for $(1 - \alpha)$]. If the probability of obtaining a result at least as extreme as the one obtained is smaller than the level of significance chosen, the null hypothesis should be considered false and the alternative hypothesis true.

Suppose a trader wished to know whether a given coin was fair. If the trader flipped the coin 20 times and heads appeared each time, the answer would be obvious. The answer is obvious because it is easy to see intuitively that when the coin is fair, the probability of obtaining such an extreme answer is very small.

On the other hand, if, say, 15 heads had occurred, the answer would have been less than obvious. It is less than obvious because it is less than obvious how the probabilities involved should be calculated. If the probabilities are represented by a distribution, the problem becomes how to divide the distribution into those probabilities that favor a fair coin and those that do not. In this case, the proper distribution is the binomial distribution. Exhibit 31 shows the probabilities involved. If the probability of throwing 15 heads is considered evidence that the coin is unfair, certainly the probability of throwing 16 heads also should be. It is certainly not reasonable to consider it evidence that the coin is fair. Therefore, the probability of throwing 15 or more heads is the probability that the coin is unfairly weighted to fall heads. If this amount is relatively small, the coin should be considered fair. Of course, if it is also possible that the coin might be weighted to fall tails, the possibilities of 5 or fewer heads (15 or more tails) must also be considered.

If the null hypothesis is that the coin is fair and the alternative hypothesis is that the coin is not fair, and if the trader accepts a (1-0.99) or 0.01 level of significance, then the evidence indicates that the coin is *fair;* that is, as the proba-

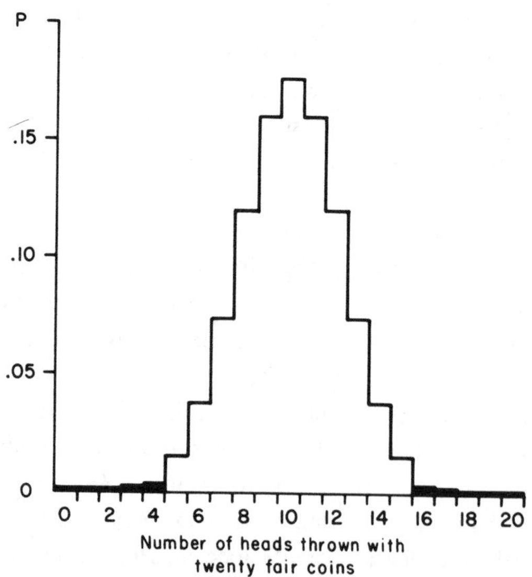

Exhibit 31. Histogram of probability distribution of 20 throws of a fair coin. Shaded area represents 5 or fewer, or 15 or more heads.

bility of 15 or more heads or 5 or fewer heads (i.e., 0.042) is larger than the level of significance chosen, the null hypothesis cannot be rejected.

The level of significance chosen and the hypothesis designated as the null hypothesis are questions of value, not questions of logic or fact. The correct decision depends on the economics of the decision that the trader must make. The null hypothesis should be the hypothesis that the trader would find prudent to assume true if there were no evidence. For example, it is clearly prudent for a trader to assume that any given trading method is worthless until proven otherwise. The hypothesis that a given trading method is worthless would be the null hypothesis. The alternative hypothesis would be that the trading method has value. The level of significance desirable depends on the cost of being wrong. More precisely, the higher the cost of acting as if the alternative hypothesis is true when it is not, the higher the level of significance should be. As it is obviously expensive to trade with useless trading methods, relatively high levels of significance seem prudent.

In a sense, tests and confidence intervals are mirror images of each other. Whereas tests provide more information on how certain a result is, confidence intervals provide more information on the results. Whereas the trader will find it useful to know, say, that he can be 0.98 certain that the probability of success on a given trade will be larger than 0.5, he will, perhaps, find it more useful to know with 0.95 certainty that the probability of success on a given trade will be larger than 0.55. I suspect, therefore, that the trader will find confidence intervals more useful than tests.

How useful tests and confidence intervals will be will depend on how large the sample size is, of course.

Clearly, for a given confidence coefficient, the larger the sample is per se and the larger the sample is as a portion of the population, the smaller the confidence limits will be. However, unless the sample is a relatively large portion of the population, say larger than 0.1, the sample size as a portion of the population is considerably less important than the sample's size per se. This is fortunate, because in the most interesting cases there may be no way of knowing how large the population really is. Indeed, in many cases the population could, theoretically at least, be infinite.

For example, we might be interested in the average price change of May wheat after a certain chart pattern. In this case, the sample would be the price behavior of May wheat for some years past. But, clearly, the population we are really interested in encompasses the future of May wheat. Who can say how large that will be? In practice, therefore, the trader will find that statistics rarely need be, or can be, adjusted for the population size.

Notice how the sample and population differed in the example above. The population of interest consists of the future price behavior of wheat but the sample consists solely of past price behavior. By definition, *not a single member of the population of interest can be sampled in a forecasting problem.*

This does not imply that past data are necessarily useless but rather that they are not necessarily helpful. To extrapolate, it is necessary to assume both that the sample was randomly selected and that the population that was really sampled is essentially the same as the population of interest.

This last assumption is a dangerous one. There are an infinite number of ways the population sampled can differ from the population of interest. For example: (1) future markets may not have the same mix of trading and trending markets as in the past; (2) a trading method may depend on information that is not really available when it is needed; (3) a trading method may depend on executions that cannot be obtained.

I do *not* mean to suggest that the last assumption should never be made, but I do believe that the trader should think about it long and hard. Moreover, such thinking should be done *before* a research project is begun. Research projects are expensive and unless the project is carefully designed, the expense can easily be wasted.

A popular rule of thumb among researchers is to allocate 20 percent of research funds to planning and analyzing. One planning technique many researchers find particularly useful is to consider how an individual who did not want to believe their conclusions would criticize them. What kind of evidence would convince a rational but unfriendly critic?

However, even if it is reasonable to assume that the population sampled is reasonably similar to the population of interest, it is not reasonable to assume that the population of interest will be like any given sample unless that sample was randomly selected. Partly, this is because a random sample is likely to be a representative sample. More important, however, if the sample is random (but *only* if it is random) the mathematical laws of probability can be applied. These are powerful laws that make it possible to make *objective* generalizations from the sample to the populations. In other words, if the sample is random, reasonable statements can be made about the population. However, if the sample is not random, these statements cannot be made, no matter how large the sample is.

If the efficient market hypothesis is true or approximately true, past data have been randomly distributed. Therefore, a method that works with *unseen* past data should work on the market itself. Unfortunately, even with the best will in the world, it is difficult not to select methods to fit the data or to select data to fit the methods. For that reason, it is generally advisable to replicate successful studies on unseen data. Of course, the best, though most expensive, data is the market itself.

Research is expensive. Although research, on average, will produce better decisions, better decisions are not infinitely valuable. The trader, therefore, should give some thought to how much time and money to invest in research.

Clearly, if a sample is randomly selected, the larger the sample size, the more useful the research will be. Indeed, the usefulness of any admissible statistic will increase with the square root of the sample size (see Exhibit 32).

On the other hand, the cost of taking a sample will almost never increase with the square root of the sample size. Almost invariably, the cost of taking a sample will consist of a fixed cost, that is, a cost that does not vary with the sample size, and a variable cost, that is, a cost that increases directly and linearly with the sample size.

This implies that there is an optimal size for any sample. What that will be depends on the cost of being wrong and the costs of taking a sample. If the cost of being wrong is small enough and the costs of taking a sample are high enough, the optimal sample size may be no sample at all (see Exhibit 33).

More often, some sample will be worth taking. However, even when this is the case, not every sample is worth taking. Notice in Exhibit 34 that when the sample is either very small or very large, the total cost curve is above the sample information value curve.

The optimal sample size is the point where the sample information value curve most exceeds the total cost curve. This is the point where the marginal reward from gathering a larger sample size just equals the cost of gathering it. For example, the optimal sample size will be the point where the value to the trader of narrowing the confidence intervals will just equal the cost of increasing the sample size by one.

There are, of course, formulas for calculating the optimal sample size. Unfortunately, they are difficult to use and make assumptions that may not be true. If the trader puts some care into guessing, he probably will be almost as well off.

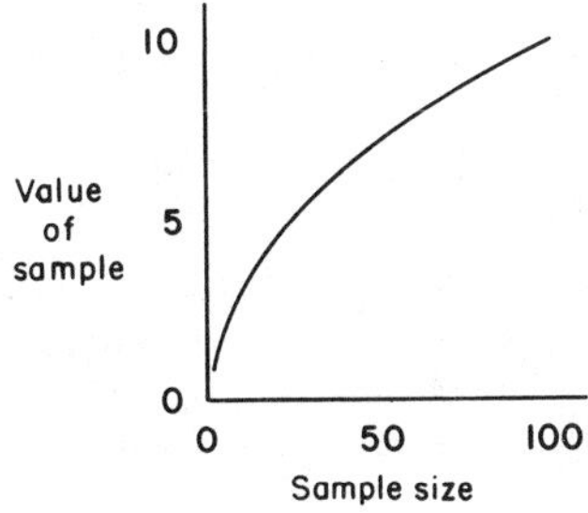

Exhibit 32. The value of a sample increases with the square root of the sample size.

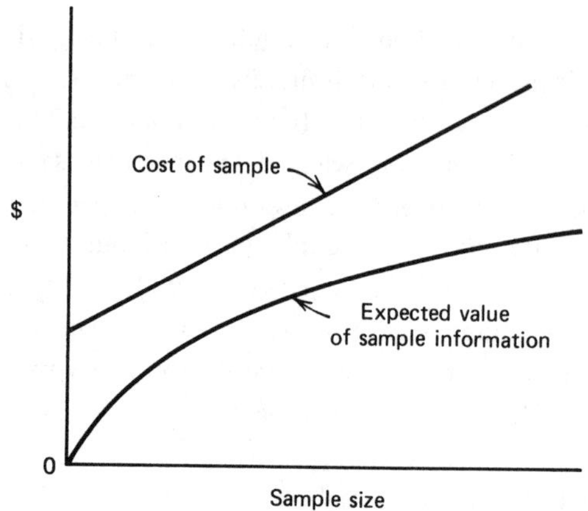

Exhibit 33. Sometimes no sample at all is worth taking.

PRACTICE

Statistics is an applied science. Still, if the trader has decided to begin his study at this point in the text, he has made a mistake. Statistical techniques work only because they are applications of theory. If the trader does not understand the applicable theories, he will be unable to meaningfully apply the techniques.

On the other hand, what theory statisticians find of most interest is of no practical importance. A statistical technique, like a car or a computer, will work whether or not its user understands why.

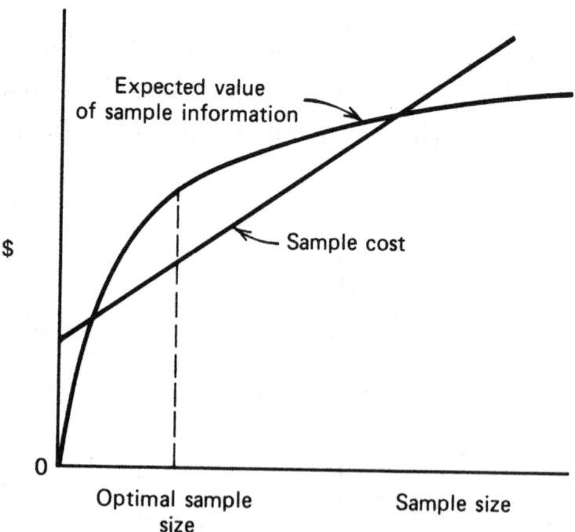

Exhibit 34. Very small and very large samples are rarely worth taking. Moreover, there is a "right" sample size.

The trader should look at a statistical technique as a black box (see Exhibit 35). It is not important that the trader understand what goes on in the box, but it is important that the trader understand what goes into and what comes out of the box.

It is necessary that the trader understand how to perform the needed calculations, but it is not necessary that the trader understand the logic of the calculations. For example, the formula for the Spearman rank correlation coefficient (r_s), which will be explained later, is:

$$r_s = 1 - \frac{6 \cdot \Sigma di^2}{N^3 - N}$$

The trader must understand how to use this formula but need not understand why, for instance, di^2 is multiplied by 6 and not 7.

Part of the input for each technique is a group of assumptions. If these assumptions are in fact met, the techniques output can be relief upon. If these assumptions are not met, the output cannot be relied upon. Clearly, the trader should carefully consider the assumptions of the available techniques before he uses them.

It is for precisely this reason that alternative methods are presented. If the assumptions of one technique are not appealing, the assumptions of another might be. Of course, if the assumptions behind none of the methods presented are appealing, the trader must seek out more sophisticated and difficult methods, if they exist, or guess.

A great deal of important data is dichotomous. In other words, the data can only take one of two forms: yes or no, in or out, up or down. Even when this is not the case, data can often be reduced to a dichotomous form: a person has blue eyes or he does not, a person is born in England or he is not.

Frequently, it is important to estimate what portion (P) of a given dichotomous population has a certain characteristic. (Note that parameters are printed

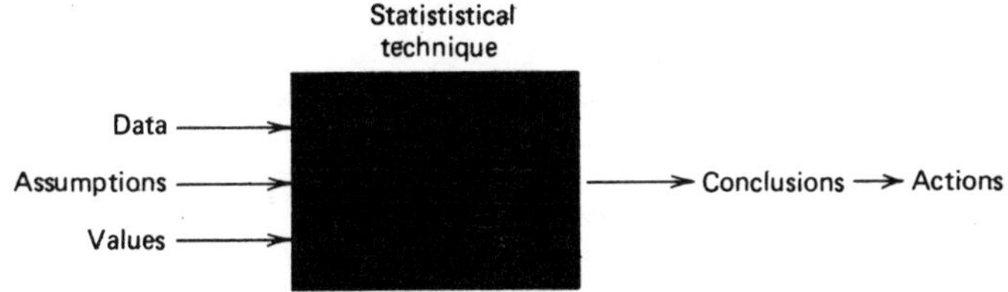

Exhibit 35. It is important that traders understand the assumptions and values of statistical techniques. It is not important that they understand the theory.

in boldface while statistics are printed sans serif, that is "T" rather than "*T*," with the exceptions of "*N*," "*P*," and χ^2. Note also that with the exceptions of "*N*" and "*R*," none of the symbols used in this chapter are used elsewhere.) For example, for money management purposes, it may be important to estimate what portion of future trades will be profitable.

There are several ways to estimate **P** if it can be assumed that:

1. Each event can be classified into one of two groups: Y and ~Y.
2. The probability **P** of an event being classified Y remains constant from event to event.
3. The *N* events are independent.
4. The *N* events have been randomly selected.

The most obvious estimator is P' (the $'$ merely indicates that it is the first indicator considered. The $''$ indicates it is the second indicator considered, etc.), where

$$P' = \mathsf{Y}/N$$

P' has a number of virtues. The first and most obvious is that it is easy to calculate. Its second virtue is mathematical. It can be shown that the sample statistic is more likely to be P', if in fact the population parameter is **P**, than it is if it is any other value. In other words, if, say, $P' = 0.4$, this is more likely to occur when $\mathbf{P} = 0.4$ than it is at any other time.

Unfortunately, when N is small, P' is sometimes clearly unreasonable. For example, if a trader has traded corn only three times, but has traded successfully each time, then

$$\mathsf{Y} = 3$$

$$N = 3$$

and, given certain assumptions, his probability (P') of profiting on any given trade would seem to be

$$P' = \frac{3}{3}$$

$$= 1.0$$

which is clearly unreasonable.

A possibly more reasonable estimator is P'', which is constructed as follows:

$$P'' = \frac{\sqrt{N}P' + 0.5}{\sqrt{N} + 1}$$

For example, if:

$$Y = 3$$

$$N = 4$$

then

$$P'' = \frac{\sqrt{4} \cdot 0.75 + 0.5}{\sqrt{4} + 1}$$

$$= \frac{2 \cdot 0.75 + 0.5}{2 + 1}$$

$$= \frac{1.5 + 0.5}{2 + 1}$$

$$= \frac{2}{3}$$

$$= 0.667$$

which is clearly more reasonable than ($P' = 0.75$).

P'' is a weighted average of P' and 0.5, with the weighting depending on how large N is. When N is large, P' and P'' are virtually identical. However, when N is small, the divergence can be considerable. Clearly, for the commodity trader, P'' is often a more prudent estimator than P'.

A still more prudent procedure would be to use P' as an estimate of **P** but to construct a confidence interval about P'. Clearly, it is more reasonable to use P' as an estimator of **P** than it is to use another estimator, because P' is more likely to equal **P** than any other estimator is. On the other hand, it is clearly unreasonable to expect P' to *exactly* equal **P**. A confidence interval is a way of showing how reasonable an estimate of **P** the estimate P' really is.

If the sample is relatively large, say larger than 30, confidence limits can be easily calculated. How this is done will be described later. Unfortunately, these techniques are not valid when the sample size is small, in which case Table 1 in Appendix 3 must be used. The small sample procedure will now be described.

1. Select a confidence coefficient α. If no value if acceptable, use the next largest value.
2. Calculate Z. If only one confidence limit is to be calculated, $Z = \alpha$. If both are to be calculated, $Z = 1 - ((1 - \alpha)/2)$.
3. Locate the section of the table where N is equal to the sample size.
4. Under column Y locate the row where Y is equal to the number in the sample with the attribute of interest.
5. The lower confidence limit $PL(\alpha)$ is the value where the selected row and column intersect.
6. Under column Y locate the row where Y is equal to $N - Y$.
7. The upper confidence limit $PU(\alpha)$ is one minus the value where the selected row and column intersect.

For example, assume that a trader has traded wheat twice, but both times successfully. In this case, P', of course, is 1. Assume the trader wishes to locate the 0.9 confidence intervals. Using Table 1 in Appendix 3 and following the procedure above, the confidence levels located are $PU(\alpha) = 1.0000$ and $PL(\alpha) = 0.224$.

Clearly, the most likely value for **P** is 1.0000. Unfortunately, there is a 0.9 probability that **P** is as large as 1.0000 or as small as 0.224. Considering the size of this range, it does not seem reasonable that P' is a reliable estimate of **P**.

However, when $N \geqslant 30$, confidence intervals can easily be calculated. We shall do so now.

1. Decide whether one or both confidence limits are to be calculated.
2. Select a confidence coefficient α.
3. Calculate Z. If only one confidence limit is to be calculated, $Z = \alpha$. If two, $Z = 1 - [(1 - \alpha)/2]$.
4. Locate $\tilde{Z}$. $\tilde{Z}$ is the number of standard deviations from the mean that has a probability of Z. These values can be found on Table 2 in Appendix 3.
5. Calculate:

$$Pu(\alpha) = P' + \tilde{Z}\sqrt{\frac{P'(1 - P')}{N - 1}}$$

$$PL(\alpha) = P' - \tilde{Z}\sqrt{\frac{P'(1 - P')}{N - 1}}$$

For example, assume that a trader wants to be 0.95 certain of both the upper and lower confidence limits when $P' = 0.6$ and $N = 100$. Therefore:

$$\alpha = 0.95$$

$$Z = 1 - [(1 - 0.95)/2]$$

$$\tilde{Z} = 0.975$$

Using Table 2 in Appendix 3, if $Z = 0.975$ then $\tilde{Z} = 1.96$

$$PU(0.95) = 0.6 + 1.96 \sqrt{\frac{0.6(1 - 0.6)}{100 - 1}}$$

$$= 0.6 + 1.96 \sqrt{\frac{0.24}{99}}$$

$$= 0.6 + 1.96 \cdot \sqrt{0.0024242424}$$

$$= .60 + 1.96 \cdot .049236596$$

$$= .60 + .096503728$$

$$= .696503728$$

$$PL(\alpha) = 0.6 - 1.96 \sqrt{\frac{0.6(1 - 0.6)}{99}}$$

$$= .60 - .096503728$$

$$= .503496272$$

All of these techniques assume that the events are independent. In many cases this is a reasonable assumption. In many cases, however, it is not.

There are two types of dependency, positive and negative. Positive dependency means that large values are followed, on average, by large values, and small values by small values. Negative dependency means that large values are followed, on average, by small values, and small values by large values.

"Large" and "small" are relative terms. If the values can be positive or negative, positive dependency means that, on average, positive values are followed by positive values, and negative values by negative values.

A run test is a means of testing whether dichotomous data are dependent. A run is a group of consecutive or successive events; for example, in the series below, where each event follows the event to its left, there are 26 events:

++--0++0++-+-+--0++0-+-+--

However, when the ties, which are indicated by zeros, are dropped, there are 22 events and 14 runs:

++--++++-+-+--++-+-+--

The procedure for testing for dependency will now be described.

1. Decide whether to test for positive dependency, negative dependency, or both.
2. Select a level of significance $(1 - \alpha)$.
3. Calculate Z. If only positive or negative dependency is to be tested for, $Z = (1 - \alpha)$. If both positive and negative dependency are to be tested for, $Z = (1 - \alpha)/2$.
4. Locate $\tilde{\tilde{Z}}$. $\tilde{\tilde{Z}}$ is the number of standard deviations from the mean that has a probability of Z. These values can be found in Table 2 in Appendix 3.
5. Calculate K.

$$K = \frac{N(r - 0.5) - 2n_1n_2}{\sqrt{\dfrac{2n_1n_2(2n_1n_2 - N)}{N - 1}}}$$

where N = the sample size

r = the number of runs

n_1 = one of the two types of events

n_2 = the other type of event.

(Naturally, $n_1 + n_2 = N$)

6. a. Positive dependency is significant at the $(1 - \alpha)$ level if

$$K > \tilde{Z}$$

Otherwise, it is not.

b. Negative dependency is significant at the $(1 - \alpha)$ level if

$$K < \tilde{Z}$$

Otherwise, it is not.

c. Positive or negative dependency is significant at the $(1 - \alpha)$ level if

$$K > |\tilde{Z}|$$

where the horizontal bars indicate that the absolute value of $\tilde{Z}$ is to be considered. In other words, a negative sign for $\tilde{Z}$ should be ignored. If K is not larger than the absolute value of $\tilde{Z}$, there is no significant dependency at the $(1 - \alpha)$ level.

For example, if all of a trader's decisions are optimal, his or her profits and losses will be independent. Contrariwise, if his profits and losses are not independent, the trader can change his behavior to incorporate this information and improve his reward/risk ratio. Assume that a trader has had a series of profitable and unprofitable trades that could be represented by the data given above. Assume, also, that the trader will not change his trading behavior unless the results are significant at the $(1 - \alpha)$ or 0.10 level. If both negative and positive dependency are to be tested for:

$$Z = (1 - 0.90)/2$$

$$= 0.1/2$$

$$= 0.05$$

$$\tilde{Z} = 1.65$$

Using the data above and assigning 12 to n_1, then:

$N = 22$, $n_1 = 12$, $n_2 = 10$, and $r = 14$. Thus:

$$2n_1n_2 = 2 \cdot 12 \cdot 10$$

$$2n_1n_2 = 240$$

$$K = \frac{22(14 - 0.5) - 240}{\sqrt{\dfrac{240(240 - 22)}{22 - 1}}}$$

$$= \frac{22(13.5) - 240}{\sqrt{\dfrac{240(218)}{21}}}$$

$$= \frac{297 - 240}{\sqrt{\dfrac{52320}{21}}}$$

$$= \frac{57}{\sqrt{2491.428571}}$$

$$= \frac{57}{49.91421212}$$

$$= 1.141959325$$

Because 1.141959325 is not larger than the absolute value of 1.65, the trader should not change his trading behavior.

The relationship between one dichotomous variable and another is frequently important. For example, it might be interesting to know how often an indicator that allegedly forecasts the direction of next week's closing wheat prices actually does forecast next week's wheat prices.

Clearly, four pieces of information are needed to estimate the relationship. The information needed is a, the number of times the index correctly forecasted a price rise; b, the number of times the index incorrectly forecasted a price rise; c, the number of times the index incorrectly forecasted a price decline; and d, the number of times the index correctly forecasted a price decline. This information can be tabled as in Exhibit 36.

The relationship between the two dichotomous variables can be estimated by the adjusted correlation coefficient C if it can be assumed that:

1. Each event can be classified into one of two groups; Y and ~Y, by each of two independent criteria.

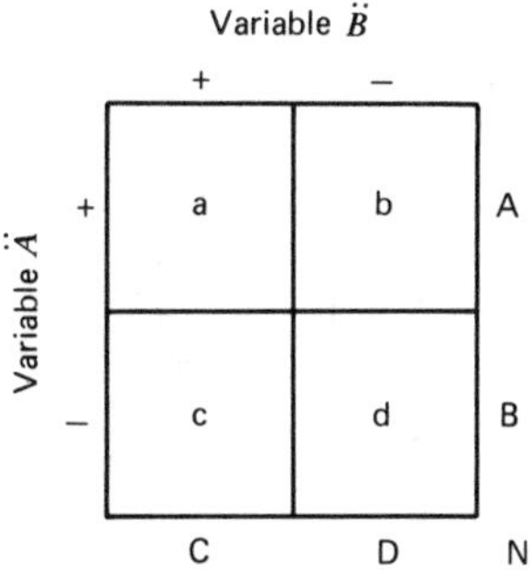

Exhibit 36. a, b, c, and d represent sample information and A, B, C, and D represent the margin totals. N is the sample size.

2. The probability **P** of an event being classified Y remains constant from event to event for each of the two independent criteria.
3. The N events are independent.
4. The N events have been randomly selected.
5. a, b, c, and d or their expected values are all greater than or equal to 1. The expected value of, say, b, that is, EX(b) is equal to the product of the appropriate marginal totals divided by the sample size. Thus:

$$\text{EX(a)} = \text{A} \cdot \text{C}/N$$

$$\text{EX(b)} = \text{A} \cdot \text{D}/N$$

$$\text{EX(c)} = \text{B} \cdot \text{C}/N$$

$$\text{EX(d)} = \text{B} \cdot \text{D}/N$$

where A, B, C, and D are all marginal totals. For example, using the data in Exhibit 37:

$$\text{EX(b)} = 5 \cdot 2/7$$

$$= 1.4$$

Naturally, when C = 0, there is no relationship between the sample variables; when C = 1, the relationship is perfect. The relationship will be positive if ad > bc, negative if ad < bc, and nonexistent if ad = bc. The adjusted correlation coefficient is calculated as follows:

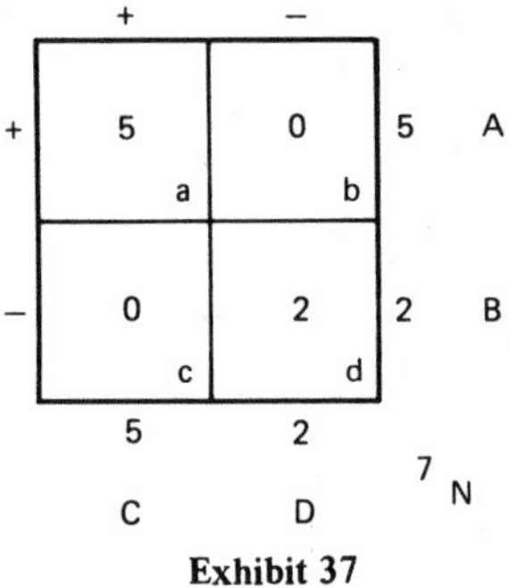

Exhibit 37

$$C = \sqrt{\frac{\chi^2}{\chi^2 + N}} \Big/ .707$$

when

$$\chi^2 = \frac{N\left(|ad - bc| - \frac{N}{2}\right)^2}{(a + b)(c + d)(a + c)(b + d)}$$

N = the sample size

These formulas are actually quite easy to use. Let us assume, for example, that over the last 90 weeks, a trader has counted the number of times a given index has and has not forecasted the weekly change in May wheat and arranged the information in Exhibit 38. Therefore:

$$\chi^2 = \frac{90\left(|37 \cdot 34 - 13 \cdot 6| - \frac{90}{2}\right)^2}{(37 + 13)(6 + 34)(37 + 6)(13 + 34)}$$

$$= \frac{90(|1258 - 78| - 45)^2}{4{,}042{,}000}$$

$$= \frac{90(|1180| - 45)^2}{4{,}042{,}000}$$

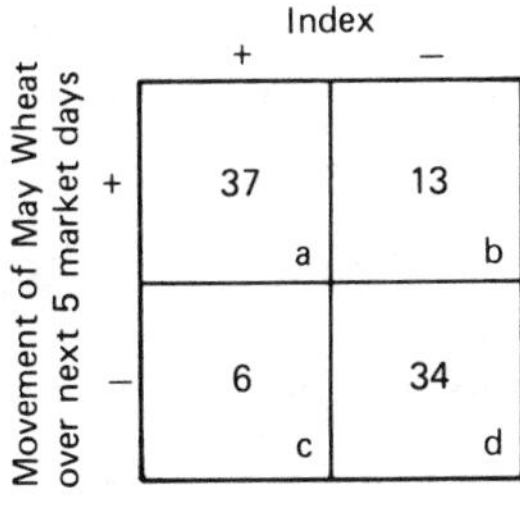

Exhibit 38

$$= \frac{90(1135)^2}{4{,}042{,}000}$$

$$= \frac{90 \cdot 1{,}288{,}225}{4{,}042{,}000}$$

$$= \frac{115940250}{4{,}042{,}000}$$

$$= 28.68388174$$

Therefore:

$$C = \sqrt{\frac{28.68388174}{28.68388174 + 90}} \bigg/ .707$$

$$= \frac{\sqrt{0.2416830434}}{0.707}$$

$$= \frac{0.4916126965}{0.707}$$

$$= 0.6953503487$$

Clearly, C may or may not be significant. If the assumptions above were satisfied and if the actual or expected values of a, b, c, and d are all greater than or equal to 5, the significance can easily be determined. This technique will be described shortly. However, if all of the actual or expected values are not greater than 5, the following, and more tedious, technique must be used:

1. Decide whether to test for only positive or negative relationships, or both.
2. If you have decided to test for a positive or a negative relationship but not both, check to see that the sign of the relationship is the same as the sign of C. If it is not, there is no relationship.
3. Select a level of significance $(1 - \alpha)$.
4. Calculate Z. If you have decided to test for both positive and negative relationships, $Z = (1 - \alpha)/2$. If you have decided to test for either positive or negative relationships, but not both, $Z = 1 - \alpha$.
5. Determine the sample values a + b and c + d.
6. Find the sample values a + b in Table 3 in Appendix 3 under the heading "Totals in the Right Margin."
7. In the same section of the table, but to the right, locate the sample values c + d under that heading.
8. To the right, in the next section of the table, locate the sample value b. If the sample value b is not available, go to step 8 (Alternative).
9. If the sample value d is equal to or less than the value in the column under the chosen value of Z in the row identified with the sample values for a + b, c + d, and b, the data are significant at level of significance $(1 - \alpha)$.
8. (Alternative) In the same section of the table where the sample value b was to be found, locate sample value a.
9. (Alternative) If the sample value c is equal to or less than the value in the column under the chosen values of Z and in the row identified with the sample values for a + b, c + d, and a, the data are significant at that level.

For example, suppose a trader has observed the behavior of an index and the subsequent behavior of platinum and tabled the data as in Exhibit 37. Let us also assume that the trader has decided to use the index if it demonstrates positive dependency and 0.95 significance during the test period. In this case, therefore, $Z = 0.95$.

Using the data in Exhibit 37, a + b = 5 and c + d = 2. In this case, b does not equal 5, but a does. After locating the proper rows and columns on Table 3 in Appendix 3, we find that the sample value for c must be equal to or less than 0 for the data to be significant at the $(1 - \alpha)$ level.

If, in fact, the actual or expected values are all greater than or equal to 5, the procedure is as follows:

1. Decide whether to test for a positive relationship or negative relationship or both.
2. If you have decided to test for a positive or a negative relationship but not both, check to see that the sign of the relationship is the same as the sign of C. If it is not, there is no relationship.
3. Select a level of significance $(1 - \alpha)$.
4. Calculate Z. If you have decided to test for either a positive or a negative relationship, $Z = \alpha$. If you have decided to test for both positive and negative relationships, $Z = 1-[(1 - \alpha)/2]$.
5. Locate ZZ on Table 4 in Appendix 3. ZZ is the value opposite Z.
6. If the value of χ^2 calculated above is equal to or larger than ZZ, then C is significant at the $(1 - \alpha)$ level.

For example, assume that a trader wanted 0.90 certainty before he used the method that generated the data in Exhibit 38. Let us also assume that he wanted to test for positive or negative relationships. The expected values are all obviously over 5, so the technique above can be used. $Z = 0.95$ and Table 4 in Appendix 3 reveals that the χ^2 value must be larger than or equal to 3.84 for the trader to be 0.95 certain that the method is valid. As the χ^2 generated was, in fact, 28.6, the method seems to be valid.

One of the most frequent and important research tasks is estimating an average value. Unless, for example, trading can be expected to be profitable on average, it clearly makes no sense to trade.

There are several ways to estimate X, if it can be assumed that:

1. The data can be measured on a ratio scale. That is, a scale with a zero point and with constant differences between any two numbers. Price and weight are examples.
2. The true mean **X** is the same for each event.
3. The N events are independent.
4. The N events have been randomly selected.

A useful and obvious estimator for the population's arithmetic mean **X** is the sample's arithmetic mean X′. This is simply the sum of the sample value divided by the sample size. For example: 300, -950, 45, -50, -150, 200, 400 has a total of -205 and sample size of 7. The sample arithmetic mean is, therefore, -205 ÷ 7 = -29.28.

Another estimator is the sample median X''. The sample median is the sample's middle value when the sample has been ordered by magnitude and the sample size is odd. When the sample size is even, the median is the arithmetic average of the middle two values. Ranking the data above produces the following: -950, -150, -50, 45, 200, 300, 400. The median in the example above is 45.

Note that the mean and median differ in the example above. This will happen whenever the sample is not symmetric, that is, skewed. Because the mean gives more weight to extreme values than the median does, it will shift more than the median will in the direction of the extreme values, that is, in the direction of the skew (see Exhibit 60).

In many ways, the sample mean is the most desirable average. After all, we are generally interested in the population mean, not the population median. However, because the mean is more affected by extreme values than the median is, it is a less stable and, therefore, in many ways a less desirable measure of location. The sample median can be used in any situation where the mean can be used, but the converse is not true.

A third estimator is the sample midrange X'''. The sample midrange is simply the arithmetic mean of the sample's two most extreme values. For example, ranking the data above produces the following: -950, -150, -50, 45, 200, 300, 400. The most extreme values are, of course, -950 and 400, and the sample midrange is:

$$X''' = \frac{-950 + 400}{2}$$

$$X''' = \frac{-550}{2}$$

$$X''' = -275$$

The only real virtue of the sample midrange is its simplicity. This, of course, is also a drawback. When the sample is of even modest size, the midrange is grossly inferior to the mean and median. Still, if the sample size is quite small, the sample midrange is an acceptable and quick but not too dirty technique.

Another virtue of the sample midrange is that confidence limits can easily be constructed. This is also a quick but not too dirty technique. We will describe it now.

1. Decide whether only the upper or lower or both the upper and lower confidence limits are to be constructed.
2. Select a confidence coefficient α.
3. Calculate the sample size N.
4. Locate the range adjustment factor (RAF) in Table 5 in Appendix 3. This is located where the column for the appropriate confidence coefficient and the row for the appropriate sample size intersect. The far left column indicates the sample size. If only the lower or upper confidence limit is to be constructed, the confidence coefficients are located on the bottom row. If both the lower and upper confidence limits are to be constructed, the top row contains the confidence coefficients.
5. Note whether the adjustment is to be placed inside or outside the range. Table 5 in Appendix 3 makes this clear.
6. Calculate the sample range W.
7. Calculate the range adjustment RA.

$$\mathrm{RA} = \mathrm{RAF} \cdot \mathrm{W}$$

8A. If the range adjustment is to be made inside:

$$\mathrm{X}'''\mathrm{U}(\alpha) = \mathrm{R}(N) - \mathrm{RA}$$

$$\mathrm{X}'''\mathrm{L}(\alpha) = \mathrm{R}(1) + \mathrm{RA}$$

8B. If the range adjustment is to be made outside:

$$\mathrm{X}'''\mathrm{U}(\alpha) = \mathrm{R}(N) + \mathrm{RA}$$

$$\mathrm{X}'''\mathrm{L}(\alpha) = \mathrm{R}(1) - \mathrm{RA}$$

(where R(N) indicate the sample's largest value and R(1) the sample's smallest value.)

For example, assume that a trader has developed a theory that he believes, but is not certain, has forecasting power. Nevertheless, the trader has decided he will trade with it if a trial run demonstrates 0.95 certainty that the method has forecasting power. Even if the method is highly unprofitable during the trial, the theory could still be used with the buy and sell orders reversed, so both confidence limits must be constructed.

Assume that a trial run produces the following gross profits and losses: -50, 300, 400, -150, 100, 200, 250, -200, -50. Using the data above:

$$X''' = \frac{400 + (-200)}{2}$$

$$X''' = \frac{200}{2}$$

$$X''' = 100$$

$$W = 400 - (-200)$$

$$= 600$$

Table 5 in Appendix 3 reveals that when $N = 9$, $\alpha = 0.95$ and both confidence limits are to be constructed, RAF = 0.2 and the adjustment is to be made to the inside. Therefore:

$$\text{RAF} = 0.2 \cdot 600$$

$$= 120$$

and

$$X'''U(\alpha) = 400 - 120$$

$$= 280$$

$$X'''L(\alpha) = -200 + 120$$

$$= -80$$

Since the confidence limits contain zero, the trader should not use the method.

Unfortunately, this technique becomes progressively less powerful as the sample size increases. An alternative is to use a technique based on the mean absolute deviation (MAD) rather than the sample range (W). In addition to the assumptions above, this technique assumes that the population is distributed normally, or approximately normally. A technique for constructing confidence intervals will now be described:

1. Decide whether an upper confidence limit, a lower confidence limit or both are to be calculated.
2. Decide on a confidence coefficient α.
3. Calculate Z. If only one confidence limit is to be calculated, $Z = \alpha$. If both confidence limits are to be calculated, $Z = 1 - [(1 - \alpha)/2]$.
4. Calculate the sample size N.
5. Compute the sample mean X'.
6. Compute the sample mean absolute deviation (MAD). This is calculated by subtracting each value in the sample, in turn, for the mean. Second, all negative signs are dropped. Finally, the average of all the resulting values is calculated.
7. Find HNZ in Table 5 in Appendix 3. Move down the far left column until you find the sample size N. Then move across the row until you find the column under the value Z.
8. Calculate $X'U(\alpha)$ and/or $X'L(\alpha)$

$$X'U(\alpha) = X' + [(\text{MAD} \cdot \text{HNZ})/\sqrt{N}]$$

$$X'L(\alpha) = X' - [(\text{MAD} \cdot \text{HNZ})/\sqrt{N}]$$

For example, assume that a trader was willing to trade oats only if he could be 0.95 confident that his trading method was profitable on a net basis. Let us also assume that during the trial run, the method produced the following profits and losses: 50, 150, 350, -200, -75, 300, -25, 250. Using the above data, the trader need calculate only a lower confidence limit, $Z = 0.95$ and $N = 8$. Therefore:

$$\text{HNZ} = 3.092$$

$$\sqrt{8} = 2.8284271$$

and

$$50 - 100 = |-50| = 50$$

$$150 - 100 = |50| = 50$$

$$350 - 100 = |\ 250| = 250$$

$$-200 - 100 = |-300| = 300$$

$$-75 - 100 = |-175| = 175$$

$$300 - 100 = |\ 200| = 200$$

$$-25 - 100 = |-125| = 125$$

$$\underline{250} - 100 = |\ \underline{150}| = \underline{150}$$

$$800 \qquad\qquad 1300$$

$$\div\ 8 \qquad\qquad \div\ 8$$

$$X' = 100 \qquad\qquad MAD = 162.5$$

Therefore:

$$XL(\alpha) = 100 - \frac{162.5 \cdot 3.092}{2.828471}$$

$$= 100 - 177.64014$$

$$= -77.64014$$

Confidence intervals for the median cannot generally be set without extensive tables. This is unfortunate, as these techniques, unlike the above techniques, do not demand that the population be distributed even approximately normally. However, if the trader is willing to construct both limits and to limit himself to one of three confidence coefficients, then limits can be easily calculated. We shall describe the method now.

1. Decide on a confidence coefficient α.
2. Select the appropriate value for $\exists$.

α	$\exists$
0.90	0.80
0.95	1.00
0.99	1.30

3. Arrange the sample in order of rank and give each value a rank from R(1) for the smallest to R(N) for the largest. N is, of course, also the sample size.
4. Calculate Π.

$$\Pi = \frac{N + 1}{2} - \exists\sqrt{N}$$

rounded off to the nearest integer.

5. Calculate ΠΠ.

$$\Pi\Pi = (N + 1) - \Pi$$

6. $X''U(\alpha) = R(\Pi\Pi)$

   $X''L(\alpha) = R(\Pi)$

For example, assume that a trader wishes to construct 0.90 confidence intervals for the trial run of a new copper trading method, and that his sample is: 50, 150, 350, -200, -75, 300, -25, 250.

In this case, ∃ = 0.8. The sample is ranked below:

$$R(8) = 350$$

$$R(7) = 300$$

$$R(6) = 250$$

$$R(5) = 150$$

$$R(4) = 50$$

$$R(3) = -25$$

$$R(2) = -75$$

$$R(1) = -200$$

$$\Pi = \frac{8 + 1}{2} - 0.8\sqrt{8}$$

$$= \frac{9}{2} - 0.8 \cdot 2.8284271$$

$$= 4.5 - 2.2627416$$

$$= 2.$$

$$\Pi\Pi = (8 + 1) - 2$$

$$= 9 - 2$$

$$= 7$$

$$X''U(\alpha) = R(7)$$

$$= 300$$

$$X''L(\alpha) = R(2)$$

$$= -75$$

It is often useful to know the relationship between two variables. One method of doing this is to plot the data on a dot chart called a scatter diagram. In Exhibit 39 each dot represents the relationship between the level of a proprietary

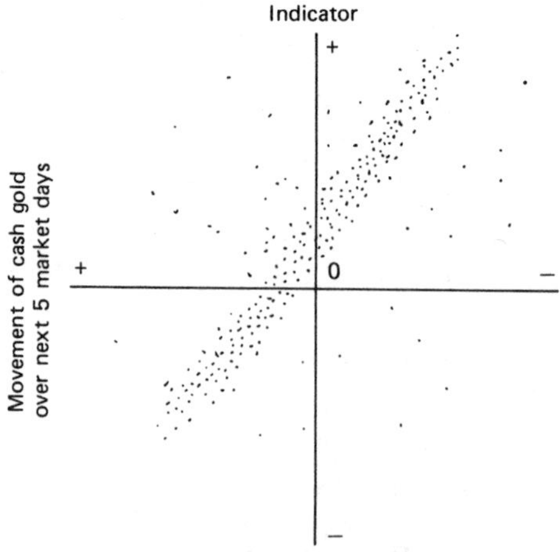

Exhibit 39. A scattergram of a positive relationship.

indicator and the net change in the price of gold over the next week. In this case, the relationship is positive, that is, large values of one variable are accompanied or followed, on average, by large values of the other variable, and small values of one variable by small values of the other. Exhibit 40 illustrates a negative relationship, that is, large values of one variable are accompanied or followed, on average, by small values of the other variable, and small values of one variable by large values of the other. Exhibit 41 illustrates a third alternative, that is, that there is no relationship at all between the variables.

Despite the usefulness of the scatter diagram, it does not provide a measure of the relationship of the two variables. One of many ways to express that relationship is with the Spearman rank correlation coefficient (r_s). This coefficient expresses the relationship between pairs of ranked variables, X(i) and Y(i), by means of a number from negative one to positive one inclusive. If the coefficient is one, this indicates perfect positive correlation between the variables. For example:

X(i)	Y(i)
6	6
5	5
4	4
3	3
2	2
1	1

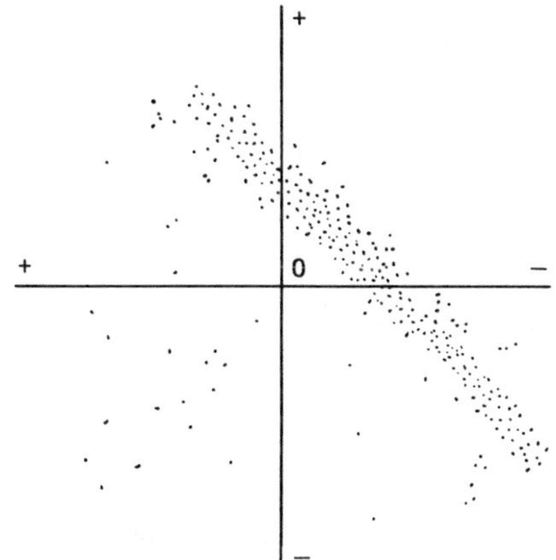

Exhibit 40. A scattergram of a negative relationship.

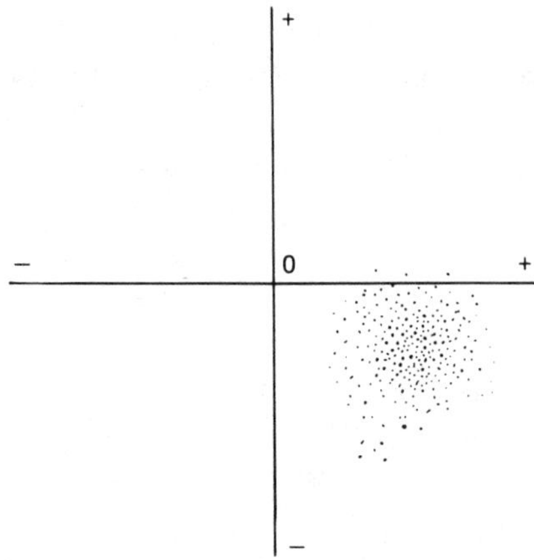

Exhibit 41. A scattergram of a nonexistent relationship.

If, on the other hand, the coefficient is negative one, that indicates a perfect but negative correlation between the variables. For example:

X(i)	Y(i)
6	1
5	2
4	3
3	4
2	5
1	6

If the coefficient is zero, that indicates no correlation whatever. An approximate example is:

X(i)	Y(i)
6	1
5	6
4	3
3	4
2	5
1	2

The calculation of the Spearman rank correlation coefficient will now be described.

1. If the data is not already in ranked form, it must be reduced to ranked form.
2. For each pair of ranked data, calculate di. di is the difference between the ranks.
3. Calculate di^2 for each value. This is simply the di value squared.
4. Calculate Σdi^2. This is the sum of all the di^2 values.
5. Multiply di^2 by 6.
6. Take the sample size N and cube it, that is, multiply it by itself twice.
7. The result is N^3. Subtract N from N^3.
8. Divide the results of step 5 by the results of step 7.
9. If the results of step 8 are subtracted from 1, the result is the Spearman correlation coefficient (r_s). Algebraically, this is:

$$r_s = 1 - \frac{6 \cdot \Sigma di^2}{N^3 - N}$$

For example, let us suppose that a trader has invented an index that he believes can forecast the gold market over the next three days. The index values are listed in the X(i) column in the matrix below, and the corresponding changes in the gold price over the next three days are listed in column Y(i). In other words, when the index registered 150, the net change in the gold price over the next three days was $25. In the next two columns, R(X) and R(Y), the variables X and Y are ranked. The next column, di, calculates the difference between columns R(X) and R(Y), and the column next to that, di^2, squares the difference. The sum of these squares is then calculated and plugged into the formula. The sample size, which is also the largest rank, and the sample size cubed are then plugged into the formula and the formula is calculated.

X(i)	Y(i)	R(X)	R(Y)	di	di^2
150	25	6	4	2	4
90	-100	2	2	0	0
125	300	4	6	-2	4
70	250	1	5	-4	16
140	-200	5	1	4	16
100	-50	3	3	0	0
160	500	7	7	0	0

$di^2 = 40$

$$7^3 = 7 \cdot 7 \cdot 7$$

$$= 343$$

$$r_s = 1 - \frac{6 \cdot 40}{343 - 7}$$

$$= 0.2857$$

r_s is, of course, a statistic, and may or may not equal the parameter r_s. Fortunately, it is relatively easy to test the significance of r_s. The procedure will now be described.

1. Select a level of significance $(1 - \alpha)$.
2. Decide whether the test will be for positive relationships, negative relationships, or both.
3. If both relationships are to be tested for, the available values of $(1 - \alpha)$ are in the top row of Table 7 of Appendix 3. If only positive or negative relationships but not both are to be tested for, the second row gives the available values.
4. Note the sample size *N*. The far left column contains all available sample sizes between 6 and 100. Locate the row with the appropriate sample size.
5. Move across the row until you locate the rightmost value that is smaller than the absolute value of r_s.
6. Move up this column to whichever of the top two rows is appropriate. If the $(1 - \alpha)$ level is larger than or equal to the $(1 - \alpha)$ level selected earlier, the data are not significant at the selected level.

For example, if a trader decides to conduct a two-sided test of the problem above with a significance of (1 - 0.95) or 0.05, the appropriate value in Table 7 in Appendix 3 is 0.786. As the value for the sample only equals 0.2857, r_s is not significant at the 0.05 level.

Chapter Six

Trading and Tradeoffs

Many traders fail to plan not because they do not know the virtues of planning, but because they are not sure what a good trade would look like. There is some market folklore on this topic (e.g., don't take a trade unless the potential profit is three times the potential loss), but most of it is either irrelevant or worse, wrong.

Which trades are worth accepting is suggested by probability theory and interest rate theory. Interest is the time value of money, and time is a major factor in selecting trades. Simple interest can be calculated as follows:

$$V(t) = V(0)[(1 + \iota)^t]$$

where $V(t)$ = the value at the end of t periods

$V(0)$ = the value at time 0

ι = the interest rate

t = the number of periods

The order in which the calculations are performed will generally affect the outcome. Calculations within parentheses are performed before calculations outside them. Furthermore, multiplication takes place before division, both take place before exponentiation, and all of these take place before addition or subtraction. Exponentiation is indicated by a superscript such as the Y in the expression X^Y. The Y indicates that the X is to be multiplied by itself Y times; for example, $5^4 = 5 \cdot 5 \cdot 5 \cdot 5 = 625$. Therefore, if $V(0) = 10$, $\iota = 0.08$, and $t = 15$, then:

$$V(t) = 10[(1 + 0.08)^{15}]$$

$$= 10[(1.08)^{15}]$$

$$= 10(3.172169114)$$

$$= 31.72169114$$

When interest is compounded, the proper formula is:

$$V(t) = V(0)\left[\left(1 + \frac{\iota}{q}\right)^{qt}\right]$$

where q = the number of times interest is compounded per time period

Therefore, if $q = 4$ and the other numbers are as they were above, then:

$$V(t) = 10\left[\left(1 + \frac{0.08}{4}\right)^{(4 \cdot 15)}\right]$$

$$= 10[(1 + 0.02)^{60}]$$

$$= 10[(1.02)^{60}]$$

$$= 10(3.281030739)$$

$$= 32.81030739$$

When compounding is continuous, q becomes infinite and the formula becomes:

$$V(t) = V(0)[e^{(\iota t)}]$$

where $e = 2.71828$

For example, if $V(0) = 10$, $\iota = 0.08$, and $t = 15$ as above, then:

$$V(t) = 10[2.71828^{(0.08 \cdot 15)}]$$

$$= 10[2.71828^{(1.2)}]$$

$$= 10(3.320114243)$$

$$= 33.20114243$$

The interest rate formula can be used to examine the tradeoff between trading profitability and trading frequency. Traders are generally cautioned not to overtrade, but if the trader can trade profitably, frequent trading would seem to be a virtue because it allows the trader to increase his return on capital. Indeed, as the trader can compound his profits, it would seem that trading frequency is more important than profitability.

Using ι as a measure of profitability and q as a measure of frequency, Exhibit 42 illustrates the effect of increasing the frequency of trading.

Notice that while compounding increases the return, the marginal increase—that is, the amount the return is raised by compounding just one more time—continually decreases until it reaches the limit when compounding is continuous. Clearly, it is simply not that important to trade frequently.

On the other hand, Exhibit 43 shows that the marginal return from increasing the interest rate increases without limit. Notice, for example, that the difference between the compound returns for $\iota = 1$ and $\iota = 0.99$ in the eleventh year is larger than the compound returns for $\iota = 0.5$. Oddly enough, as Exhibit 44 shows, even the importance of compounding is a function of profitability. Clearly, most traders would be better off trying to find very profitable trades than trying to trade often.

There is no reason to assume that a very profitable trade need have a large potential gain. Indeed, potential loss is probably more important because it becomes increasingly more difficult to break even, much less profit, with larger and larger losses. In fact, the gain necessary to break even (E) is:

$$E = 1/(1 - \Lambda)$$

where Λ = the proportion of capital lost

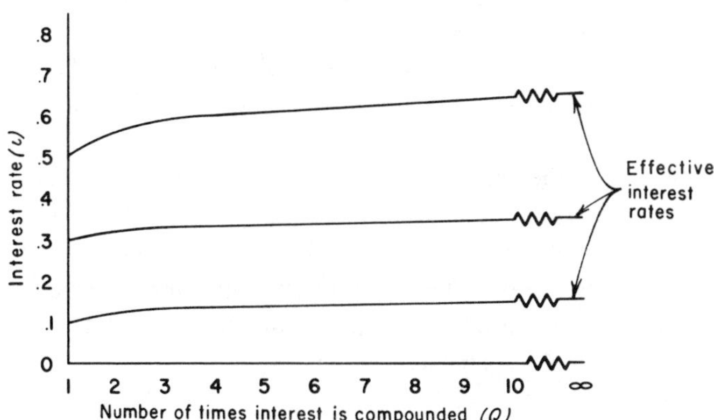

Exhibit 42. Compounding earnings by frequent trading becomes progressively less important as the rate of compounding increases.

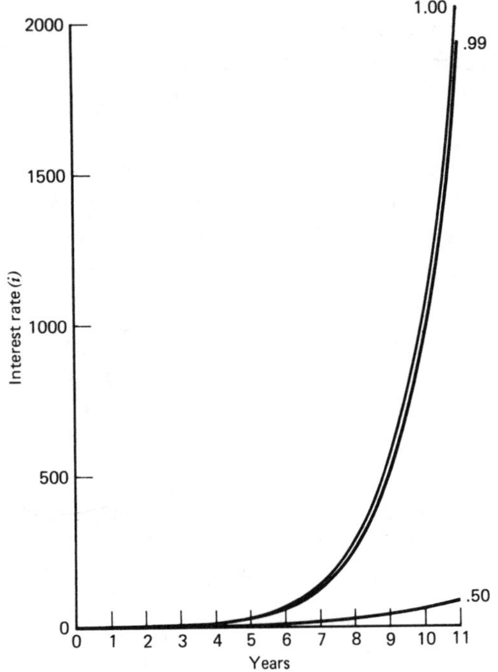

Exhibit 43. The marginal returns from increasing the interest rate increase without limit.

If a trader loses 0.2 of his trading capital, he must then make $E = 1/(1 - 0.2) = 1.25$ on his remaining capital to break even. Exhibit 45 charts this relationship. As the reader will observe, large losses will almost certainly doom a trader.

Nevertheless, it may still be reasonable to risk a large proportion of the available funds if the probability of loss is small enough. The value of a trade, after all, is a probability-weighted average of the trader's potential risks and rewards.

Therefore, unless the trader understands some probability theory, at least intuitively, he can't really evaluate a trade. Richard A. Epstein,[1] for example, has catalogued some of the most common and most dangerous financial fallacies and, not surprisingly, many of them are misunderstandings of probability. The fallacies he presents are "gambling" fallacies, but that is cold comfort indeed. Commodity trading is also a gamble.

---

[1] Epstein, R A., *The Theory of Gambling and Statistical Logic,* Academic Press, New York, 1977, 393–394. The examples in brackets in sections 2, 5, 6, and 7 are my own.

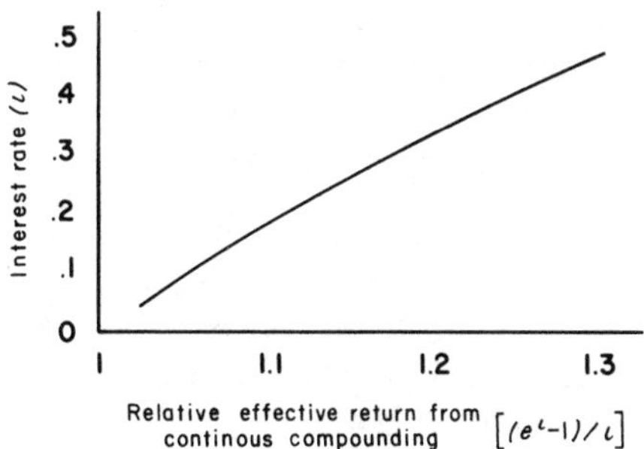

Exhibit 44. The importance of compounding is a function of profitability.

1. A tendency to overvalue wagers involving a low probability of a high gain and undervalue wagers involving a relatively high probability of low gain. This tendency accounts for some of the "long-shot" betting at race tracks.
2. A tendency to interpret the probability of successive independent events as additive rather than multiplicative. Thus the chance of throwing a given number on a die is considered twice as large with two throws of the die as it is with a single throw. [For example, the odds of throwing a six twice in succession with a fair die is $(\frac{1}{6} \cdot \frac{1}{6}) = \frac{1}{36}$, not $\frac{1}{12}$.]
3. After a run of successes a failure is inevitable, and vice versa [the Monte Carlo fallacy].

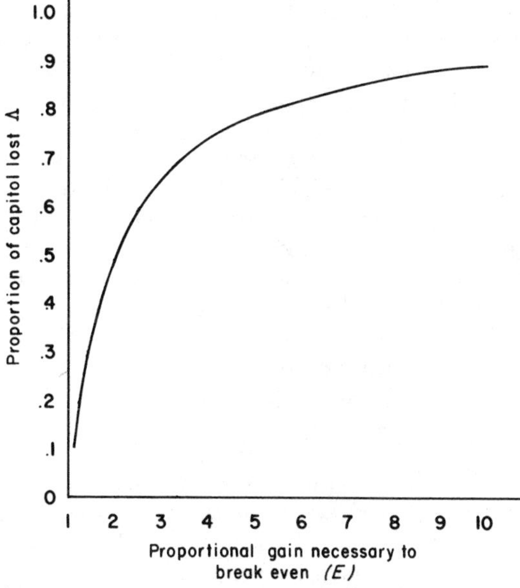

Exhibit 45. Large losses will almost certainly doom a trader.

4. The psychological probability of the occurrence of an event exceeds the mathematical probability if the event is favorable and conversely. For example, the probability of success of drawing the winning ticket in a lottery and the probability of being killed during the next year in an automobile accident may both be one chance in 10,000; yet the former is considered much more probable from a personal viewpoint.
5. The prediction of an event cannot be detached from the outcomes of similar events in the past, despite mathematical independence. [For example, the odds of throwing a head with a fair coin is the same both before and after a run of ten heads.]
6. When a choice is offered between a single large chance and several small chances whose sum is equal to the single chance, the single large chance is preferred when the multiple chances consist of repeated attempts to obtain the winning selection from the same source (with replacement); however, when there is a different source for each of the multiple chances, they are preferred. [For example, the odds that a head will appear on one toss with a fair coin and that at least six heads will appear when eleven fair coins are each tossed once is exactly the same. But many people will prefer the latter bet to the former.]
7. The value of the probability of a multiple additive choice tends to be underestimated and the value of a multiplicative probability tends to be overestimated. [For example, the odds of throwing a one or a two or a three with one throw of a fair die is $(\frac{1}{6} + \frac{1}{6} + \frac{1}{6}) = \frac{3}{6}$, whereas the odds of throwing a one three times in a row is $(\frac{1}{6} \cdot \frac{1}{6} \cdot \frac{1}{6}) = \frac{1}{216}$. However, most people underestimate the odds of the first bet and overestimate the odds of the second bet.]
8. When a person observes a series of randomly generated events of different kinds with an interest in the frequency with which each kind of event occurs, he tends to overestimate the frequency of occurrence of infrequent events and to underestimate that of comparatively frequent ones. Thus one remembers the "streaks" in a long series of wins and losses and tends to minimize the number of short-term runs.
9. A tendency to overestimate the degree of skill involved in a gambling situation involving both skill and chance.
10. A strong tendency to overvalue the significance of a limited sample selected from a relatively large population.
11. The concept of "luck" is conceived as a quantity stored in a warehouse to be conserved or depleted. A law of conservation of "luck" is implied, and often "systems" are devised to distribute the available "luck" in a fortuitous manner. Objectively, "luck" is merely an illusion of the mind.
12. The sample space of "unusual" events is confused with that of low probability events. For one example, the remarkable feature of a bridge hand of 13 spades is its apparent regularity, not its rarity (all hands are equally probable). For another, if one holds a number close to the winning number in a lottery, one tends to feel that a terribly

> bad stroke of misfortune has caused one *just* to miss the prize. Bertrand Russell's remark that we encounter a miracle every time we read the license number of a passing automobile is encompassed by this fallacy. The probability of an "unusual" occurrence should be equated to the ratio of the number of unusual (by virtue of symmetry or other aesthetic criteria) events to the total number of events.

Clearly, the trader or gambler who can avoid the fallacies above has an advantage over those who cannot. Statistics and probability theory can be of use here. Statistics was discussed earlier. Probability theory will now be discussed.

A probability is a number between zero and one inclusive, where zero indicates a given event has no possibility of occurring and one indicates that the event is certain to occur. Although probabilities can rarely be determined, they can be estimated in several ways.

1. **Judgment.** The simplest and most obvious way of estimating a probability is to guess. Clearly, the usefulness of a guess will depend on the experience and reasoning ability of the guesser. This may not be a particularly rigorous approach, but it's better than nothing and sometimes it's the only approach possible.
2. **Theory.** In some cases, probabilities can be determined mathematically. For example, if the probability of throwing a head with a fair coin is 0.5, then the probability of throwing three heads in a row is 0.125. With this approach the trader must know the assumptions underlying the theory and must determine or estimate how closely they match the real world. If the assumptions do not match the real world, the theory is irrelevant. In other words, if the probability of throwing a head on a given throw is not 0.5, then the probability of throwing three heads in a row is not 0.125.
3. **History.** In many cases the probability of something happening in the future can be assumed to be the same as, or reasonably close to its past relative frequency. For example, if a trading method was profitable on half of its trades to date most traders would be willing to assume that it will continue to be profitable half of the time.

Several definitions must be learned before the mathematics of probability can be discussed. A *simple* probability is the probability of a given event occurring. It is written $P(\quad)$. This is read "the probability of." Events are represented by arbitrary letters; for example, throwing a head with a given coin could be represented by an $\ddot{H}$, in which case the probability of throwing a head would be written $P(\ddot{H})$. A *joint* probability is the probability of two events, say $\ddot{H} + \ddot{T}$, both occurring. If the probability of throwing a tail with the same coin is $P(\ddot{T})$, then the probability of throwing a head and a tail is written $P(\ddot{H},\ddot{T})$. This probability is zero, of course. A *conditional* probability is the probability that one event will occur, given that another event has occurred; for example, if the probability of throwing a head on the first toss of a fair coin is $P(\ddot{J})$ and the probability of throwing a head on the second toss is $P(\ddot{K})$, then the probability of throwing a head when a head has just been thrown would be written $P(\ddot{K}|\ddot{J})$.

Statistical *independence* exists for two events, say $\ddot{K} + \ddot{J}$, if the probability of $\ddot{K}$ occurring does not depend on whether $\ddot{J}$ has occurred. Another way of putting it is that the probability of event $\ddot{K}$ occurring equals the conditional probability of event $\ddot{K}$ occurring, given that event $\ddot{J}$ has occurred. This can be written $P(\ddot{K}) = P(\ddot{K}|\ddot{J})$. For example, with a fair coin the probability of throwing a head will not depend on the previous throw; that is, it is independent of the previous throw. Consider, as an example of statistical *dependence*, the probability of selecting at random a coin dated 1980 from six coins, three dated 1980 and three dated 1978. The probability of success on the first selection is 0.5. But note that if the coin is not replaced, the probability of success on the second selection depends on whether the first coin selected was dated 1980. If the first coin selected was dated 1980, the probability that the second one selected will be dated 1980 is 0.4; otherwise the probability is 0.6.

Statistical dependence is important in calculating *joint* probabilities. If two events are statistically independent, their joint probability—that is, the probability that both of them will occur—is the product of their individual probabilities. This can be written as $P(\ddot{K},\ddot{J}) = P(\ddot{K}) \cdot P(\ddot{J})$.

For example, if the probability of tossing heads with one bent coin is $P(\ddot{U}) = 0.4$, and the probability of tossing heads with another bent coin is $P(\ddot{V}) = 0.1$, then the probability of tossing heads with both is $P(\ddot{U},\ddot{V}) = P(0.4) \cdot P(0.1) = 0.04$.

If two events are statistically dependent, the probability of both events occurring is the simple probability of one of the events occurring (it does not matter which one) times its conditional probability. This can be written as $P(\ddot{Y},\ddot{Z}) = P(\ddot{Y}) \cdot P(\ddot{Y}|\ddot{Z})$, where $\ddot{Y}$ and $\ddot{Z}$ are arbitrary events.

For example, the probability of selecting a coin dated 1980 from three dated 1980 and three dated 1978 is $P(\ddot{Y}) = 0.5$. The probability of selecting a second coin at random dated 1980 is $P(\ddot{Z}) = 0.4$, where $P(\ddot{Z}) = P(\ddot{W}|\ddot{Y})$; that is, where $\ddot{W}$ represents the second coin dated 1980. In other words, $P(\ddot{Z})$ is shorthand for $P(\ddot{W}|\ddot{Y})$, the probability that a second coin dated 1980 will be selected at random, given that the first coin selected was dated 1980. Therefore, the probability of selecting two coins in a row dated 1980 is $P(\ddot{Z}|\ddot{Y}) = P(0.5) \cdot P(0.4) = 0.2$.

The probability of either of two events occurring is equal to the sum of their simple probabilities minus their joint probabilities. This can be written as $P(\ddot{Z}$ or $\ddot{Y}) = P(\ddot{Z}) + P(\ddot{Y}) - P(\ddot{Z},\ddot{Y})$.

For example, the probability of tossing at least one head with two bent coins when the probability of tossing a head with one is 0.7 and the probability of tossing a head with the other is 0.4 is:

$$P(\ddot{Z} \text{ or } \ddot{Y}) = P(0.7) + P(0.4) - P(0.28)$$

$$= P(0.82)$$

Note that because the coin tosses are independent:

$$P(\ddot{Z},\ddot{Y}) = P(0.7) \cdot P(0.4)$$

$$= 0.28$$

If the two events are *mutually exclusive,* that is, if both cannot occur, then the formula above simplifies to:

$$P(\ddot{W} \text{ or } \ddot{V}) = P(\ddot{W}) + P(\ddot{V})$$

For example, with a fair coin the probability of throwing a tail is 0.5; therefore, the probability of throwing either a head or a tail is:

$$P(\ddot{H} \text{ or } \ddot{T}) = P(0.5) + P(0.5)$$

$$= 1.0$$

The probability, of course, is not always equal to 1.0.

The virtue of probability theory is that it allows the trader to compare investments and speculations without losing sight of their relative risks. Consider, for example, two bets. The first bet is at odds of 2 to 1 on one flip of a fair coin. The second bet is at odds of 8 to 1 on one flip of a bent coin. The trader, after examining the coin, believes that the probability of it landing in his favor is 0.2. Before going further, the trader might consider whether he would accept one of the bets and if so, which one and why.

One measure of the potential profitability of a bet is its expected value (EX). This value is calculated by multiplying each potential profit or loss by the probability that the profit or loss will in fact take place.

When the profits or losses can take only two values, the expected value is particularly easy to calculate. The expected value (EX) is:

$$EX = PW - (1 - P)L$$

where W = the potential winnings

L = the potential losses

P = the proportion of winning trades

Therefore, for the first bet:

$$EX = 0.5 \cdot 2 - 0.5 \cdot 1 = 0.5$$

and for the second bet:

$$EX = 0.2 \cdot 8 - 0.8 \cdot 1 = 0.8$$

The fact that the second bet has a higher expected value means that is probability-weighted *average* return is higher. Expected value is a measure of risky returns, but it is *not* a risk-adjusted measure of return; that is, it does not measure how risky the return is.

Consider for example, the following two trading methods:

Method I	Method II
$W = 2$	$W = 101$
$L = 1$	$L = 100$
$P = 0.5$	$P = 0.5$
$EX = (2 \cdot 0.5) - (1 \cdot 0.5) = 0.5$	$EX = (101 \cdot 0.5) - (100 \cdot 0.5) = 0.5$

Although both trading methods have the same expected value, the second method is clearly riskier. It is riskier because its profits and losses are more widely dispersed (see Exhibit 46).

Logically, risk is merely a cost of trading. If the cost is excessive, the trader will be ruined. However, even if the cost is modest, the account will *never* grow as quickly as the arithmetic average would indicate. This is called "variance slippage." Variance is the square of the standard deviation, which in turn is a measure of the width or dispersion of a distribution (see Exhibit 47). If the distribu-

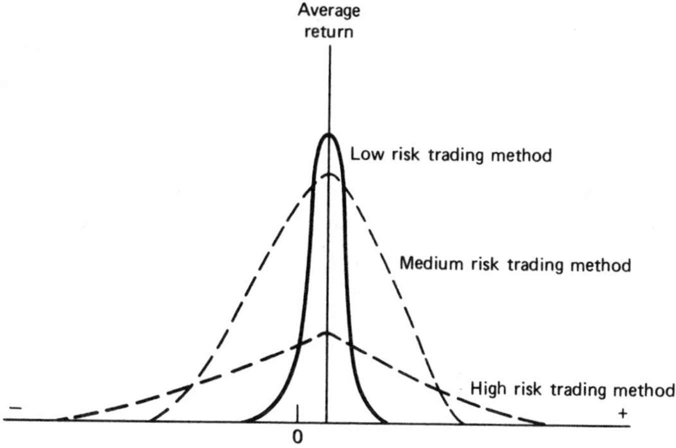

Exhibit 46. The wider the distribution of returns, the larger the risk.

tion of interest is of profits and losses, variance can be used as a measure of risk. Variance slippage means that as long as there is any risk or variance, the account will never grow as quickly as the arithmetic average of the trading profits would indicate. Moreover, the larger the variance, the more the arithmetic average will overestimate the real growth (see Appendix 5).

The rate at which the account can really be expected to grow is a useful measure of risk and reward. If E. O. Thorp's strategy for minimizing risk and maxi-

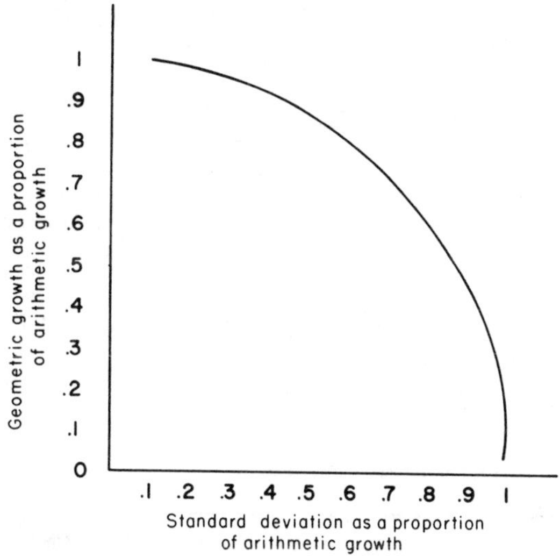

Exhibit 47. A portfolio's long-term compound growth rate declines as its risk, measured by the standard deviation of returns, increases.

mizing the (e log) growth of capital is followed, the growth rate can easily be calculated or estimated.[2] Actually, Thorp's formula only calculates capital growth correctly when P, W, and L completely describe the distribution of potential profits and losses. Since this is not the case, Thorp's formula will also overestimate account growth, although by a lesser amount. Unfortunately, at the current state of the art, there is no alternative except to use complicated and expensive Monte Carlo techniques. Be that as it may, Thorp's strategy is to bet a fixed fraction (f) of the capital where:

$$f = \epsilon / B$$

$$\epsilon = (B + 1)P - 1$$

where $B = W/L$

and where W = the potential winnings

L = the potential losings

P = the proportions of winning trades

For example, if $W = 3$, $L = 1$, and $P = 0.6$, then $B = 3$ and $\epsilon = 1.4$, in which case $f = 0.47$ and Thorp's strategy would be to bet 0.47 of the trading capital.

How quickly capital will grow is a function of B and P. According to Thorp, the growth function (g) is:

$$g = P[\log(1 + Bf)] + \{(1 - P)[\log(1 - f)]\}$$

"Log" here refers to the natural logarithm. This function can be found on several pocket calculators. It has also been extensively tabled (see Table 13 in Appendix 3).

$$g = 0.6\{\log[1 + (3 \cdot 0.47)]\} + \{(1 - 0.6)[\log(1 - 0.47)]\}$$

$$g = 0.6(\log 2.41) + 0.4(\log 0.53)$$

$$g = 0.6(0.8796) + 0.4(-0.6349)$$

[2] Thorp, E. O., The Kelly Money Management System, *Gambling Times*, December 1979, pp. 91 and 92.

$$g = (0.52776) + (-0.25396)$$

$$g = 0.2738$$

Clearly, the larger g is, the more quickly capital can be expected to grow. How large the account will be after any given number of trades can never be known, of course, but the most likely or expected value can be calculated as follows:

$$\text{EX}(N) = V(0)(e^{Ng})$$

where EX(N) = the expected value at the end of n trades

N = the number of trades

Using the data above and assuming that $V(0) = 10$ and $N = 5$, then:

$$\text{EX}(N) = 10[2.71828^{(5 \cdot 0.2739)}]$$

$$= 10(2.71828^{1.364})$$

$$= 10(3.9118)$$

$$= 39.118$$

Because these formulas are objective it is possible to derive some generalizations about what constitutes a reasonable risk or a potentially profitable trade.

First, such rules of thumb as "don't accept a trade unless the potential profit is at least three times the potential loss" clearly are of no use whatsoever because they do not incorporate the probabilities of winning and losing.

Second, if the expected gross profit (GP) is:

$$\text{GP} = PW - (1 - P)L$$

and the expected gross of profit to loss (GR) is:

$$\text{GR} = PW/(1 - P)L$$

then the expected gross ratio of profit to loss is of considerably more importance than the expected gross profit. This can be deduced from the fact that the difference between winning and losing is not a part of the formula for f, whereas their ratio is. An example may make this clearer. Consider two trading methods with the following properties:

Method I	Method II
$W = \$4$	$W = \$3$
$L = \$2$	$L = \$1$
$P = 0.5$	$P = 0.5$

Plugging these numbers into the formulas for GP and GR we obtain:

$$\text{GP} = 4(0.5) - 2(1 - 0.5) = 1 \qquad \text{GP} = 3(0.5) - 1(1 - 0.5) = 1$$

$$\text{GR} = 4(0.5)/2(1 - 0.5) = 2 \qquad \text{GR} = 3(0.5)/1(1 - 0.5) = 3$$

Notice that although gross profit for both methods is the same, the gross ratio of profit to loss is higher for Method II. Plugging the appropriate numbers into the formulas for B, ϵ, f, and g, we obtain:

Method I	Method II
$B = 4/2 = 2$	$B = 3/1$
$\epsilon = [(2 + 1)0.5] - 1 = 0.5$	$\epsilon = [(3 + 1)0.5] - 1 = 1$
$f = 0.5/2 = 0.25$	$f = 1/3 = 0.3333\ldots$
$g = 0.058891517$	$g = 0.143841035$

Note that g is higher for Method II than it is for Method I. Clearly, Method II is superior.

For the trader who must pay commission and execution costs (CEC), the expected net profit (ENP) and the expected net ratio of profit to loss (RPL) are the relevant criteria, of course. The formulas are:

$$\text{ENP} = P(W - \text{CEC}) - [(1 - P)(W + \text{CEC})]$$

$$\text{RPL} = P(W - \text{CEC})/[(1 - P)(W + \text{CEC})]$$

where ENP = expected net profit

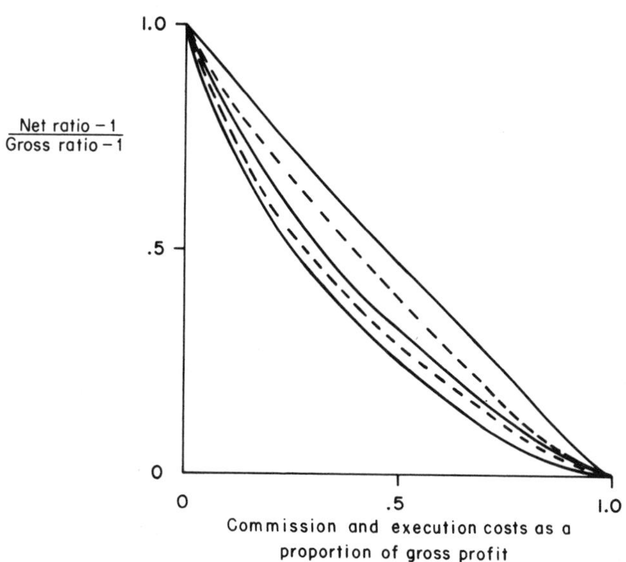

Exhibit 48. Each curve represents a different gross ratio. It is as important to minimize commissions and execution costs as it is to maximize gross profits.

RPL = expected net ratio of profit to loss

CEC = commission and execution costs

Exhibit 48 shows that the larger CEC/GP, the smaller RPL/GR. It is also clear that increasing GR is less important than reducing CEC/GP. Clearly, it is important both to minimize commission and execution costs and to maximize the expected gross profit.

The above analysis implies that prudent trading is a waiting game. The trader must carefully watch and forecast the market but only trade when the potential loss (L) is less than his (or her) account balance, when the expected loss (i.e., $L(1 - P)$) is a small proportion of his account balance, when the expected net ratio of profit to loss is large, and when the commission and execution costs are only a small proportion of the expected gross profit.

Naturally, this approach will not guarantee success. From what little evidence exists, I suspect Bernard Kummerli was using an approach something like this when he dropped $30 million in cocoa futures.[3] Clearly, there is no such thing as a trade that is too carefully planned.

[3] "Smith, A.," *Supermoney*, Popular Library, New York, 1972, pp. 122–155.

Chapter Seven

Trading Plans

INTRODUCTION

In many ways, commodity trading is a loser's game. The winning commodity trader, like the winner in tennis or war, is the one who makes the least mistakes. Not all mistakes are fatal, of course, but one mistake that will almost certainly doom a trader is to trade without a plan.

Any trading plan will be superior to no trading plan because every plan will consider strategy and tactics in more detail than the trader would otherwise. A trading plan, for example, will never allow a trader to take a position for no reason at all, and then wait to get lucky. Yet sadly, many traders will do just that.

An unwritten plan is better than no plan at all, and a written plan is better than an unwritten one. This is because a written plan will be more carefully thought out, more detailed, and more conscientiously followed than an unwritten plan.

A written plan will also allow the trader to audit his own performance. Periodic audits are critical; a trader who does not perform them will continue to make the same mistakes. However, without a written trading plan, audits are impossible. When important sums of money are involved, it is difficult not to lie to oneself. Worse, the trader who does lie to himself will rarely be able to admit it later unless he is confronted with evidence, such as a written trading plan.

A written trading plan is a set of documents, forms, and worksheets. A reasonably complete set might include a strategic plan, a tactical plan, a watch sheet, a log book, a work sheet, and an operating statement.

Naturally, a given trader need not use all of the tools described. Nor is there any reason he (or she) cannot invent others. Clearly, the tools used should depend on the trader's philosophy, psychology, forecasting skills, and capital. The reader should, therefore, feel free to modify the tools presented to fit his (or her) own style of trading.

This chapter has been influenced by a number of sources. Unfortunately, I have found it *very* difficult to decide which material to credit. Therefore, instead of footnoting the article heavily and probably uselessly, I have decided simply to list the few articles and books I found useful and to suggest that the reader read them all. I believe the reader will still find them useful.

R. Teweles et al., *The Commodity Futures Game,* McGraw-Hill, New York, 1974.

R. Teweles et al., Notes From a Trader (various topics), *Commodities,* September 1976, p. 28; October 1976, p. 46; November 1976, p. 44; December 1976, p. 30; February 1977.

J. R. Maxwell, Sr., *Commodity Futures Trading Orders,* Speer Books, Port Angeles, Wash., 1974.

Commodity Trader's Survival Kit, Success Profiles (no date, location, or author).

STRATEGIC PLANS

The strategic trading plan deals with the broadest and most general problems of trading: How much money will I dedicate to trading? How much time? How will I forecast the market? How will I convert these forecasts into trades? How will I allocate money to trades?

A good strategic trading plan should be consistent, viable, and authoritative. A consistent plan is simply one with no self-contradictions; for example, it may be reasonable to trade on the basis of fundamentals, to trade many commodities, or to spend little time trading, but it is scarcely reasonable to expect to do all three.

A viable trading plan is one that is consistent with the "real world;" that is, the trader should really have the skills and resources that the trading plan demands. Any self-delusion here, and many more traders delude themselves than not, will insure defeat.

An authoritative plan allows the trader to make judgments about tactical plans. A good tactical plan is consistent with the strategic plan, a bad one is not; for example, if for strategic reasons a trader decided to trade only long-term, fundamentally based trends, even to consider technical input would be a violation of the strategic plan.

There is nothing sacred about a strategic plan, and if a better one can be constructed, it certainly should be. Nevertheless, the plan should be changed only after a greal deal of thought, and never to avoid missing a trade.

The reason is essentially mathematical, All trading involves a risk of ruin, a risk that the trader will lose his trading capital. This risk can be expressed as a number from 0 to 1 inclusive, where 0 indicates no risk of ruin and 1 indicates ruin is certain. When wins and losses are equal, the risk of ruin (R) can be calculated from the formula

$$R = \left(\frac{1 - \mathcal{A}}{1 + \mathcal{A}}\right)^{\partial}$$

where $\mathcal{A} = P - (1 - P)$

P = the proportion of winning trades

∂ = the units of trading capital

For example, if the trader wins or loses $500 each time he trades, and if he wins 0.6 of the time and if, after dedicating the necessary funds to margin, he starts with \$5,000, then $\partial = 10$, $P = 0.6$, $\mathcal{A} = 0.2$, and $R = 0.02$.

Now assume the same trader finds that a net loss of one unit of capital bothers him so much that he quits trading. In effect, then, this trader had one unit of capital, not ten. The risk of ruin under these conditions is 0.67. Clearly, this trader would have been better off not trading at all.

Changes in the trading plan can decrease the risk of ruin, of course, but changes that are not considered carefully and at leisure almost always do just the opposite.

TACTICAL PLANS

The form of the tactical trading plan should depend on the strategic plan. Some strategic plans need virtually no tactical planning. For example, most trend-following techniques require little more than an order log; fundamentalists, on the other hand, may need extensive tactical plans.

A tactical plan can be constructed freehand, but the use of forms insures that the trader will consider certain factors each time he trades. Which factors should be considered is a strategic, not a tactical, decision. A fairly general and extensive tactical form is displayed in Exhibit 49; naturally, the trader should feel free to modify the form to fit his own style and strategy.

The reasons for most of the data in sections A and B should be fairly obvious. The trade number and opening date allow the trade to be located and reviewed later. The closing date insures that a trade is not forgotten.

Section B allows both net long and short positions and spreads to be recorded. If a long or short position is taken, the commodity, month, and number of contracts should be listed under the appropriate headings. If a spread is taken (the form allows spreads with as many as four commodities), each commodity must be listed under long or short, with the appropriate month and contracts listed below. The months and contracts are not always obvious, so completing this section might be delayed until parts C and D are completed.

The number of contracts traded is partly a strategic and partly a tactical problem. Part of the strategic plan should be a money management system, which should allocate a maximum amount of risk acceptable for the trade. Tactical analysis should then suggest how much risk should be accepted per contract.

The acceptable risk per contract may be larger or smaller than the amount of risk acceptable for that trade. If it is larger, of course, the trade cannot be accepted. If it is equal or smaller, the maximum risk acceptable is divided by the

A. Date opened ________________ Trade no. ________________

Date closed ________________

B.

	Long	Short	Long	Short
Commodity				
Month				
Number of contracts				

C. Maximum risk acceptable ________________ Stop loss risk ________________

Net risk per contract ________________ Commission ________________

Margin per contract ________________ Probable skid ________________

Total risk (gross or net) ________________ Gross risk per contract ________________

D. Bullish factors:

Bearish factors:

Conclusion:

E. Entry plan:

Entry log:

Entry No.	Log No.	Date	Order	Fill
1				
2				
3				

Exhibit 49. Tactical trading form.

F. Exit plan:

Landmarks:

Perils:

Exit log:

Exit No.	Log No.	Date	Order	Fill
1				
2				
3				

G. Trade narrative:

Profit ____________________ Loss ____________________

Evaluation:

Exhibit 49. *(continued)*

risk acceptable per contract. The result, with any remainder dropped, is the number of contracts to trade.

Depending on the margin requirements, the acceptable risk per contract may be calculated on either a gross or a net basis. On a net basis, the acceptable risk is the commission, the probable skid, and the stop loss risk. The stop loss risk is the difference between the entrance price and the stop loss.

Stop loss location is a major trading decision and is worth a considerable amount of thought. Although a stop loss is a money management tool, its location should somehow be a function of the price forecast. Clearly, a price movement opposite the one forecasted is prima facie evidence that the forecast is wrong. If the trader can decide at what point the evidence is strong enough to abandon the trade, he has his stop loss point, his stop loss risk, and his net risk per contract.

Unfortunately, net risk per contract may not be an acceptable measure of risk. In some cases gross risk, which is the net risk per contract plus the margin needed to trade the contract, should be used.

The importance of margin will depend on the money management strategy. Prudent money management demands that a certain proportion of the trading capital be kept from the market at all times. If these funds are large enough, they can be used for margin, and margin need not affect the number of contracts traded. If these funds are not large enough, however, then risk must be calculated on a gross basis.

Section D is the most important part of the trading plan. All rational trading is based on an explicit or implicit forecast. When the trade and the forecast are not identical, the forecast must somehow be transformed into a trade. Clearly, the more explicit the forecast, the easier this will be to do.

The format presented requires the trader to evaluate the bullish and bearish factors in narrative form. Forcing oneself to evaluate the arguments against a desired trade might have a sobering effect. Another approach that some traders may prefer is a checklist format requiring the trader to evaluate certain indicators or data each time a trade is contemplated. Which data and indicators are to be evaluated is a strategic question, of course.

The conclusion should be the direction and distance the price is likely to move, the contract that should be traded, and the location of the stop. In addition, the data necessary to structure the portfolio, such as the probability of the trade being profitable, must be estimated.

Once sections A-D are completed, the trade can be initiated. This cannot be done without giving orders, and the trader will find it virtually impossible to consider the orders he might give and the conditions under which he might give them too carefully.

Section E consists of an entry plan and an entry log. An entry plan is simply a narrative analyzing the orders to be given and conditions under which they will be used. Because it is sometimes necessary to initiate several orders before obtaining a fill, a moderately long entry log is provided. A more detailed description of the trading orders can be provided in an order log, which is discussed later. The reader should note that the entry log and the order log should be cross-referenced.

If a position is accepted, it must eventually be exited. This will happen for one of five reasons, and the exit plan in part F must provide for all of them.

1. **The Trade Shows a Loss.** At some point a loss will become larger than the trader can afford and the trade will have to be abandoned. This loss can be planned or unplanned. A planned loss is better than an unplanned loss because

no reasonable plan will allow a significant portion of the capital to erode. Yet unplanned losses often do just that.

A stop loss insures that the loss will be planned. However, although stop losses are critical, they are not the only means of exiting a losing trade. Conceivably, the reader may have an indicator or method of analysis that will indicate that the forecast is no longer to be trusted. If so, the exit plan for losing trades may read, "exit when indicator $\ddot{X}$ gives a signal or when a stop loss at price $\ddot{Y}$ is touched, whichever comes first."

2. The Trade is Profitable. Ideally, both a risk level and a profit objective should be determined before the trade is begun. Unfortunately, for some trading methods there is no reasonable way to set objectives. An alternative might be an indicator or method of analysis that signals when profits should be taken.

Again, having more than one method of exiting a trade has its advantages. A reasonable plan might read, "exit when the price reaches $\ddot{Y}$ or indicator $\ddot{X}$ gives a signal, whichever comes first."

3. Nothing Happens. Occasionally, the price will float between the stop loss and the profit objective without touching either. In some cases this will indicate that the analysis was wrong and the trade should be closed. In other cases where the forecast indicates only the direction of the trend and not its extent or timing, theoretically it would not be valid to close out the trade without an exit signal.

Unfortunately, futures have limited lives, and every trade must be closed eventually. If manipulating stops and profit objectives is not a viable way of closing the trade, an arbitrary date must be picked, preferably before delivery notice has been received, and the trade closed on that date. Choosing the closing date when the trade is initiated has the advantage that the trader will not be affected by price movements irrelevant to his analysis.

4. A Better Trade Becomes Available. Prudent money management allows only a certain proportion of the funds available to be committed to the market at any one time. If more good trades become available than can be supported, theoretically the trader should upgrade his portfolio, closing his worst open trades and accepting the best new ones. If the trader does not have the discipline to do this–if, for example, he keeps his worst trades while accepting others–his chances of success are almost nonexistent.

On the other hand, upgrading is difficult and expensive and the benefits need not exceed the costs. If the marginal costs, that is, the commission and execution costs, exceed the marginal profits, the portfolio should not be upgraded.

Some traders should not upgrade even if this is not the case. Upgrading demands that the trader realistically evaluate trades in progress. Unfortunately, when hard cash is on the line, objectivity can be difficult or impossible for many traders. A good trading plan must consider a trader's psychology as well as his finances.

5. **The Situation Changes.** Every trade is based on an explicit or implicit forecast. Clearly, if the forecast is no longer reasonable, the trade should be closed, whether it is profitable or not.

It is critical that every conceivable reason the trade might be abandoned be considered in the trading plan. Not to do so insures that the estimates needed for money management will be wrong. It also insures that decisions on whether to close a trade will sometimes have to be made while the trade is still open; for many traders, perhaps even most, this insures that the decision will be made irrationally.

A trade may no longer be reasonable because of foreseeable or unforeseeable events. A foreseeable event might be a government crop report that differs from the expected. An example of an unforeseeable event cannot be given, of course. If an example could be given, it would be foreseeable. Still, it's safe to say that many traders might not even consider the possible effects of a radical change in government policy on a potential trade. For those traders, if a radical change in government policy took place, it would be unforeseen.

How the trader should handle the unexpected is partly a strategic and partly a tactical problem. The trader has only two choices. He can act on what limited information he has at the time, or he can ignore the situation. If the trader decides to act, he must act quickly or not at all. To do this rationally demands ice water for nerves and an encyclopedic knowledge of market fundamentals.

For most traders, a more reasonable approach is to ignore the situation. If the trader has a stop in place, and if a catastrophic price change does not take place, he cannot be hurt too badly. Although the trader might lose money he would not have lost if he had acted quickly, over the long run he will lose less. If a trader cannot make decisions rationally, he must give up trading or he must find a way to trade rationally without making those decisions.

Another alternative is to make decisions only within limits set before the trade begins; the sections "Landmarks" and "Perils" prescribe these limits. Landmarks are events indicating that the trade is going according to plan; perils that it is not. The distinction is somewhat arbitrary. For example, a government crop report might be both a landmark and a peril. Still, the distinction is useful enough to be worth keeping in mind.

Somehow the exit plan must be executed. This cannot be done without giving orders and a log is provided for recording them.

Section G provides for a review of the completed trade. The profit or loss must be recorded, the actions taken summarized, and the trading plans and trade reviewed. Separating the trade narrative and the evaluation should be useful. The actions taken will never change, but the evaluations will, as the trader grows.

WATCH SHEET

One drawback of tactical plans is that the market changes as they are being developed. By the time a perfect plan could be constructed, if one could be constructed at all, the contract to be traded would probably have expired.

One solution to this problem is to scale down the tactical plan to reach some kind of compromise between urgency and completeness. Another solution is the watch sheet.

The watch sheet is simply a dated listing or summary of whatever news, announcements, gossip, data, information, or analysis the trader thinks might help him forecast the market. Along with the trader's own ideas, analyses, and forecasts, the original unsummarized data can be clipped and kept in an appended file.

Which data should be recorded and how the data should be used depends on the trader's strategic plan. There is no reason for the trader to record every piece of data, just as there is no reason that the trader must always be able to forecast the market. The trader must merely be right, on average, when he does forecast the market.

One approach might be to watch the market until a clear bullish or bearish pattern emerges and then create a tactical plan to exploit it. Another approach would be to watch the market until it makes a mistake and then trade against it. It is not enough that the trader disagree with the market's price; the trader must also understand why the market prices as it does and disagree with its analysis. The trader then develops a tactical plan to exploit the market's mistake.

In any case, the watch sheet will allow the trader to develop the tactical plan in far more detail and far more rapidly than he could without it.

ORDER LOG

A trading order converts a plan into a trade. Regardless of how well wrought a plan is, if the order is ill-conceived or carelessly given, the trade is almost certainly doomed.

Because the order and limits given can change a trade's reward/risk ratio, sometimes drastically, it is nearly impossible to consider too carefully which orders to give. However, as the usable number of orders and limits is fairly small, a reasonable amount of skill can be acquired quickly (see Exhibits 50 and 51).

Some strategic plans allow the trader few or no alternatives. Such plans may give the trader no choice of orders and even no choice of tactics. In such cases, there may be no reason to have a tactical plan, and the simplest of order logs will suffice.

In other cases, there will be no reason to keep an order log. The trading plan must contain entry and exit logs; the trade could hardly be analyzed without them. If only one or two commodities are traded at a time, the trader hardly needs both a tactical plan and an order log.

However, many traders will benefit from using both. Having a separate order log allows the trader more control; for example, it allows him to analyze the orders apart from the trades.

An order log may be arbitrarily complex. How complex it should be should depend on the number of alternatives the trader wishes to consider every time he trades.

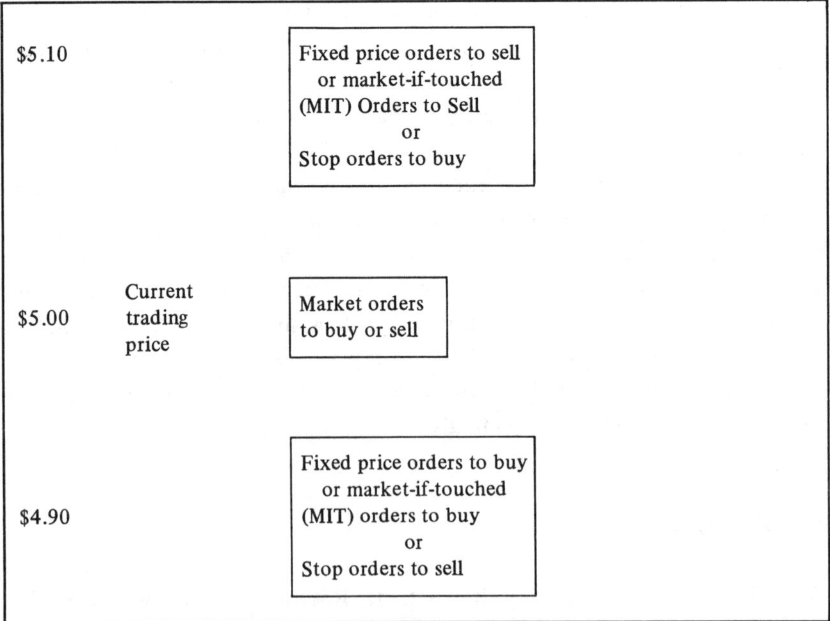

Exhibit 50. Where various trading orders may be placed in relation to current trading price. Adapted from Maxwell, J. R., *Commodity Futures Trading Orders,* Speer Books, Port Angeles, Wash., 1974, p. 22.

For most traders, a log like the one in Exhibit 52 should suffice. The order number allows the order log to be cross-referenced with the tactical plan. The date column should contain the date and the time the order is given to the broker. This information can be useful if there is a problem with the fill. The trade number and the entry/exit number allow the tactical plan to be cross-

Type of Order	Relation to the Market		Class of Order		Usable Limitations		
	Above	Below	Day	Open	Price	Life	Time
Market			X		X		X
Market-if-touched	S	B	X	X	X	X	X
Fixed-price	S	B	X	X	X	X	X
Stop	B	S	X	X	X	X	X

B = Buy, S = Sell, X = Use is permitted.

Useful Combinations

Above the Market	Below the Market
Buy stop	Sell stop
Sell MIT	Sell stop
Buy stop	Sell MIT
Buy stop	Fixed-price buy
Fixed-price sell	Sell stop

MOC Combinations

Market-if-touched, fixed-price, and stop orders may be placed with the "or market on close" stipulation.

Exhibit 51. Usable order and limit combinations. From Maxwell, J. R., *Commodity Futures Trading Orders,* Speer Books, Port Angeles, Wash., 1974, p. 54.

Order log

Order No.	Date	Trade No.	Order	Limits	Fill

Exhibit 52. Adapted from Maxwell, J. R., *Commodity Futures Trading Orders,* Speer Books, Port Angeles, Wash., 1974, p. 2.

referenced with the order log. If the trade requires more than one attempt for entry or exit, which is often the case, this data can be important.

The order column should list the commodity, the option, the number of contracts, the type of order, and whether the order is a buy or sell. If the commodity is traded on more than one exchange, the exchange should be listed, too.

Any limits on the order should be listed in the next column. Limits can be useful in shifting the return/risk ratio. The use of a special column insures that the trader will at least consider limiting his order before he places it.

The fill column should indicate if an order is canceled. If the order is filled, the column should indicate the date of the fill, the time, and the price at which the order was filled. This data can be useful in evaluating the cost of placing various types of orders, your skill at placing them, or your broker's efficiency in having them executed. Unfortunately, if the data indicate a problem, it's not always easy to tell where the problem lies.

Trading orders must not only be carefully considered, they must be carefully given. Any error here will destroy the trading plan. However, properly used, the order log will insure that the orders a trader gives his broker are the orders he intends to give. The trader should write the order in the log and then *read* the order to his broker; the broker should then record the order, and repeat it, and the trader should confirm it.

WORK SHEET

Money is a trader's largest and most important tangible asset. Money can take several forms, such as equity, margin, or net trading power. If funds are not in the right form at the right time, interest will be lost or trades foregone or abandoned. As funds can generally be changed into different forms only at a price, the trader would be well-advised to watch his funds carefully.

It is simply impossible to manipulate something meaningfuly unless you know what you're manipulating. Most traders control their funds, if they control them at all, on the basis of a monthly account statement from their brokerage firm and an occasional question to their account executive. This information is neither detailed enough nor frequent enough for meaningful control. If trading decisions are made on a daily basis, funds must also be managed on a daily basis. Fortunately, fund management is comparatively easy.

An operating statement and a work sheet must be prepared daily. Because data from the work sheet are needed to complete the operating statement, the work sheet must be completed first.

The work sheet (see Exhibit 53) consists of a number of short, identical, numbered forms. How many of these forms will have to be filled in on any given day will depend on how many trades are open after the close.

The numbers at the top of each segment insure that the segments are completed in the proper sequence. This number and the date insure that the previous day's data are not included in the current analysis.

Listing the commodity and position insures that the sign and values for the calculations that follow are correct. The current open profit or loss is the latest closing price minus the entry price, times the dollar value of a unit change, if the trader was long. The dollar value will depend upon the contract traded and the number of contracts traded. If the trader was short, the sign of the results must be changed. If spreads are being traded, price differences rather than prices must be recorded. The mechanics, however, are the same.

Subtracting the stop loss point from the last close gives the open risk; whether the trader is long or short, the open risk is always positive. If the trader is not using a stop loss, perhaps because he is trading spreads, his losses may be potentially unlimited. For budgeting purposes, then, the trader must select some arbitrary large amount as his open risk.

OPERATING STATEMENT

The operating statement is a short form that the trader should complete each day he has a position open after the close. The object of the calculations is the trader's net power, or his ability to accept new trades.

Before a new position is accepted, the trader must calculate how much trading power it will demand. If this demand exceeds the trader's net power, the trade cannot be accepted. As Teweles, Harlow, and Stone[1] note

---

[1] Notes From a Trader, R. Teweles et al., *Commodities,* December 1976, p. 30.

Failure to consider net power can force a trader to choose among three choices, none of which are good:
1) Depositing more money than he wishes to utilize for commodity trading,
2) Reducing or eliminating an open position too soon, or,
3) Changing stops which were set logically.
. . .such an approach makes an already difficult game almost impossible to win.

Date	No.
Number contracts held	Commodity position
Last close	$
minus entry price	
Difference (correct for sign)	$
times dollar value unit change	
Open profit or loss	
Last close	$
minus stop loss	$
Difference (ignore sign)	$
times dollar value unit change	
Open risk	$

The double line is an accounting convention that indicates that the numbers below the line are not related to the numbers above. Consider a trader who's 74th trade was short one contract of December Wheat on the Chicago Board of Trade. The value of each one-cent change for one contract is $50.00. Assume that the trader had sold the wheat at $5.12, put in a stop at $5.20 and that the contract last closed at $5.14. The form is completed as follows:

Date: October 22, 1982	No. 74
Number contracts held: 1	Commodity position: December Wheat
Last close	$5.14
minus entry price	$5.12
Difference (correct for sign)	–$0.02
times dollar value unit change	$50.00
Open profit or loss	–$100.00
Last close	$5.14
minus stop loss	$5.20
Difference (ignore sign)	$0.06
times dollar value unit change	$50.00
Open risk	$300.00

Exhibit 53. Daily work sheet.

Fortunately, net power is easy to calculate. We will do so now (see Exhibit 54). The available trading capital is the funds the trader has dedicated to trading. Profitable and unprofitable trades and additions and withdrawals of capital and interest affect the available trading capital; open trades do not. If the trader keeps some of his funds in a money market fund where they are not immediately available, he must reduce the available trading capital by that amount. The result, of course, is the account balance.

Available trading capital	$
minus money market reserve	
Account balance	$
minus margin	
plus open profits	
minus open losses	
Gross trading power	$
minus open $ risk	
minus commission	
minus execution costs	
Net trading power	$

Consider as an example a trader who has $11,043.00 committed to trading of which $3,000.00 is in a money market fund. Assume that the trader had three open positions, the wheat trade discussed in Exhibit 53, and a corn and an oat trade. The margin for these trades is, let us say, $750.00, $600.00, and $400.00, respectively, and the margin total is $1,750.00. The wheat trade has an open loss of -$100.00. The corn and oat trades have open profits of $12.00 and $233.00. The open risk for the contracts is $300.00, $200.00, $350.00, respectively, for a total of $850.00. The commissions are $50.00 apiece for a total of $150.00. The execution costs are estimated as $50.00, $64.00, and $40.00, respectively, for a total of $155.00. The form is completed as follows:

Available trading capital	$11,043.00
minus money market reserve	3,000.00
Account balance	$ 8,043.00
minus margin	1,750.00
plus open profits	223.00
minus open losses	100.00
Gross trading power	$ 6,416.00
minus open $ risk	850.00
commission	150.00
execution costs	155.00
Net trading power	$ 5,261.00

Exhibit 54. Operating statement.

If the trader did not have any open trades, the account balance and the gross trading power would be equal. When there are open trades, the account balance must be decreased by the margin needed to sustain those trades and increased or decreased, respectively, by the open profits or losses. Margin levels, unfortunately, are not constant and if the trader believes they might be raised, he should increase his allowance for margin.

The gross trading profit minus the commissions, the open dollar risk, and the execution costs gives the net trading profit. The open dollar risk has already been calculated and commissions are easily available. The execution costs of a trade are the slippages between the trading order and its execution. If the trade is still pending, execution costs on both the open and close must be estimated; otherwise, only the close need be. Execution costs, of course, depend on the liquidity of the market. Market liquidity can change rapidly, and it can be expensive to underestimate the net power; thus it is better to overestimate execution costs than underestimate them.

A trader's gross trading power is the amount of money the trader might use to open new positions or even withdraw from the account–if he is certain that he will never lose a trade. If the trader believes he might occasionally lose a trade, he should use net power instead.

Chapter Eight

Avoiding Avoidable Risk Through Portfolio Theory

The virtue of applying portfolio theory to commodity trading has been lauded at length—and well it should be. Modern portfolio theory is almost the only area of trading where there is certainty. Unfortunately, it is possible to abuse even the most powerful techniques. Recently, the promotional literature of several wire houses and advisory services have implied that portfolio trading will produce certain or near certain profits. Naturally, it will do no such thing.

Portfolio trading need be nothing more than trading several commodities simultaneously. Portfolio theory, on the other hand, is the use of probability theory to account and budget for certain types of risk. As there are few facts more well established about commodity trading than its risk, this task is critical. However, trading a portfolio will no more insure market success than having an accountant will.

Although portfolio theory is an important tool, it is not the only tool needed. Claims to the contrary notwithstanding, portfolio theory will not forecast the market. Given forecasts and their probable error, however, it will suggest the amount and type of diversification advisable. In most cases portfolio theory will indeed suggest trading a portfolio, but not in all cases. If a trader cannot forecast the market correctly on average, diversification will only insure ruin. If such a trader must trade, the most reasonable plan would be to trade infrequently. An even better plan, of course, would be to give up trading.

However, a trader or fund manager who can forecast the market can increase his or her reward/risk ratio by diversifying. In other words, the trader can increase the return for a given amount of risk, reduce the risk for a given return, or even increase the return and reduce the risk by diversifying (see Exhibit 2).

The virtues of diversification are well known, and the usual application is to trade as many commodities as possible, the reasoning being that trading another commodity will always lower the risk and generally raise the return. However, because there are costs involved, diversification may lower the return and only minimally reduce risk.

The two primary costs of diversification are research costs and transaction costs. Research costs may be minimal if the trader or fund manager has a computerized trading method that does not vary from commodity to commodity. On the other hand costs may be extensive if the trader must personally analyze each commodity. Transaction costs consist of commission and execution costs. Commissions will generally go up as the number of contracts traded per commodity go down, which will happen with diversification. Execution costs depend on the

---

Parts of this chapter were originally published in slightly different form: Gehm, F., Avoiding "avoidable" risk through portfolio theory, *Commodities Magazine,* 250 S. Wacker Dr., Chicago, IL 60606, July 1980, pp. 46–50.

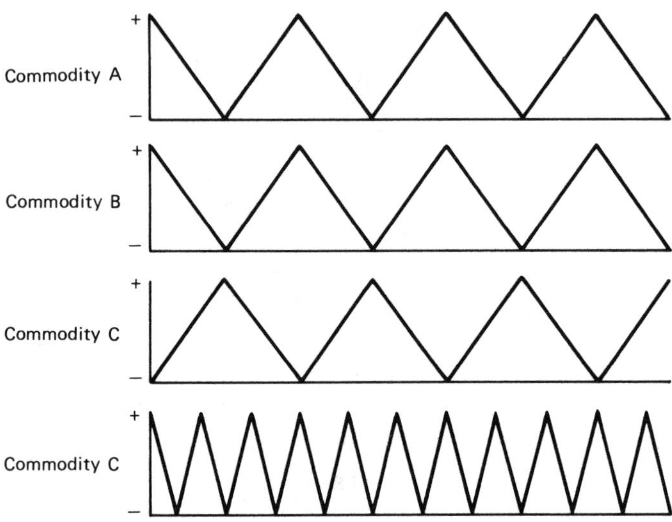

Exhibit 55. The correlation coefficient C expresses the relationship between two variables by a number from +1 to –1 inclusive. Profits and losses from trading commodities $\ddot{A}$ and $\ddot{B}$ are perfectly correlated (C = +1); a $500 profit in Commodity $\ddot{A}$ would be accompanied by a $500 profit in Commodity $\ddot{B}$, for example. Trading profits and losses from $\ddot{B}$ and $\ddot{C}$ are negatively correlated (C = –1); a $500 profit in Commodity $\ddot{B}$ would be accompanied by a $500 loss in Commodity $\ddot{C}$. Profits and losses in $\ddot{C}$ and $\ddot{D}$ have no correlation (C = 0). For a more general explanation, see Chapter 5.

liquidity of the market; if the trader is trading in large amounts they can go down with diversification.

Assuming that none of the streams of profits and losses from any of the commodities are perfectly correlated with each other (see Exhibit 55) and that each commodity can be traded profitably, it can be proven that trading yet another commodity can always lower the risk. Unfortunately, the amount that each additional commodity lowers the risk diminishes quickly, as Cornell's Harold Bierman's formula shows.[1]

If we assume that the risks, returns, and profit correlations for all commodities are equal (see Exhibit 56) and that N is the number of commodities traded, the proportion of the risk eliminated of the total avoidable risk (T) is:

$$T = (N - 1)/N$$

(See Exhibit 57.) The proportion of the total avoidable risk avoided by trading another commodity (A) is:

[1] Bierman, H., Diversification: Is there Safety in Numbers?, *Journal of Portfolio Management*, Fall 1978, Vol. 5, No. 1, pp. 29–32.

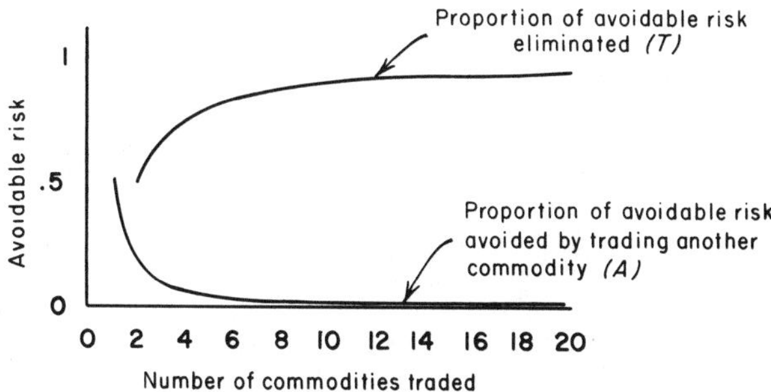

Exhibit 56. The amount that each additional commodity reduces the "avoidable" risk diminishes quickly.

$$A = 1/[N(N + 1)]$$

If, for example, $N = 5$, then $T = 0.8$ and $A = 0.03$.

The amount of avoidable risk is a function of the portfolio correlation coefficient. A correlation coefficient is a number between one and minus one inclusive where one indicates a perfect and positive correlation, minus one indicates a perfect but negative correlation, and zero indicates no correlation at all. Bierman assumes that negative correlations do not exist, which is almost certainly true.

The total avoidable risk can never be lowered below the portfolio's correlation coefficient–no matter how large a portfolio is traded. If the risk and return for all commodities in the portfolio are equal and the correlation coefficient is 0.8, the risk can never be lowered below 0.8 of the risk on a single commodity. An examination of Exhibit 57 shows, in this case, that there is little reason to diversify beyond two or three commodities.

Number of Commodities Traded							
1	1	1.00	1.00	1.0000	1.0000	1.0000	1.000
2	1	0.90	0.75	0.6250	0.6000	0.5500	0.500
3	1	0.87	0.67	0.5000	0.4664	0.3997	0.333
4	1	0.85	0.63	0.4375	0.4000	0.3250	0.250
5	1	0.84	0.60	0.4000	0.3600	0.2800	0.200
10	1	0.82	0.55	0.3250	0.2800	0.2400	0.100
20	1	0.82	0.53	0.2875	0.2400	0.1900	0.050
∞	1	0.80	0.50	0.2500	0.2000	0.1000	0.000
Correlation Coefficient of Commodities Traded	1	0.80	0.50	0.2500	0.2000	0.1000	0.000

Exhibit 57. Amount of remaining "avoidable" risk. From Bierman, H., Diversification: Is There Safety in Numbers?, Reprinted with permission of *The Journal of Portfolio Management,* Fall 1978, Vol. 5, No. 1, p. 30.

Indeed, for many traders (or fund managers), an optimal portfolio should contain nowhere near as many commodities as it might. Theoretically, the trader should continue to diversify until the costs of trading the next commodity just equals the benefits (see Exhibit 10). In practice, there is generally a great deal of uncertainty involved in these estimates, yet estimates must be made.

As a matter of fact, it would be remarkable if the risks, returns, and correlations were consistent over even a medium-sized portfolio. To the extent that these factors differ, the formula will only give an approximation.

One of the problems in using formulas such as those presented here is that all of them make assumptions known to be false. Unfortunately, there is no alternate to using such formulas except guessing.

Two dangerous assumptions are that profits and losses are independent and that catastrophic losses are *very* rare. In fact, as perusal of any historical chart book will demonstrate, catastrophic losses are rare—or at least catastrophic price changes are. More important, catastrophic risk is often foreseeable. Techniques for managing catastrophic risk are discussed in Chapter 9.

A substantially capitalized and diversified account could withstand even catastrophic loss as long as price movements are independent and such losses are very rare. For the most part, price movements do seem to be independent. However, monetary and political pressures can cause diverse commodities to move together. At such times diversification is of little use. If the trader cannot forecast such changes, he (or she) can at least hedge against them by keeping a considerable proportion of his (or her) assets in cash. In such a case, it is probably prudent to commit even less capital to the market than the formulas that follow recommend.

A more interesting, difficult, costly, but perhaps more profitable technique is to risk approximately the same amount on the long and short sides at any given time. One reason it is difficult to use this technique is that there are other, often conflicting criteria for choosing which commodities to trade.

Clearly, more money should be devoted to those commodities with higher reward/risk ratios, all other things being equal. The Sharpe ratio (SR) is one method of adjusting for risk and reward.[2] Here reward is the expected mean return per trade (EX) and risk is the expected standard deviation of returns (SD). In addition, a measure is needed of the riskless rate of return; this might be the interest received (I) if there were no trading. By definition, the Sharpe ratio of any commodity is:

---

[2]Sharpe, W. F., Capital Asset Prices: A Theory of Market Equilibrium under Conditions of Risk, *Journal of Finance*, September 1964, Vol. 19, pp. 425–444.

$$SR = (EX - I)/SD$$

Although with a preprogrammed calculator the mean and standard deviation are not difficult to calculate, beta estimates are even easier. Beta estimates demand only a reasonable high estimate (H), a reasonable low estimate (l), and a "most likely" estimate (M). It does not particularly matter how the reader interprets "reasonable" as long as he (or she) is consistent. Beta EX and SD estimates can be calculated as follows:

$$EX = \frac{H + 4M + l}{6}$$

$$SD = \sqrt{\frac{(H - l)^2}{2}}$$

For example, if $H = 250$, $M = 75$, and $l = -200$, then:

$$EX = \frac{(250 + (4 \cdot 75) + (-200)}{6}$$

$$= 58.33$$

$$SD = \sqrt{\frac{[250 - (-200)]^2}{2}}$$

$$= 318.20$$

(Recall that subtracting a negative number is the same as adding a positive one.)

For technical reasons, beta estimates are not as good as the mean and standard deviation, but they do allow intuitive traders and traders with little or no data to use the technique that follows.

Another alternative is to use the mean absolute deviation (see Chapter 5) in place of the standard deviation. For technical reasons, this may be a better technique than either the standard deviation or its beta estimate.

Unfortunately, the commodity trader must make approximations that the stock market trader need not. First, although I is not difficult to measure for a stock portfolio, it is difficult to measure for a commodity portfolio, and in practice is often ignored. Second, whereas stock purchases and sales can be made simultaneously, commodity trades rarely can be. It therefore seems more reasonable to calculate a commodities Sharpe ratio on the basis of, say, monthly profits and losses rather than on the basis of profits and losses per trade. The effect, of course, is that risk that might otherwise have been avoided is not. Be that as it may, Edwin Elton, Martin Gruber, and Manfred Padbury, all of New York University, have shown that the Sharpe ratios for a group of commodities can be used to allocate funds.[3] The techniques that follow are simplifications of their work. The Sharpe ratios for the commodities are summed and the Sharpe ratio for each commodity is divided by the resulting sum. The resulting proportion for a given commodity is the proportion of available funds that should be allocated to it.

Unfortunately, this procedure will occasionally construct unbalanced portfolios (e.g., 0.75 of the funds in one commodity). One method of correcting for this is to set an upper limit to the proportion of funds allocated to any given commodity. If this is done the proportion of funds allocated to the remaining commodities must be adjusted (see Exhibit 58).

A second problem with this method is that it does not adjust for the correlations between the returns from various commodities. For a medium-sized portfolio, one approach would be to select the commodity with the highest Sharpe ratio from each group of related commodities (e.g. grains, meats) and construct the portfolio from these commodities.

Another approach is to use the above techniques to construct portfolios for each group of related commodities and then to combine these portfolios into a single portfolio by using the same techniques again. There are, of course, more sophisticated methods, but these are too complex to describe here.

Allocating funds among commodities is only part of the trader's or fund manager's job. He must also decide what proportion of the available funds to commit to the market at any given time.

Clearly, the more of the available funds the trader commits to the market at any one time, the more quickly his account will grow, but the more probable it is that the trader will eventually be ruined. All trading involves the risk of ruin, the risk that the trader will lose his trading capital or a large enough portion of it that he will quit trading. This risk can be expressed as a number from 0 to 1 inclusive, where 0 indicates no risk of ruin and 1 indicates that ruin is certain.

Clearly, if the trader accepts "bad" or even "fair" bets, eventual ruin is inevitable. In other words, if

---

[3] Elton, E. J., Gruber, M. J., and Dadberg, M. W., Optimal Portfolios from Simple Ranking Devices, *Journal of Portfolio Management*, Spring 1978, Vol. 4, No. 3, pp. 15–19.

Commodity	Mean Return	Standard Deviation of Return(s)	Sharpe Ratio	Portfolio Weighting
A	50	100 =	0.5000 ÷ 3.9166 =	0.1277
B	75	90 =	0.8333 ÷ 3.9166 =	0.2128
C	60	80 =	0.7500 ÷ 3.9166 =	0.1915
D	100	75 =	1.3333 ÷ 3.9166 =	0.3404
E	40	80 =	0.5000 ÷ 3.9166 =	0.1276
Total			3.9166	1.0000

The Sharpe ratio is the mean return of a commodity divided by its standard deviation of returns. The portfolio weighting for a commodity is its Sharpe ratio divided by the sum of the Sharpe ratios.

However, assume that the trader will commit no more than 0.25 of available funds to any commodity. Commodity D is therefore assigned a weighting of 0.25 and the other commodities recalculated. Divide the Sharp ratio for a commodity by the sum of the Sharpe ratios for those commodities not assigned a weighting. Multiply this by the proportion of the portfolio that remains to be allocated. Because one commodity already has been set at 0.25, the remaining commodities must be multiplied by (1 - 0.25) = 0.75.

Commodity	Set at Upper Boundary	Sharpe Ratio	Portfolio Weight of Remaining Commodities	Portfolio Weighting
A		0.5000 ÷ 2.5833 = 0.1936 × 0.75 =	0.1452	0.1452
B		0.8333 ÷ 2.5833 = 0.3226 × 0.75 =	0.2419	0.2419
C		0.7500 ÷ 2.5833 = 0.2903 × 0.75 =	0.2177	0.2177
D	0.25			0.25
E		0.5000 ÷ 2.5833 = 0.1936 × 0.75 =	0.1452	0.1452
Total	0.25	2.5833	0.7500	1.0000

Exhibit 58

$$PW \leqslant (1 - P)L$$

where P = the proportion of winning trader

W = average amount won

L = average amount lost

The symbol $\leqslant$ indicates that the variable on the left is smaller than or equal to the variable on the right. Ruin is certain if the trader plays long enough.

However, if the trader only accepts "good" bets, ruin is no longer certain but merely possible. A good bet is one where

$$PW > (1 - P)L$$

The symbol > indicates that the variable on the left is greater than the variable on the right.

How large a trader's risk of ruin is depends on how well-capitalized he (or she) is relative to the amount he (or she) risks on any given trade. If a trader accepts only good bets and wishes to reduce his risk of ruin, he can do so merely by reducing the scale of his trading.

Of course, if the scale of trading is reduced far enough, trading may not be worth the effort. The formulas that follow will allow the trader to judge the tradeoffs involved. However, to use the formulas that follow, the proportion of time the portfolio is profitable must be known, as well as the profit expected when the portfolio is profitable and the loss expected when it is not.

If the portfolio is equally weighted among the commodities traded, if the risk and reward of trading the commodities are identical, and if the profits and losses are independent, this can be calculated easily.

For a properly constructed, small- or medium-sized portfolio, independence is probably a reasonable assumption. Identity of reward and risk is probably not a reasonable assumption for any portfolio. However, the technique is usable and conservative if the trader uses the commodity with the *lowest* reward/risk ratio. Similarly, equal weighting is not a reasonable assumption, but the technique is usable and conservative if the trader uses n rather than N in the formulas that follow. n is calculated by dividing 1 by the portfolio's largest weighting and rounding the answer down to the largest whole number. For example, in Exhibit 58 the largest portfolio weighting is 0.3404. In this case, $n = \frac{1}{0.3404} = 2$, rounded down. If the upper boundary is set at 0.25, $n = \frac{1}{0.25} = 4$.

These techniques make two pessimistic or, if you will, conservative assumptions. The techniques assume, first, that the portfolio is, in effect, only as large as it would be if all the commodities were weighted as heavily as the most heavily weighted one. Second, they assume that none of the commodities has a higher reward/risk ratio than the commodity with the least favorable one.

There are, of course, techniques that make more reasonable assumptions, but they are much more difficult and tedious to use.

The objects of the calculations to follow are:

P = the proportion of the time the portfolio is profitable.

W = the average winnings if, in fact, the portfolio is profitable.

L = the average losses if, in fact, the portfolio is not profitable.

The data used are:

$\mathfrak{p}$ = the probability of a given trade for a given commodity being profitable.

$\mathfrak{w}$ = the average winnings if, in fact, the trade is profitable.

$\mathfrak{l}$ = the average losses if, in fact, the trade is not profitable.

Clearly, the amount won or lost any time the portfolio is traded (G) will depend on how many of the commodities have, in fact, been traded profitably (K). There are obviously $n + 1$ possible values for K and G and these values can easily be calculated and tabled. In fact:

$$G = (\mathfrak{w}K) - [\mathfrak{l}(n - K)]$$

where K is, in turn, each number from 0 to n inclusive. Exhibit 59 displays the tabled values for $\mathfrak{p} = 0.4$, $\mathfrak{w} = \$200$, $\mathfrak{l} = \$100$ and $n = 5$.

The probability of any given K occurring (Q) can be extracted from a table of binomial probabilities if $\mathfrak{p}$, K, and n are known. The appropriate values for Exhibit 59 have been extracted from Table 8 in Appendix 3.

K	G		Q		M	
0	-500.00	×	0.078	=	-39.00	
1	-200.00	×	0.259	=	51.80	90.00
2	100.00	×	0.346	=	34.60	
3	400.00	×	0.230	=	92.00	
4	700.00	×	0.077	=	53.90	
5	1000.00	×	0.010	=	10.00	190.50

Exhibit 59. K is in turn each of the numbers from 0 to n inclusive. G is calculated from K by inserting $\mathfrak{w}$, $\mathfrak{l}$, n, and K into the formula:

$$G = (\mathfrak{w}K) - [\mathfrak{l}(n - K)]$$

Q is extracted from the table of binomial probabilities (Table 8 in Appendix 3). M is calculated by multiplying $G \times Q$.

The probability of the portfolio being profitable is the sum of the probabilities of all the different ways the portfolio might be profitable. Reading down the table in Exhibit 59, we see that the lowest positive value for G is 1, at which value $K = 2$. Therefore, if the portfolio is to be traded profitably, then $K \geqslant 2$. The probability that the portfolio will be profitable (P) is the sum of all the Q values from $K = n$ to $K = 2$ inclusive. In this particular case, $P = (0.010 + 0.077 + 0.230 + 0.346) = 0.663$. P can also be extracted from a table of cumulative binomial probabilities (see Table 9 in Appendix 3).

Given the above assumptions, if the portfolio is, in fact, profitable, the profit will be one of the positive G values. However, for budgeting purposes a probability-weighted average of the positive G values should be used. For each value of K, an $\mathcal{M}$ value, which is the product of the G and Q values, must be calculated. For $K = 5$, for example, $\mathcal{M} = G \times Q = 1000 \times 0.010 = 10.00$. These values are also tabled in Exhibit 59. The sum of all the $\mathcal{M}$ values for $K \geqslant 2$ (that is, for all cases where the portfolio would be traded profitably) divided by P is the probability-weighted average for winning, or W. In the example above,

$$W = \frac{(10.00 + 53.90 + 92.00 + 34.60)}{0.663}$$

$$= 287.33.$$

Similarly, the sum of all $\mathcal{M}$ values for $K \leqslant 1$ (that is, for all cases where the portfolio would be traded unprofitably) divided by $1 - P$ is the probability-weighted average for losing, or L. In the example above,

$$L = \frac{(51.80 + 39.00)}{0.337}$$

$$= 269.43$$

Blackjack expert and California State University professor Peter Griffin has developed a formula that approximates the risk of ruin (R) when wins do not equal losses.[4] When wins, on average, do equal losses, the formula in Chapter 7

[4]Griffin, P., *The Theory of Blackjack*, Gamblers Press, Las Vegas, Nevada, 1981, p. 000. Dr. Griffin's formulas, alas, are only approximations. When wins do not equal losses the true risk of ruin can only be calculated using difference equations, which are too complicated to explain here.

can be used; indeed, that formula *must* be used when this is the case. However, this is so rarely the case that Professor Griffin's formula will almost certainly suffice. Griffin's formula, though tedious, is not as difficult as it looks; it is as follows:

$$R = \Psi^{\Theta}$$

where
$$\Psi = \frac{1 - \mathcal{P}}{\mathcal{P}}$$

$$\mathcal{P} = 0.5 + \frac{\mathrm{EX}}{2\sqrt{\Gamma}}$$

EX = the expected mean return per trade

Γ = the expected squared mean return per trade

$$\Theta = \frac{\mathcal{C}}{\sqrt{\Gamma}}$$

$\mathcal{C}$ = the beginning capital minus the level of ruin

The expected mean return per trade (EX) is the probability weighted sum of all of the values that the trade might take. The expected squared mean return per trade (Γ) is the probability weighted sum of all of the squared values that the trade might take.

A trader's capital is the amount he has available for trading. Unfortunately, because some of this money must be allocated to margins and other costs, not all of it is available for trading. If funds that are not available for trading are lost, the trader is ruined. At the very least, a trader's level of ruin must be set high enough to cover the needed margins, commissions, executions costs, and other expenses. Therefore, a trader's "real" beginning capital $\mathcal{C}$ is his beginning capital minus those funds that are not available for trading, or his net power.

Some traders prefer to set higher levels of ruin. This, of course, increases the risk of ruin (R) but provides some insurance against catastrophic loss. The trader must decide for himself the value of this tradeoff.

The trader must also decide when to quit trading or how to withdraw winnings. One alternative is to trade until a desired level of capital is reached and then quit. In this case, Professor Griffin's formula is:

$$R = 1 - \frac{\Psi^{\Theta} - 1}{\Psi^{\xi} - 1}$$

where
$$\xi = \frac{\mathfrak{X}}{\sqrt{\Gamma}}$$

and where Ψ, Θ, EX, Γ, and $\mathscr{C}$ are defined as above.

Although it makes no sense to intend to trade forever, the first formula will give an acceptable answer if a trader's desires are large enough. The first formula will always give a higher risk of ruin than the second, more complicated formula will. In other words, if the simplified formula gives an acceptable risk of ruin, the more complex formula will, also. If the trader's desires are more modest, he must subtract his level of ruin from whatever amount he believes would be sufficient for him to retire from trading. The result is his "real" desired capital ($\mathfrak{X}$).

An example may make the use of Professor Griffin's technique clearer. Assume that a trader was interested in opening a \$5000 account. Previous research had convinced him that he would need to devote \$1500 to margins and other fixed expenses; that he could expect his portfolio to be profitable 0.6 of the time on a weekly basis; and that his portfolio would produce profits of \$750, on average, when it was profitable, and losses of \$250, on average, when it was not. Assume, also, that the trader had decided to abandon trading if his account balance fell to \$2000, and to retire from trading and invest his money in mutual funds if his balance reached \$10,000.

Given the information above:

$$\mathscr{C} = 5000 - 2000$$

$$= 3000$$

$$\mathfrak{X} = 10000 - 2000$$

$$= 8000$$

Possible Value $\ddot{X}$	Probability $P(\ddot{X})$	$\ddot{X} \cdot P(\ddot{X})$	$\ddot{X}^2 \cdot P(\ddot{X})$
750	0.6	450	337,500
-250	0.4	-100	25,000
	1.0	EX = 350	Γ = 362,500

Therefore:

$$= 0.5 + \frac{350}{2\sqrt{362{,}500}}$$

$$= 0.5 + \frac{350}{2 \cdot 602.0797289}$$

$$= 0.5 + \frac{350}{1204.159458}$$

$$= 0.5 + 0.2906591795$$

$$= 0.7906591795$$

$$\Psi = \frac{1 - 0.7906591795}{0.7906591795}$$

$$= \frac{0.2093408205}{0.7906591795}$$

$$= 0.2647674573$$

$$\Theta = \frac{3000}{\sqrt{362{,}500}}$$

$$= \frac{3000}{602.0797289}$$

$$= 4.982728791$$

$$\xi = \frac{8000}{\sqrt{362{,}500}}$$

$$= \frac{8000}{602.0797289}$$

$$= 13.28727678$$

$$R = 1 - \frac{0.2647674573^{4.982728791} - 1}{0.2647674573^{13.28727678} - 1}$$

$$= 1 - \frac{0.001331345728 - 1}{0.00000002145073926 - 1}$$

$$= 1 - \frac{-0.9986686543}{-0.9999999786}$$

$$= 1 - 0.9986686757$$

$$= 0.0013313243$$

Although the calculations are tedious, the answer is important. Knowing that the risk of ruin is relatively small can provide valuable peace of mind during the inevitable runs of losing trades. Notice that the simplified formula still gives an acceptable answer:

$$R = 0.2647674573^{4.982728791}$$

$$= 0.001331345728$$

Another alternative is to periodically withdraw trading capital.[5] One method of doing this is to withdraw a portion of each winning trade. This, of course, reduces the size of the average win, thus increasing the risk of ruin, all other things being equal.

A third alternative is to remove an amount equal to the average loss (L) every t trades. This effectively reduces the proportion of winning trades and increases the risk of ruin, all other things being equal. Of course, the effective proportion of winning trades (EP) must now be used instead of the proportion of winning trades (P) in the formulas above. The relationship is:

[5] Snow, P., How Big a Position Should You Take?, *Commodities*, November 1976, pp. 30 and 31. Snow's work should be avoided because many of his formulas are wrong.

$$\text{EP} = \frac{P}{1 + \dfrac{1}{t}}$$

If, for example, $P = 0.6$ and $t = 5$, then:

$$\text{EP} = \frac{0.6}{1 + \dfrac{1}{5}}$$

$$= \frac{0.6}{1 + 0.2}$$

$$= \frac{0.6}{1.2}$$

$$= 0.5$$

A fourth and easier alternative is to allow the trading capital to build up to some predetermined level $\mathscr{X}$ and then to withdraw enough money to drop the capital to $\mathscr{C}$. If the trader's risk of ruin between withdrawals is R, then if N withdrawals are made the risk of being ruined at least once (NRR) is

$$\text{NRR} = 1 - (1 - R)^N$$

For example, if $R = 0.05$ and $N = 10$, then:

$$\text{NRR} = 1 - (1 - 0.05)^{10}$$

$$= 1 - (0.95)^{10}$$

$$= 1 - 0.60$$

$$= 0.40$$

Again, removing trading funds sharply increases the chance of ruin, but then a trader who has repeatedly removed capital from the market may not care.

If the trader is willing to commit enough funds to the market, a superior technique can be used. Blackjack expert and University of California professor Edward O. Thorp has developed a formula that will minimize the risk of ruin, among other things.[6] Unlike Griffin's technique, Thorp's technique will not calculate a risk of ruin, but the risk of ruin will be relatively small. Interestingly enough, under some conditions, which do not exist in the real world, the risk of ruin is zero. Be that as it may, in addition to minimizing the risk of ruin, Thorp's technique will also minimize the average time needed for trading capital to grow by any given amount and maximize the (e log) growth of trading capital. According to Thorp, there is a considerable profit penalty for not using his technique. Thorp's technique calculates the most prudent and profitable *fixed* fraction (f) of the trading capital that can be committed to the market by any given trader or system.

For example, if the trader has a \$10,000 account and his $f = 0.2$, he should commit \$2000 to the market. If he loses the \$2000, he should then commit \$1600. On the other hand, if the account grows to, say, \$12,000, he should commit \$2400.

The formula for f is simple:

$$f = \frac{\epsilon}{B}$$

where

$$\epsilon = (B + 1)P - 1$$

and

$$B = \frac{W}{L}$$

---

[6]Thorp, E. O., The Kelly Money Management System, *Gambling Times*, December 1980, pp. 91-92. Incidently, when wins equal losses the correct formula is $f = P - (1-P)$. For example, if $P = .6$ then:

$$\begin{aligned} f &= 0.6 - (1-0.6) \\ &= 0.6 - 0.4 \\ &= 0.2 \end{aligned}$$

Unfortunately, in the real world wins rarely equal losses and the more complicated formula in the text must be used.

Using the data calculated above ($P = 0.663$ and $B = W/L$, or \$287.33/\$269.43 = 1.0664), then

$$\epsilon = (1.0664 + 1)0.663 - 1$$

$$= 0.3700$$

and

$$f = \frac{0.3700}{1.0664}$$

$$= 0.3470$$

If $\epsilon \leqslant 0$, then it would be prudent not to trade, and if $f \geqslant 0.5$, it would probably be prudent to use 0.5 instead.

For most traders it will be virtually impossible to use these formulas exactly. Judgment therefore must be used. For example, Thorp's formula may suggest trading 0.175 of the available capital, but trading four contracts may demand 0.152, whereas five contracts will demand 0.19. If the trader commits a larger fraction of his capital than f, he risks ruin. If he commits a smaller fraction, his capital will not grow as quickly as it could. In this case it would be better to trade four contracts. In all cases it is better to trade conservatively.

There is another reason the formulas above cannot be used exactly. To calculate f it is necessary to know the size and composition of the portfolio. But to know that, it is necessary to know f!

Iterative or trial and error techniques provide one method of avoiding the paradox. The trader can assume an f and then construct a portfolio to fit it. That portfolio can then be used to calculate another f and the process repeated until the answer stabilizes.

Suppose, by way of analogy, that the trader wished to calculate the square root of $\ddot{X}$ but lacked any method of doing it exactly. One solution would be to divide $\ddot{X}$ by an arbitrary number $\ddot{Y}$. If the result $\ddot{Z}$ does not equal $\ddot{Y}$, then $\ddot{X}$ should be divided by the average of $\ddot{Y}$ and $\ddot{Z}$ and the process repeated until $\ddot{Y}$ is arbitrarily close to $\ddot{Z}$.

For example, assume that the trader wishes to find the square root of 81, which is 9, of course. Dividing 81 by, say, 5 produces 16.2. As the numbers are not even approximately equal, the process should be repeated by dividing 81 by $(5 + 16.2)/2 = 10.6$. The result this time is 7.641509434. As the numbers are still not approximately equal, the process should be continued by dividing 81 by (10.6 + 7.641509434)/2 = 9.120754717. The result this time is 8.880844022.

Notice that the result draws progressively closer to the correct answer, but that with each iteration the improvement becomes more trivial. With enough repetitions the result can be brought arbitrarily close. How close is close enough depends on how much work each iteration is and how much each iteration changes the answer.

This process is tedious when done by hand, but then the process need be done only rarely.

Theoretically, Thorp's technique should be used only once; Thorp's technique was created to calculate the optimal fixed fraction of capital to devote to trading. However, as the trader's equity grows or shrinks, it becomes inefficient or impossible to use the portfolio that was used to calculate *f*. If *f* is calculated on the basis of a relatively modest and conservative portfolio, the portfolio might be upgraded or downgraded as needed without necessarily changing *f*. You need to recalculate *f* only when the account size has changed substantially. For example, a trader who could theoretically begin trading with a five-commodity portfolio might calculate *f* on the basis of a three-commodity portfolio and trade however many commodities *f* allowed. Only when the portfolio had grown to seven or eight or dropped to two or three would *f* be recalculated.

For some traders, the cost of using the techniques described above will exceed the benefits. Still, these techniques should be considered carefully because the trader who does not use them will be accepting needless risk, and there is no reward for doing so. I admit that using some of these techniques, is difficult; but whoever said commodity trading would be easy?

Chapter Nine

Avoiding Catastrophic Risk

One of the most serious problems facing the trader is the possibility of catastrophic loss. A catastrophic loss is a loss much larger than the trader budgeted for, much larger than the margin demanded by the exchange. Traders have been financially ruined by a single bad trade; without doubt, it will happen again.

There seem to be two popular attitudes toward catastrophic risk. The first is that the probability of a trader actually being afflicted is so small that it is hardly worth considering. The second attitude is that the mere possibility of decimating a large portion of one's wealth should be sufficient to discourage all but the most foolhardy.

Both attitudes contain an element of truth. Clearly, every trader and potential trader should seriously consider the possibility of sustaining a catastrophic loss. It is also clear that those who find the possibility unbearable should not trade, whereas those who can accept such losses can, at least, consider trading.

Catastrophic risk is the risk the trader accepts in addition to the risk of losing his trading capital. Obviously, if the trader commits *all* of his assets to trading, he is accepting no catastrophic risk; this seems to apply to many young traders. A trader who has $12,000 in assets and who commits $10,000 to trading need worry little about catastrophic loss; if the trader sustains such a loss, he goes bankrupt, but for him bankruptcy will be little different than a long series of losing trades.

This approach, of course, would not be prudent for most traders, especially for most older traders. Although it reduces the risk of catastrophic loss, it increases the total risk. The total risk increases because the risk of losing trading capital is much much higher than the risk of catastrophic loss. For almost anyone to commit a large portion of their assets to trading is a bad idea.

For most traders a more useful approach would be to shelter some assets from seizure. I am informed that assets can be legally sheltered in several ways. For example, money kept in a qualified retirement plan is safe from seizure—until retirement; money kept in a short-term trust is safe from seizure—until the money reverts to its settler-creator; and money transferred to other family members before a loss takes place is safe from seizure, but the money is no longer the giver's. As the law is far more capricious than the commodity market, the trader would be well advised to consult a lawyer before depending on any legal method of sheltering money.

The trader who cannot shelter the majority of his assets—no doubt this includes the majority of traders—would be well advised to take half an hour or so and imagine what would happen if he (or she) lost $30,000 for each contract he were trading. How would he feel? How would his wife (or her husband) feel? How would his children and neighbors feel? How would he feel about how they felt?

Without doubt, catastrophic loss is horrible. For many, no potential profit is worth the risk. For others, trading can be worth the risk–if the probability of sustaining a catastrophic loss is small enough.

At one time economists thought they knew exactly how likely price changes of any given size would be. At that time, economists believed commodity price changes were normally distributed. If price changes were, in fact, normally distributed and if the mean and standard deviation of the distribution were known, then *everything* that could be known about that distribution would be known.

Exhibit 28 is a drawing of a normal distribution. Like all such drawings, it is incorrect. It is incorrect because the tails of the distribution do not go to infinity, which they should, theoretically. In practice, of course, this is scarcely important; beyond, say, three standard deviations from the mean, the tails can hardly be seen.

Indeed, if price changes were, in fact, distributed normally, price changes larger than three standard deviations from the mean should occur less than 0.01 of the time, whereas changes larger than 10 standard deviations should almost never happen. If price changes were normally distributed, catastrophic risk would not be a serious problem.

Unfortunately, catastrophic risk is a serious problem.

It came as quite a shock to economists when Mandelbrot[1] announced that certain speculative prices were not normally distributed. The distributions looked normal. Moreover, there were strong mathematical reasons why these distributions should be normal. Nevertheless, Mandelbrot insisted they were not. What Mandelbrot had noticed was that the tails of these distributions were much thicker than they would have been if the distributions were, in fact, normal; therefore, the distributions were not, in fact, normal.

Mandelbrot believed that the appropriate distribution was the stable Paretian family. This announcement was not greeted with any particular pleasure. The mathematics of the normal distribution had been thoroughly studied; the mathematics of the stable Paretian family were hardly understood at all.

Indeed, the distribution is really understood in only three special cases: the coin toss, the normal, and the Cauchy, which we will discuss later. These cases are actually relatively simple. Indeed, all three distributions can be completely described by two variables, such as the mean and standard deviations.

On the other hand, the stable Paretian family requires four variables to describe it: location, scale, skewness, and kurtosis. Location is the central tendency

---

[1] Mandelbrot, B., The Variation of Certain Speculative Prices, *Journal of Business,* Vol. 36, No. 4, 1963, pp. 394–419.

of a distribution; it might be measured by the mean or median. Scale is the width or dispersion of the distribution; it might be measured by the standard deviation or the mean absolute deviation. Skewness is the symmetry of a distribution (see Exhibit 60), and kurtosis is the thickness of the distribution tails (see Exhibit 61).

The most important of the distribution's variables is kurtosis. *The kurtosis of the distribution determines which statistical tools can be used to measure the other three variables.* The kurtosis ($\mathcal{K}$) of a stable Paretian distribution is measured on a scale of zero to two, exclusive of zero, inclusive of two. When the distribution is symmetrical and when $\mathcal{K}$ equals two, the distribution is normal. When the distribution is normal, the mean is a valid measure of location and the standard deviation is a valid measure of dispersion.

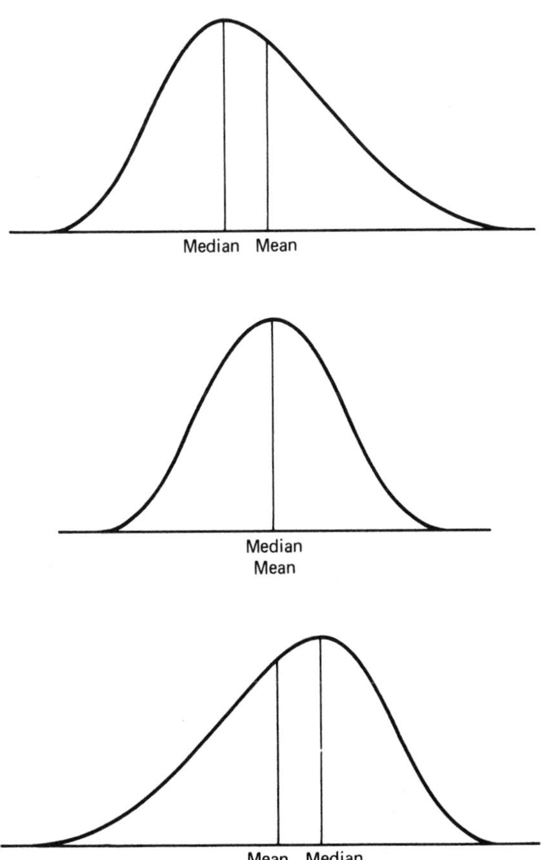

Exhibit 60. Skewness can be positive (a), nonexistent (b), or negative (c).

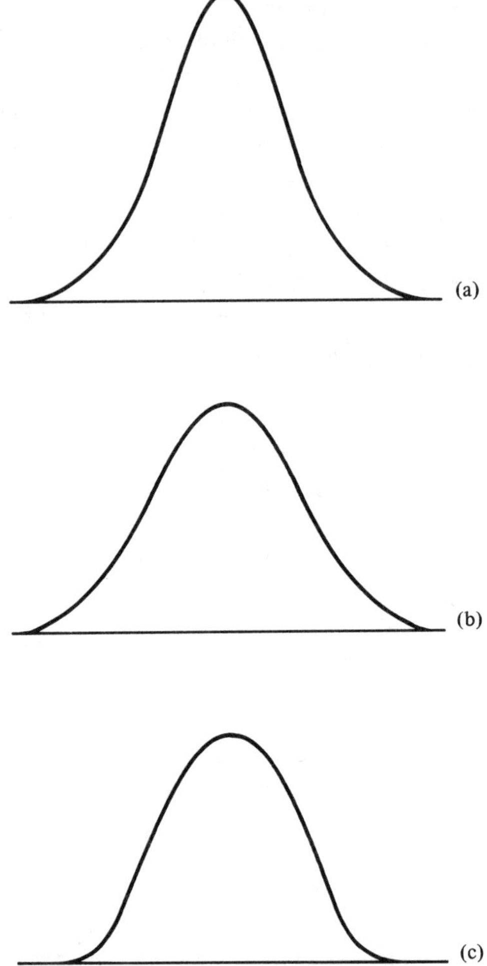

Exhibit 61. Kurtosis can be peaked (a), nonexistent (b), or flat-topped (c).

However, as $\mathcal{K}$ drops below two, the standard deviation rapidly becomes meaningless. Fortunately, the mean absolute deviation is a valid measure of dispersion as long as $\mathcal{K}$ is larger than one; unfortunately, the mean absolute deviation and even the mean itself are only valid measures as long as $\mathcal{K}$ is larger than one. When $\mathcal{K}$ equals one and when the distribution is symmetrical, the distribution is Cauchy. When the distribution is Cauchy or, more generally, when $\mathcal{K}$ is equal to or smaller than one, it becomes extremely difficult to trade rationally (see Exhibit 62).

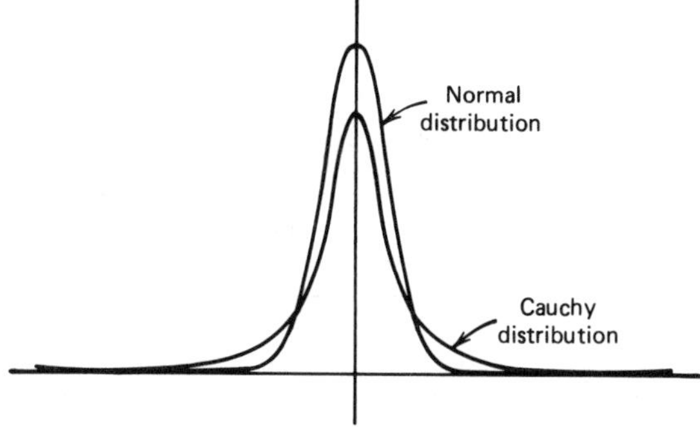

Exhibit 62. The proper commodity price distribution seems to be somewhere between the normal and the Cauchy, at least if skewness can be ignored. Unfortunately, the student's *t* distribution, the stable Paretian family of distributions, and perhaps other distributions and families of distributions subsume this range.

The problem is that there is no really desirable, generally usable, valid measure of location for Cauchy-like distributions. The most desirable measure of location would be the arithmetic average, the mean. But when $\mathcal{K}$ is equal to or smaller than 1, the mean is not a valid measure. This means that a trading method that had been profitable on average would give no assurance whatsoever that the method could be expected to remain profitable. A sample size of a billion would be as useless as a sample size of one.

Location can still be measured. The median is still a valid measure of location for Cauchy-like distributions, for example. However, the median is not really a desirable measure because it does not really tell the trader what he wants to know; it is simply available while the mean is not.

Fortunately, prices do not appear to have a Cauchy distribution, at least no published study of price behavior that I am aware of has found one. Unfortunately, estimates of $\mathcal{K}$ vary radically from sample to sample, so it is difficult to say exactly what $\mathcal{K}$ is, though it seems to be somewhere between one and two (see Exhibit 63).

Interestingly enough, the stable Paretian family is not the only distribution that provides descriptions ranging from the normal to the Cauchy, inclusive. The student's distribution, which is far better known and understood, does so, also.[2]

The student's distribution, which is invariably symmetrical, requires only

[2] Praetz, P. D., The Distribution of Share Price Changes, *Journal of Business,* Vol. 45, January 1972. Pages 49–55 appear to describe the first research on this topic; unfortunately, however, Praetz's work is seriously flawed. More reliable is Blattberg, R. C., and Gomedes, N.J., A Comparison of the Stable and Student Distributions as Statistical Models for Stock Prices, *Journal of Business,* Vol. 47, No. 2, April 1974, pp. 244–280.

	Estimates of Degrees of Freedom for Student Model		Estimates of the Characteristic Exponent for the Stable Model		Log-Likelihood Ratios for
	Daily Data	Weekly Data	Daily Data	Weekly Data	Daily Data
Union Carbide	7.6562	23.315	1.71	1.80	14.46
Dupont	6.1215	8.267	1.67	1.76	12.81
Procter and Gamble	3.3021	5.937	1.52	1.80	14.64
Sears	2.8021	4.089	1.55	1.62	9.61
Standard Oil of California	4.8368	5.206	1.62	1.84	17.72
Standard Oil of New Jersey	3.5694	27.040	1.61	1.76	7.85
Swift	4.3281	14.417	1.60	1.78	17.03
Texaco	5.3455	9.657	1.65	1.83	15.48
Bethlehem Steel	4.7830	6.175	1.64	1.77	10.75
Chrysler	6.3715	9.666	1.73	1.77	10.04
Eastman Kodak	5.3542	3.598	1.72	1.47	7.88
United Aircraft	4.8455	10.394	1.66	1.89	8.71
U.S. Steel	13.2600	13.452	1.87	1.80	2.99
Westinghouse	6.1128	8.929	1.73	1.75	10.50
General Electric	4.8368	7.287	1.66	1.70	14.38
General Foods	5.0955	5.281	1.67	1.77	10.19
General Motors	5.0955	6.493	1.68	1.78	9.29
Goodyear	4.8368	11.162	1.65	1.77	8.24
International Harvester	5.1042	8.570	1.72	1.73	4.72
International Nickel	3.8194	6.044	1.58	1.65	11.30
International Paper	5.1042	8.096	1.68	1.60	10.78
Johns Manville	5.8542	8.783	1.77	1.72	6.54
Allied Chemical	5.0417	89.984	1.73	1.94	7.43
Alcoa	4.8368	5.725	1.67	1.86	8.16
American Can	3.3198	4.735	1.65	1.61	7.89
American Telephone and Telegraph	2.5347	2.349	1.45	1.45	10.29
American Tobacco	2.8021	3.351	1.49	1.59	14.29
Anaconda	8.9323	6.731	1.76	1.61	11.27
Woolworth	3.3194	2.561	1.60	1.45	12.61
Owens Illinois	4.5781	9.182	1.60	1.66	14.10

Exhibit 63. Estimated results for daily rate of return. Notice that in all cases the log-likelihood ratio favors the student's distribution. (A ratio below one would favor the stable model.) Notice also that in 26 of 30 cases, the distribution becomes more normal, that is, the degrees of freedom increase as the sum size or the differencing interval increases. Reprinted from Blattberg, R., and Gonedes, N. J., A Comparison of the Stable and Student Distributions as Statistical Models for Stock Prices, *The Journal of Business,* Volume 47, No. 2, April 1974, pp. 244–280, by permission of University of Chicago Press © 1974, University of Chicago Press.

three variables to describe it: location, scale, and kurtosis. Location and scale can be measured the same way they can be for the stable Paretian distribution. Kurtosis, however, is measured by a variable known as the degrees of freedom (ν) which can take any value from one to infinity, inclusive. When $\nu = 1$, the distribution is Cauchy; when ν is infinite, the distribution is normal.

The stable Paretian distribution and the student's distribution differ in several ways. The most obvious is that the stable distribution can describe skewed data, which the student's distribution cannot. A more important difference is that the standard deviation of the stable Paretian distributions rapidly becomes a meaningless measure of scale as $\mathcal{K}$ drops below two. On the other hand, the standard deviation of the student's distribution only becomes meaningless when ν is relatively close to one. This allows the trader to use many more and many more powerful statistical tools than he could otherwise.

Another important difference is that the stable Paretian distribution is stable, whereas the student's distribution is not. If the distribution is stable, kurtosis will remain constant, regardless of the differencing interval, that is, the time period between the events being measured. On the other hand, location, scale, and skewness will increase in proportion to any increase in the differencing interval. For example, if the distribution is stable and if the mean daily price change is $\ddot{X}$, the standard deviation of the mean daily price change is $\ddot{S}$, and the kurtosis is $\ddot{\mathcal{K}}$, then the mean weekly (5-day) price change will be $5\ddot{X}$, the standard deviation of the weekly price change will be $5\ddot{S}$, and the kurtosis of the weekly price change will be $\ddot{\mathcal{K}}$.

On the other hand, if the distribution is not stable, that is, if it converges, the distribution's kurtosis will decrease as the differencing interval increases. This will have no effect on the mean, which will remain stable, but the skewness and standard deviation will decrease as the differencing interval increases. For example, if the distribution is not stable and if the mean daily price change is $\ddot{X}$, the standard deviation is $\ddot{S}$, and the kurtosis $\ddot{\mathcal{K}}$, then the mean weekly price change will be $5\ddot{X}$, the standard deviation will be less than $5\ddot{S}$, and the kurtosis will be less than $\ddot{\mathcal{K}}$.

Interestingly enough, academic studies of stock price behavior have found that the distributions converge. Although there is considerable kurtosis in daily price data, there is considerably less in weekly data (Exhibit 63). Indeed, when monthly data is considered, kurtosis may disappear almost completely.

The available evidence indicates that stock and probably commodity price distributions resemble a student's distribution more closely than they do a stable Paretian distribution. Unfortunately, stock price distributions and possibly commodity price distributions are frequently skewed.[3] As the student's distribution cannot describe skewed data, the student's distribution cannot adequately describe some price behavior.

The fact is that no one knows how commodity prices are *really* distributed, and without this information it is impossible to accurately calculate risk either catastrophic and otherwise. In other words, *part of the risk a trader must accept is not knowing the full extent of his risk.*

On the other hand, if the trader plans carefully, the probability of sustaining a catastrophic loss might be smaller than the above analysis suggests. In other words, to some extent catastrophic loss is probably avoidable.

There are both strategic and tactical approaches to eliminating or minimizing catastrophic risk. Strategic approaches do not involve forecasting; tactical approaches do. Strategic approaches will be discussed first.

A trader with exposed assets can eliminate catastrophic risk only by legally shifting the risk to someone else or by trading only certain limited-risk speculations. Some money managers and brokerage firms are willing to limit the trader's risk to his investment, in effect insuring the trader against catastrophic loss. In return, they demand large advisory fees or commissions and partial or total control over trading.

Limited-risk speculations allow the trader considerably more control. These speculations include options and certain spreads. For legal reasons, commodity options are not currently available on any legitimate exchange, but the law is capricious and this may change.

If options again become available, the trader obviously should restrict himself to those that can be expected to be profitable on average. Whether this can be expected of any given option will depend on the price the trader must pay for it and the probability of the underlying commodity moving as forecasted. In recent years, a great deal of work, academic and otherwise, has been done on option pricing;[4] the trader would be well advised to become familiar with some of it before he buys his first option.

Spreads per se are neither more nor less dangerous than outright positions; however, certain spreads, which are known as carrying charge spreads, will indeed limit the trader's risk. Unfortunately, the logic and location of these spreads are so well known that there is little point in describing them here. If there is little risk in trading them, there is also little reason. Indeed, there are so many

---

[3] Simkowitz, M. A., and Beedles, W. L., Asymmetric Stable Distributed Security Returns, *Journal of the American Statistical Association*, June 1980, pp. 306–312.

[4] A reasonable place to start is with Cootner, P., (ed.), *The Random Character of Stock Market Prices*, M.I.T., Cambridge, Mass., 1964.

traders trying to exploit these spreads that it would be remarkable if there were any profit potential left.

The problem with these techniques is that they are quite expensive in terms of profit potential. It is clearly pointless, for example, to buy an option that is so expensive that there is no chance or almost no chance of selling it profitably. This, unfortunately, is all too often the case. In such cases, the trader would be better off either accepting the risk of catastrophic loss or foregoing trading altogether.

There are at least two strategies that will reduce catastrophic risk, although they will not eliminate it. One strategy is to minimize the number of contract days held; this will be explained later. Another strategy is to limit trading to times and places where limits are enforced; this, in effect, limits trading to legitimate American exchanges.

American exchanges enforce two types of price limits. The first limits the amount that the price can move above or below the previous day's closing price; this is called the "daily limit." The second limits the range of a given day's trading; this is called the "daily range." Often, but not always, the daily range is twice the daily limit, in which case it does not matter whether the upper or the lower limit is reached first. For example, if the previous day's closing price for May wheat was $2.53, the daily limit is $.20, and the daily range is $.40, the price of May wheat could not go higher than $2.73 or lower than $2.33. However, if the daily range was less than twice the daily limit—if, say, it was $.20—and May wheat traded at, say, $2.60 before dropping below $2.53, it could go no lower than $2.40.

Trading need not stop when the price hits a limit. Occasionally, for example, the price will hit both limits during a day's trading, sometimes more than once. A rational price change larger than the limits allow will still happen, but it will happen over several days' time. For example, it took the Mexican peso five days to drop from .078 to .048. Presumably, without limits, it would have dropped that distance in a single day (see Exhibit 64).

On the other hand, limits will impede large irrational price changes. This is not necessarily a virtue, however. Profits can only be made when the market acts irrationally; a more rational market will be a less potentially profitable one. Nevertheless, if the trader is willing to give up some profit potential, he will find the risks of catastrophic loss less on exchanges that enforce price limits.

Unfortunately, not all exchanges have price limits. British exchanges, for example, do not. Furthermore, American exchanges do not enforce price limits during the last month a contract is traded. Therefore, prices are unusually volatile during this time, and it is not a prudent time to trade (see Exhibit 65).

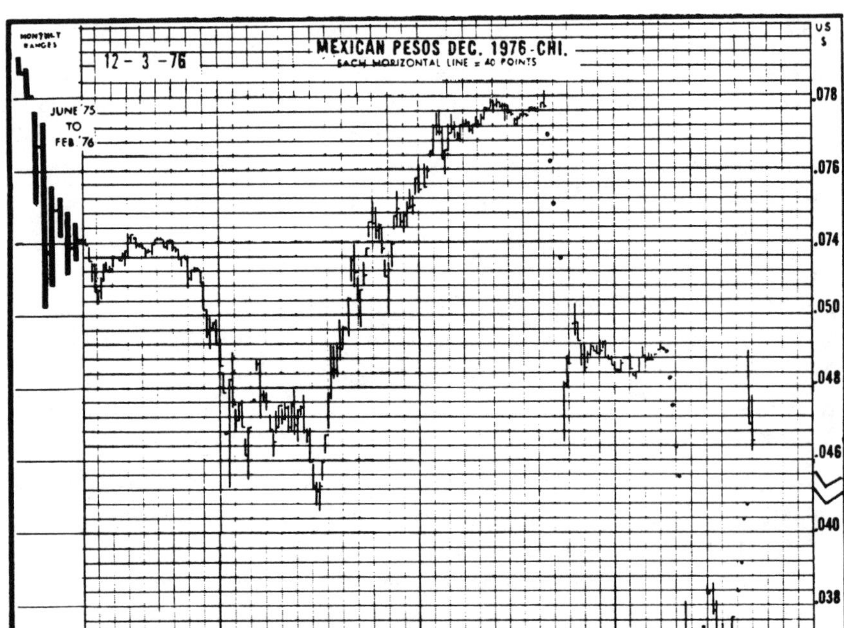

Exhibit 64. December 1976 Mexican peso (International Money Market). From Commodity Chart Service.

The second strategy for reducing catastrophic risk is to minimize and properly distribute the number of contract days held. The number of contract days held, over some period of time, is the sum of the number of contracts the trader holds on each day that he holds one or more. For example, if a trader buys three contracts on Monday's opening and sells them on Tuesday's opening, and then buys one contract on Wednesday's opening and sells it on the following Monday's opening, he has held eight contract days over the calendar week.

All other things being equal, the greater the number of contract days a trader holds, the greater the catastrophic risk. All other things being equal, the trader who buys eight contracts on Wednesday's open and sells them all on the next open is accepting the same catastrophic risk as the trader above.

But all other things are never equal. If a catastrophic loss is likely to bankrupt the trader, it may make more sense to aggregate the number of contract days

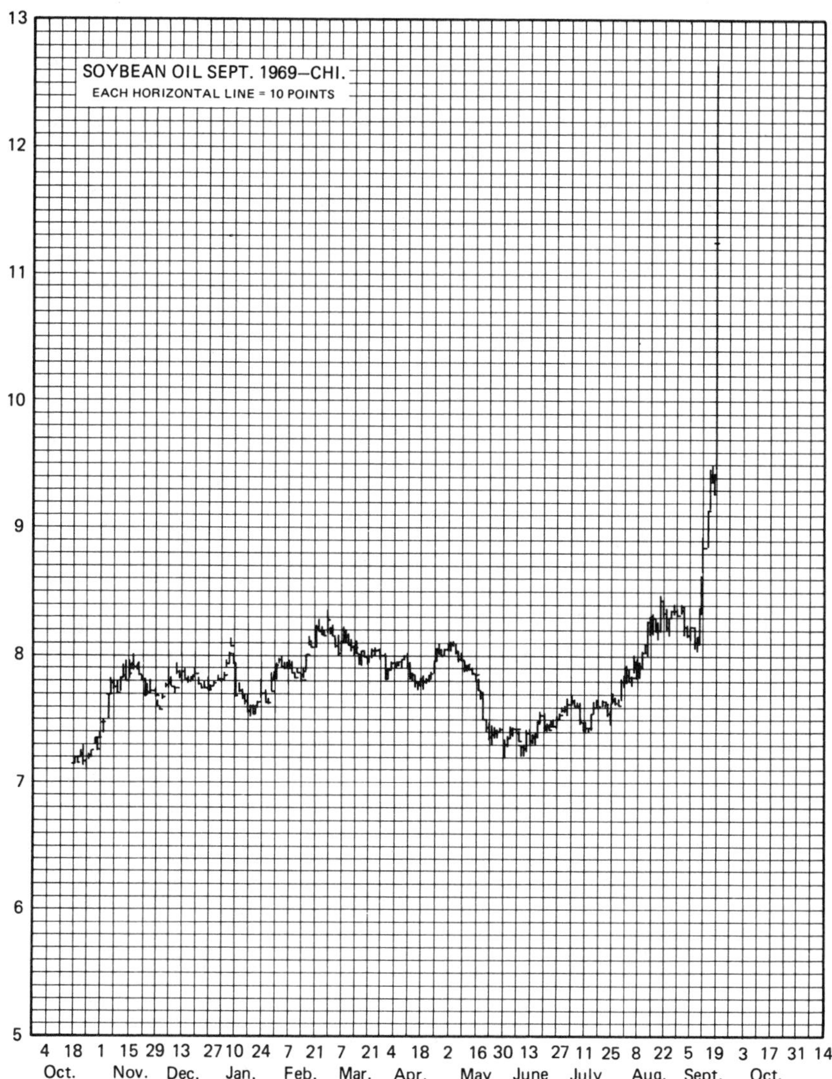

Exhibit 65. September 1969 soybean oil; July 1972 wheat (Chicago Board of Trade). From Commodity Chart Service.

held as much as possible. This minimizes the probability of a catastrophic loss but increases the size of the loss if, in fact, a loss takes place. But then, the magnitude of the loss need not concern the trader if he goes bankrupt; legally, going bankrupt with $50,000 in debts is exactly the same as going bankrupt with

\$5,000,000 in debts.[5] On the other hand, if catastrophic losses are not likely to bankrupt the trader, but only cause him considerable pain, it makes more sense to equally distribute the number of contract days held as much as possible. This will maximize the probability of being affected but will minimize the effect if, in fact, a disaster takes place.

There is another reason that all other things are never equal, and that is that the ability to trade profitably is, among other things, a function of the number of contract days held.

The tradeoffs involved can best be analyzed in terms of E. O. Thorp's[6] formula for account growth. Thorp's formula for the growth function (g) is:

$$g = \{P[\log(1 + Bf)]\} + \{(1 - P)[\log(1 - f)]\}$$

where

$$f = \frac{\epsilon}{B}$$

$$\epsilon = (B + 1)P - 1$$

$$B = \frac{W}{L}$$

and where

W = the average profit if, in fact, a trade is profitable

L = the average loss if, in fact, a trade is unprofitable

P = the proportion of winning trader

---

[5] Planning for a possible bankruptcy is *not* fraud as long as the trader honestly presents his or her financial position to the brokerage firm. Brokerage firms are very well aware of the risk of catastrophic loss and are free to reject the account. Incidentally, the behavior of most brokerage firms is less than honorable here. Many firms will not open accounts for individuals whose total assets do not substantially exceed the amount they will devote to trading. This protects the company against a default if the trader suffers a catastrophic loss, of course, and there is nothing unethical about this. What is unethical is the implication that this practice is enforced only for the protection of the trader, not for the mutual protection of the trader and the firm. Worse, most brokerage firms give little or no warning of the risks involved.

[6] Thorp, E. O., The Kelley Money Management System, *Gambling Times*, December 1979, pp. 91–92.

Here "log" refers to the natural logarithm. This function can be found on several pocket calculators. It is also available in Table 13 in Appendix 3.

In the formula above, f is the proportion of trading funds that can prudently be committed to the market. The number of contract days a trader can hold is clearly a function of f, among other factors. Still, while the terms are not synonymous, there is no obvious systematic difference between them. The proportion of funds that can prudently be committed to the market (f) can therefore be used as a surrogate for the number of contract days held.

As would be expected, account growth is a function of f, which is itself a function of P, the proportion of winning trades and B, the win/loss ratio. In terms of the growth function (g), neither P nor B is more important than the other. However, f is affected much more by changes in P than by changes in B. Indeed, an increase in P that will produce the same increase in g that an increase in B would produce will produce a larger increase in f.

This implies that at least as far as minimizing catastrophic risk is concerned, it is more important to select trades with large win/loss ratios than to select trades that are almost certain to win. These matters are not always under the trader's control, but when they are, the choice is clear.

Tactical approaches involve forecasting the market. These will be discussed next.

The extent to which the market can successfully be forecasted is the extent to which its causes can be understood, of course. Because massive changes in price are caused by massive changes in the fundamentals, it is necessary to study these. Case studies of catastrophic price changes reveal at least four different types of fundamental change.

The first, most obvious, and most unpleasant type of massive fundamental change is a sudden emergence or disappearance of a powerful new source of supply or demand. The 1972 wheat market (see Exhibit 66) is an example. The sharp increase in the price of wheat was caused by a sharp increase in the foreign demand for wheat. Russian demand for wheat had not been an important market factor for years, and there was no reason to believe it would be then. Russian buying, in effect, was a powerful, random, exogenous shock to the market.[7]

A second, less obvious, but more predictable type of massive fundamental change is the sudden but conditional emergence or disappearance of a source of supply or demand. The 1977 orange freeze provides an example of this type of catastrophe (see Exhibit 67). At certain times of the year the orange crop is susceptible to frost damage; at other times it is not. If a trader can forecast the seasons, he can forecast the danger of being in the orange juice market; he need not

---

[7] My thanks to Randy Sheldon of the Chicago Board of Trade for reviewing the material on wheat.

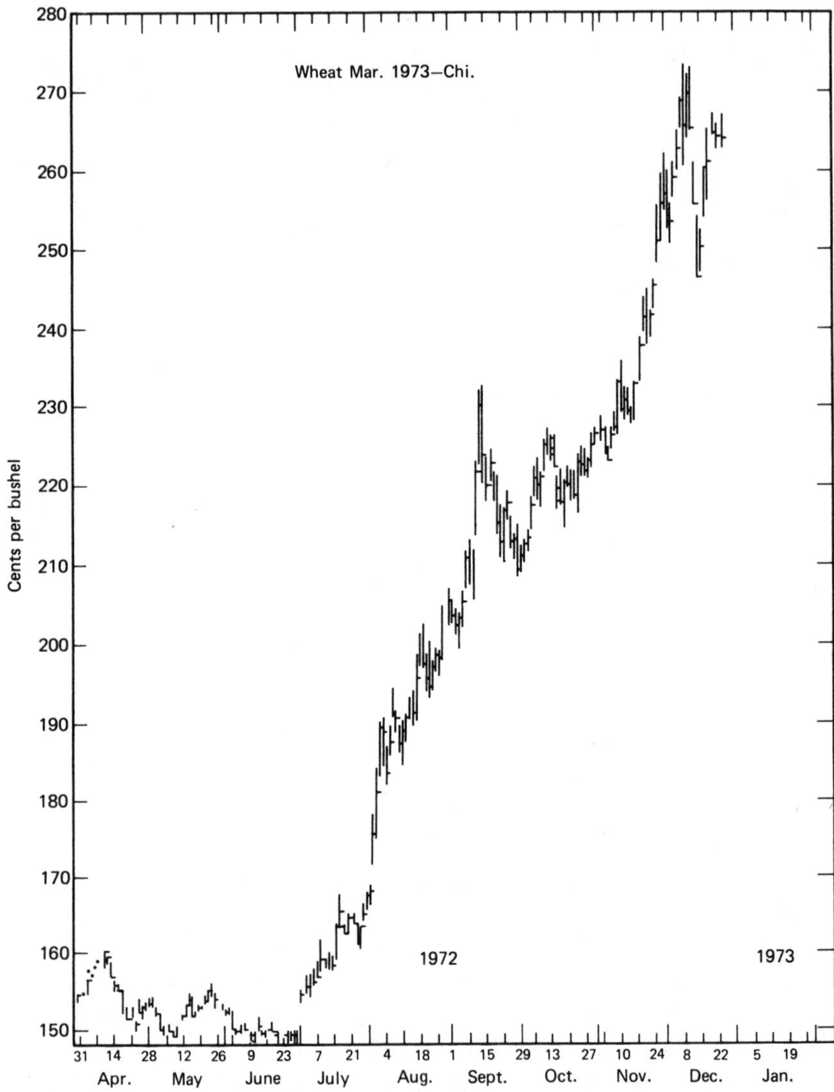

Exhibit 66. March 1973 wheat (Chicago Board of Trade). From Commodity Chart Service.

be able to forecast the weather. An orange freeze is, in effect, a powerful, conditional, exogenous shock to the market.[8]

A third, still less obvious, but still more predictable type of massive fundamental change is a *gradual* change in the fundamentals that causes a sudden

[8]My thanks to Tom Greene of the New York Cotton Exchange for reviewing the material on orange juice.

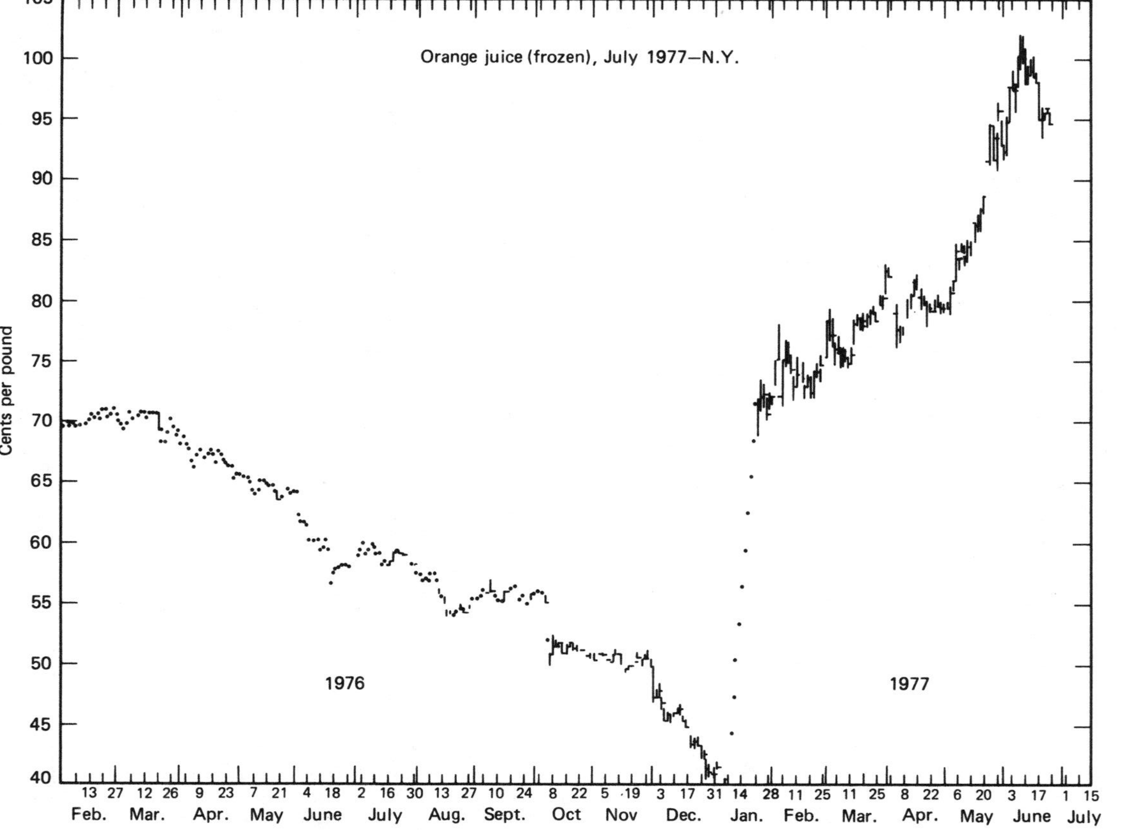

Exhibit 67. July 1977 orange juice. From Commodity Chart Service.

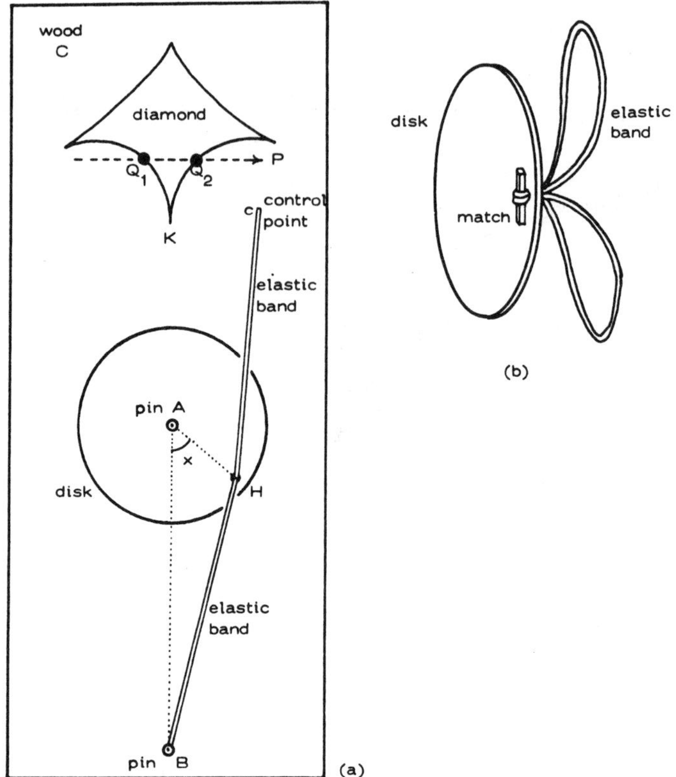

Exhibit 68. (a) a catastrophy machine; (b) how to attach the elastic bands. From Zeeman, E. C., *Catastrophy Theory: Selected Papers, 1972-1977*, Addison-Wesley, Reading, Mass., 1977, p. 9.

emergence or disappearance of a form of supply or demand. The trader will find it easier to understand this concept if he takes the time to make and play with the toy in Exhibit 68.

> The materials needed are 2 elastic bands, 2 drawing pins, half a matchstick, a piece of cardboard and a piece of wood. Taking the unstretched length of an elastic band as our unit of length, cut out a cardboard disk of diameter about 1 unit. Attach the two elastic bands to a point near the edge of the disk—the easiest way to do this is to pierce a small hole at $\ddot{H}$, push little loops of the elastic bands through the hole, and secure them by slipping the matchstick through the loops and pulling tight [as in Exhibit 68]. Now pin the centre of the disk to the piece of wood with drawing pin $\ddot{A}$ (with the elastic bands on the top and the matchstick underneath), and

> make sure that it spins freely. Fix the other drawing pin B into the wood, so that AB is about 2 units, and then hook one of the elastic bands over B. The machine is now ready to go.
>
> Hold the other end of the other elastic band; where you hold it is the *control point* C. Therefore the control space C is the surface of the wood. Meanwhile the *state* of the machine is in the position of the disk, and this is measured by the angle X = BAH. When the control C is moved smoothly, the state X will follow suit, except that sometimes instead of moving smoothly, it will suddenly jump.[9]

The control point corresponds to the market's fundamentals and the state to the market price. The sudden jump corresponds to a catastrophic price change.

A real world example is the 1976 Mexican peso devaluation (see Exhibit 64). For decades, the Mexican government had pegged the price of the peso to the U.S. dollar. It had done this by buying pesos whenever they fell below the price of \$.078 per peso. At the same time, the Mexican government had inflated the money supply relative to that of the United States. In other words, although in terms of the U.S. dollar the price of the peso was stable, its value was steadily eroding. It was obvious, therefore, that if the peso was devalued, anyone holding pesos at that time would lose a great deal. It was also obvious that unless radical and unlikely changes in the fundamentals took place, sooner or later the Mexican government would have to devalue the peso. When the Mexican government finally devalued the peso, prices collapsed.

A fourth, more obvious, and still more predictable type of massive fundamental change is one that takes place in a market so unstable that one massive fundamental change can be expected to follow another A real world example is the 1979-80 gold market (see Exhibit 69). In one sense, the cause of each catastrophic price change differed: Each change was caused by a different radical change in the international political economy. However, in another sense, the causes were the same—international political instability. The trader need not have understood international political economics to have understood the danger of trading gold.

The above analysis permits or demands several conclusions. The first is that the degree to which a trader can avoid catastrophic risk depends on his knowledge of market fundamentals. In most of the cases above, the technical trader could not have avoided catastrophe.

This seriously limits the trader's ability to diversify. As few traders understand the fundamentals of more than one or two commodities in any depth, few

[9] Zeeman, E. C., *Catastrophe Theory: Selected Papers, 1972-1977,* Addison-Wesley, Reading, Mass., 1977, pp. 8 and 10.

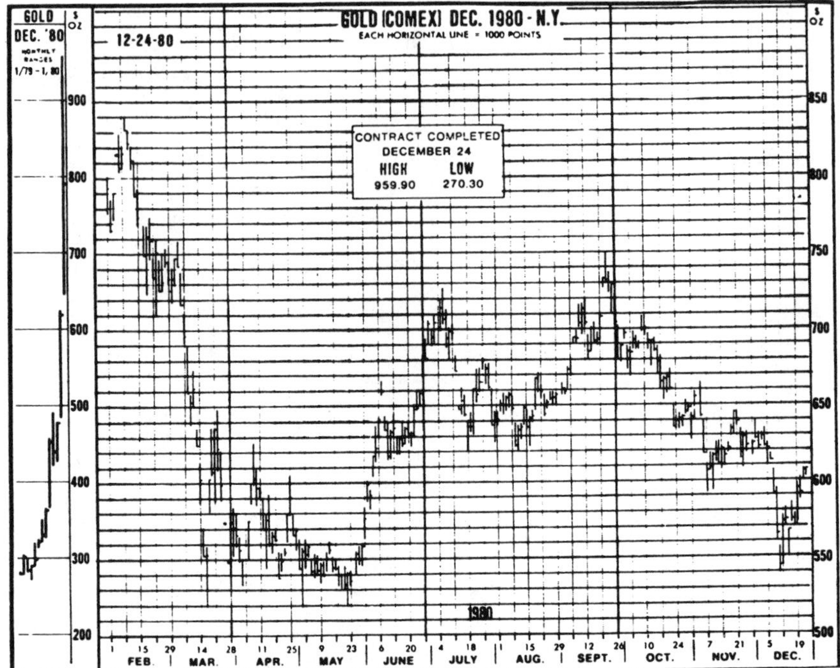

Exhibit 69. December 1980 gold (International Money Market). From Commodity Chart Service.

traders can trade more than one or two commodities with relative safety. If the trader accepts a smaller portfolio to reduce the probability of sustaining a catastrophic loss, he will have to trade more contracts per commodity, all other things being equal, which will increase the size of the loss, if, in fact, a loss takes place.

A second conclusion is that efforts to avoid catastrophic risk are clearly subject to diminishing returns (see Exhibit 8). Some catastrophic risks may be easily avoided; for example, even the most cursory examination of the 1979–80 gold market would have revealed the danger of trading in it. Indeed, the most cursory glance at the price charts should have revealed the market's instability.

Unfortunately, the charts would not reveal the danger of trading the Mexican peso. Fortunately, the fundamentals would. Clearly, as long as the peso was pegged to the dollar, the *only* purpose a futures contract for the peso could have had would be to provide a place to hedge against, or to gamble on, the peso's potential devaluation. It should have been clear at the time that those who best understood the economics believed there was a reasonable chance of a devaluation. Else, why a contract?

Interestingly enough, if the trader read the financial press, he would have seen that the devaluation was imminent. Several weeks before the devaluation, the Mexican government took out full-page ads in *The Wall Street Journal* and other publications to announce that the peso would not be devalued. Such announcements frequently precede devaluations.

In the case of orange juice, the situation is somewhat different. A freeze is a mere possibility, not an inevitability. However, the fact that oranges are subject to periodic freezes is well known; thus a trader who had made a reasonably thorough study of the fundamentals should have been able to avoid this disaster.

Unfortunately, in the case of the 1972 wheat market there is simply no reason to believe the average trader could have anticipated the risk. Indeed, with the exceptions of the governments of the U.S. and USSR and, perhaps, some of the larger grain companies, no one was aware of the potential turmoil until it was too late.

Clearly, if an individual is going to trade commodities, he is going to have to accept some risk of catastrophic loss. As more and more risk is avoided, it clearly will become progressively harder to avoid what remains, until finally there will be risk that can be avoided only at an excessive price, if it can be avoided at all.

The problem, of course, is not avoiding risk but selecting the "right" risks, that is, risks that promise an adequate reward. This is not an easy task.

If the trader is willing to assign probabilities to the possible successes and failures of various investments or speculations, there are a number of techniques that can almost certainly be of value. One of these will be discussed later.

Unfortunately, it is difficult and occasionally impossible to assign probabilities to many events. There are often historical probabilities, of course, but they may be unrepresentative or unstable. Alternatively, the probabilities may depend on how the trader plays the game.

This is obviously true for many simple games such as tic-tac-toe or chess, and it may even be true for the vastly more complicated game of commodity trading. This suggests that the trader may be able to lower the probability of sustaining a catastrophic loss by prudent trading.

On the other hand, the trader may *not* be able to lower the probability of sustaining a catastrophic loss by prudent trading. Indeed, one version of the contrary opinion theory argues that the market always, or almost always, acts so as to surprise the greatest number of traders. This theory may not be true, but it *is* reasonable, and it is well worth keeping in mind.

When the trader cannot or will not assign probabilities to future events, the decision must be made under uncertainty, as opposed to risk or certainty. Decision making under uncertainty is more abstract, more nebulous, and more difficult than other types of decision making. For these reasons it should be handled in a formal, structured manner.[10]

Unfortunately, it is difficult to tell if a decision made under uncertainty is wrong. In a sense, an investment chosen under uncertainty can only be wrong if the investment is inconsistent with the trader's values or if another investment dominates it. Determining whether either is the case demands the construction of a payoff matrix. We will describe that now.

A payoff matrix is a table showing what the results would be if a trader selected one of several investments, and then one of several mutually exclusive and exhaustive states of nature occurred. A state of nature is a potential state of the commodities fundamentals. It might be an act of nature, such as a freeze or a drought, or it might be a government action, such as a ban on imports or exports.

Constructing a payoff matrix will be the trader's biggest obstacle to applying the techniques described below. Much of the time, hard data will be nonexistent. Yet somehow the trader must decide which of a nearly infinite number of investments are worth considering, which of an infinite number of states of nature are most important, and how the various states of nature affect the various investments.

Clearly, simplifying assumptions must be made. If the assumptions are reasonable, the decisions made will be good. If not, not.

For example, let's consider a trader who believed that if there were no new fundamental developments and if neither the U.S. nor the Swiss governments intervened, the U.S. dollar was almost certain to fall against the Swiss franc. Unfortunately, these are big ifs. If, in fact, the U.S. or Swiss government did intervene, the trader could expect big losses. Although the trade obviously carries considerable risk, the risk is difficult to quantify because government actions are notoriously capricious (see Exhibit 70).

Although there are an infinite number of possible scenarios, it is likely that only a relatively small number will seem important. Often, many of these will fall into groups, and when this is the case, one state of nature can represent many scenarios. For example, the state of nature, "small positive change in the fundamentals," might represent a positive change in the relative balance of payments, a positive relative change in the inflation rates, a positive relative change in the inflation rates, or a positive relative change in export-import policies.

---

[10] Epstein, R. A., *The Theory of Gambling and Statistical Logic,* Academic Press, New York, 1977, pp. 49–52.

		State of Nature			
		$\ddot{K}$	$\ddot{L}$	$\ddot{M}$	$\ddot{N}$
	$\ddot{A}$	(300)	1200	1400	(6000)
Investment	$\ddot{B}$	(50)	300	350	(500)
	$\ddot{C}$	5	5	5	5

Investment

$\ddot{A}$ is a position long in Swiss franc futures, $\ddot{B}$ is a position in Swiss mutual funds, $\ddot{C}$ is a position in U.S. Treasury Bills.

State of Nature

$\ddot{K}$ indicates a small positive change in U.S. fundamentals, $\ddot{L}$ indicates no change in U.S. fundamentals, $\ddot{M}$ indicates a small negative change in U.S. fundamentals, $\ddot{N}$ indicates massive U.S. or Swiss intervention in the current market.

Exhibit 70

Although there are a large number of investments that might be considered, there are only a few that are obviously related to changes in the relative strengths of the U.S. and Swiss economies. The relationship of the first two investments displayed in Exhibit 70 is obvious, of course. The third investment, T-bills, is essentially a do-nothing alternative.

The next step in this type of analysis is to examine the matrix for dominance. One investment dominates another if and only if it has at least as high a payoff for every state of nature and a higher payoff for at least one state of nature. When this is the case, the dominated investment can be removed from the matrix. For example, in Exhibit 71, investment $\ddot{D}$ clearly dominates investment $\ddot{E}$. Investment $\ddot{E}$ can therefore be ignored and removed.

The second step is to select a set of decision rules. There are a number of different decision rules available, any of which may be reasonable, depending on the trader's psychology, values, and philosophy of nature.

The *maximax* rule is reasonable if the trader is optimistic, if the trader values success more than he fears failure, or if he believes that nature is beneficent, that it will cooperate with him to produce the state most to the trader's liking. Although this belief does not seem reasonable, many traders adhere to it. Be that as it may, the rule is:

$$\max(i)\ [\max(j)\mathrm{Pf}(ij)]$$

where Pf(ij) indicates the payoff for the ith investment and the jth state of nature; i and j are arbitrary investments and states of nature. The rule demands

		State of Nature			
		$\ddot{K}$	$\ddot{L}$	$\ddot{M}$	$\ddot{N}$
Investment	$\ddot{A}$	130	250	140	20
	$\ddot{B}$	200	80	150	100
	$\ddot{C}$	180	300	40	110
	$\ddot{D}$	140	220	130	60
	$\ddot{E}$	130	100	130	20

No matter what state of nature occurs, investment $\ddot{D}$ always has a payoff equal to or larger than that of investment $\ddot{E}$. Investment $\ddot{D}$ therefore dominates investment $\ddot{E}$, and investment $\ddot{E}$ can be dropped from the table.

		State of Nature			
		$\ddot{K}$	$\ddot{L}$	$\ddot{M}$	$\ddot{N}$
Investment	$\ddot{A}$	130	250	140	20
	$\ddot{B}$	200	80	150	100
	$\ddot{C}$	180	300	40	110
	$\ddot{D}$	140	220	130	60

Exhibit 71

that the trader first locate the maximum (max) or most favorable payoff for each investment. The trader must then locate the investment with the most favorable of the most favorable payoffs (see Exhibit 72).

The *maximin* rule is reasonable if the trader is pessimistic, if the trader fears failure more than he values success, or if he believes that nature is malevolent, that it will conspire against him to produce the state of nature least to the trader's liking. If certain versions of the theory of contrary opinions are true, this is a reasonable belief for most traders most of the time. If this theory is not true, of course, this is not a reasonable belief. Be that as it may, the rule is:

$$\max(i)[\min(j)\mathrm{Pf}(ij)]$$

	$\ddot{K}$	$\ddot{L}$	$\ddot{M}$	$\ddot{N}$		
$\ddot{A}$	130	<u>250</u>	140	20	<u>250</u>	
$\ddot{B}$	<u>200</u>	80	150	100	<u>200</u>	
$\ddot{C}$	180	<u>*300*</u>	40	110	<u>*300*</u>	<u>*300*</u>
$\ddot{D}$	140	<u>220</u>	130	60	<u>220</u>	

Exhibit 72. The most favorable payoff for each investment is underlined and is in the column to the right of the matrix. The most favorable of the most favorable payoffs is underlined and is also in italics. The *maximax* rule suggests acquiring investment $\ddot{C}$.

where Pf(*ij*) again represents the payoff of the *i*th investment and *j*th state of nature. The rule demands that the trader first locate the minimum (min) or least favorable payoff for each investment. The trader must then locate the investment with the most favorable of the least favorable payoffs (see Exhibit 73).

The *Hurwicz* rule is reasonable if the trader is less than completely committed to optimism or pessimism, to the value of success or fear of failure, or to a belief in a psychology of nature. Actually the Hurwicz rule contains a full range of the values above, including the maximax and maximin rules as special cases. The rule is:

$$\max(i)\{\Omega\,[\max(j)\mathrm{Pf}(ij)] + [1 - \Omega]\,[\min(j)\mathrm{Pf}(ij)]\}$$

where Pf(*ij*) again is the payout for the *i*th investment and the *j*th state of nature. Ω represents the trader's optimism or pessimism by a number from 0 to 1 inclusive, where 0 indicates complete pessimism and 1 indicates complete optimism. When Ω equals 0 the rule is, in effect, the maximin rule and when Ω equals 1 the rule is, in effect, the maximax rule. Naturally, when Ω equals any other number, both optimism and pessimism are represented to some degree.

The Hurwicz rule may seem formidable, but it is really quite easy to apply. The trader must first represent or quantify his feelings about himself and about the market by selecting a value from 0 to 1 inclusive. The trader must then locate the maximum or most favorable payoff and the minimum or least favorable payoff for each investment. The trader must then multiply the maximum value by Ω, multiply the minimum value by 1 - Ω, and then add the resulting values for each investment. The trader then locates the investment with the maximum or largest resulting sum (see Exhibit 74).

Obviously, if the trader is going to use the Hurwicz rule, Ω must be chosen with care. One approach, perhaps as good as any, is to use whatever value for Ω seems intuitively appealing. Another and slightly more tedious approach is to assign Ω whatever value of Ξ would make the trader indifferent as to which investment he acquired from those displayed in Exhibit 75.

	K̈	*L̈*	*M̈*	*N̈*		
Ä	130	250	140	<u>20</u>	<u>20</u>	
B̈	200	<u>*80*</u>	150	100	<u>*80*</u>	<u>*80*</u>
C̈	180	300	<u>40</u>	110	<u>40</u>	
D̈	140	220	130	<u>60</u>	<u>60</u>	

Exhibit 73. The least favorable payoff for each investment is underlined and is in the column to the right of the matrix. The most favorable of the least favorable payoffs is underlined and is also in italics. The *maximin* rule suggests acquiring investment *B̈*.

		$\ddot{K}$	$\ddot{L}$	$\ddot{M}$	$\ddot{N}$	ϕ $\quad$ $1-\phi$	
Investment	$\ddot{A}$	130	<u>*250*</u>	140	*20*	0.2 • <u>*250*</u> + 0.8 • *20* = 66	
	$\ddot{B}$	<u>*200*</u>	*80*	150	100	0.2 • <u>*200*</u> + 0.8 • *80* = *104*	*104*
	$\ddot{C}$	180	<u>*300*</u>	*40*	110	0.2 • <u>*300*</u> + 0.8 • *40* = 92	
	$\ddot{D}$	140	<u>*220*</u>	130	*60*	0.2 • <u>*220*</u> + 0.8 • *60* = 92	

Exhibit 74. The most favorable payoff for each investment is in italics and underlined and in the column to the right of the matrix. The least favorable payoff for each investment is in italics and in the second column to the right of the matrix. The third column to the right of the matrix contains a weighted average of these. When Ω = 0.2, the *Hurwicz* rule suggests acquiring the largest of the weighted averages, investment $\ddot{B}$.

On the other hand, Ω does not always have to be carefully chosen. Indeed, the care taken in choosing Ω should clearly depend on whether changing it will change the investment selected. The easiest way to see this relationship is to graph the value for each investment for each value of Ω from 0 to 1 inclusive (see Exhibit 76).

The *minimax regret* rule embodies different values than the rules above. In many ways this rule is the one most appropriate for the *professional* money manager. The professional money manager is generally, and unfairly, supposed to be omniscient. Indeed, he (or she) will generally be criticized whenever the results are less than the best possible. When this is the case, minimizing the cost or regret of picking the wrong investment is desirable. The rule is:

$$\min(i)[\max(j)\mathrm{Tr}(ij)]$$

where Tr(*ij*) represents the trader's regret that he selected the *i*th investment when the *j*th state of nature occurs. Obviously, the first step in this analysis is to calculate the regret for each combination of investment and state of nature. This is done by subtracting each payoff from the maximum possible payoff for that state of nature. When tabled, the result is the regret matrix. The next step is to locate the maximum regret for each investment and then to select the investment with the smallest or minimum maximum regret (see Exhibit 77).

		State of Nature	
		$\ddot{K}$	$\ddot{L}$
Investment	$\ddot{A}$	0	1
	$\ddot{B}$	Ξ	Ξ

Exhibit 75. Whatever value of Ξ will make a trader indifferent between investments $\ddot{A}$ and $\ddot{B}$ is an acceptable value for Ω.

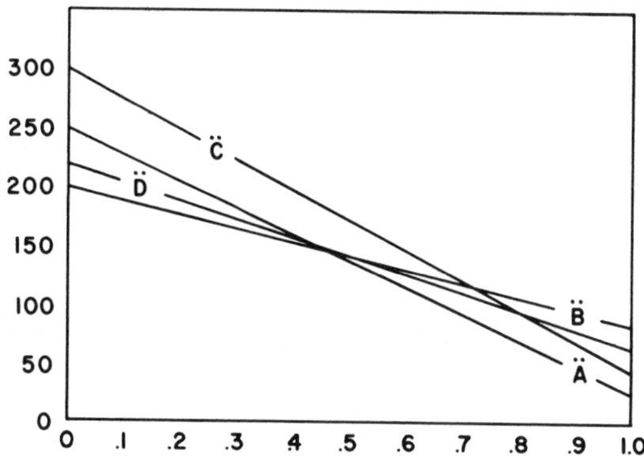

Exhibit 76. The Hurwicz chart allows the trader to see the implications of all possible values of Ω.

If the trader is willing to assign probabilities to future events, he will have to make a risky decision rather than an uncertain one. This is a considerable improvement. Indeed, when probabilities are available, it is *always* possible to make at least as good a decision, and possibly a much better one, than could have been made without them.

Unfortunately, precisely because techniques for making decisions under risk use more information than techniques for making decisions under certainty, such techniques are more difficult to use. The only technique that is presently within the range of most traders is the certainty equivalent.

Certainty equivalents are a practical application of utility theory. Utility

	K̈	*L̈*	*M̈*	*N̈*
Ä	130	250	140	20
B̈	200	80	150	100
C̈	180	300	40	110
D̈	140	220	130	60

	K̈	*L̈*	*M̈*	*N̈*		
Ä	70	50	10	90	90	
B̈	0	220	0	10	220	
C̈	20	0	110	0	110	
D̈	60	80	20	50	80	80

Exhibit 77. A regret matrix is calculated by subtracting each payoff from the maximum payoff for that state of nature. The maximum payoffs are underlined in the top table. The regret matrix is below. Next, the largest regrets for each investment are located. These are underlined and in the column to the right of the matrix. The *minimax regret* rule suggests acquiring the smallest of the maximum regrets, which in this case is investment *D̈*.

theory,[11] in turn, is an attempt to explain why different people do not always value goods and services in the same way.

The utility of a good or service, such as money, is the psychological value or satisfaction a person receives from owning or consuming the good or service. The more value or satisfaction the person receives, the higher the utility is for that good or service at that time, for that person.

For example, if an individual who has no money at all is given a single dollar, he (or she) will almost certainly value that dollar a great deal. However, if that individual continued to receive dollars until he had a million of them, he almost certainly would not value the next dollar as much as he valued the first.

The pleasure or satisfaction or utility that money provides cannot be measured as easily or as accurately as pounds or inches can, but it can be measured by an arbitrary unit called, for lack of a better term, "Utils." "Utils" stand for utility. Utility can be measured in a number of ways, but the easiest way is simply to ask people how much satisfaction or pleasure or utility a given amount of a specific good or service would give them, and then scale their answers.

For example, except under the most extraordinary circumstances, no reasonable individual would find any pleasure or utility in being broke. Therefore, it seems reasonable to equate a loss large enough to bankrupt a trader with a lack of utility. Second, an arbitrarily large amount of money should be given an arbitrarily small amount of Utils. For example, a profit of $100,000 might be given 10 Utils. Third, a utility curve is constructed by filling in the utility of other dollar values. In other words, the trader must ask himself, "If a loss large enough to bankrupt me has no utility, and a $100,000 profit has 10 Utils, how many Utils are $\ddot{X}$ dollars worth?" The value of $\ddot{X}$ would be, in turn, a series of potential profits or losses such as $5,000, $10,000 - $5,000, - $10,000.

Once a utility curve has been constructed, a trader's potential profits and losses can be transformed into Utils and the Utils can be averaged. The resulting average can then be transformed back into dollars with the utility curve. The result, which is called a certainty equivalent, is the psychological value of the trade or investment *in dollars* for a given trader at a given time.

If the utility curve has been carefully constructed, a trade with a certainty equivalent of, say, $50 will have a cash value of $50 to the trader at that time. In other words, the trader should be indifferent about a choice between a trade with a certainty equivalent of $50 and $50 in cash. Indeed, if he (or she) is not indifferent, the utility curve has not been properly constructed.

---

[11] See Swalm, R. O., Utility Theory–Insights Into Risk Taking, *Harvard Business Review*, November–December 1966, p. 123–135.

If the trader has a choice among several trades with varying certainty equivalents, the best trade for him at that time is the one with the highest certainty equivalent. For example, suppose a trader who has the utility curve displayed in Exhibit 78 is offered two bets ($\ddot{X}$ and $\ddot{Y}$) on a single toss of a fair coin where the following conditions hold: for $\ddot{X}$, wins equal losses equal \$50; for $\ddot{Y}$, wins equal losses equal \$500. In dollar terms, the expected value of both bets is the same—0.

$$\ddot{X} = [0.5(\$50)] + [0.5(-\$50)]$$

$$= (\$25) + (-\$25)$$

$$= \$0$$

and

$$\ddot{Y} = [0.5(\$100)] + [0.5(-\$100)]$$

$$= (\$50) + (-\$50)$$

$$= \$0$$

However, the certainty equivalents of the two bets are not equal. For the dollar values of interest, the approximate utility values (u) are:

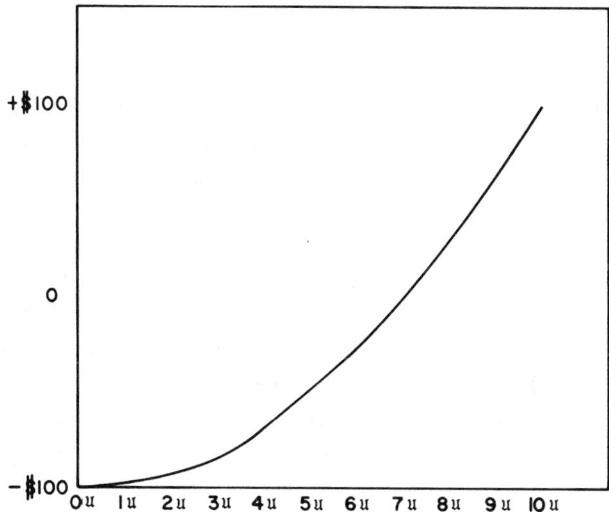

Exhibit 78. A utility curve represents an individual's feelings about a good or service such as money.

$$\$100 = 10 \text{ u}$$

$$50 = 8.6 \text{ u}$$

$$0 = 7 \text{ u}$$

$$-7.52 = 6.8 \text{ u}$$

$$-50 = 5 \text{ u}$$

$$-100 = 0 \text{ u}$$

Therefore:

$$\ddot{X} = [0.5(8.6\text{ u})] + [0.5(5\text{ u})]$$

$$= (4.3\text{ u}) + (2.5\text{ u})$$

$$= 6.8$$

$$\ddot{Y} = [0.5(10\text{ u})] + [0.5(0\text{ u})]$$

$$= (5\text{ u}) + (0\text{ u})$$

$$= 5\text{ u}$$

The certainty equivalents of 6.8 u and 5 u are -\$7.52 and -\$50, respectively. If the trader *must* choose one of the bets, the first is better for the particular trader at that time. The fact that neither of the bets has a positive certainty equivalent means that for this trader, neither of the bets is truly desirable. Indeed, the negative certainty equivalents indicate that the trader at that time would be willing to pay up to \$7.52 and \$50 to avoid bets $\ddot{X}$ and $\ddot{Y}$, respectively.

\$50 may seem an excessive amount to pay to avoid bet $\ddot{Y}$, but this means nothing more than that the reader's utility for money differs from that of the trader in question. There is nothing remarkable in this, however. On the contrary, it would be remarkable if any two individuals ever had the same utility for money, or if one individual held the same utility for any reasonably long period of time.[12]

---

[12] A decision based on a given utility curve obviously is valid only as long as the curve accurately represents the trader's feelings. According to Swalm (p. 134), the available evidence suggests that utility curves *are* stable for long periods, curiously enough.

On the other hand, it may be that after considering the bet, the trader decides that \$50 *is* an excessive amount to pay to avoid bet $\ddot{Y}$. If this is the case, the utility curve was not drawn rationally or carefully. If the curve was not drawn carefully, the trader must simply begin again. If the curve is irrational, there is little hope. A trader may not be able to draw a rational curve if his feelings about money are uncertain, unstable, or intransitive. Such an individual should not trade. As "Adam Smith" notes, "If you don't know who you are, this is an expensive place to find out.[13]

[13]"Smith, A," *The Money Game*, Dell, New York, 1969, p. 41.

Chapter Ten

Cashing in on Cash Management

Prudent money management demands that a certain portion of the money committed to trading be kept off the market. If the amount of money is reasonably large, it will generally be invested in T-bills or money market funds, raising the return from trading at little or no risk.

There is a delightful irony here. Most traders devote most of their energy to trading, where success is uncertain at best, while little energy is devoted to cash management, where success is almost certain.

There are no doubt many reasons why traders do not devote the energy to cash management that they might. For one thing, shuffling funds from one account to another is nowhere near as exciting as trading; for another, shuffling funds is nowhere near as profitable as trading can be. Still, as the efforts involved are slight and the returns relatively certain, the trader who is more interested in profits than trading should find the techniques useful.

Essentially, cash management is an inventory problem. To trade, funds must be left with a broker. If the account is large enough, the broker might allow some of these funds to be invested in T-bills.[1] But even then the returns are lower than the returns available elsewhere; this is the cost of carrying an inventory. Furthermore, there are fixed costs for transferring funds. The purpose of a cash management model is to minimize the total costs of maintaining a cash inventory (see Exhibit 79).

A cash management model is a set of rules for transferring cash from one account to another. During the last 30 years, financial researchers have produced a variety of models embodying a variety of assumptions. For the commodity trader, it seems to me the most reasonable model is that of Miller and Orr.[2]

Miller and Orr assume that net cash flows (receipts minus expenditures) are random in both sign and size, that the probability of earning or losing funds is equal, that the distribution is stable and approximately normal, and that funds can be transferred instantly at some fixed cost. Although several of the assumptions are unrealistic, the model does represent real-world cash flows fairly well (see Exhibit 80).

Part of this chapter was originally published in slightly different form: Gehm, F., Cashing in on Cash Management, *Commodities Magazine*, 250 South Wacker Drive, Chicago IL, 60606, April 1980, pp. 60–62.

[1] A number of brokerage firms now provide in-house money market funds. In many cases there are no costs for transferring funds. However, the available evidence indicates that at this time the returns these funds provide are less than those available elsewhere.

[2] Miller, M., and Orr, D., A Model for the Demand for Money by Firms, *Quarterly Journal of Economics 80,* August 1966, pp. 413–435.

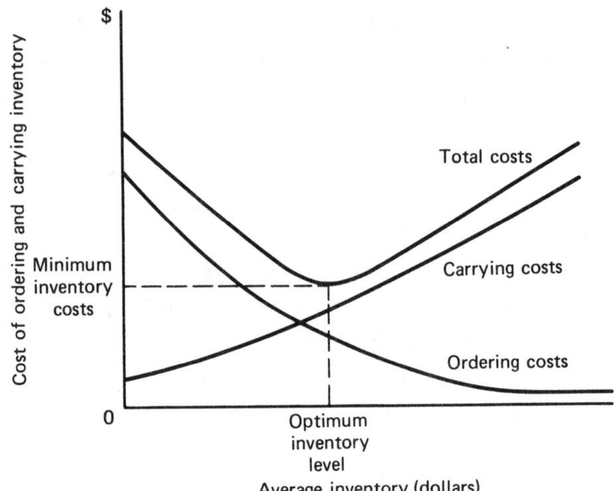

Exhibit 79. Inventory models attempt to minimize the total cost of holding an inventory by mathematically locating the point where the marginal transfer costs just equal the marginal holding costs.

Although there are cash management models embodying more reasonable assumptions, they are more difficult to understand and use. In general, I believe the cost of attempting to understand and use these models would exceed their advantages over Miller and Orr's model.

The Miller and Orr model assumes that there is a lower limit (g), set by the

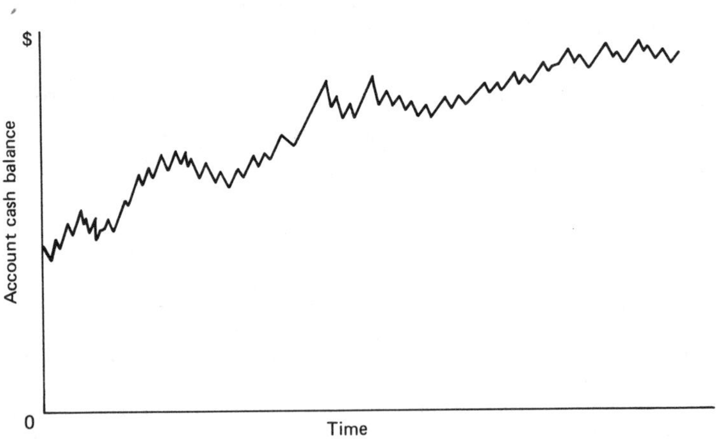

Exhibit 80. Typical cash flow behavior according to Miller and Orr. From Miller, M. and Orr, D., A Model for the Demand for Money by Firms, *Quarterly Journal of Economics 80*, August 1966.

user, below which the cash balance cannot remain. The model generates a desired balance ($\mathcal{D}$) and an upper limit ($\mathcal{U}$). When the balance rises to $\mathcal{U}$, the balance is returned to $\mathcal{D}$ by subtracting $\mathcal{U} - \mathcal{D}$ from it. Similarly, $\mathcal{D} - g$ is added to the balance when it drops to g (see Exhibit 81).

The desired balance and the upper limit are functions of the costs of transferring funds from one account to another, the standard deviation of daily net cash flows, the appropriate daily interest rate difference, and the lower limit.

The cost of transferring funds consists of whatever costs the brokerage house and money market fund inflict for wiring and receiving the funds, and the cost of the work the trader must perform to transfer the funds. The latter costs, of course, depend primarily on how highly the trader values his own time. In any case, the larger the cost of transferring funds, the less reason there is to do it often, and the higher the desired balance and the upper limit should be.

The appropriate daily interest rate difference is the difference between the daily interest paid by the money market fund and the interest, if any, paid by the brokerage house. The larger this difference is, the more costly it is to keep a cash inventory, and the lower the desired balance and the upper limit should be.

The standard deviation of the daily net cash flows is a measure of the variability of trading profits and losses. The more variable profits and losses are, the more reasonable it is to try to minimize the number of times funds are switched

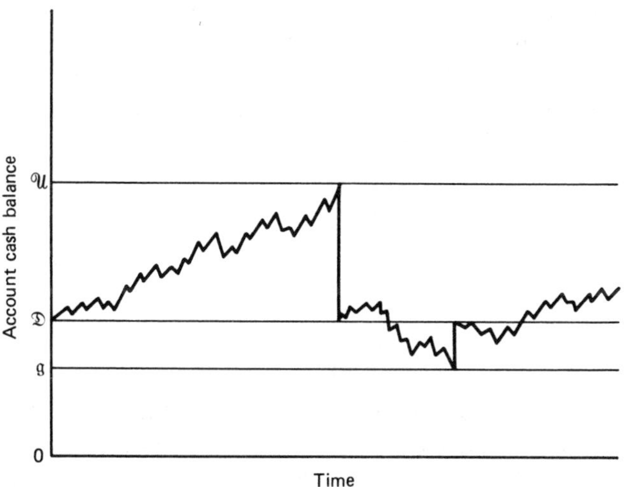

Exhibit 81. The Miller and Orr model demands that funds be added to the account when the balance drops to g and withdrawn when it rises to $\mathcal{U}$. From Miller, M., and Orr, D., A Model for the Demand for Money by Firms, *Quarterly Journal of Economics 80*, August 1966.

back and forth; in this case, the desired balance and upper limit should be set high.

Naturally, none of the factors discussed above are stable; thus Miller and Orr's model must be updated regularly. Fortunately, the model can be updated easily with a pocket calculator.

Miller and Orr's formulas are:

$$\mathcal{D}' = \sqrt[3]{\frac{3\mathcal{T}SD^2}{4\,\mathcal{I}}}$$

$$\mathcal{U}' = 3\mathcal{D}'$$

where $\mathcal{T}$ = cost of transferring funds from one account to another

SD = standard deviation of daily net cash flows

$\mathcal{I}$ = the appropriate daily interest rate difference, which can be calculated easily on a pocket calculator (see Exhibit 82).

An alternative to calculating the standard deviation is to calculate the adjusted sample range. The range (the highest value minus the lowest value) is calculated and divided by $D(N)$ which is the expected value of the range of a sample size N, given certain assumptions. $D(N)$ can be found in Table 10 in Appendix 3. For mathematical reasons the Miller-Orr model assumes that $\mathcal{G} = 0$. The fact that this is virtually never a reasonable assumption only means that once the model's user determines the appropriate lower limit, call it $\mathcal{G}'$, then:

$$\mathcal{G} = \mathcal{G}'$$

$$\mathcal{D} = \mathcal{D}' + \mathcal{G}'$$

$$\mathcal{U} = \mathcal{U}' + \mathcal{G}'$$

$\mathcal{G}'$ is the minimum amount of funds that must be allocated to trading according to the current trading plan. An example may make this clearer. Suppose the reader has just opened a \$10,000 account and is planning to purchase a September wheat contract. The commission for this is, say, \$50, and the initial margin is \$1000. Furthermore, let us assume execution costs of \$50 and a \$750 stop. Clearly, the account balance cannot be allowed to decline below \$1850 if the trade is to be maintained.

Use of Miller and Orr's formula is fairly easy to use with a preprogrammed calculator. Ideally, the calculator should have several addressable memories and the ability to calculate standard deviations and either roots or powers. The Commodore S61 is one of several that will accomplish this. However, the techniques can still be used if the calculator (or its user) cannot calculate standard deviations.

Assume: 1. That the minimum amount of funds to be allocated to trading is \$3000. 2. That the cost of transferring funds is \$15. 3. That the brokerage firm pays 12 percent interest per year, whereas the money market fund selected pays 15 percent; and 4. That the trader lacks the ability to calculate standard deviation but wishes to estimate the standard deviation of net changes in the account balance from the adjusted sample range of the changes of the last 10 days (more data might be better), which were: \$50, –\$500, \$300, -\$610, \$10, \$425, -\$115, -\$290, \$600, -\$90.

Given the above data:

$$\mathcal{G}' = 3000$$

$$\mathcal{T} = 15$$

$$i = \frac{(0.15 - 0.12)}{365} = 0.0000821978082$$

$$SD = \frac{600 - (-610)}{3.0775} = 393.1762794$$

Of course, 600 and –610 are the highest and lowest values for the sample; 3.0775 is extracted from Table 10 in Appendix 3. (Incidentally, the standard deviation of the sample, as estimated by my pocket calculator, is 391.0157712.)

This data must be plugged into Miller and Orr's formula:

$$\mathcal{D}' = \sqrt[3]{\frac{3\mathcal{T}SD^2}{4\ \mathcal{I}}}$$

Thus:

$$\mathcal{D}' = \sqrt[3]{\frac{3 \cdot 15 \cdot 393.1762794 \cdot 393.1762794}{4 \cdot 0.0000821978082}}$$

$$= \sqrt[3]{2.115917593^{10}}$$

$$= \$2,765.99$$

Finally,

$$\mathcal{U}' = 3\mathcal{D}'$$

$$= \$8,297.63$$

Exhibit 82

$$\mathfrak{G} = \mathfrak{G}'$$

$$= \$3000.00$$

$$\mathfrak{D} = \mathfrak{D}' + \mathfrak{G}'$$

$$= \$2{,}765.88 + \$3{,}000.00$$

$$= \$5{,}765.88$$

$$\mathfrak{U} = \mathfrak{U}' + \mathfrak{G}'$$

$$= \$8{,}297.63 + \$3{,}000.00$$

$$= \$11{,}297.63$$

The three outside the root sign $\sqrt[3]{X}$ indicates the cube root of X is to be found, or the number, say Y, which when multiplied by itself three times equals X (e.g., $Y \cdot Y \cdot Y = X$). If the calculator has powers but not roots, raising the number to the 0.33333333. . . power will give the same result as finding the cube root.

The power of a number or the number's superscript is the number of times that the number is to be multiplied by itself (e.g., $X^3 = X \cdot X \cdot X$). Note that $\sqrt[Y]{X} = X^{1/Y}$.

Exhibit 82. (Continued.)

Thus \$1850 constitutes the money allocated to this trade. If more than one contract or commodity will be traded, then the total amount of money allocated to trading, or $\mathfrak{G}'$, becomes the relevant figure. The remaining funds, in this case \$8150, constitute the trader's net power,[3] that is, his ability to accept new trades.

Setting $\mathfrak{G}'$, of course, is a matter of judgment. It demands an estimate of the number of acceptable trades that will be found in the near future. Some trading plans include a long-term map of the specific commodities and number of contracts that will be traded; other plans give little or no warning before a trade is signaled.

Even in the latter case, however, prudent money management will put limits on the number and types of contract that can be accepted, and these limits can be used to estimate $\mathfrak{G}'$. Indeed, it is generally preferable to overestimate $\mathfrak{G}'$: The

[3] Techniques for calculating and managing net power are discussed in Chapter 7. The first and virtually the only discussion of net power in the literature is Teweles, R., et al., *The Commodity Futures Game: Who Wins? Who Loses? Why?*, McGraw-Hill, New York, 1974, pp. 66–68.

cost of doing so is only foregone interest, whereas the cost of underestimating $\mathcal{G}'$ is foregone trading.

A danger in using the model must be pointed out. The model will always generate some definite numbers for $\mathcal{D}$ and $\mathcal{U}$, and many individuals may tend to use these without thinking. Unfortunately, judgment must be used as well, because the model does not incorporate all the factors that should influence the decision.

There may be times, for example, when the funds should be allowed to rise above $\mathcal{U}$, such as when an exceptional number of good trades are expected or when the exchanges are expected to raise margin levels. Conversely, if few good trades are expected or the exchanges are expected to lower margin levels, funds might be reduced to $\mathcal{D}$ before they reach $\mathcal{U}$.

The assumption that funds can be transferred instantly may create problems. For a fee, many money market funds and brokers will wire funds, so for many traders, this is not an unrealistic assumption. Furthermore, if it is only the broker who will not wire funds, there is no real problem; the trader will merely lose a small amount of interest income while funds are in transit. However, if the money market fund will not wire funds or the broker will not accept wired funds, then the trader must either keep enough funds with the broker to tide him over while funds are in transit, or forego trading during that period. Another solution, or course, might be to change brokers or funds.

Chapter Eleven

A Timing Method for Fundamentalists

THE FUNDAMENTAL TIMING INDEX: INTRODUCTION

By itself, a price forecast is not a trading plan. If, for example, the current price of May wheat were $2.50 a bushel and the trader believed it should be priced at $3.00 to clear, obviously, the trader should buy. But should he buy today? Should be wait until tomorrow? Is it already too late to buy? More generally, how can these problems be resolved?

The fundamental timing index may provide a substantial portion of the fundamentalist's tactical plan. Specifically, it turns forecasts into trades; that is, given a price forecast, it provides entry, exit, and stop points. In other words, the trader will know what to do under all circumstances.

There are, of course, other methods for solving the same problem and under some circumstances they may even be more useful. Therefore, after the construction and theory of the fundamental timing index is discussed, the advantages and disadvantages of the index and its competitors will be discussed.

THE FUNDAMENTAL TIMING INDEX: CONSTRUCTION

Volatility Average

Construct a moving average of the difference between each day's close and the previous day's close, ignoring whether the difference is positive or negative. This moving average should be at least 15-days long and possibly longer, as we shall see later.

Potential Profit

Subtract today's close from the target price, that is, the price at which you believe the commodity or stock should be selling. Ignore whether the difference is positive or negative.

Days to Profit

Divide the potential profit by the volatility average. Ideally, the volatility average should be two or three times the length of the number of days to profit. If the length of the volatility average is not longer than the days to profit, the former must be lengthened and the process repeated.

Decision Average

Construct an average of the closing price of the last few days. The number of days should be the same as the number of days to profit.

Decision Rules

1. **Entry Points.** (a) If an entry position is sought and today's closing price is below the target price but above the decision average, a buy signal is given and the commodity or stock is purchased at tomorrow's opening. (b) If an entry position is sought and today's closing price is above the target price but below the decision average, a sell signal is given and the commodity or stock is sold short at tomorrow's opening. (c) If an entry position is sought and neither of the above conditions exist, no position is taken and all indexes are recalculated after tomorrow's close.

2. **Exit Points.** After a position is taken, a stop order is placed at twice the volatility average under the entry point if the trader is long, and twice the volatility average over the entry point if the trader is short. Profits are taken at the target price. In addition, all four indexes are recalculated each day. If the closing price of a commodity that was bought drops below the decision average, the commodity is sold. If the closing price of a commodity that was sold short rises above the decision average, the short is covered. All open positions are closed out on the first day of the delivery month and no new position taken thereafter.

THE FUNDAMENTAL TIMING INDEX: RATIONALE

Logic

The logic of the fundamental timing index should be fairly obvious. A moving average is a mechanical tool for defining trends. The longer a moving average, the longer the trends it will identify, the less sensitive it will be to price changes, and the less losing trades or whipsaws it will generate. The fundamental timing index correlates the length of the moving average with the price's proximity to the target price. Obviously, if the current price is a considerable distance from the target price, a short moving average would be inappropriate: Although it might be profitable, it would simply not identify trends of a fundamentally relevant length. As the current price approaches the target price, the size of the fundamentally relevant trends decreases until it ceases to exist when the target price is reached. The fundamental timing index therefore takes profits at the target price and shrinks the moving average as it follows the price to the target. In addition, a stop is placed to protect the trader from a sudden market turn.

Limitations

Assuming the trader can forecast target prices with some accuracy, the fundamental timing index has one major limitation–the market may not trend. Indeed, there is considerable evidence, academic and otherwise, that the market does not trend.[1] The very popularity of the maxim, "trade with the trend" should make it suspect.[2,3] Everyone cannot profit, yet almost everyone attempts to trade with the trend. On the other hand, for the fundamentalist, the market need not trend with the consistency it must for the trend follower. If indeed the reader has found a market inefficiency, the market must by definition trend in its direction–eventually.

Alternatives

Unlike the technician, the fundamentalist has only a limited number of ways to choose entry, exit, and stop points. To the best of my knowledge, the following list is exhaustive.

1. **The Fundamental Timing Index.**
2. **Random Selection.** Assuming the near term cannot be forecast successfully, the trader does not attempt to "time" his trades but over-margins and rides out any, hopefully only intervening, move.[4] This is a reasonable approach. Even if the assumption isn't true, the approach is merely inefficient.
3. **Eclectic Selection.** Here the trader combines fundamental analysis with a technical approach; for example, chart analysis. If the technical method has forecasting power this is a valid approach. However, it is also a dangerous approach. It is possible, for example, that the technical method will identify trends only when the fundamental analysis is in error. Careful strategic planning is necessary to make this approach work.

---

[1] See Cootner, P. H., ed., *The Random Character of Stock Market Prices,* M.I.T., Cambridge, Mass. 1964.

[2] See Hays, D., Why Pros Like Trends . . . and Trade Contrarily, *Commodities,* February 1977, pp. 30–31, 58, 60.

[3] Rome, M., Simple Systems vs. the Computer *Commodities,* August 1977, pp. 38–41.

[4] Lofton, T., A Different Approach to Commodity Futures, *Commodities,* September 1974, pp. 10–13.

Generally, however, the technical approach is chosen for its psychological value and no effort is made to investigate its forecasting power. This is a popular and useless approach.

4. **Seasonal Selections.** Some seasonal approaches give exit and entry dates; others give time periods within which action should take place. A reasonable approach.
5. **News Analysis.** If a trader possesses a piece of important information no one else possesses, or believes that the market has misinterpreted a news piece, immediate action may be indicated. A reasonable approach.

In my opinion, the fundamental timing index is clearly better than methods 2 and 3. It should not be used however, when methods 4 and 5 are available.

Optimization

No attempt has been made to "optimize" the system; for there is no reason to believe that optimizing the fundamental timing index on the basis of any one method of forecasting price targets would be valid for any other method of forecasting price targets. The reader, of course, may believe the fundamental timing index lacks some desirable properties and modify it on an a priori basis. Assuming that reasoning skills are randomly distributed among my readers, this can only lead to a further dispersal of entry, exit, and stop points, which is desirable.

Motives

Quite obviously, this book was written to make money, but if this chapter really contains a profitable trading method, why, the reader may be asking himself, doesn't your author trade it himself, rather than sell it?

The previous sentence contains an error. What is being sold is not "a profitable trading method," but a timing system with several unusual and interesting properties. If the reader cannot forecast prices accurately, this timing system will be of no use. Entry, exit, and stop points will vary as the target price varies, and assuming that forecasting skill is randomly distributed among my readers, there is little danger of the system being overexposed.

I believe a similar argument can be made for the rest of the book. Although the techniques presented here can change a trader's reward/risk ratio, they cannot make a winner out of a trader who cannot forecast the market accurately.

To be useful, forecasting techniques must be obscure or esoteric; money management techniques need not be.

Chapter Twelve

Conclusion

This is a practical, not a theoretical, book and yet it has a thesis. The thesis is that commodity trading can be profitable, if it can be profitable at all, only if it is handled in a professional manner, that is, if the work is performed in an organized, disciplined manner, and the best, most modern managerial tools are used.

Like all theses, this one is conditional, that is, it is true only under certain conditions. Many of the conditions have been stated in the text, but I believe three are important enough to be stated here.

1. "Nothing is as easy as it looks."[1]
2. There are no decision rules with which to choose decision rules.[2]
3. The only important problem is what to do next.[2]

---

[1] Block, Arthur, *Murphy's Law and Other Reasons Why Things Go ƃuoɹM!* Price/Stern/Sloan, Los Angeles, 1977, p. 11.

[2] Anonymous, Bloggin's Working Rules in *The Scientist Speculates,* I. J. Good, ed., Capricorn Books, New York, 1962, p. 213.

Appendix One

List of Symbols

Symbols not accompanied by explanations are intervening symbols, that is, they are essentially mathematical shorthand for a group of symbols.

$+$	Add
Σ	Summation
$-$	Subtract
$/$	Divide
$\div$	Divide
$\times$	Multiply
$\cdot$	Multiply
$!$	Factorial
$>$	Greater than
$\geqslant$	Greater than or equal to
$<$	Less than
$\leqslant$	Less than or equal to
$=$	Equal to
$\sim$	Not
$\simeq$	Approximately equal
$\vert\ \vert$	Absolute value
$'$	First estimator (statistics only)
$''$	Second estimator (statistics only)
$'''$	Third estimator (statistics only)
$\$$	Dollars
$\sqrt{\ }$	Root
$\ddot{A}$ through $\ddot{Z}$	Arbitrary values
A through D	Marginal totals
a through d	Individual cell values
A $\mathscr{A}$	Proportion of total avoidable risk avoided by trading another commodity
$a-a'$	Available portfolio boundary
AE	Average erosion (population value)
AE	Average erosion (sample value)
α	Confidence coefficient
$(1-\alpha)$	Level of significance

B	
BK	Breakeven point
BOT	Cumulative account equity value bottom
BOT(t)	Day number of cumulative account equity value bottom
$\mathscr{C}$	Beginning trading capital minus the level of ruin
C	Adjusted correlation coefficient
CEC	Commissions and execution costs
Γ	Expected squared mean return per trade
$\mathscr{D}$	Desired cash balance
$\mathscr{D}'$	
di	Difference in ranks
$D(N)$	Expected value of range of sample size N
E	Proportional gain necessary to break even
Δ	
ϵ	
e	2.718281828
∂	Units of trading capital
EF	
EP	Effective proportion of winning trades
ENP	Expected net profit
EX	Expected value
$EX(\ )$	Expected value of
EX( )	Expected value of (statistics only)
∃	
f	Proportion of trading capital that should be committed to the market
FC	Fixed costs
G	
$\mathfrak{g}$	Lower cash limit
$\mathfrak{g}'$	Minimum amount of funds that must be dedicated to trading
g	Growth function
g	Growth function
GA	Geometric average
GP	Expected gross profit
GR	Expected gross ratio of profit to loss

H	Reasonably high estimate
HNZ	
Θ	
$\mathcal{J}$	Interest rate difference
i	Arbitrary investment
I	Riskless rate of return
ι	Interest rate
j	Arbitrary state of nature
$\mathcal{K}$	Kurtosis
K	Number of commodities traded profitably
K	Run test value
L	Potential Loss
l	Reasonable low estimate
$\mathfrak{l}$	Loss on a given trade
Log	Natural Logarithm
Λ	Proportion of capital lost
λ	Simplified weighted average
$\mathcal{M}$	
M	Most likely estimate
$\mathfrak{M}$	Most likely reward
$\mathfrak{m}$	Minimum reward
MAD	Mean absolute deviation
Max ( )	Locate the maximum value
Min ( )	Locate the minimum value
N	Number of interest, sample size
n	Measure of portfolio size
n_1	Number of one type of event
n_2	Number of another type of event
NRR	Probability of surviving N withdrawals in a row without ruin
ν	Degrees of freedom
Ξ	
ξ	
$\mathbf{P}$	Proportion (population)
P	Proportion (sample), probability

$\mathscr{P}$	
$\mathfrak{p}$	Probability of a given trade being profitable
P( )	Probability of
P( )	Conditional probability
P(,)	Joint probability
P(or)	Probability of either of two events
P(|)	Conditional probability
Pf( )	Payoff
PU( )	Upper confidence level
PL( )	Lower confidence level
Π	
$\Pi\Pi$	
Q	
q	Number of times interest is compounded per time period
R	Risk of ruin
r	Number of runs
RA	
RAF	Range adjustment factor
RPL	Expected net ratio of profit to loss
r_s	Spearman rank correlation coefficient
r_s	Spearman rank correlation coefficient (sample)
R( )	Rank sample number
SR	Sharpe ratio
SD	Standard deviation
$\mathscr{T}$	Fixed cost of transferring funds
T	Proportion of risk eliminated from the total avoidable risk
t	Number of time periods
TR	Total revenue
Tr	Trader's regret
TOP	Cumulative account equity value top
TOP(t)	Day number of cumulative account equity value top
$\mathscr{U}$	Upper cash balance level

$\mathcal{U}'$	
UE	Unacceptable erosion proportion
$\mathfrak{U}$	Utility value or Util
VC	Variable costs
V(t)	Value at the end of t periods
V(0)	Value at time 0
W	Potential win
W'	
W	Sample range
$\mathfrak{w}$	Win on a given trade
X	Mean (population)
X	Mean (sample)
X(i)	Rank i of variable X.
XL(α)	Lower α confidence limit of the mean
XU(α)	Upper α confidence limit of the mean
χ^2	Chi square
ψ	
Y	Member of one of two mutually exclusive groups
Y(i)	Rank i of variable y
Ψ	
Z	
$\tilde{Z}$	Number of standard deviations from mean with probability Z or P
$\mathfrak{z}$	Trading capital goal-level of ruin
ZZ	
Ω	Trader's optimism or pessimism

Appendix Two

Mathematical Review

Mathematics is a language. Like English and other languages, it consists of sentences which consist, in turn, of nouns, verbs, adjectives, and adverbs. Like English and other languages, the components of mathematics can be meaningfully assembled only in certain ways. This appendix discusses and teaches some basics of mathematical grammar.

For myself and, perhaps, for most people, learning a new language is difficult and dull. Without doubt the trader will find mathematical sophistication to be of considerable value. Certainly, without mathematics, the trader will be unable to use many of the techniques in this book. This is, perhaps, not a fatal handicap. Often the awareness of a problem is most of its solution. Still, when mathematical techniques are available, it is almost always costly to ignore them.

To use this appendix and, therefore, this book, the trader must be able to add, subtract, multiply, and divide. The trader who cannot do this needs more help than can be provided here. Such a trader should start with a basic book on arithmetic or, perhaps, a tutor.

Unfortunately, some individuals will not be able to use even the most basic book. Almost all books make the assumption that the reader is merely uninformed or bewildered. Unfortunately, this is not always the case. Many people, including many mature and intelligent people, are *afraid* of mathematics and even of arithmetic. These people must deal with this fear first, of course. Therapy or the use of a self-help book on overcoming mathematical anxiety can be of use here.

There are a number of excellent books on basic mathematics. The best, or one of the best, is *Mathematics for Statistics* by W. I. Bashaw, from which most of the rest of this appendix is excerpted.[1] I have made as few changes as possible. I have not altered the statistical slant of the explanations, although it is not quite appropriate here. Nor have I changed Bashaw's symbol system to match my own. I believe that these will be minor annoyances. I have not made the appropriate changes because I believe many traders will want to study Bashaw's book in more detail. Indeed, I recommend this. Bashaw's book covers more material than this book does, of course. Moreover, it provides many problems that the trader can use to test his ability.

Parentheses indicate material that has been changed or added. All such material is my responsibility, of course. All other material is by Bashaw.

---

[1] Bashaw, W. I., *Mathematics for Statistics,* Wiley, New York, 1969.

PROPORTIONS AND PERCENTAGES

Introduction

Perhaps the most common statistics ever calculated and reported are frequency counts, proportions, and percentages.

Proportions and percentages have the same utility. Their purpose is to clarify the interpretation of certain data—usually frequency counts. For example, suppose a particular city contains 4162 Democrats. This statistic really is not very informative. But it would be highly meaningful if you knew that the same number was one-half of the registered voters. The number one-half can be written as a proportion—$\frac{1}{2}$ or .5—or it can be written as a percentage—50% or 50 percent. Both the percentage and the proportion numerals are interpretable, whereas the raw frequency count is relatively unhelpful.

A second major use is in the calculation of probabilities, a major objective of statistical studies. Empirical probability estimates are often proportions.

A point of frequent confusion is the relationship between frequencies, proportions, and percentages. You must learn these relationships and be able to convert quickly any of these into any of the others. A special section of this appendix will be devoted to these conversions.

Basic Definitions

Introduction

This section will define each of these concepts: frequency, ratio, proportion, and percentage. The calculation of each will be explained.

FREQUENCY

The word "frequency" is used in statistics to mean the number of things that have a specific description. We have used one example—the number of persons in a specific city who were registered Democrats. If we polled a city population and asked each person his political affiliation, the number of persons saying "Democrat" is the frequency of occurrence of the response "Democrat." If we obtained the number of responses "Republican," "Socialist," "Independent," and other possible party affiliations, we could get a *frequency distribution* of political party membership for the city. A frequency distribution of political party membership would give the exact number of persons polled who are members of each party.

Here are some more examples of common data often reported in terms of frequencies of occurrence and frequency distributions; the number of traffic accidents each month; the number of persons contracting cancer; the number of unemployed adults; the number of enrollees in each of several training programs; the number of children who earn A's, B's, C's, D's, or F's on their report card; and the number of automobiles sold by various manufacturers.

In summary, a *frequency* is determined by a *count* of persons or things or any events of interest. A *frequency distribution* gives the frequency counts for a set of related events or alternative events.

RATIO

"Ratio" is a general mathematical term that will be used often. The word "ratio" refers to a number that is a quotient of two given numbers. The ratio of 3 to 1 is $3 \div 1$, or 3; the ratio of 2 to 6 is $2 \div 6$, or $\frac{1}{3}$; the ratio of 1 to 10 is $1 \div 10$, or .1; and the ratio of 4 to 7 is $4 \div 7$, or $\frac{4}{7}$.

PROPORTION

In statistics, the word "proportion" usually refers to a particular ratio—the ratio of a frequency to the *sum* of *all* of the frequencies in a frequency distribution. If in our political poll we found 4162 Democrats out of 8324 registered voters, we say that "the proportion of Democrats is .5," which means that "half of the voters are Democrats."

In most uses of "proportion," the term refers to the ratio of a part to a whole. Because of this, proportions are usually fractions between zero and one (or equal to zero or one).

Since proportions are usually the ratio of parts to wholes, the interpretation of all proportions is quite easy. A proportion of zero means that there exists no such part, while a proportion of one means the part comprises the whole. These meanings hold whether we are talking about persons, events, things, or whatever.

Let's take an example. Suppose a teacher grading an exam gives the following marks to 20 children: five receive A's, ten receive B's, four receive C's, and one receives an F. The proportion of papers marked "A" is $\frac{5}{20}$, or $\frac{1}{4}$. The proportion marked "B" is $\frac{1}{2}$. What proportion receives "C," "D," or "F"? The answers are $\frac{1}{5}$, 0, and $\frac{1}{20}$, respectively.

Suppose the teacher has another class of 40 students and in this class gives 25 A's, 10 B's, and 5 C's. The two classes are quite different in size. The teacher gave 10 B's in both classes; however, *relatively* more B's were assigned to class one since the proportion of B's in class one is $\frac{1}{2}$, while the proportion of B's in class two is only $\frac{1}{4}$. Can you see how, using proportions, we can make the two classes comparable despite the fact that one was twice as large as the other? In which class did the teacher assign more A's? The proportion of A's in class one is .25, while the proportion in class two is 625, so relatively more A's were assigned in class two.

EXPONENTS AND RADICALS

Introduction

This section serves two purposes. One is to familiarize you with the mathematical language and notation of exponents and radicals. The second is to help you use the special notation as shortcuts in certain arithmetic problems.

DEFINITIONS AND TERMINOLOGY

Exponents

Exponents provide a shorthand method of writing out multiple multiplications. In particular, if a number is to be multiplied by itself one or more times, the exponential notation is quite helpful. Consider the relationship $3 \times 3 \times 3 \times 3 = 81$. This can be rewritten in exponential notation as $3^4 = 81$. Here, the numeral "4" is the *exponent.* The symbols instruct the reader to multiply three by itself four times ($3 \times 3 \times 3 \times 3$). Here are some more examples:

$$2^2 = 2 \cdot 2 = 4$$

$$2^3 = 2 \cdot 2 \cdot 2 = 8$$

$$2^4 = 2 \cdot 2 \cdot 2 \cdot 2 = 16$$

$$4^3 = 4 \cdot 4 \cdot 4 = 64$$

$$7^2 = 7 \cdot 7 = 49$$

The sentence "$3^4 = 81$" is read, "Three raised to the fourth power is 81" or, more simply, "Three to the fourth power is 81." The exponent "^{2}" is usually read as "squared" rather than "raised to the second power." Thus, "$5^2 = 25$" is read, "Five squared equals 25."

Roots

Determining a root is the inverse operation of powering. Thus, the question, "What is the square of five?" calls for powering five, i.e., $5^2 = 5 \cdot 5 = 25$. On the other hand, the question, "What is the *square root* of 25?" calls for determining the number, which, when multiplied by itself, yields a product of 25. The operator for square root determination (or extraction) is the radical sign: $\sqrt{\ }$. Thus, "$\sqrt{25} = ?$" is read, "What is the square root of 25?" The answer, of course, is five, since $5 \cdot 5 = 25$.

We can also seek higher order roots just as we can use any number as an exponent. The symbols "$\sqrt[3]{125} = ?$" means, "What number when multiplied by itself three times yields 125?" The equation "$\sqrt[6]{64} = ?$" means, "What number when multiplied by itself six times yields 64?" The answers are 5 and 2, respectively, since $5 \cdot 5 \cdot 5 = 125$ and $2 \cdot 2 \cdot 2 \cdot 2 \cdot 2 \cdot 2 = 64$.

Radical Sign as a Grouping Operator

The square root operator (or radical sign) can be treated exactly like a set of braces or parentheses for indicating the order of operations. For example, $\sqrt{16 + 9}$ is to be treated as identical to $\sqrt{(16 + 9)}$. The answer that is correct in terms of standard convention is 5 and not 7. The numbers 16 and 9 must be added *before* obtaining the square root—$\sqrt{16 + 9} = \sqrt{25} = 5$, and it does *not* equal $4 + 3$ or 7.

Multiplication and Division with Exponents

There are several special multiplication or division problems that can be simplified by exponent manipulation. Let's look at these by considering examples.

Power of a Product

a. $[(2)(4)]^2 = [(2)(4)]\,[(2)(4)] = (2^2)(4^2)$

b. $[(7)(3)]^3 = [(7)(3)]\,[(7)(3)]\,[(7)(3)] = (7^3)(3^3)$

c. $(3 \cdot 5 \cdot 2)^2 = (3 \cdot 5 \cdot 2)(3 \cdot 5 \cdot 2) = (3^2)(5^2)(2^2)$

d. $(4 \cdot 2)^3 = (4 \cdot 2)(4 \cdot 2)(4 \cdot 2) = 4^3 2^3$

Can you see the pattern? The rule can be stated as, "A power of a product is the product of the powers."

Product of Powers of the Same Numeral

a. $5^2 \cdot 5^3 = (5 \cdot 5)(5 \cdot 5 \cdot 5) = 5^5$
b. $4^2 \cdot 4^4 = (4 \cdot 4)(4 \cdot 4 \cdot 4 \cdot 4) = 4^6$
c. $3^3 \cdot 3^3 = (3 \cdot 3 \cdot 3)(3 \cdot 3 \cdot 3) = 3^6$
d. $2^4 \cdot 2^3 = (2 \cdot 2 \cdot 2 \cdot 2)(2 \cdot 2 \cdot 2) = 2^7$

Do you see the pattern? What is the relationship of the exponents on the left to the exponents on the right? The relationships are *a*, $2 + 3 = 5$; *b*, $2 + 4 = 6$; *c*, $3 + 3 = 6$; and *d*, $4 + 3 = 7$.

The rule in these examples is to *add* the exponents. Other examples are $3^2 \cdot 3^3 = 3^{2+3} = 3^5$ and $9^5 \cdot 9^7 = 9^{5+7} = 9^{12}$. This rule is applied below.

The Power of a Power

a. $(2^3)^4 = (2^3)(2^3)(2^3)(2^3) = 2^{12}$
b. $(4^5)^2 = (4^5)(4^5) = 4^{10}$
c. $(6^3)^3 = (6^3)(6^3)(6^3) = 6^9$
d. $(5^2)^4 = (5^2)(5^2)(5^2)(5^2) = 5^8$

The pattern in the exponents should be clear. The relationships are *a*, $3 \times 4 = 12$; *b*, $5 \times 2 = 10$; *c*, $3 \times 3 = 9$; and *d*, $2 \times 4 = 8$. The rule is to *multiply* the exponents.

Division of Exponents

The principles above also apply to fractions and division. Keep in mind that a division (say, $4 \div 2$) can be treated as a multiplication ($4 \div 2 = 4 \cdot \frac{1}{2} = 2$). Some examples of the rules are:

a. $(4 \div 3)^2 = (\frac{4}{3})(\frac{4}{3}) = 4^2/3^2 = 4^2 \div 3^2$
b. $(18 \div 4)^3 = 18^3 \div 4^3$
c. $(\frac{1}{3})^2(\frac{1}{3})^3 = (\frac{1}{3})(\frac{1}{3})(\frac{1}{3})(\frac{1}{3})(\frac{1}{3}) = (\frac{1}{3})^5$
d. $(\frac{18}{7})^3(\frac{18}{7})^6 = (\frac{18}{7})^9$

e. $[(\frac{3}{4})^2]^3 = (\frac{3}{4})^2(\frac{3}{4})^2(\frac{3}{4})^2 = (\frac{3}{4})^6 = 3^6/4^6$

f. $[(\frac{7}{8})^4]^3 = 7^{12} \div 8^{12}$

Here are some new examples involving division.

a. $5^4 \div 5^2 = \dfrac{5 \cdot 5 \cdot 5 \cdot 5}{5 \cdot 5} = 5 \cdot 5 = 5^2$

b. $7^5 \div 7^2 = \dfrac{7 \cdot 7 \cdot 7 \cdot 7 \cdot 7}{7 \cdot 7} = 7 \cdot 7 \cdot 7 = 7^3$

c. $3^6 \div 3^4 = \dfrac{3 \cdot 3 \cdot 3 \cdot 3 \cdot 3 \cdot 3}{3 \cdot 3 \cdot 3 \cdot 3} = 3 \cdot 3 = 3^2$

d. $3^9 \div 3^4 = 3^{9-4} = 3^5$

e. $18^4 \div 18^2 = 18^{4-2} = 18^2$

Can you see the pattern in the exponents? The rule is to *subtract* the exponents in these examples. This rule can be extended to cover problems like $6^3 \div 6^5$, as we shall see in the next subsections.

Special Exponents

Exponent of One

An exponent of one does *not* mean "multiply a number by itself once," as this will be confused with the exponent "two." It means that there is no powering indicated at all. Usually, then, the exponent of one is unnecessary and is not written. For example $6^1 = 6$, and we usually write "6" instead of "6^1." However, it is sometimes helpful to think of a numeral without an exponent as having an exponent equal to one. For example, in the problem

$$7^5 \div 7^4$$

we use the subtraction rule to get $5 - 4 = 1$; so the answer is "7^1." However, we usually write this answer as "7" and not "7^1."

Exponent of Zero

The zero exponent is helpful on some occasions. Like the exponent of one, its meaning is a standard convention. Let's look at some more exponential patterns.

$$3^5 = 3 \cdot 3 \cdot 3 \cdot 3 \cdot 3 = 243$$

$$3^4 = 3 \cdot 3 \cdot 3 \cdot 3 \qquad = 81 = 243 \div 3$$

$$3^3 = 3 \cdot 3 \cdot 3 \qquad = 27 = 81 \quad \div 3$$

$$3^2 = 3 \cdot 3 \qquad = 9 \quad = 27 \quad \div 3$$

$$3^1 = 3 \qquad = 3 \quad = 9 \quad \div 3$$

$$3^0 = ?$$

There are no factors of three belonging in the last line since the zero exponent directs us to use *no* factors. We could say $3^0 = 0$, but this is not consistent with the pattern on the right. The last element, to use the same pattern, is $3 \div 3$, which, of course, is one. For *mathematical consistency*, we *define* 3^0 as 1.

Here are some more examples of why the exponent of zero *always* means "one" no matter what the base number is:

$$7^5 \div 7^5 = 1 \quad \text{but} \quad 7^{5-5} = 7^0$$

$$5^4 \div 5^4 = 1 \quad \text{but} \quad 5^{4-4} = 5^0$$

Negative Exponents

Exponents with minus signs also have a standard conventional meaning. In general, they represent *reciprocals.* Let's look at a continuation of the pattern of powers of three presented in the last subsection:

$$3^3 = 3 \cdot 3 \cdot 3 = 81 \div 3 = 27$$

$$3^2 = 3 \cdot 3 \qquad = 27 \div 3 = 9$$

$$3^1 = 3 \qquad = 9 \quad \div 3 = 3$$

$$3^0 = \qquad = 3 \quad \div 3 = 1$$

Let's continue the pattern using minus signs:

$$3^{-1} = 1 \div 3 = \frac{1}{3}$$

$$3^{-2} = (\tfrac{1}{3}) \div 3 = \frac{1}{9}$$

$$3^{-3} = (\tfrac{1}{9}) \div 3 = \frac{1}{27}$$

or, in another form

$$3^{-1} = \frac{1}{3}$$

$$3^{-2} = \frac{1}{3}^{2}$$

$$3^{-3} = \frac{1}{3}^{3}$$

$$3^{-4} = \frac{1}{3}^{4}$$

Consider these examples, also.

a. $$7^3 \div 7^5 = \frac{7 \cdot 7 \cdot 7}{7 \cdot 7 \cdot 7 \cdot 7 \cdot 7} = \frac{1}{7 \cdot 7} = \frac{1}{7^2}$$

and

$$7^3 \div 7^5 = 7^{3-5} = 7^{-2}$$

b. $$6^2 \div 6^5 = \frac{6 \cdot 6}{6 \cdot 6 \cdot 6 \cdot 6 \cdot 6} = \frac{1}{6^3}$$

and

$$6^2 \div 6^5 = 6^{2-5} = 6^{-3}$$

NEGATIVE NUMBERS

Introduction

It is difficult to do any statistical calculations without knowing fundamental operations on negative numbers. Negative numbers are numbers "less than zero." At one time, mathematicians used the terms "directed" or "signed" numbers for negative numbers.

The basic operations–addition, subtraction, multiplication, and division–must be so well known that they are second nature to you.

The Real Number System and the Number Line

The "real number system" is the set of numbers that is used in almost all statistical work. You should already be thoroughly familiar with at least the positive real numbers–these include the counting numbers (integers) and all fractions that can be expressed as ratios or decimal fractions. Also included are numbers called "irrational numbers," which are nonintegers that cannot be expressed as fractions. Examples of these are $\sqrt{2}$ and $\sqrt{3}$. These two numbers cannot be expressed exactly by numerals that are in decimal or ratio notation. However, they are among the real numbers. At the end of this chapter you will see some examples of "nonreal" or "imaginary" numbers, which are not numbers in the real number system.

The real number system includes numbers less than zero. In order to distinguish between these two sets of numbers, we call those exceeding zero "positive" numbers. Numbers less than zero are called "negative" numbers. Negative numbers are expressed as numerals preceded by a minus sign, while positive numbers are indicated by numerals preceded by either a plus sign or no sign.

Negative numbers are common in everyday use. Certainly, everyone uses negative numbers to discuss the winter temperature. In financial affairs, we can use negative numbers. In fact, an overdrawn bank account can be considered as an account containing a negative amount of money. Let's use banking as an example. Suppose I have $100 in my account and in one day I write three checks in the amounts $50, $30, and $45. My checkbook stub should show:

1.	2.	3.
$100	$50	$20
- 50	- 30	- 45
$ 50	$20	?

The final entry should be "–25," indicating that the account is overdrawn by $25.

A common tool for conceptualizing number systems is by a "number line." Since the number line can also help demonstrate some fundamental operations, let's use it to help us understand negative numbers.

Think of a straight line that has no end–an infinitely long line. Let's mark a spot on the line with a zero. The zero will be the basic reference point. Here is a sketch of part of our number line. We will call the right side the positive side and

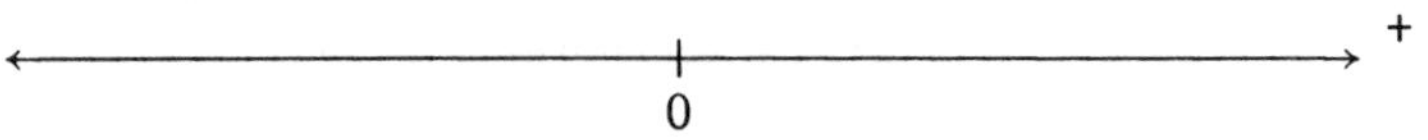

+

0

mark it with a plus sign. The left side is the negative side and is marked with a minus sign.

Notice that the terms "positive," "negative," "plus," and "minus" are, in a way, quite arbitrary labels that are used to distinguish two sets of numbers or to distinguish the two sides of the number line. We could have used the terms "left" and "right" instead of "negative" and "positive." However, the language is not arbitrary in the sense that we need a common, standard vocabulary, so we will continue to use the customary mathematical terminology.

Let's define an arbitrary unit of length and subdivide the line into sections of this unit length, starting at the zero point and working both ways. At the end of each length we will mark the line.

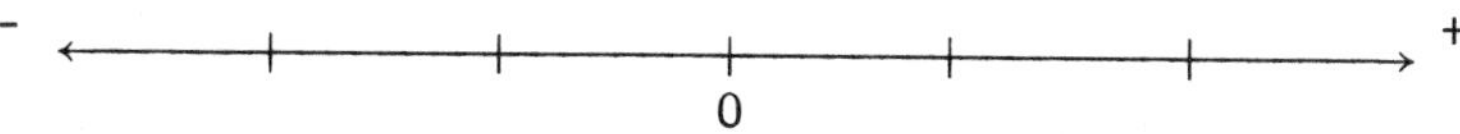

Let's define our unit as having a length of "one" (or "one unit"–this could be one inch, one yard, one millimeter, or one of any arbitrary unit). Now we label our marks on the line with signed numbers, as in the next diagram. If you think

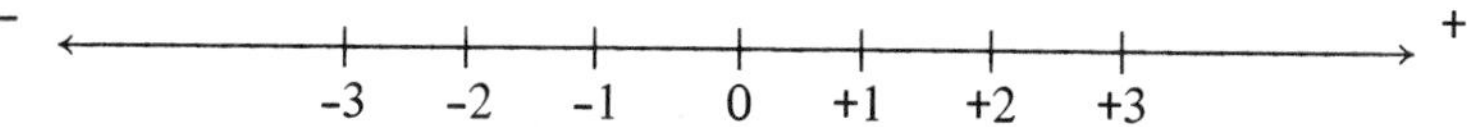

of the line as infinite in length, you can conceptualize any real number as having a corresponding point somewhere on the line. The number "100" corresponds to a point 100 units to the right of 0. The number "-50" corresponds to a point 50 units to the left of 0.

In fact, we can now *define a negative number* as any number corresponding to a point on the number line to the left of zero. This is a perfectly good definition.

Fractions and irrational numbers are also on the line somewhere. For example, the interval from +1 to +2 contains an infinite number of points, each corresponding to fractional numbers. Contained in this interval are points corresponding to $1\frac{1}{2}$, 1.1032, $1\frac{3}{4}$, 1.9995, $\sqrt{2}$, $\sqrt{3.9}$, and any of an infinite number of other numbers that are greater than +1, but less than +2.

Addition of a Positive Number to a Real Number

Let's learn to add using the number line. The addition operation will be defined as "move to the right on the number line." The problem, "What is 5 + 2?" will be defined as follows. Start at 5 on the number line and move right two units. The answer is the number corresponding to the stopping place. Since "7" is the numeral on the line at the stopping point, 5 + 2 = 7.

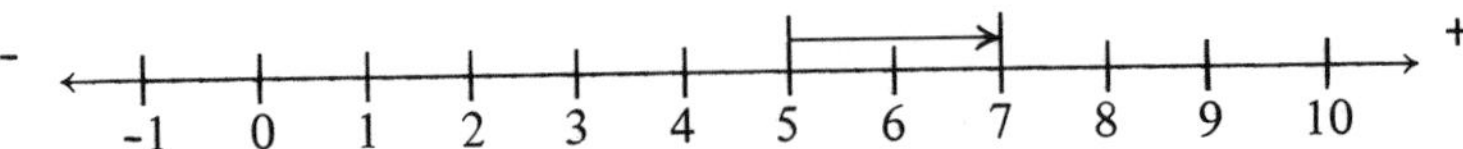

Well, that was simple enough. But what about (–5) + 2 = ? Locate "–5" on the number line and move to the right two places. The answer is seen to be –3.

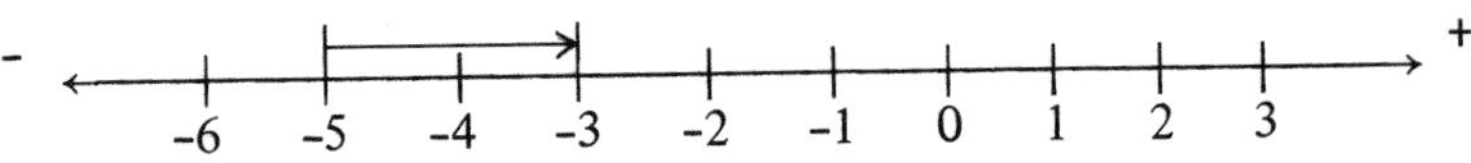

Do these with the number line.

a. (-2) + 3 = ?
b. (-6) + 4 = ?
c. (-1) + 4 = ?
d. 1 + 2 = ?

The answers are *a*, + 1; *b*, –2; *c*, + 3; and *d*, + 3. Be sure you can use the number line to add a positive number to either a positive or negative number.

Now, let's look at some patterns. You may wish to check these on the number line.

4 + 2 = 6	2 + 2 = 4	1 + 5 = 6
2 + 2 = 4	1 + 2 = 3	0 + 5 = 5
0 + 2 = 2	0 + 2 = 2	-1 + 5 = 4
-2 + 2 = 0	-1 + 2 = 1	-2 + 5 = 3
-4 + 2 = -2	-2 + 2 = 0	-3 + 5 = 2
-6 + 2 = -4	-3 + 2 = -1	-4 + 5 = 1
-8 + 2 = -6	-4 + 2 = -2	-5 + 5 = 0
-10 + 2 = -8	-5 + 2 = -3	-6 + 5 = -1

Study the patterns involving one positive addend and one negative addend. In every case, the answer can be obtained by *taking the difference between the addends and adding the sign of the addend which is most different from zero* (i.e., which is largest if you ignore the sign). Thus, -1 + 5 is 5 - 1 with a plus sign, or +4; and -6 + 5 is 6 - 5 with a minus sign, or -1. This "rule" is the standard way of doing additions like these.

Subtraction of a Positive Number from a Real Number

Subtraction can be defined as "moving left on the number line." Thus, "6 - 4 = ?" is defined as follows. Locate "6" on the number line and move *left* 4 units. Find the number corresponding to the stopping place. Do the example. The answer is, of course, 2.

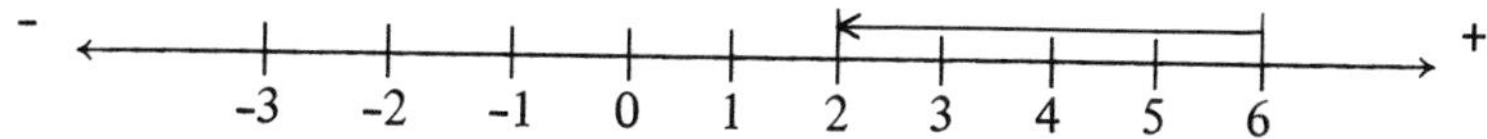

Let's do some more. What is 4 - 7? This problem is undefined unless you have a number system with negative numbers. Locate "4" on the line and move left seven units.

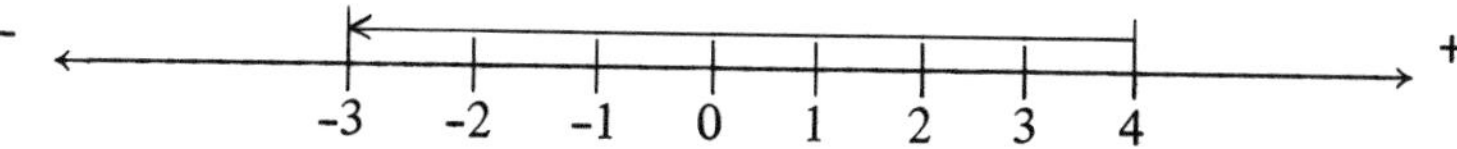

What is (-1) - 1? Start at "-1" and move left one unit.

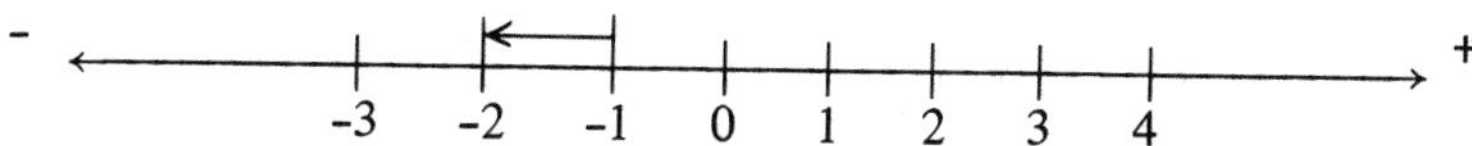

The answers are -3 and -2, respectively.

Now, let's look at some patterns. Use the number line to check these.

8 - 6 = 2	6 - 4 = 2
6 - 6 = 0	5 - 4 = 1
4 - 6 = -2	4 - 4 = 0
2 - 6 = -4	3 - 4 = -1
0 - 6 = -6	2 - 4 = -2
-2 - 6 = -8	0 - 4 = -4
-4 - 6 = -10	-2 - 4 = -6

Most of these subtractions follow the rule given in the previous subsection. However, a new case arises—the subtraction of a positive number from a negative number. The rule here is to add the numbers together and give the sum a negative sign (-4 - 2 = ?; 4 + 2 = 6, so -4 - 2 = -6). In terms of moving on the number line, you start to the left of zero and move further left. The rule is easily clarified by thinking of the number line.

Addition of Negative Numbers to Real Numbers

The addition of a negative number to a real number can be handled by changing the sign of the number to a plus sign, and subtracting instead of adding. For example, 5 + (-2) is the same as 5 - (+2), or 5 -2. Also, 3 + (-5) is the same as 3 - (+5), or 3 - 5.

This trick illustrates a basic principle: subtraction is merely the addition of a negative number. When you work in the real number system, which has negative numbers, you see that there really is no need to have an operation called "subtraction" because it is merely the addition of a negative number.

Subtraction of Negative Numbers from Real Numbers

The subtraction of negative numbers is a little more complex. It will be more readily understood after we take a look at multiplication of negative numbers. For now, let's be dogmatic and do the subtraction by rule only. The rule is to change the number to a positive number and add instead of subtracting. That is, change *both* the operation *and* the sign. Thus,

$$5 - (-1) = 5 + (+1) = 5 + 1 = 6$$

$$2 - (-4) = 2 + (+4) = 2 + 4 = 6$$

$$-8 - (-2) = -8 + (+2) = -8 + 2 = -6$$

Here are some patterns that will show that the above rule does make sense:

$$8 - (+4) = 8 - 4 = 4$$

$$8 - (+3) = 8 - 3 = 5$$

$$8 - (+2) = 8 - 2 = 6$$

$$8 - (+1) = 8 - 1 = 7$$

$$8 - (0) = 8 - 0 = 8$$

$$8 - (-1) = 8 + 1 = 9$$

$$8 - (-2) = 8 + 2 = 10$$

$$8 - (-3) = 8 + 3 = 11$$

In each of these examples, the minuend is a constant "8." The subtrahend decreases by one as we come down the rows. Therefore, the answers must always increase by one as we come down the rows, since we subtract one less each time. We see that the rule is necessary to get answers that keep the pattern consistent.

It might help to think of walking down the number line in the positive direction and turning around whenever you get a minus sign. In this analogy, the double minus sign would mean "turn around twice" and you are again facing in the positive (add) direction.

Multiplication of Real Numbers

Two Factor Multiplication

There are three possible cases of multiplication with real numbers. These are a positive number times a positive number (which, of course, is what you already know quite well), a positive number times a negative number (or vice versa, which is still the same case), and, finally, a negative number times a negative number.

It helps to reconsider the nature of multiplication in general. Multiplication is merely repeated addition. So 6×3 is the same as $6 + 6 + 6$ or, equivalently, $3 + 3 + 3 + 3 + 3 + 3$. Multiplication involving a single negative number can be handled by this fundamental principle. For example, $3 \times (-6)$ is $(-6) + (-6) + (-6)$, or -18. Also, -6×3 is $(-6) + (-6) + (-6)$, or -18. Here are some more equalities: $3 \times (-6) = -6 \times 3 = -3 \times 6 = 6 \times (-3)$.

The minus sign can be considered as a third factor of -1, that is, $3 \times (-6) = 3 \times 6 \times (-1)$. All three factors can be commuted in several ways, each way being another way to write -18, for example, $3 \times 6 \times (-1)$, $(-1) \times 3 \times 6$, and $6 \times (-1) \times 3$.

A third way to look at the product of a negative and positive number is by patterns. Consider this set of problems:

$$6 \times 3 = 18$$

$$6 \times 2 = 12$$

$$6 \times 1 = 6$$

$$6 \times 0 = 0$$

$$6 \times (-1) = ?$$

In each row, the second factor decreases by one, so the product *must* decrease by six as we come down the rows. Therefore, the last entry must be six less than zero, or -6. We can thus continue as follows:

$$6 \times 0 = 0$$

$$6 \times (-1) = -6$$

$$6 \times (-2) = -12$$

$$6 \times (-3) = -18$$

The multiplication of two negative numbers is not as easy to demonstrate from the general definition of negative numbers. Let's do this one by patterns:

$$-6 \times 3 = -18$$

$$-6 \times 2 = -12$$

$$-6 \times 1 = -6$$

$$-6 \times 0 = 0$$

$$-6 \times -1 = ?$$

As we decrease the second factor by one in each row, the answer must *increase* by six. So the last entry must be six more than zero, or +6. We can continue the pattern:

$$-6 \times 1 = -6$$

$$-6 \times 0 = 0$$

$$-6 \times (-1) = 6$$

$$-6 \times (-2) = 12$$

$$-6 \times (-3) = 18$$

A very important special case is the product (-1)(-1). Let's find the product, using patterns:

$$(-1)(3) = -3$$

$$(-1)(2) = -2$$

$$(-1)(1) = -1$$

$$(-1)(0) = 0$$

$$(-1)(-1) = ?$$

The answer must be zero plus one, or +1.

We can use our knowledge that (-1)(-1) = 1 and our ability to commute multiplication factors to get some additional insight into multiplying two negative numbers. As an example, consider (-6) × (-3). This can be rewritten as four factors: (-1)(6)(-1)(3). Let's commute 6 and -1 to give (-1)(-1) (6)(3). Since (-1)(-1) is one, we have (-6)(-3) = 6 • 3 = 18.

Another Look at Subtraction

Now we can return to the problem of subtracting negative numbers. The problem 6 - (-2) can be treated as 6 + (-1)(-2), or 6 + 2 = 8.

Multiplication of Several Factors

The preceding sections dealt with multiplying only two factors. But, several factors can be multiplied together, where some are positive and some are negative.

For example, what is (-6)(3)(4)(-2)(-3)? Let's convert each negative number into a positive number times -1 and commute the entire system. We can write:

$$(-1)(6)(3)(4)(-1)(2)(-1)(3) =$$

$$(-1)(-1)(-1)6 \cdot 3 \cdot 4 \cdot 2 \cdot 3 =$$

$$(-1)(-1)(-1)(432) =$$

But $(-1)(-1) = +1$, so $(-1)(-1)(-1) = (+1)(-1)$, or -1, so the answer is -432.

Let's not spend a great deal of time here. It is sufficient to say that when the number of minus signs in a product of several factors is odd, the answer is negative. If there is an even number of minus signs, the answer is positive. For example:

$$(-2)(-2)(-2)2 = -16$$

$$(-2)(2)(2)(2) = -16$$

$$(-2)(2)(-2)(2) = 16$$

$$(-2)(-2)(-2)(-2) = 16$$

Division of Real Numbers

Since division is merely a form of multiplication, there is nothing particularly new here. Here is an example of each possible case.

1. $6 \div 2 = 6 \times (\frac{1}{2}) = 3$
2. $(-6) \div 2 = (-6) \times (\frac{1}{2}) = -3$
3. $6 \div (-2) = 6 \times (-\frac{1}{2}) = -3$
4. $(-6) \div (-2) = (-6) \times (-\frac{1}{2}) = 3$

In ratio notation, the same examples are as follows.

1. $6/2 = 3$
2. $-6/2 = -3$
3. $6/-2 = -3$
4. $-6/-2 = 3$

Exponents and Radicals Involving Negative Numbers

Exponentiation

There is no particular problem involving the exponentiation of a negative number, since this is merely two, or several, factor multiplication. The sign of the product depends on whether the exponent is even or odd. Here are some examples.

1. $3^2 = 9 \quad (-3)^2 = 9$
2. $3^3 = 27 \quad (-3)^3 = -27$
3. $3^4 = 81 \quad (-3)^4 = 81$
4. $3^5 = 243 \; (-3)^5 = -243$
5. $(-2)^2 + (-2)^3 = 4 - 8 = -4$
6. $3^2 + (-3)^3 + 3^4 = 9 - 27 + 81 = 63$

Negative Exponents

Negative exponents are special division notation and were discussed in the previous section. We can show some patterns that illustrate the definitions of special exponents:

$$\begin{array}{ll} 2^3 = 8 & 3^3 = 27 \\ 2^2 = 4 & 3^2 = 9 \\ 2^1 = 2 & 3^1 = 3 \\ 2^0 = 1 & 3^0 = 1 \\ 2^{-1} = \frac{1}{2} & 3^{-1} = \frac{1}{3} \\ 2^{-2} = \frac{1}{4} & 3^{-2} = \frac{1}{9} \\ 2^{-3} = \frac{1}{8} & 3^{-3} = \frac{1}{27} \end{array}$$

The rules for using negative numbers are also useful in what we have called exponential algebra. Here are some examples.

1. $(2^{-2})(2^{-3}) = 2^{(-2)+(-3)} = 2^{-5}$
2. $(3^2)^{-1} = 3^{(2)(-1)} = 3^{-2}$
3. $(2^4)^{-2} = 2^{(4)(-2)} = 2^{-8}$
4. $(2^{-3})^{-2} = 2^{(-3)(-2)} = 2^6$
5. $(2^3)(2^{-2})(2^{-1}) = 2^{3+(-2)+(-1)} = 2^0 = 1$

Negatives Under Radicals

Suppose you are working a numerical problem and it reduces to $\sqrt{-4}$. Where do you go from here? This is *not* the same thing as $-\sqrt{4}$, which is, of course, -2. The expression "$\sqrt{-4}$ = ?" means, "Find a number such that when you multiply it times itself, you will get -4." Neither +2 nor -2 is such a number, because $(+2)(+2) = +4$ and $(-2)(-2) = +4$. The number $\sqrt{-4}$ cannot be handled in any way that has been previously discussed, since it is *not* an element in the real number system.

VARIABLES, CONSTANTS, AND PARAMETERS

Introduction

The purpose of this section is to introduce some algebraic language. The topics are fundamental, yet they can be a source of unusual perplexity and confusion when not understood. The use of symbols other than arabic numerals will be introduced. Also, words and terms will be explained.

There will be no calculations to learn; however, don't let this fact fool you into glossing over this material. Mathematics is supposed to be a science of logical thinking and logical thinking is difficult if terminology and fundamental principles are mastered poorly.

Things and Names of Things

Let's start our algebraic studies with a very fundamental proposition: an object and the name of the object are two different things. Now, no one would argue that this book and the letters "b," "o," "o," and "k," taken in the given order, are the same things. One is a concrete object. The letter combination is a name, a set of symbols, a label. The object is called the *referent* of the symbol "book." Certainly there is no problem distinguishing the symbol "cow" from its referent.

However, in mathematical writings and understanding, often there is considerable confusion between symbols and their referents. Let's try to keep clear the distincition between a symbol and its referent.

Throughout this book, we will use a symbolization that is almost standard ("almost" in the sense that it usually is used by persons who are careful in distinguishing symbols from referents–many writers are not). When we wish to discuss a symbol as a symbol, it will be enclosed in quotation marks. When there are no quotation marks, then what is meant is the referent of the symbol. Here are some correct examples.

1. A cow is a mammal. How do you pronounce "cow?"
2. Soft-covered books are generally called "paperback books."
3. The word "friend" is misspelled in your paper. John is my best friend.
4. There is too much confusion among the use of "to," "too," and "two."

Hopefully, this text will be consistent in the use of quotation marks to designate names.

One source of difficulty in algebra often is the student's confusion in the distinction between numbers and the symbols for numbers. Symbols for numbers are called "numerals," When we wish to talk about a number, we will write a numeral. When we wish to talk about a numeral, we will write the numeral and put quotation marks around it. Here are some correct examples.

1. Two ways to write "two" are "2" and "1 + 1."
2. "1,000,000" has six "0's." 1,000,000 is 10^6.
3. The statement "2(1 + 3) = 5" is wrong; it should be "2(1 + 3) = 8" because 1 + 3 = 4 and 2 × 4 = 8.

The number-numeral confusion arises largely because numbers are abstract concepts. You cannot point to a number as you can a book or a cow. The referent of the numeral "5" is a *concept* that we might call "fiveness," which is developed over years of experience with numbers. Fiveness becomes understood by a child largely with the aid of finger and toe counting.

Why should we bother with this discussion? It is because algebra introduces some unusual symbols and notations that are clarified by distinguishing symbols from their referents. Consider the number five. It has many symbols associated with it, all of which are equivalent in the sense that *each has the same referent.* Here are several of the infinite number of ways to write a symbol for the number five.

Five	4 + 1
V	$\sqrt{25}$
𝍸	55 ÷ 11
710 - 705	The remainder of 65 ÷ 12

Each of these expressions has the same referent. They are all different names for the same thing.

Letters as Names of Numbers

Since numerals are human inventions, the use of a particular numeral for referring to a particular number is somewhat arbitrary. For example, I could use the letter "a" as a symbol for one and the letter "b" as a symbol for two. Then I could say things like

"$a + a = b$," "$b - a = a$," or "$(b)(a) = b$"

Each of these sentences is true and is meaningful *in context.* Arabic numerals are necessarily used in order to be able to communicate, but there should be nothing mysterious about using nonnumeric symbols for numbers.

The common equation for relating the circumference of a circle to the radius of the circle is $C = 2\pi r$. This formula includes the Arabic "2," the Greek letter "π," and the letters "C" and "r." The "2" refers, of course, to the number two. The "π" refers to a number that is close to, but not exactly equal to, $\frac{22}{7}$. It is not a rational number, that is, it cannot be written *exactly* in decimal *or* ratio notation; therefore, notation other than decimal notation is used—the Greek letter pi. The number pi is no less a number than two or four. It is merely inconvenient that it cannot be written exactly in decimal or ratio notation, so a letter is used for convenience to denote pi.

The letters "C" and "r" are also used for convenience. By using them, the formula becomes applicable for any circle, which is certainly more convenient than needing an infinite number of equations, one for each possible circle size. The letters "r" and "C" refer to specific numbers wherever the formula is used in the context of an application.

Basic Definitions

Introduction

This section defines many terms used extensively in mathematics and statistics. An important consideration in the use of any of these terms, just as in the use of any word, is the *context* in which the word or term is used. Keep the context in mind, and you can avoid some of the confusion that many students have. In particular, whether or not a numeral or other symbol refers to a constant or not, or whether it refers to a parameter or not, is a matter of context. A "5" can refer to a specific value of a variable, a known constant, a parameter that is known, or any of several things, depending on the context in which it is used.

The first several subsections deal with distinctions between constants and variables. It is unfortunate that the use of the terms "constant" and "variable" is so standard, since they connote movement versus nonmovement or change versus nonchange, but only in relatively rare instances is there actual movement or change related to a mathematical variable in the behavioral sciences. The terms "variable" and "constant" are borrowed largely from physics where it makes sense to talk, for example, about an object falling in space with time (a variable) constantly increasing, distance fallen (a variable) constantly increasing, and the force of gravity acting on the object with a constant effect.

CONSTANTS

Definition. The word "constant" refers to symbols or numerals that have only one number for their referent. Again, you must keep context in mind when you use the word "constant."

Arabic Numerals Used to Denote Constants. Usually, constants are symbolized by Arabic numerals. Some texts even erroneously define "constants" in this way. In the formula $C = 2\pi r$, the symbols "2" and "π" refer to numbers that are constants in the formula. Here is another expression: $y^2 + 3y + 6$. The constants in this second example consist of 2, 3, and 6, corresponding to Arabic numerals "2," "3," and "6."

Letters Used to Denote Constants. Letters can also be used as constants. For example, we can multiply 2 times π and use "k" as the symbol for 2π. Then "$C = 2\pi r$" can be written "$C = kr$," in which the "k" refers to the constant 2π. The symbol "π," of course, is also a letter, but it is a Greek letter.

Here is another example. Consider this set of expressions:

$$0 + x = 1$$

$$1 + x = 2$$

$$2 + x = 3$$

$$3 + x = 4$$

$$4 + x = 5$$

If all of these statements are *simultaneously* true, then "x" must refer to a *constant*—namely, the number one.

So, a constant can be either an Arabic numeral, a letter, or any other symbol as long as, in context the *symbol has a single number as its referent.*

VARIABLES AND RANGES OF VARIABLES

Definition. The word "variable" refers to a symbol with more than one number as a referent. The term "range of a variable" means the set of all referents to which the variable might refer. Usually, the context will determine the range of a variable. Here is an example: $y = x^2$. If nothing else is known but that y and x are variables referring to real numbers, then one can infer that x has as its range *all real numbers,* while y has as its range *all positive real numbers* plus zero. (Since a negative number squared is always a positive number, y cannot be negative.) However, the context of the problem might specify that numbers to which x can refer consist only of integers between 0 and 5; then the variable x has a range of {0, 1, 2, 3, 4, and 5}, whereas the variable y has a range of {0, 1, 4, 9, 16, and 25}.

Letters Used to Denote Variables. Usually letters are used as symbols for variables. However, it is important to remember that letters can also refer to constants. But this presents no particular problem if you consider that a constant is merely a special case of a variable—a constant is a variable with a range consisting of only one number.

PARAMETER

The term "parameter" is difficult because it refers to numbers that are simultaneously constants from one point of view and variables from another. Let's consider an example. Let's define a variable and call it "x." The variable x is a score on an inventory of mathematics background. Scores are defined as follows:

$x = 0$ if the interviewee had no high school math
$x = 1$ if the interviewee had only one math course
$x = 2$ if the interviewee had two courses
$x = 3$ if the interviewee had more than two courses

So the range of x is 0, 1, 2, and 3. Now let's define four groups of college freshmen, using the variable x. Let's assume that each of these four groups will be assigned to different college math sequences. Across all groups, x is a variable, but *within the groups*, x is constant. We can call x a parameter–it is number *unique to the subgroup*, but which has different values over *all* students. In this case, the *parameter* actually *defines the subgroups.*

Here is another example. The equation $X + Y = A$ is a general expression for all pairs of numbers X and Y that add up to A. A, X, and Y are all variables; however, A is also a parameter. If a particular number is substituted for A, one particular set of X and Y pairs is possible. A different number for A would lead to different X and Y pairs. Thus, A is a parameter since it defines the (X, Y) sets. Here are some examples of pairs of X and Y for three values of the parameter A.

$A = 0$		$A = 2$		$A = 4$	
X	Y	X	Y	X	Y
-1	1	1	1	2.5	1.5
-2	2	2	0	4	0
-3	3	0	2	-9	13
2	-2	-4	6	7	-3
10	-10	3	-1	2	2

You can see how a parameter acts as both variable and constant. A is a variable in the sense that any number is in its range. However, for a particular set of the (X, Y) pairs, A is constant. It is a *parameter* that defines the elements in the sets of (X, Y) pairs.

COEFFICIENTS

The word "*coefficient*" is used often in discussing the symbols in an algebraic expression. It can be considered as a synonym for the word "factor."

Consider the equation

$$y = 5x + 1$$

The symbols "$5x$" can be used as an example. We can say "5 is the coefficient of x," or "x is the coefficient of 5," since both 5 and x are factors of $5x$.

Traditionally, "coefficient" was used only for nonvariables, and some texts might still use this old definition. That is, in "$y = 5x + 1$," some texts might say that only "5" is a coefficient since "x" refers to a variable. However, the modern usage of "coefficient" allows us to call "5" a coefficient of x and call "x" a coefficient of 5.

Consider this algebraic expression:

$$5ax.$$

The coefficient of x is $5a$, the coefficient of a is $5x$, and the coefficient of 5 is ax.

EQUATIONS AND INEQUALITIES

Equations and inequalities are mathematical sentences. They are statements like any good English declarative sentences; and like any declarative sentences, they can be true or they can be false. Here is an example of an equation that is a true sentence:

$$[7 + 2(10)]/3 = 9$$

Here is an example of an equation that is not true: $2 + 2 = 5$. Both are perfectly good statements, but one is true and one is not.

An *equation* is a mathematical sentence that specifies that two numbers are equal. It always contains an equal sign (=). Or, in other words, an equation specifies that two expressions are names for the same number. The equation

$$[7 + 2(10)]/3 = 9$$

says that "$[7 + 2(10)]/3$" and "9" have as their referents the same number (namely, 9).

The equation $X^2 + B = C + 1$ means that whatever the referent of X, B, and C, "$X^2 + B$" and "$C + 1$" are equivalent names for the same referent number. Again, the equation may be true or false, just like any English sentence.

An inequality also is a sentence that is either true or false. There are five inequality signs to know. These are "$\neq$," "$>$," "$<$," "$\geqslant$," and "$\leqslant$."

The symbol "$\neq$" means "is not equal to" and is illustrated by the true sentence "$2 + 2 \neq 5$." The symbol "$>$" is read "is greater than." The true sentence "$5 > 2 + 2$" is read, "Five is greater than 2 + 2." The symbol "$<$" is read "is less than." The true sentence, "$2 + 2 < 5$" is "two plus two is less than five." Notice that the arrow in the inequality sign always points to the smaller quantity. Here are some more examples of true inequalities. Assume a and b are positive numbers:

$$7 + 2 > 8 \qquad 1 + 1 \neq 3$$
$$\sqrt{3} > 1 \qquad \sqrt{a + 1} > \sqrt{a}$$
$$\sqrt{3} < 2 \qquad ab < a(b + 1)$$

The two examples "$\sqrt{3} > 1$" and "$\sqrt{3} < 1$" can be combined into a compound sentence "$1 < \sqrt{3} < 2$" which can be read "$\sqrt{3}$ is less than 2 *and* it is greater than 1" or "$\sqrt{3}$ is *between* 1 and 2." The latter reading is preferred since it is clearer and briefer. Also notice that the last two sentences are true without regard to the numbers to which "a" and "b" refer (as long as they are positive numbers).

The symbols "$\geqslant$" and "$\leqslant$" are read "is greater than *or* equal to" and "is less than *or* equal to," respectively. Here are some examples:

$$7 + 2 \geqslant 8 \qquad \sqrt{24} \leqslant 5$$
$$7 + 2 \geqslant 9 \qquad \sqrt{25} \geqslant 5$$
$$9 \leqslant 7 + 2 \qquad \sqrt{25} \leqslant 5$$
$$9 \leqslant 17 + 1 \qquad a + 10 \geqslant 10 \text{ if } a \geqslant 0$$

Equations and inequalities are of utmost importance.

MODELS

The word "model" is a generic term used in research to denote any of a variety of explanations of phenomena. Many models are expressed mathematically as equations or functions (discussed next), so it is appropriate to discuss models in this chapter. Some models are merely verbal descriptions of phenomena; some are sophisticated mathematical theories.

At one extreme we might say, "Behavior is a product of heredity and environment," while at the opposite extreme we might say, "The total energy (E) contained in any physical object is expressed by $E = mc^2$, where m is a parameter depending on the mass of the object and c is a constant." Usually statisticians try to formulate explanations of research results or expected research results in some sort of equation involving variables, constants, and parameters.

The model that is the most commonly used statistical model is the normal (or Gaussian) equation. When this is graphed, it has a bell-shaped appearance. The model is used often in grading ("grading on the curve"), in applying test scores, and in statistical inference. The equation can be written

$$P = (1/\sqrt{2\pi})e^{-(x-\mu)^2/2}$$

where P and x are variables, μ is a parameter, and all other symbols refer to known constants. More general, or complex, versions can be written that involve other subgroup parameters. Both "π" and "e" refer to known constants that are irrational numbers (i.e., they can't be expressed by an Arabic numeral in decimal or ratio notation). The equation is a model for the frequency with which x takes on the various values in its range. The parameter "μ" corresponds to the subgroup average score. The problem of the statistician is to estimate this parameter for various subgroups.

Another common model is the linear model. This is an equation that says an event (variable) is determined largely by a weighted sum of other variables. The linear model is used extensively in prediction problems. The "weights" are parameters associated with the particular group of persons or things for which predictions will be made. The statistical problem in prediction is to estimate these parameters.

PRIMES

Primes (′) are also commonly used to distinguish several different numbers that are similar in some way. Thus, we can write three daily temperature measurements with subscripts as "T_1," "T_2," and "T_3." Or, we can use prime notation and say T', T'', and T'''. (In this sentence we are violating the quotation mark rule for symbols, but the use of quotation marks here would be quite confusing.)

Here is an example. Let Y be a variable we have measured. Let Y' be an estimate of the same variable based on a different measuring instrument. Y and Y' are similar, yet different, numbers.

TILDES

The *tilde* (˜) also is used for the same purpose. We might have three measurements of Y. We can denote these by "Y," "Y'," and "$\tilde{Y}$."

CARATS

The *carat* (^) is used similarly. We could distinguish four measurements of Y as "Y," "Y'," "$\tilde{Y}$," and "$\hat{Y}$."

Factorials

Another special multiplication operator is the factorial. The factorial sign "!" indicates a special repeated multiplication which is used frequently in statistical applications.

Here are several examples:

$$3! = 3 \cdot 2 \cdot 1 = 6$$

$$4! = 4 \cdot 3 \cdot 2 \cdot 1 = 24$$

$$6! = 6 \cdot 5 \cdot 4 \cdot 3 \cdot 2 \cdot 1 = 720$$

In general, $$n! = n(n - 1)(n - 2) \ldots 3 \cdot 2 \cdot 1,$$

where n is an *integer.* (Note that when n equals zero, $n!$ is defined as one.)

The Summation Operator, Σ

(The summation sign Σ indicates that a group of constants or variables are to be added together. In this text it is used to indicate that all members of a particular group are to be added. For example, if $X(i)$ takes the values 5, 2, 7, and 1, then:

$$\Sigma X(i) = 5 + 2 + 7 + 1$$

$$= 15$$

In all texts other than this one, $\Sigma X(i)$ would be written ΣX_i. It is also possible to indicate that more than one variable is to be added or that less than the entire range of variables should be added by suitably modifying the summation sign. Such cases, however, do not appear in this book and will not be discussed here.)

LOGARITHMS

Introduction

Not too long ago, the logarithm concept and methodology was taught because it was a necessary calculation aid. Today there is seldom a need to use logarithms to speed up calculations, since we have mechanical calculators and electronic calculators and computers.

However, logarithms occur naturally in mathematical formulations independent of their use as computational aids. You will eventually learn to use statistical formulas that contain logarithm functions. There also might be rare occasion to use logarithms as a calculation aid.

For these reasons, we will go into a discussion of logarithm concepts and show how logs and antilogs are determined by tables, how logs are used in multiplication and division, and show special statistical applications of logs. The distinction between common logarithms and natural logarithms will be discussed, since, more often than not, natural logarithms will be more useful to you than common logarithms.

Basic Definitions

General Definition of a Logarithm

A logarithm is an *exponent* used in a special way. We know that any real number (or a close approximation) can be written in decimal notation. In addition, any real number greater than zero can be written as some power of any other real number.

For example, 9 can be written as "3^2" and 27 can be written as "3^3." Any numbers between 9 and 27 can be written as "3" with a fractional exponent—an exponent between 2 and 3. The number $\frac{1}{3}$ is written "3^{-1}" and $\frac{2}{3}$ can be written "3^{-2}."

Since many numbers must be written with fractional exponents, tables and graphs are used to give these exponents. In our example, all of the numbers were powers of 3, so we say we were working in a *base-3* system. A table for a base-3 system would give, for selected numbers, the power to which 3 must be raised to give each of the numbers. Here is a small base-3 table.

Number	Exponent (logarithm)
81	4
27	3
9	2
3	1
1	0
$\frac{1}{3}$	-1
$\frac{1}{9}$	-2
$\frac{1}{27}$	-3

A full table would show fractional values between these entries.

The word "logarithm" is a synonym for "exponent." However, that synonym is used only in the context in which we are working because "logarithm" is meaningless unless the base is known. We could label the second column as either "exponent" or "logarithm." This language is clarified by the symbols

$$\text{"}\log_3 81 = 4\text{"}$$

which is read, "The log of 81 to the base 3 is 4," or, "The base-3 log of 81 equals 4." "$\text{Log}_3\ 81 = 4$" means, literally, "$3^4 = 81$" (see Table 1).

The value of logs is apparent from a problem like this: to what power must 3 be raised to obtain 81?" Or, equivalently "Solve $3^x = 81$ for x." We rewrite the question as

$$\text{"}\log_3 81 = x\text{"}$$

Table 1

Log	Antilog
4	81
3	27
2	9
1	3
0	1
−1	$\frac{1}{3}$
−2	$\frac{1}{9}$
−3	$\frac{1}{27}$

and look up "81" in our base 3 table. The table gives us $x = 4$ since $3^4 = 81$. The number 81 will be called the *antilog* of 4 (4 is the log). Thus, our base-three table could have looked like Table 1.

Moreover, exponential algebra is simplified using log tables. We know that $3^u \cdot 3^v = 3^{u+v}$ and $3^u \div 3^v = 3^{u-v}$. Also, $(3^u)^v = 3^{u,v}$ and $\sqrt[u]{3} = 3^{1/u}$. These "rules" of exponential algebra can readily be used with log tables.

Here is a set of eight problems (see Table 2) showing the application of logs to exponential algebra. Study them carefully. See how the *addition* of logs is used for *multiplication* and the *subtraction* of logs is used for *division.* Work out the multiplications to be sure that the log procedure is correct.

Table 2

Problem	Logs from Table 1	Solution	Antilog from Table 1
1. 3×9	$\log_3 3 = 1$ $\log_3 9 = 2$	$1 + 2 = 3$	antilog $3 = 27$
2. $(\frac{1}{27}) \cdot 81$	$\log_3 (\frac{1}{27}) = -3$ $\log_3 81 = 4$	$(-3) + 4 = 1$	antilog $1 = 3$
3. $27 \div 9$	$\log_3 27 = 3$ $\log_3 9 = 2$	$3 - 2 = 1$	antilog $1 = 3$
4. $9 \div (\frac{1}{9})$	$\log_3 9 = 2$ $\log_3 (\frac{1}{9}) = -2$	$2 - (-2) = 4$	antilog $4 = 81$
5. 9^2	$\log_3 9 = 2$	$2 \cdot 2 = 4$	antilog $4 = 81$
6. $\sqrt{81}$	$\log_3 81 = 4$	$(\frac{1}{2}) \cdot 4 = 2$	antilog $2 = 9$
7. $\frac{81 \cdot 27}{9 \cdot 3}$	$\log_3 81 = 4$ $\log_3 27 = 3$ $\log_3 9 = 2$ $\log_3 3 = 1$	$4 + 3 - 2 - 1 = 4$	antilog $4 = 81$
8. $((\frac{1}{27})\sqrt{81})^2$	$\log_3 (\frac{1}{27}) = -3$ $\log_3 81 = 4$	$2(-3 + (\frac{1}{2})4) = -2$	antilog $-2 = \frac{1}{9}$

Let's continue the discussion of base 3 by graphing. This is an easy, but crude, way to get the fractional values for our table. A graph shows all values in the range that is graphed, but accuracy is quite limited, and this must be kept in mind. The graph (see Exhibit 83) shows the relationship of N (the antilog) to $\log_3 N$. It is the graph of the function $y = \log_3 N$.

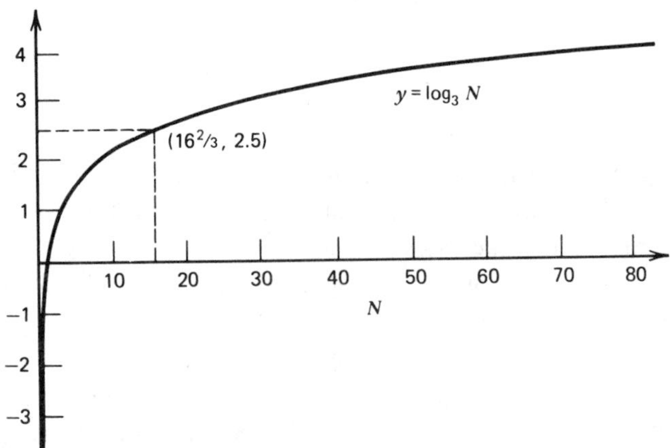

Exhibit 83. From Bashaw, W. I., *Mathematics for Statistics*, Wiley, New York, 1969, p. 254.

Exhibit 83 shows the general shape of curves of the form $y = \log x$. Log curves cross the horizontal axis at +1, that is, $\log_b 0 = 1$ for any base $(b^0 = 1$ for any number $b)$. The base is given by the abscissa of the point at which the curve passes $\log_b N = 1$ (b is 3 in Exhibit 83). Accuracy is extremely bad below $\log_b N = 0$ because the curve approaches zero asymptotically. Frequently, graphs are scaled on a "log scale" that stretches out the horizontal axis, allowing greater accuracy.

Let's use the graph to approximate some arithmetic. Here are some problems.

a. $16\frac{2}{3} \times 3\frac{1}{3} = ?$
b. $43\frac{1}{3} \div 23\frac{1}{3} = ?$
c. $\sqrt{55} = ?$

APPROXIMATE SOLUTIONS

a. $\log_3 16\frac{2}{3} + \log_3 3\frac{1}{3}$ is approximately $2.5 + 1.2 = 3.7$. The antilog of 3.7 is about $56\frac{2}{3}$. (The precise product is $55\frac{5}{9}$.)
b. $\log_3 43\frac{1}{3} - \log_3 23\frac{1}{3}$ is about 3.5 - 2.8, or .7. The antilog of .7 is about 2. (The precise answer is $1\frac{6}{7}$.)
c. $\frac{1}{2}$ (log 55) is about (.5)(3.7) or 1.85. The approximate antilog of 1.85 is 7.5. To two decimal places, $\sqrt{55}$ is 7.42.

We could do much better with a very large, well-drawn graph, but the principles are illustrated fairly well with even the crude graph.

Common and Natural Logs

It has been stated that log systems can be devised for any base; that is, for any real number all other real positive numbers can be expressed as a power of the base. We have used base 3 as an example. A base of 2 is used occasionally, especially in computer applications. Base 10 is so widely used that logs to base 10 are called "*common logarithms.*" The irrational number e is also used as a base. Since the number e and logs of e occur naturally in many mathematical developments, base e logs are called "*natural logarithms.*"

For review, explain these statements.

a. $\log_{10} 1000 = 3$
b. $\log_e 10 = 2.3026$

Statement *a* means, "10^3 = 1000" and statement *b* means, "*e* raised to the power 2.3026 is 10."

Common logs are used so frequently that the base 10 need not be indicated. The symbol "log" *without an indicated base* almost always will mean "log to the *base 10.*"

Natural logs are also common enough to have a special symbol. The usual symbol is "ln" ("n" for "natural"). So, statements *a* and *b* can quite correctly be written as

$$\log 1000 = 3 \qquad \text{and} \qquad \ln 10 = 2.3026$$

Common Logs

Let's now study thoroughly the common log (base 10) system. A fundamental principle used with logarithms is that any positive real number can be factored into a power of 10 and a number between 1 and 10. For example, study this pattern.

$$7180 = 7.18 \times 10^3$$

$$718 = 7.18 \times 10^2$$

$$71.8 = 7.18 \times 10^1$$

$$7.18 = 7.18 \times 10^0$$

$$.718 = 7.18 \times 10^{-1}$$

$$.0718 = 7.18 \times 10^{-2}$$

$$.00718 = 7.18 \times 10^{-3}$$

Our rule for converting multiplication into addition of logs can now be used to determine the logs for each number in the left-hand column by finding only the number log 7.18. Remember that

$$\log 10^3 = 3$$

$$\log 10^{-3} = -3$$

and, in general, log $10^k = k$, for any number k. ("Log 10^k" means, "To what power must 10 be raised to obtain 10^k?" The answer is obvious: 10 must be raised to the kth power to obtain 10^k, so log $10^k = k$.) Let's construct a short table of logs and antilogs for the "718" example (see Table 3).

Table 3

Antilog	Log
7180	log 7.18 + log 10^3 = log 7.18 + 3
718	log 7.18 + log 10^2 = log 7.18 + 2
71.8	log 7.18 + log 10^1 = log 7.18 + 1
7.18	log 7.18 + log 10^0 = log 7.18 + 0
.718	log 7.18 + log 10^{-1} = log 7.18 − 1
.0718	log 7.18 + log 10^{-2} = log 7.18 − 2
.00718	log 7.18 + log 10^{-3} = log 7.18 − 3

It is apparent that the logs of all numbers in the antilog column are based on the same number–log 7.18. We need to determine only log 7.18 from a common logarithm table to know all of the logs corresponding to the numbers in the antilog column. To four decimal places, log 7.18 = .8561. Let's use this number to complete the "718" table (see Table 4). The last three entries require further information on standard notation. They could be written accurately as "-.1439," "-1.1439," and "-2.1439," respectively, where these numerals are determined by the indicated subtractions. However, it is more convenient in logarithm handling to keep the numeral ".8561" as part of the log numeral since ".8561"

Table 4

Antilog	Log
7180	.8561 + 3
718	.8561 + 2
71.8	.8561 + 1
7.18	.8561 + 0
.718	.8561 − 1
.0718	.8561 − 2
.00718	.8561 − 3

identifies the antilog "7.18." So, logs of numbers between zero and one are usually not written as negative numbers. Here are two common ways of writing negative logs; the second way usually is preferred:

$$\log .718 = \bar{1}.8561 \quad \text{or} \quad 9.8561 - 10$$

$$\log .0718 = \bar{2}.8561 \quad \text{or} \quad 8.8561 - 10$$

$$\log .00718 = \bar{3}.8561 \quad \text{or} \quad 7.8561 - 10$$

So, finally we have our completed "718" log table (see Table 5).

Table 5

Antilog	Log
7180	3.8561
718	2.8561
71.8	1.8561
7.18	0.8561
.718	9.8561 – 10
.0718	8.8561 – 10
.00718	7.8561 – 10

Let's learn two new terms. The ".8561" part of the log numeral is called the "*mantissa.*" The mantissa identifies the antilog, but it does not say where the decimal point is to be located. By writing negative logs in the standard notation, we can easily use tables to identify antilogs from logs and logs from antilogs. Most log tables list only mantissas, and mantissas usually are tabled only for antilogs between one and ten. No other values need to be tabled.

The part of the log numeral that identifies the decimal point location is called the "*characteristic.*" Table 5, the characteristics are "3," "2," "1," "0," "9 - 10," "8 - 10," and "7 - 10."

The terms "characteristic" and "mantissa" and the concepts just outlined can be clarified by additional examples. Let's consider the numbers 0, 2, and 6. The mantissa of the logs of 0, 2, and 6 are 0, .3010, and .7782, respectively. Let's build a log table for various numbers based on products of 10 and the numbers 0, 2, and 6 (Table 6).

Study the patterns. See how the mantissas can always identify whether or not the antilog numeral has a "1," "2," or "6" in it. Also, see how the characteristics identify the location of the decimal point.

Let's do some arithmetic problems using the "0, 2, 6" table. Remember that

Table 6

Antilog	Log
1,000	3.0000
600	2.7782
200	2.3010
100	2.0000
60	1.7782
20	1.3010
10	1.0000
6	0.7782
2	0.3010
1	0.0000
.6	9.7782 - 10
.2	9.3010 - 10
.1	9.0000 - 10
.06	8.7782 - 10
.02	8.3010 - 10
.01	8.0000 - 10
.006	7.7782 - 10
.002	7.3010 - 10
.001	7.0000 - 10

multiplication is handled by log addition and division is handled by log subtraction. The examples are as follows.

1. $(600 \cdot 20) \div 60$
2. $.6 \div 60$
3. $.02 \times 600 \div 2$

The solutions are as follows.

1. $2.7782 + 1.3010 - 1.7782 = 2.3010$.
   The answer is 200 since log 200 = 2.3010.
2. $(9.7782 - 10) - 1.7782 = 8.0000 - 10$.
   The answer is .01 since log .01 = 8.0000 - 10.
3. $(8.3010 - 10) + (2.7782) - (.3010) = 10.7782 - 10$.
   This is the same as 0.7782, so the answer is 6.

Common Log Tables

We have seen that the characteristic gives the decimal point location in the antilog and the mantissa determines the antilog numeral. Any positive real number can be written as a log. The characteristic will tell the location of the decimal point and the mantissa will tell the numeral. To convert antilogs to logs and logs to antilogs, we need a table that gives only mantissas, since the characteristic is only a decimal point indicator.

Tables for mantissas of common logarithms are in many standard arithmetic and statistics books. It should be apparent that such tables can be quite long, since the log function has an infinite range. The appendix gives an abbreviated common log table. Tabled are mantissa values for numbers between one and 999. The table can be used for almost any number by the choice of the *characteristic.* It is a one-way table whose columns refer to the last digit of the entering number. Here is one row of the table as an example.

	0	1	2	3	4	5	6	7	8	9
24	3802	3820	3838	3856	3874	3892	3909	3927	3945	3962

The tabled number for 241 is .3820. The tabled number for 248 is .3945. Do you see how the columns are used merely to save space? The log of 241 is 2.3820. The log of 24.8 is 1.3945. The log of 2480 is 3.3945. Do you see how logs are obtained from the table?

The accuracy of the table is limited to three significant figures in the antilogs and four significant figures in the logs. Antilogs can be carried to four decimal places by linear interpolation.

Natural Log Tables

Natural logs appear frequently in statistical formulas and for this reason are of special interest. We can frequently avoid natural logs by always converting natural logs into common logs, and vice versa.

The conversion is

$$\ln N = 2.3026 \log N$$

or

$$\log N = (2.3026)^{-1} \ln N$$

The constant 2.3026 is ln 10 taken to four decimal places.

Natural logs can be used for arithmetical calculations just as common logs are used. But the problem of the irrational base makes this a little difficult since the characteristic is determined by powers of e, rather than 10. It is not easy, without a lot of experience with e, to decide upon the characteristic of a number like 42.31. How many times must 2.7183 be powered to get 42.31?

So, the importance of the natural log table is not so much for calculations as for merely looking up values and using these in statistical formulas.

TABLES AND TABLE READING

Introduction

Research investigators use statistical tables constantly. In addition, a major research task is often the construction of tables. Most students can use statistical tables with little difficulty; however, occasionally a student or two will have trouble interpreting a table. Many students have trouble interpolating and extrapolating tables.

A statistical table is essentially a number list that defines a functional relationship. A one-way table defines a one-to-one correspondence that could be used in constructing a graph of the function underlying the table. A two-way table defines a two-to-one correspondence. It is used to table functions of two variables. If additional variables need to be included in the function being tabulated, the table usually is broken up into several one- or two-way tables.

Most common statistical functions appear in tables. The purpose of the tables is to present values of the function of interest that can be located and used quickly and accurately.

A major problem in tables arises from the fact that they usually deal with variables that have an infinite number of elements in their range. Since this is true, tables can show only selected values. A table of squares, for example, can show the squares of integers from 1 to 1000. It could show squares of integers from 1 to 10,000 but only show every fifth integer. Frequently, a table of squares will show squares of only the numbers between 1 and 10, but will show them for every number in increments of .01, that is, 1.00, 1.01, 1.02, . . . , 9.99, 10.00. Obviously, the accuracy and utility of tables depends on such things as the increment between entries, the number of entries, and the number of decimal places to which entries are carried.

The standard techniques for determining values that do not appear in a table are *interpolation* and *extrapolation.* Interpolation is the process of estimating a number that is between two tabled numbers. Extrapolation is the process of estimating numbers beyond the range of tabled entries. Usually, extrapolation is quite difficult to do accurately and is to be avoided. Interpolation, on the other hand, can be highly accurate and useful.

In this section some examples of one-way and two-way tables will be used. Interpolation in both one- and two-way tables will be explained, and extrapolation will also be discussed.

One-Way Tables

A one-way table can be constructed to show the ordered number pairs relating one variable to another variable by any functional relationship. We have already used one-way tables for logarithms. The log table shows number pairs consisting of a log and its antilog.

Many statistical tables show the theoretical frequency distribution of some random variables. The most important example of a one-way frequency distribution table is the normal curve table. This appears in almost every statistics book.

Not all normal curve tables contain the same information, so you should read the description of the table carefully before you use it. Usually the information tabled is, for any number c, the probability of obtaining such a number *or a smaller number.* That is, it tables c and $P\{z \leqslant c\}$ for selected numbers c, where c are numbers in the range of the variable z. Table 7 is a small table of the normal

Table 7

c	$P\{z \leqslant c\}$
2.5	.99
2.0	.98
1.5	.93
1.0	.84
.5	.69
.0	.50
−.5	.31
−1.0	.16
−1.5	.07
−2.0	.02
−2.5	.01

curve. Probability values corresponding to $c < -2.50$ can be considered as zero and values for $c > 2.50$ can be considered as one.

The table can be read in two ways. One way is to choose c and look up $P\{z \leqslant c\}$. For $c = 2.0$, we find $P\{z \leqslant c\} = .98$. The second way is to choose $P\{z \leqslant c\}$ and look up c. We can ask, "For what c does $P\{z \leqslant c\} = .16$?" The table gives the answer, $c = -1.0$.

A normal curve table can be laid out in a way that makes it look like a two-way table. Such a presentation is intended to save space, and possibly to save the researcher time by cutting down the size of the table that must be examined. For example, our little table takes eleven lines. If we wanted to show values in increments of .25 instead of .5, the table would have 21 lines. If we used increments of .01, the table would take up a great deal of space. Let's construct part of our table in increments of .25, but lay it out so that fractional units appear in columns of a matrix.

c	.00	.25	.50	.75
2	.98	.99	.99	1.00
1	.84	.89	.93	.96
0	.50	.60	.69	.77

To use this table, we need to read it as a two-way table, when in fact, it is merely a one-way table cast into a matrix to preserve space. What is $P\{z \leqslant c\}$ if $c = 1.25$? The integral part of "c" instructs you to use the "1" row. The fractional part of "c" instructs you to use the ".25" column. $P\{z \leqslant c\}$ is .89. This technique for condensing one-way tables was used in the log tables of the preceding chapter.

Interpolation in One-Way Tables

Suppose we wished to know $P\{z \leqslant 1.35\}$ using a normal table. We could look it up in a better table, of course, but suppose we do not have one and must use the little table presented in matrix form in the last section. It does not tell a value of P for $c = 1.35$, but it does show P for $c = 1.25$ and $c = 1.50$. Using these values, we know that

$$.89 < P\{z \leqslant 1.35\} < .93$$

The standard technique for determining a good estimate between .89 and .93 is *linear interpolation.* We assume that the relationship between P and z is *linear.* Of course, we know that this is not the case because P is an S-shaped curve when plotted (try it). But *in the short range from 1.25 to 1.50,* a straight line might fit the plots quite well. We thus assume linearity in the very short line of interest. There are several ways to use this "local" linearity assumption. For pedagogic reasons, let's graph the two points (c, $P\{z \leqslant c\}$) that we know, namely (1.25, .89) and (1.50, .93). These can be connected with a straight line (the assumption of "local" linearity). The graph can then be read at the point where $c = 1.35$ intersects the line. The ordinate is the desired answer. By using units of length .005, we can get fairly good accuracy. The solution is plotted in Exhibit 84. The answer is approximately $P\{z \leqslant 1.35\} = .906$. Even better accuracy would be obtained by more careful graphing and using smaller increments on the graph.

The graphic procedure clearly illustrates why this is called "linear interpolation." We can also solve the problem arithmetically. We know two points and wish to determine an intermediate point. Let's write our problem out in this manner:

c	P
1.50	.93
1.35	?
1.25	.89

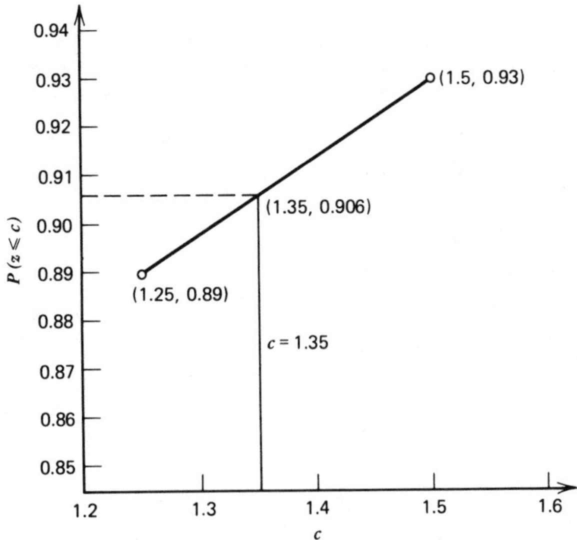

Exhibit 84. From Bashaw, W. I., *Mathematics for Statistics*, Wiley, New York, 1969, p. 269.

Notice that 1.35 is .10 units above 1.25 and .15 units below 1.50. That is, it is $\frac{2}{5}$, or .4, of the distance between 1.25 and 1.50. It seems reasonable to believe that our answer, then, is also greater than .89 by about .4 of the distance between .93 and .89. We calculate .93 - .89 = .04 and (.4)(.04) = .016. The interpolated answer is .89 + .016, or .906, which is identical to the result from the graph. The result is the same because the very same principles are involved; in one case we did the work geometrically and in the other case it was done arithmetically. The use of a better table of the normal curve yields $P\{z \leqslant 1.35\} =$ .9115. The difference between .9115 and our answer of .906 is one of table accuracy (our table only shows two decimal places) and of nonlinearity. A better table would have allowed the interpolation to be within a much narrower band, thus the "local" linearity assumption would not have led us so far off. In any case, both .9115 and .906 are equal to .91 when rounded to two places.

Two-Way Tables

Two-way tables are matrices listing a three variable function—a two-to-one correspondence between one variable and two other variables. The last section shows how a one-way table can be presented in matrix form giving a two-dimensional appearance. Another type of confusing "matrix-appearing" table is a combination of several related one-way tables shown together in matrix form. It is common, for example, to show several trigonometric functions of angles in one table. This is actually several one-way tables put together to conserve page space and to expedite looking up numbers.

In this section we discuss "real" two-way tables that are based on a two-to-one correspondence between a set of three variables. It is important to make the distinction because of the interpolation problems in a two-way table.

A commonly used two-way statistics table is the F-table. An F-table shows values of a variable called "F" as a function of two constants (parameters) called

Table 8

	d_2			
d_1	1	3	5	7
2	18.51	19.16	19.30	19.36
4	7.71	6.59	6.26	6.09
6	5.99	4.76	4.39	4.21
8	5.32	4.07	3.69	3.50

"degrees of freedom." We will call the two parameters d_1 and d_2. Table 8 is a partial F-table. The tabulated entries are values of F. To read the table, we must know d_1 and d_2. (These are known in any statistical application of an F-table.) If $d_1 = 6$ and $d_2 = 1$, then $F = 5.99$. If $d_1 = 8$ and $d_2 = 3$, then $F = 4.07$. These can be written $F(6, 1) = 5.99$ and $F(8, 3) = 4.07$. What is $F(2, 5)$ and $F(6, 3)$? They are 19.30 and 4.76, respectively.

Here is another example (see Table 9). This is a portion of a chi-square (χ^2) table. The tabled numbers are values of a variable called "χ^2." The row names are parameters (degrees of freedom), which we can call "d." The column names are probabilities of obtaining values of χ^2 equal to or less than the table entry. Let χ_t^2 be the table values. Then the column names refer to $P\{\chi^2 \leqslant \chi_t^2\}$.

Table 9

	$P\{\chi^2 \leqslant \chi_t^2\}$						
d	.90	.80	.70	.50	.30	.20	.10
1	.02	.06	.15	.46	1.07	1.64	2.71
3	.58	1.00	1.42	2.37	3.67	4.64	6.25

So, we can read the table this way: "If $d = 1$, then $P\{\chi^2 \leqslant .15\} = .70$."

Interpolation in Two-Way Tables

It should be apparent that there are no unique problems in reading tables showing two-way classifications. However, interpolation can be a problem, if interpolation must be made relative to both row and column classifications. Look at the F-table (Table 8). If you wanted to know $F(2, 2)$ or $F(3, 4)$, you could estimate these using simple linear interpolation as discussed earlier. But how would you find $F(3, 2)$? This involves interpolating in two directions.

Two-way interpolation is handled in three steps. Let's find an estimate of $F(3, 2)$ as an example. First, let's define by two one-way interpolations new row values corresponding to $d_1 = 3$, namely $F(3, 1)$ and $F(3, 3)$. Observe that 3 is halfway between 2 and 4. So, we calculate two new values, each halfway between the numbers above and below them. Our calculations are as follows:

Step 1. Find $F(3, 1)$.

$$F(3, 1) = 7.71 + \frac{18.51 - 7.71}{2}$$

$$= 7.71 + \frac{10.80}{2}$$

$$= 7.71 + 5.40 = 13.11$$

Step 2. Find $F(3, 3)$.

$$F(3, 3) = 6.59 + \frac{19.16 - 6.59}{2}$$

$$= 6.59 + \frac{12.57}{2}$$

$$= 6.59 + 6.285 = 12.875$$

We have obtained interpolated values for $F(3, 1)$ and $F(3, 3)$. We want $F(3, 2)$, so we must interpolate between 13.11 and 12.875.

Step 3. Find $F(3, 2)$ from $F(3, 1)$ and $F(3, 3)$.

$$F(3, 2) = 12.875 + \frac{13.11 - 12.875}{2}$$

$$= 12.875 + \frac{.235}{2}$$

$$= 12.875 + .1175 = 12.9925$$

Our two-way interpolation yields 12.99.

The entire process can be worked by defining first interpolated column entries for $d_2 = 2$. Let's do it again, first finding $F(2, 2)$ and $F(4, 2)$.

Step 1. Find $F(2, 2)$.

$$F(2, 2) = 18.51 + \frac{19.16 - 18.51}{2}$$

$$= 18.835$$

Step 2. Find $F(4, 2)$.

$$F(4, 2) = 6.59 + \frac{7.71 - 6.59}{2}$$

$$= 7.15$$

Step 3. Find $F(3, 2)$ from $F(2, 2)$ and $F(4, 2)$.

$$F(3, 2) = 7.15 + \frac{18.835 - 7.15}{2}$$

$$= 12.9925$$

The result is the same as before.

Let's do an example from the χ^2 table (see Table 9). What χ_t^2 value corresponds to $d = 2$ and $P = .22$? Let's first find values for $d = 2, P = .30$ and $d = 2$, $P = .20$.

Step 1. Find $\chi_t^2(2, .30)$.

$$\chi_t^2(2, .30) = 1.07 + \frac{3.67 - 1.07}{2}$$

$$= 2.37$$

Step 2. Find $\chi_t^2(2, .20)$.

$$\chi_t^2(2, .20) = 1.64 + \frac{4.64 - 1.64}{2}$$

$$= 3.14$$

Step 3. Find $\chi_t^2(2, .22)$.

$$\chi_t^2(2, .22) = 2.37 + (.8)(3.14 - 2.37)$$

$$= 2.986$$

The answer 2.986, can be obtained also by first finding $\chi_t^2(1, .22)$ and $\chi_t^2(3, .22)$. Try it and see if you can get 2.986.

COMPUTATIONAL ACCURACY

Introduction

This section deals with the accuracy to which calculations should be taken when using decimal notation. Frequently, textbooks list fairly rigid formal rules for computational accuracy, a point of view that is probably unnecessary. The accuracy of statistical calculations is usually based on a strange mixture of formal and informal guidelines that are determined by the nature of the problem, the formality of the report that will be written, the complexity of the statistical procedure, and other considerations.

The general guideline is to carry as many decimal places as you reasonably can throughout all calculations. Any rounding that is necessary should be postponed to the final steps, as long as this is practical.

An example of a unique traditional guideline is the correlation coefficient. It is rare to see a correlation coefficient in a published report that does not have exactly two-place accuracy. One-place accuracy or accuracy greater than three places is almost never reported. This is without regard to the accuracy of the original data. Other statistics are also frequently reported in this same standard manner.

However, the formal guidelines for computational accuracy are generally based on the accuracy of the basic data. The general principle is that a computation can be no more reliable than the most unreliable figure upon which it is based.

There is a tendency for persons doing statistical calculations to report results in a way that implies more accuracy than is warranted. For example, you might ask several persons to tell you their income to the nearest \$1000. Then if you report that the average income is \$5,431.29 you are obviously implying that your measurement of income was highly accurate. In fact, it was quite poor. The average probably should have been reported as "about \$5000" or "over \$5000" or "between \$5000 and \$6000." The answer cannot be any more accurate than to the nearest thousand since the data were that imprecise.

This example shows that there is a need for guidelines, if only rough ones. In addition, there are a few technical terms in this section that should be a part of your vocabulary.

Significant Figures

The term "*significant figures*" or "*significant digits*" is helpful in discussing calculation accuracy. A decimal system numeral is said to have as many significant figures as there are *nonzero digits plus zeros placed between nonzero digits.* Let's look at some examples.

Numerals with one significant figure:

1; 4; 6; 60; 500; 9,000,000; .04; .0006

Numerals with two significant digits:

12; 34; 1.2; .00021; 7,400; 620,000; .0014

Numerals with three significant figures:

312; 417; 2.18; .244; .0244; 405; 20,600; .0104

Numerals with four significant digits:

5416; 412.5; 63,250; 31.24; 50.15; 1,012; 4.001; .001427

An exception to this definition is zeros to the right of a decimal point *and* to the right of nonzero digits. Such zeros are counted as significant figures. These numerals all have exactly four significant digits:

.1014; .2010; .4000; 500.0; .004610; .004600; .01000

This exception is based on the observation that these "extra zeros" are unnecessary *except* to indicate significance. In general, the difference between "5" and "5.0" in statistical data is as follows.

> "5" usually means "a number greater than 4.5 but less than 5.5," while "5.0" usually means "a number greater than 4.95 but less than 5.05." That is, "5.0" shows more measurement accuracy than "5."

Zeros to the right of all nonzero digits are ambiguous if there is no decimal point. Conceivably, "6000" could have one, two, three, or four significant figures. You would usually assume that "6000" has only one significant figure (the "6"). Sometimes dots or bars are used, so that three significant digits might be indicated by "6000" or "60$\bar{0}$0." In applied work, however, this usage is fairly rare, so that "6000" would usually mean "a number greater than 5500, but less than 6500."

Rounding

"*Rounding*" is the process of discarding unwanted significant figures. The usual reason for rounding is so that a computational result will have no greater accuracy implied than is justified. Another reason is to reduce computational difficulty—it is easier to work with few digits in each numeral.

Frequently, the purpose for which the numeral will be used dictates rounding. For example, suppose a city spends exactly $415,219.26 on city recreation in a given year. The city auditors need to know the numeral to the penny. A newspaper reporter might use the numeral "$415,000," lay persons discussing the budget might say "$400,000," or even "one-half million." Each person uses the accuracy necessary for his own purposes.

There are standard rules for rounding that should be known. Let's use the budget figure above as an example.

Significant Digits	Numeral
8	415,219.26
7	415,219.30
6	415,219
5	415,220
4	415,200
3	415,000
2	420,000
1	400,000

In lines 6, 4, 3, and 1, the last significant digit retained is the same digit that was used in the preceding line. These were "rounded down" in the sense that the rounding process involved merely dropping nonzero digits. Each numeral in lines 6, 4, 3, and 1 refers to a number *less than* 415,219.26.

The last significant figure retained in lines 7, 5, and 2 has been increased by one over the corresponding digit of the preceding line. These have been "rounded up." The resulting numerals refer to numbers all *larger than* 415,219.26.

If the portion to be discarded is a numeral with a starting digit of "4," "3,"

"2," "1," or "0," then we round down. If the digit is "6," "7," "8," or "9," we round up. If the digit is "5," we round up if the "5" is followed by any nonzero digit. Check the example using these rules. Here is another example:

4,516,293

This numeral can be rounded to any of these numerals:

4,516,290
4,516,300
4,516,000
4,520,000
4,500,000
5,000,000

It is rounded to "4,500,000" because the portion discarded, "16,293," refers to a number less than 50,000. It is rounded to "5,000,000" because the portion discarded, "516,293," refers to a number *greater* than 500,000. Therefore, you basically determine whether or not the portion "rounded off" starts with five or more or less to decide whether you round up or down.

Suppose, however, the numeral ends with "5." For example, should "65" be rounded to "60" or "70?" The decision is quite arbitrary; however you should be consistent. A commonly used rule is to round up if the digit preceding the "5" is odd and round down if the digit preceding the "5" is even. Thus, we would have "65" rounded to "60" but "75" rounded to "80." In the long run, you will increase the numerals about one-half the time and decrease them about one-half the time using this rule.

Computational Accuracy

If a and b are two real numbers, then $a + b$, $a - b$, ab, or a/b can have no more accuracy than *a or b, whichever is least accurate.* Also, $\sqrt{a}$ can be no more accurate than a. The word "accuracy" means, basically, the degree to which a number is free of measurement or rounding error.

Most statistical techniques are based on fallible measurement. Perhaps the only truly error-free numbers are frequency counts such as census data. Examples of measures that are likely to be error free include the number of children in a teaching experiment, the number of white rats that turn right in a T-maze, and the number of heads that occur in 20 tosses of a coin—other examples can be constructed, but most, if not all, will deal with frequency counts of one sort or another.

So, most statistical data have measurement error. The error can be small—as in measuring weight with a very good scale—or it can be quite large—as in measuring school achievement with a poorly made classroom examination.

In the case that we have non-error-free numbers, the general rule of accuracy can be interpreted in terms of significant figures—a computational result, in general, deserves no more and no fewer significant figures than *any* number used in the computation. That is, the least accurate number sets the accuracy of the result.

Let's look at some examples. Suppose we wish to add the error-free numbers 16,594 and 12,724, but we will carry only three significant figures in order to simplify the addition. We have

$$\begin{array}{r} 16{,}600 \\ +12{,}700 \\ \hline 29{,}300 \end{array}$$

The sum has only three significant figures, so it is usually assumed that the "real sum" is somewhere between 29,250 and 29,350. The real sum is, in fact, 29,318, and this is indeed in the interval.

Suppose that we had chosen to round only one of the numbers. We have

$$\begin{array}{r} 16{,}594 \\ +12{,}700 \\ \hline 29{,}294 \end{array}$$

The sum, if it is left as it is, implies that the "real sum" is between 29,293.5 and 29,294.5, which is not true. If the sum is rounded to four digits, (29,290), we might believe that the "real sum" is in the interval 29,285 to 29,295, which is also not true. Only when the sum is rounded to three digits do we get an interval containing the "real sum." The sum, to three significant figures, is 29,300, which is the sum rounded according to the rule. This rounded sum implies that the "real sum" is in the interval 29,250 to 29,350, which is true.

The major error is in reporting a result in a way that implies more accuracy than is justified. The accuracy of the sum is limited to the accuracy of the least accurate addend. Results can be slightly more accurate than the least accurate number, but accuracy *seldom extends beyond one additional significant figure.*

Computational errors in lengthy statistical calculations can be additive. For this reason, rounding should be postponed until a result is reached. Let's suppose we wish to add these numbers, which are based on fallible measurement: 260, 2140, 3040, 70.45, and 82.35. The smallest number of significant figures is two, so we could round each number before adding. We would get 5510, which is rounded to 5500. If we added before rounding, we would get 5592.80 which is rounded to 5600. The "5600" is a more accurate sum that is "5500." The first solution involved a constant bias–each number was rounded down and these rounding errors were accumulated. The second solution involved only one rounding error.

Approximations

It seems appropriate to end with a very important suggestion. Rough rounding of all numerals to a few (one or two) places can lead to very quick approximate solutions. Such approximate solutions are helpful in checking more careful calculations for gross errors. This trick is especially helpful in keeping track of decimal points. You might also use rough approximate answers to solve text examples and problems quickly, although some problems require detailed calculations that can be overlooked with the approximate solutions.

Final Word on Rounding

Rules of accuracy are more often violated than not in statistical textbooks and research reports, so don't take these rules too academically. Many statistical text problems lose their value as pedagogic devices if rules of accuracy are followed too strictly. For example, rounding at intermediate steps might lead you to a result slightly different from that in the text, leading you to believe that you have misunderstood a basic principle. Moreover, a few statistical procedures are quite sensitive to rounding error, so frequent rounding is to be avoided in some cases.

Appendix Three

Tables

Only working tables are included in this section. Expository tables are distributed throughout the text.

1. Selected Confidence Limits for the Binomial Distribution
2. Critical Values of the Unit Normal Distribution
3. Critical Values for d (or c) in the Fisher-Yates Test
4. Critical Values of the χ^2 Distribution for One Degree of Freedom
5. Factor from the Range to the Adjustment for Extreme Values
6. Critical Values of the Distribution of the Mean Absolute Deviation
7. Critical Values of Spearman's Rank Correlation Coefficient
8. Binomial Distribution–Individual Terms
9. Binomial Distribution–Cumulative Terms
10. Selected Range Adjustment Factors for Unit Normal Distribution
11. Selected Values for the Exponential Distribution
12. Tables of Common Logarithm–Five Places
13. Tables of Natural or Naperian Logarithms, .01-11.09

Table 1. Selected Confidence Limits for the Binomial Distribution[a, b]

N	Y	Confidence Coefficient (z) .90	.95	.99
1	0	0.000	0.000	0.000
	1	.100	.050	.010
2	0	0.000	0.000	0.000
	1	.051	.025+	.005+
	2	.316	.224	.100
3	0	0.000	0.000	0.000
	1	.035–	.017	.003
	2	.196	.135+	.059
	3	.464	.368	.215+
4	0	0.000	0.000	0.000
	1	.026	.013	.003
	2	.143	.098	.042
	3	.320	.249	.141
	4	.500	.473	.316

N	Y	Confidence Coefficient (z) .90	.95	.99
5	0	0.000	0.000	0.000
	1	.021	.010	.002
	2	.112	.076	.033
	3	.247	.189	.106
	4	.379	.343	.222
	5	.621	.500	.398
6	0	0.000	0.000	0.000
	1	.017	.009	.002
	2	.093	.063	.027
	3	.201	.153	.085–
	4	.333	.271	.173
	5	.458	.402	.294
	6	.655+	.598	.464
7	0	0.000	0.000	0.000
	1	.015–	.007	.001

N	Y	Confidence Coefficient (z) .90	.95	.99
	2	.079	.053	.023
	3	.170	.129	.071
	4	.279	.225+	.142
	5	.316	.341	.236
	6	.500	.446	.357
	7	.684	.623	.500
8	0	0.000	0.000	0.000
	1	.013	.006	.001
	2	.069	.046	.020
	3	.147	.111	.061
	4	.240	.193	.121
	5	.255–	.289	.198
	6	.418	.315+	.293
	7	.582	.500	.410
	8	.745+	.685–	.549

[a]Calculated by Edwin L. Crow, Eleanor G. Crow, and Robert S. Gardner according to a modification of a proposal of Theodore E. Sterne. Reprinted by permission of Biometrika Trustees.

[b]The observed proportion in a random sample of size n is Y/N. The table gives the lower confidence limit for the population proportion PL(Z), as a function of N and Y. The upper confidence limit PU(Z) = 1 – (lower confidence limit, entered with $N - Y$ instead of Y).

Table 1. *(continued)*

N	Y	Confidence Coefficient (Z) .90	.95	.99
9	**0**	0.000	0.000	0.000
	1	.012	.006	.001
	2	.061	.041	.017
	3	.129	.098	.053
	4	.210	.169	.105+
	5	.232	.251	.171
	6	.390	.289	.250
	7	.485–	.442	.344
	8	.609	.557	.402
	9	.768	.711	.598
10	**0**	0.000	0.000	0.000
	1	.010	.005+	.001
	2	.055–	.037	.016
	3	.116	.087	.048
	4	.188	.150	.093
	5	.222	.222	.150
	6	.341	.267	.218
	7	.352	.381	.297
	8	.500	.397	.376
	9	.648	.603	.488
	10	.778	.733	.624

N	Y	Confidence Coefficient (Z) .90	.95	.99
11	**0**	0.000	0.000	0.000
	1	.010	.005–	.001
	2	.049	.033	.014
	3	.105–	.079	.043
	4	.169	.135+	.084
	5	.197	.200	.134
	6	.302	.250	.194
	7	.315+	.333	.262
	8	0.423	0.369	0.340
	9	.577	.500	.407
	10	.685–	.631	.500
	11	.803	.750	.641
12	**0**	0.000	0.000	0.000
	1	.009	.004	.001
	2	.045+	.030	.013
	3	.096	.072	.039
	4	.154	.123	.076
	5	.184	.181	.121
	6	.271	.236	.175–
	7	.294	.294	.235–
	8	.398	.346	.302
	9	.500	.450	.321

N	Y	Confidence Coefficient (Z) .90	.95	.99
	10	.602	.550	.445+
	11	.706	.654	.555–
	12	.816	.764	.679
13	**0**	0.000	0.000	0.000
	1	.008	.004	.001
	2	.042	.028	.012
	3	.088	.066	.036
	4	.142	.113	.069
	5	.173	.166	.111
	6	.246	.224	.159
	7	.276	.260	.213
	8	.379	.327	.273
	9	.455+	.413	.302
	10	.530	.480	.406
	11	.621	.566	.477
	12	.724	.673	.571
	13	.827	.755–	.698
14	**0**	0.000	0.000	0.000
	1	.007	.004	.001
	2	.039	.026	.011
	3	.081	.061	.033

Table 1. *(continued)*

N	Y	Confidence Coefficient (Z) .90	.95	.99
	4	.131	.104	.064
	5	.163	.153	.102
	6	.224	.206	.146
	7	.261	.206	.195–
	8	0.355–	0.312	0.249
	9	.406	.371	.286
	10	.422	.389	.364
	11	.578	.500	.392
	12	.635–	.611	.500
	13	.739	.688	.608
	14	.837	.794	.714
15	0	0.000	0.000	0.000
	1	.007	.003	.001
	2	.036	.024	.010
	3	.076	.057	.031
	4	.122	.097	.059
	5	.154	.142	.094
	6	.205+	.191	.135–
	7	.247	.191	.179
	8	.325+	.294	.229
	9	.325+	.332	.273
	10	.400	.369	.328
	11	.500	.448	.373
	12	.600	.552	.461
	13	.675–	.631	.539
	14	.753	.698	.627
	15	.846	.809	.727
16	0	0.000	0.000	0.000
	1	.007	.003	.001
	2	.034	.023	.010
	3	.071	.053	.029
	4	.114	.090	.055+
	5	.147	.132	.088
	6	.189	.178	.125+
	7	.235+	.178	.166
	8	.299	.272	.212
	9	.305+	.272	.261
	10	.381	.352	.295+
	11	.450	.429	.357
	12	.550	.500	.421
	13	.619	.571	.475+
	14	.695–	.648	.549
	15	.765–	.728	.643
	16	.853	.822	.736
17	0	0.000	0.000	0.000
	1	.006	.003	.001
	2	.032	.021	.009
	3	.067	.050	.027
	4	.107	.085–	.052
	5	.140	.124	.082
	6	.175+	.166	.117
	7	.225+	.166	.155+
	8	.277	.253	.197
	9	.290	.254	.242
	10	.364	.337	.242
	11	.432	.406	.338
	12	.500	.456	.380
	13	.568	.511	.413
	14	.636	.583	.500
	15	.710	.663	.587
	16	.775–	.746	.654
	17	.860	.834	.758

Table 1. *(continued)*

N	Y	Confidence Coefficient (Z) .90	.95	.99
18	0	0.000	0.000	0.000
	1	.006	.003	.001
	2	.030	.020	.008
	3	.063	.047	.025+
	4	.101	.080	.049
	5	.135-	.116	.077
	6	.163	.156	.110
	7	.216	.157	.145+
	8	.257	.236	.184
	9	.277	.242	.226
	10	.349	.325-	.228
	11	.416	.375-	.314
	12	.464	.381	.318
	13	.518	.444	.397
	14	.581	.556	.466
	15	.651	.619	.534
	16	.723	.675+	.603
	17	.784	.758	.682
	18	.865+	.843	.772
19	0	0.000	0.000	0.000
	1	.006	.003	.001
	2	.028	.019	.008
	3	.059	.044	.024
	4	.095+	.075+	.046
	5	0.130	0.110	0.073
	6	.151	.147	.103
	7	.209	.150	.137
	8	.238	.222	.173
	9	.265+	.232	.212
	10	.337	.312	.218
	11	.386	.345-	.293
	12	.386	.365-	.305+
	13	.440	.426	.383
	14	.560	.500	.436
	15	.614	.574	.485-
	16	.663	.635+	.545-
	17	.735-	.684	.617
	18	.791	.768	.695-
	19	.870	.850	.782
20	0	0.000	0.000	0.000
	1	.005+	.003	.001
	2	.027	.018	.008
	3	.056	.042	.023
	4	.090	.071	.044
	5	.126	.104	.069
	6	.141	.140	.098
	7	.201	.143	.129
	8	.221	.209	.163
	9	.255-	.222	.200
	10	.325-	.293	.209
	11	.358	.293	.274
	12	.367	.351	.293
	13	.422	.411	.363
	14	.500	.467	.399
	15	.578	.533	.424
	16	.633	.589	.500
	17	.672	.649	.576
	18	.745+	.707	.625+
	19	.797	.778	.707
	20	.874	.857	.791
21	0	0.000	0.000	0.000
	1	.005+	.002	.000
	2	.026	.017	.007
	3	.054	.040	.022
	4	.086	.068	.041

Table 1. *(continued)*

N	Y	Confidence Coefficient (Z) .90	.95	.99
	5	.121	.099	.065+
	6	0.130	0.132	0.092
	7	.191	.137	.122
	8	.191	.197	.155
	9	.245	.213	.189
	10	.306	.276	.201
	11	.306	.276	.257
	12	.353	.338	.283
	13	.407	.398	.339
	14	.458	.449	.347
	15	.542	.494	.409
	16	.593	.545	.466
	17	.647	.602	.534
	18	.694	.662	.591
	19	.755+	.724	.653
	20	.809	.787	.717
	21	.877	.863	.799
22	**0**	0.000	0.000	0.000
	1	.005–	.002	.000
	2	.024	.016	.007
	3	.051	.038	.021
	4	.082	.065–	.039

N	Y	Confidence Coefficient (Z) .90	.95	.99
	5	.115–	.094	.062
	6	.115–	.126	.088
	7	.181	.132	.116
	8	.181	.187	.147
	9	.236	.205+	.179
	10	.289	.260	.194
	11	.289	.264	.242
	12	.340	.326	.273
	13	.393	.383	.318
	14	.444	.418	.334
	15	.500	.424	.396
	16	.556	.500	.450
	17	.607	.576	.495+
	18	.660	.611	.546
	19	.711	.674	.604
	20	.764	.736	.666
	21	.819	.795–	.727
	22	.885+	.868	.806
23	0	0.000	0.000	0.000
	1	.005–	.002	.000
	2	.023	.016	.007

N	Y	Confidence Coefficient (Z) .90	.95	.99
	3	.049	.037	.020
	4	.078	.062	.038
	5	0.110	0.090	0.059
	6	.110	.120	.084
	7	.173	.127	.111
	8	.173	.178	.140
	9	.228	.198	.171
	10	.273	.247	.187
	11	.274	.255–	.229
	12	.328	.317	.265+
	13	.381	.360	.298
	14	.431	.360	.323
	15	.478	.409	.384
	16	.521	.457	.420
	17	.569	.543	.429
	18	.619	.591	.500
	19	.672	.640	.571
	20	.726	.683	.614
	21	.772	.745+	.677
	22	.827	.802	.735–
	23	.890	.873	.813

Table 1. *(continued)*

N	Y	.90	.95	.99
		Confidence Coefficient (Z)		
24	**0**	0.000	0.000	0.000
	1	.004	.002	.000
	2	.022	.015+	.006
	3	.047	.035–	.019
	4	.075–	.059	.036
	5	.105–	.086	.057
	6	.105–	.115–	.080
	7	.165–	.122	.106
	8	.165–	.169	.133
	9	.221	.191	.163
	10	.259	.234	.181
	11	.264	.246	.216
	12	.317	.308	.257
	13	.370	.339	.280
	14	.413	.347	.313
	15	.447	.396	.362
	16	.447	.443	.364
	17	.553	.500	.416
	18	.577	.557	.464
	19	.630	.604	.536
	20	.683	.653	.584
	21	.736	.692	.636

N	Y	.90	.95	.99
		Confidence Coefficient (Z)		
	22	.779	.754	.687
	23	.835+	.809	.741
	24	.895+	.878	.819
25	**0**	0.000	0.000	0.000
	1	.004	.002	.000
	2	.021	.014	.006
	3	.045–	.034	.018
	4	.072	.057	.034
	5	.101	.082	.054
	6	.101	.110	.077
	7	.158	.118	.101
	8	.158	.161	.127
	9	.214	.185+	.155+
	10	.246	.222	.175+
	11	.255–	.238	.205+
	12	.307	.296	.245+
	13	.360	.317	.245+
	14	.389	.336	.305–
	15	.389	.384	.342
	16	.432	.431	.352
	17	.500	.475–	.403

N	Y	.90	.95	.99
		Confidence Coefficient (Z)		
	18	.568	.525+	.451
	19	.611	.569	.500
	20	.638	.616	.549
	21	.693	.664	.597
	22	.745+	.697	.648
	23	.786	.762	.695+
	24	.842	.815–	.755–
	25	.899	.882	.825–
26	**0**	0.000	0.000	0.000
	1	.004	.002	.000
	2	.021	.014	.006
	3	.043	.032	.017
	4	.069	.054	.033
	5	.097	.079	.052
	6	.097	.106	.073
	7	.151	.114	.097
	8	.151	.154	.122
	9	.209	.180	.149
	10	.233	.212	.170
	11	.247	.230	.195–
	12	.299	.282	.234

Table 1. *(continued)*

N	Y	Confidence Coefficient (Z) .90	.95	.99
	13	.342	.282	.234
	14	.342	.325+	.298
	15	.377	.374	.322
	16	.419	.421	.342
	17	.460	.458	.393
	18	.540	.494	.438
	19	.581	.535–	.474
	20	0.623	0.579	0.513
	21	.658	.626	.558
	22	.701	.675–	.607
	23	.753	.718	.658
	24	.791	.770	.702
	25	.849	.820	.766
	26	.903	.886	.830
27	**0**	0.000	0.000	0.000
	1	.004	.002	.000
	2	.020	.013	.006
	3	.042	.031	.017
	4	.066	.052	.032
	5	.093	.076	.050
	6	.093	.101	.070
	7	.145+	.110	.093
	8	.145+	.148	.117
	9	.204	.175–	.143
	10	.221	.202	.166
	11	.239	.223	.185–
	12	.291	.269	.224
	13	.326	.269	.225–
	14	.326	.316	.284
	15	.365+	.364	.298
	16	.407	.402	.332
	17	.447	.430	.383
	18	.500	.437	.413
	19	.553	.500	.419
	20	.593	.563	.461
	21	.635–	.585+	.539
	22	.674	.636	.581
	23	.709	.684	.616
	24	.761	.731	.668
	25	.796	.777	.703
	26	.855–	.825+	.775+
	27	.907	.890	.834
28	**0**	0.000	0.000	0.000
	1	.004	.002	.000
	2	.019	.013	.005+
	3	.040	.030	.016
	4	.064	.050	.031
	5	0.089	0.073	0.048
	6	.089	.098	.068
	7	.139	.106	.089
	8	.139	.142	.112
	9	.197	.170	.137
	10	.208	.192	.162
	11	.232	.217	.175+
	12	.284	.258	.214
	13	.310	.259	.218
	14	.312	.307	.272
	15	.355–	.355–	.272
	16	.396	.381	.323
	17	.435+	.384	.364
	18	.473	.424	.364
	19	.527	.463	.408
	20	.565–	.537	.449
	21	.604	.576	.500

Table 1. (*continued*)

N	Y	Confidence Coefficient (Z)		
		.90	**.95**	**.99**
	22	.645+	.616	.551
	23	.688	.643	.592
	24	.716	.693	.636
	25	.768	.741	.677
	26	.799	.783	.728
	27	.861	.830	.782
	28	.911	.894	.838
29	**0**	0.000	0.000	0.000
	1	.004	.002	.000
	2	.018	.012	.005+
	3	.039	.029	.015+
	4	.062	.049	.030
	5	.086	.070	.046
	6	.086	.094	.065+
	7	.134	.103	.086
	8	.134	.136	.108
	9	.189	.166	.132
	10	.189	.184	.157
	11	.225–	.211	.165+
	12	.276	.247	.206
	13	.294	.251	.211
	14	.303	.299	.260
	15	.345–	.339	.263
	16	.385+	.339	.316
	17	.425–	.374	.346
	18	.463	.413	.354
	19	.500	.451	.397
	20	0.537	0.500	0.438
	21	.575+	.549	.477
	22	.615–	.587	.523
	23	.655+	.626	.562
	24	.697	.661	.603
	25	.721	.701	.646
	26	.775+	.749	.684
	27	.811	.789	.737
	28	.866	.834	.789
	29	.914	.897	.840
30	**0**	0.000	0.000	0.000
	1	.004	.002	.000
	2	.018	.012	.005+
	3	.037	.028	.015–
	4	.059	.047	.028
	5	.083	.068	.045–
	6	.083	.091	.063
	7	.129	.100	.083
	8	.129	.131	.104
	9	.182	.163	.127
	10	.182	.175+	.151
	11	.219	.205+	.151
	12	.265–	.236	.198
	13	.265–	.244	.206
	14	.295–	.292	.249
	15	.336	.324	.256
	16	.376	.324	.308
	17	.416	.364	.329
	18	.446	.403	.345–
	19	.476	.440	.388
	20	.508	.476	.430
	21	.545–	.524	.462
	22	.584	.560	.495–
	23	.624	.597	.531
	24	.664	.636	.570
	25	.705+	.676	.612
	26	.735+	.708	.655+
	27	.781	.756	.690
	28	.818	.795–	.744
	29	.871	.837	.794
	30	.917	.900	.849

Table 2. **Critical Values of the Unit Normal Distribution.**[a,b,c]

Z	.00	.01	.02	.03	.04	.05	.06	.07	.08	.09
0.0	.0000	.0040	.0080	.0120	.0160	.0199	.0239	.0279	.0319	.0359
0.1	.0398	.0438	.0478	.0517	.0557	.0596	.0636	.0675	.0714	.0753
0.2	.0793	.0832	.0871	.0910	.0948	.0987	.1026	.1064	.1103	.1141
0.3	.1179	.1217	.1255	.1293	.1331	.1368	.1406	.1443	.1480	.1517
0.4	.1554	.1591	.1628	.1664	.1700	.1736	.1772	.1808	.1844	.1879
0.5	.1915	.1950	.1985	.2019	.2054	.2088	.2123	.2157	.2190	.2224
0.6	.2257	.2291	.2324	.2357	.2389	.2422	.2454	.2486	.2518	.2549
0.7	.2580	.2612	.2642	.2673	.2704	.2734	.2764	.2794	.2823	.2852
0.8	.2881	.2910	.2939	.2967	.2995	.3023	.3051	.3078	.3106	.3133
0.9	.3159	.3186	.3212	.3238	.3264	.3289	.3315	.3340	.3365	.3389
1.0	.3413	.3438	.3461	.3485	.3508	.3531	.3554	.3577	.3599	.3621
1.1	.3643	.3665	.3686	.3708	.3729	.3749	.3770	.3790	.3810	.3830
1.2	.3849	.3869	.3888	.3907	.3925	.3944	.3962	.3980	.3997	.4015
1.3	.4032	.4049	.4066	.4082	.4099	.4115	.4131	.4147	.4162	.4177
1.4	.4192	.4207	.4222	.4236	.4251	.4265	.4279	.4292	.4306	.4319
1.5	.4332	.4345	.4357	.4370	.4382	.4394	.4406	.4418	.4429	.4441
1.6	.4452	.4463	.4474	.4484	.4495	.4505	.4515	.4525	.4535	.4545
1.7	.4554	.4564	.4573	.4582	.4591	.4599	.4608	.4616	.4625	.4633
1.8	.4641	.4649	.4656	.4664	.4671	.4678	.4686	.4693	.4699	.4706
1.9	.4713	.4719	.4726	.4732	.4738	.4744	.4750	.4756	.4761	.4767
2.0	.4772	.4778	.4783	.4788	.4793	.4708	.4803	.4808	.4812	.4817
2.1	.4821	.4826	.4830	.4834	.4838	.4842	.4846	.4850	.4854	.4857
2.2	.4861	.4864	.4868	.4871	.4875	.4878	.4881	.4884	.4887	.4890
2.3	.4893	.4896	.4898	.4901	.4904	.4906	.4909	.4911	.4913	.4916
2.4	.4918	.4920	.4922	.4925	.4927	.4929	.4931	.4932	.4934	.4936

2.5	.4938	.4940	.4941	.4943	.4945	.4946	.4948	.4949	.4951	.4952
2.6	.4953	.4955	.4956	.4957	.4959	.4960	.4961	.4962	.4963	.4964
2.7	.4965	.4966	.4967	.4968	.4969	.4970	.4971	.4972	.4973	.4974
2.8	.4974	.4975	.4976	.4977	.4977	.4978	.4979	.4979	.4980	.4981
2.9	.4981	.4982	.4982	.4983	.4984	.4984	.4985	.4985	.4986	.4986
3.0	.49865	.4987	.4987	.4988	.4988	.4989	.4989	.4989	.4990	.4990
3.1	.49903	.4991	.4991	.4991	.4992	.4992	.4992	.4992	.4993	.4993
3.2	.4993129	.4993	.4994	.4994	.4994	.4994	.4994	.4995	.4995	.4995
3.3	.4995166	.4995	.4995	.4996	.4996	.4996	.4996	.4996	.4996	.4997
3.4	.4996631	.4997	.4997	.4997	.4997	.4997	.4997	.4997	.4998	.4998
3.5	.4997674	.4998	.4998	.4998	.4998	.4998	.4998	.4998	.4998	.4998
3.6	.4998409	.4998	.4999	.4999	.4999	.4999	.4999	.4999	.4999	.4999
3.7	.4998922	.4999	.4999	.4999	.4999	.4999	.4999	.4999	.4999	.4999
3.8	.4999277	.4999	.4999	.4999	.4999	.4999	.4999	.5000	.5000	.5000
3.9	.4999519	.5000	.5000	.5000	.5000	.5000	.5000	.5000	.5000	.5000
4.0	.4999683									
4.5	.4999966									
5.0	.4999997133									

[a]From Croxton, Frederick E., and Cowden, Dudley J., *Practical Business Statistics,* Prentice-Hall, New York 1948, p. 511. Reprinted by permission of the publisher.

[b]Through Z = 2.99, from Rugg's *Statistical Methods Applied to Education,* by arrangement with the publishers, Houghton Mifflin Company. A much more detailed table of normal curve areas is given in Federal Works Agency. Work Projects Administration for the City of New York, *Tables of Probability Functions,* Natural Bureau of Standards, New York, 1942, Vol. II, pp. 2–238. In this appendix values for Z = 3.00 through 5.00 were computed from the latter source.

[c]Each entry in this table is the proportion of the total area under a normal curve which lies under the segment between the mean and Z standard deviations from the mean.

Table 3. Critical Values for d (or c) in the Fisher–Yates Test[a]

Totals in Right Margin		b (or a)[b]	Level of Significance			
			.05	.025	.01	.005
a + b = 3	c + d = 3	3	0	–	–	–
a + b = 4	c + d = 4	4	0	0	–	–
	c + d = 3	4	0	–	–	–
a + b = 5	c + d = 5	5	1	1	0	0
		4	0	0	–	–
	c + d = 4	5	1	0	0	–
		4	0	–	–	–
	c + d = 3	5	0	0	–	–
	c + d = 2	5	0	–	–	–
a + b = 6	c + d = 6	6	2	1	1	0
		5	1	0	0	–
		4	0	–	–	–
	c + d = 5	6	1	0	0	0
		5	0	0	–	–
		4	0	–	–	–
	c + d = 4	6	1	0	0	0
		5	0	0	–	–
	c + d = 3	6	0	0	–	–
		5	0	–	–	–
	c + d = 2	6	0	–	–	–
a + b = 7	c + d = 7	7	3	2	1	1
		6	1	1	0	0
		5	0	0	–	–
		4	0	–	–	–
	c + d = 6	77	2	2	1	1
		6	1	0	0	0
		5	0	0	–	–
		4	0	–	–	–
	c + d = 5	7	2	1	0	0
		6	1	0	0	–
		5	0	–	–	–
	c + d = 4	7	1	1	0	0
		6	0	0	–	–
		5	0	–	–	–

[a]Adapted from Finney, D. J., 1948. The Fisher–Yates test of significance in 2 × 2 contingency tables. *Biometrika,* **35**, 149–154, with the kind permission of the author and the Biometrika Trustees.

[b]When **b** is entered in the middle column, the significance levels are for d. When a is used in place of b, the significance levels are for c.

Table 3. *(continued)*

Totals in Right Margin		b (or a)[b]	Level of Significance .05	.025	.01	.005
	c + d = 3	7	0	0	0	–
		6	0	–	–	–
	c + d = 2	7	0	–	–	–
a + b = 8	c + d = 8	8	4	3	2	2
		7	2	2	1	0
		6	1	1	0	0
		5	0	0	–	–
		4	0	–	–	–
	c + d = 7	8	3	2	2	1
		7	2	1	1	0
		6	1	0	0	–
		5	0	0	–	–
	c + d = 6	8	2	2	1	1
		7	1	1	0	0
		6	0	0	0	–
		5	0	–	–	–
	c + d = 5	8	2	1	1	0
		7	1	0	0	0
		6	0	0	–	–
		5	0	–	–	–
	c + d = 4	8	1	1	0	0
		7	0	0	–	–
		6	0	–	–	–
	c + d = 3	8	0	0	0	–
		7	0	0	–	–
	c + d = 2	8	0	0	–	–
a + b = 9	c + d = 9	9	5	4	3	3
		8	3	3	2	1
		7	2	1	1	0
		6	1	1	0	0
		5	0	0	–	–
		4	0	–	–	–
	c + d = 8	9	4	3	3	2
		8	3	2	1	1
		7	2	1	0	0
		6	1	0	0	–
		5	0	0	–	–
	c + d = 7	9	3	3	2	2
		8	2	2	1	0

Table 3. *(continued)*

Totals in Right Margin		b (or a)[b]	.05	.025	.01	.005
			Level of Significance			
		7	1	1	0	0
		6	0	0	–	–
		5	0	–	–	–
a + b = 9	c + d = 6	9	3	2	1	1
		8	2	1	0	0
		7	1	0	0	–
		6	0	0	–	–
		5	0	–	–	–
	c + d = 5	9	2	1	1	1
		8	1	1	0	0
		7	0	0	–	–
		6	0	–	–	–
	c + d = 4	9	1	1	0	0
		8	0	0	0	–
		7	0	0	–	–
		6	0	–	–	–
	c + d = 3	9	1	0	0	0
		8	0	0	–	–
		7	0	–	–	–
	c + d = 2	9	0	0	–	–
a + b = 10	c + d = 10	10	6	5	4	3
		9	4	3	3	2
		8	3	2	1	1
		7	2	1	1	0
		6	1	0	0	–
		5	0	0	–	–
		4	0	–	–	–
	c + d = 9	10	5	4	3	3
		9	4	3	2	2
		8	2	2	1	1
		7	1	1	0	0
		6	1	0	0	–
		5	0	0	–	–
	c + d = 8	10	4	4	3	2
		9	3	2	2	1
		8	2	1	1	0
		7	1	1	0	0
		6	0	0	–	–
		5	0	–	–	–

Table 3. *(continued)*

Totals in Right Margin		b (or a)[b]	Level of Significance .05	.025	.01	.005
	c + d = 7	10	3	3	2	2
		9	2	2	1	1
		8	1	1	0	0
		7	1	0	0	–
		6	0	0	–	–
		5	0	–	–	–
a + b = 10	c + d = 6	10	3	2	2	1
		9	2	1	1	0
		8	1	1	0	0
		7	0	0	–	–
		6	0	–	–	–
	c + d = 5	10	2	2	1	1
		9	1	1	0	0
		8	1	0	0	–
		7	0	0	–	–
		6	0	–	–	–
	c + d = 4	10	1	1	0	0
		9	1	0	0	0
		8	0	0	–	–
		7	0	–	–	–
	c + d = 3	10	1	0	0	0
		9	0	0	–	–
		8	0	–	–	–
	c + d = 2	10	0	0	–	–
		9	0	–	–	–
a + b = 11	c + d = 11	11	7	6	5	4
		10	5	4	3	3
		9	4	3	2	2
		8	3	2	1	1
		7	2	1	0	0
		6	1	0	0	–
		5	0	0	–	–
		4	0	–	–	–
	c + d = 10	11	6	5	4	4
		10	4	4	3	2
		9	3	3	2	1
		8	2	2	1	0
		7	1	1	0	0
		6	1	0	0	–
		5	0	–	–	–

Table 3. (*continued*)

Totals in Right Margin		b (or a)[b]	Level of Significance .05	.025	.01	.005
	c + d = 9	11	5	4	4	3
		10	4	3	2	2
		9	3	2	1	1
		8	2	1	1	0
		7	1	1	0	0
		6	0	0	–	–
		5	0	–	–	–
a + b = 11	c + d = 8	11	4	4	3	3
		10	3	3	2	1
		9	2	2	1	1
		8	1	1	0	0
		7	1	0	0	–
		6	0	0	–	–
		5	0	–	–	–
	c + d = 7	11	4	3	2	2
		10	3	2	1	1
		9	2	1	1	0
		8	1	1	0	0
		7	0	0	–	–
		6	0	0	–	–
	c + d = 6	11	3	2	2	1
		10	2	1	1	0
		9	1	1	0	0
		8	1	0	0	–
		7	0	0	–	–
		6	0	–	–	–
	c + d = 5	11	2	2	1	1
		10	1	1	0	0
		9	1	0	0	0
		8	0	0	–	–
		7	0	–	–	–
	c + d = 4	11	1	1	1	0
		10	1	0	0	0
		9	0	0	–	–
		8	0	–	–	–
	c + d = 3	11	1	0	0	0
		10	0	0	–	–
		9	0	–	–	–
	c + d = 2	11	0	0	–	–
		10	0	–	–	–

Table 3. *(continued)*

Totals in Right Margin		b (or a)[b]	Level of Significance .05	.025	.01	.005
a + b = 12	c + d = 12	12	8	7	6	5
		11	6	5	4	4
		10	5	4	3	2
		9	4	3	2	1
		8	3	2	1	1
		7	2	1	0	0
		6	1	0	0	–
		5	0	0	–	–
		4	0	–	–	–
a + b = 12	c + d = 11	12	7	6	5	5
		11	5	5	4	3
		10	4	3	2	2
		9	3	2	2	1
		8	2	1	1	0
		7	1	1	0	0
		6	1	0	0	–
		5	0	0	–	–
	c + d = 10	12	6	5	5	4
		11	5	4	3	3
		10	4	3	2	2
		9	3	2	1	1
		8	2	1	0	0
		7	1	0	0	0
		6	0	0	–	–
		5	0	–	–	–
	c + d = 9	12	5	5	4	3
		11	4	3	3	2
		10	3	2	2	1
		9	2	2	1	0
		8	1	1	0	0
		7	1	0	0	–
		6	0	0	–	–
		5	0	–	–	–
	c + d = 8	12	5	4	3	3
		11	3	3	2	2
		10	2	2	1	1
		9	2	1	1	0
		8	1	1	0	0
		7	0	0	–	–
		6	0	0	–	–

Table 3. (*continued*)

Totals in Right Margin		b (or a)[b]	Level of Significance .05	.025	.01	.005
	c + d = 7	12	4	3	2	2
		11	3	2	2	1
		10	2	1	1	0
		9	1	1	0	0
		8	1	0	0	–
		7	0	0	–	–
		6	0	–	–	–
a + b = 12	c + d = 6	12	3	3	2	2
		11	2	2	1	1
		10	1	1	0	0
		9	1	0	0	0
		8	0	0	–	–
		7	0	0	–	–
		6	0	–	–	–
	c + d = 5	12	2	2	1	1
		11	1	1	1	0
		10	1	0	0	0
		9	0	0	0	–
		8	0	0	–	–
		7	0	–	–	–
	c + d = 4	12	2	1	1	0
		11	1	0	0	0
		10	0	0	0	–
		9	0	0	–	–
		8	0	–	–	–
	c + d = 3	12	1	0	0	0
		11	0	0	0	–
		10	0	0	–	–
		9	0	–	–	–
	c + d = 2	12	0	0	–	–
		11	0	–	–	–
a + b = 13	c + d = 13	13	9	8	7	6
		12	7	6	5	4
		11	6	5	4	3
		10	4	4	3	2
		9	3	3	2	1
		8	2	2	1	0
		7	2	1	0	0
		6	1	0	0	–

Table 3. *(continued)*

Totals in Right Margin		b (or a)[b]	Level of Significance .05	.025	.01	.005
		5	0	0	–	–
		4	0	–	–	–
	c + d = 12	13	8	7	6	5
		12	6	5	5	4
		11	5	4	3	3
		10	4	3	2	2
		9	3	2	1	1
		8	2	1	1	0
		7	1	1	0	0
		6	1	0	0	–
		5	0	0	–	–
a + b = 13	c + d = 11	13	7	6	5	5
		12	6	5	4	3
		11	4	4	3	2
		10	3	3	2	1
		9	3	2	1	1
		8	2	1	0	0
		7	1	0	0	0
		6	0	0	–	–
		5	0	–	–	–
	c + d = 10	13	6	6	5	4
		12	5	4	3	3
		11	4	3	2	2
		10	3	2	1	1
		9	2	1	1	0
		8	1	1	0	0
		7	1	0	0	–
		6	0	0	–	–
		5	0	–	–	–
	c + d = 9	13	5	5	4	4
		12	4	4	3	2
		11	3	3	2	1
		10	2	2	1	1
		9	2	1	0	0
		8	1	1	0	0
		7	0	0	–	–
		6	0	0	–	–
		5	0	–	–	–

Table 3. (*continued*)

Totals in Right Margin	b (or a)[b]	Level of Significance .05	.025	.01	.005
c + d = 8	13	5	4	3	3
	12	4	3	2	2
	11	3	2	1	1
	10	2	1	1	0
	9	1	1	0	0
	8	1	0	0	–
	7	0	0	–	–
	6	0	–	–	–
c + d = 7	13	4	3	3	2
	12	3	2	2	1
	11	2	2	1	1
	10	1	1	0	0
	9	1	0	0	0
	8	0	0	–	–
	7	0	0	–	–
	6	0	–	–	–

Table 4. Critical Values of the χ^2 Square Distribution for One Degree of Freedom

P	χ^2
.01	0.00016
.05	0.0039
.10	0.0158
.50	0.455
.90	2.71
.95	3.84
.99	6.63

Table 5. Factor from the Range to the Adjustment for Extreme Values[a,b]

Number in the Sample		Two-Sided Risk 10%	5%	2%	1%
2		2.66	5.85	15.41	31.33
3	0.40	0.40	0.80	1.61	2.52
4	Outside	0.06	0.24	0.54	0.87
5	Inside	0.08	0.02	0.21	0.35
6		0.15	0.07	0.06	0.16
7		0.20	0.12	0.02	0.05
8		0.24	0.17	0.08	0.02
9		0.26	0.20	0.12	0.07
10		0.28	0.22	0.15	0.11
One-Sided Risk		5%	2.5%	1%	0.5%

[a]Forman S. Acton, *Analysis of Straight-Line Data*, Dover Press, New York, 1967, p. 251. This table was originally distributed by J. W. Tukey in a dittoed paper, *Notes on Quick and Denormalized Methods of Analyzing Data*.
[b]The adjusted extreme value limits are for a typical value.

Table 6. Critical Values of the Distribution of the Mean Absolute Deviation[a]

Sample Size N	HNZ as a function of N and Z											
	.10	.20	.30	.40	.50	.60	.70	.80	.90	.95	.98	.99
2	0.224	0.460	0.721	1.027	1.414	1.946	2.776	4.353	8.929	17.969	45.001	90.024
3	0.193	0.393	0.605	0.840	1.111	1.444	1.888	2.570	3.981	5.868	9.499	13.538
4	0.182	0.369	0.566	0.780	1.022	1.308	1.673	2.195	3.161	4.280	6.113	7.868
5	0.176	0.357	0.546	0.750	0.978	1.243	1.574	2.032	2.833	3.698	5.002	6.153
6	0.173	0.349	0.534	0.732	0.951	1.205	1.516	1.940	2.657	3.399	4.461	5.355
7	0.170	0.344	0.525	0.719	0.934	1.179	1.479	1.881	2.546	3.216	4.143	4.897
8	0.168	0.340	0.519	0.711	0.921	1.161	1.452	1.840	2.471	3.092	3.933	4.601
9	0.167	0.338	0.515	0.704	0.912	1.148	1.433	1.809	2.415	3.003	3.785	4.394
10	0.166	0.335	0.511	0.699	0.904	1.138	1.418	1.786	2.373	2.936	3.674	4.241
11	0.165	0.334	0.509	0.695	0.898	1.129	1.406	1.767	2.340	2.884	3.589	4.124
12	0.165	0.332	0.506	0.691	0.894	1.122	1.396	1.752	2.313	2.842	3.520	4.031
13	0.164	0.331	0.504	0.689	0.890	1.117	1.388	1.739	2.291	2.807	3.465	3.956
14	0.163	0.330	0.503	0.686	0.886	1.112	1.381	1.729	2.273	2.779	3.418	3.893
15	0.163	0.329	0.501	0.684	0.883	1.108	1.375	1.720	2.257	2.754	3.379	3.840
16	0.163	0.328	0.500	0.682	0.881	1.104	1.370	1.712	2.243	2.733	3.346	3.795
17	0.162	0.328	0.499	0.681	0.879	1.101	1.365	1.705	2.232	2.715	3.317	3.757
18	0.162	0.327	0.498	0.679	0.877	1.098	1.361	1.699	2.221	2.699	3.292	3.723
19	0.162	0.327	0.497	0.678	0.875	1.096	1.358	1.694	2.212	2.685	3.269	3.693
20	0.162	0.326	0.497	0.677	0.873	1.094	1.355	1.689	2.204	2.672	3.249	3.667

21	0.161	0.326	0.496	0.676	0.872	1.092	1.352	1.685	2.197	2.661	3.232	3.643
22	0.161	0.325	0.495	0.675	0.871	1.090	1.349	1.681	2.190	2.651	3.216	3.622
23	0.161	0.325	0.495	0.674	0.869	1.089	1.347	1.678	2.184	2.642	3.201	3.603
24	0.161	0.325	0.494	0.674	0.868	1.087	1.345	1.675	2.178	2.633	3.188	3.586
25	0.161	0.324	0.494	0.673	0.867	1.086	1.343	1.672	2.173	2.626	3.176	3.570
26	0.161	0.324	0.493	0.672	0.867	1.084	1.341	1.669	2.169	2.619	3.165	3.555
27	0.161	0.324	0.493	0.672	0.866	1.083	1.340	1.667	2.165	2.612	3.155	3.542
28	0.160	0.324	0.493	0.671	0.865	1.082	1.338	1.665	2.161	2.606	3.146	3.530
29	0.160	0.323	0.492	0.671	0.864	1.081	1.337	1.662	2.157	2.601	3.138	3.519
30	0.160	0.323	0.492	0.670	0.864	1.080	1.335	1.660	2.154	2.596	3.130	3.508
40	0.160	0.322	0.490	0.667	0.859	1.074	1.326	1.646	2.130	2.559	3.073	3.434
60	0.159	0.320	0.487	0.664	0.854	1.067	1.317	1.633	2.106	2.524	3.019	3.362
120	0.158	0.319	0.485	0.660	0.850	1.061	1.308	1.619	2.084	2.490	2.966	3.294
∞	0.157	0.318	0.483	0.657	0.845	1.055	1.299	1.606	2.062	2.456	2.916	3.228

[a] Adapted from Herrey, A. M. J., Percentage Points of the H-Distribution for Computing Confidence Limits or Performing t-Tests by Way of the Mean Absolute Deviation, *Journal of the American Statistical Association*, March 1971, p. 188.

Table 7. Critical Values of Spearman's Rank Correlation Coefficient[a]

$(1-\alpha)(2)$:	0.50	0.20	0.10	0.05	0.02	0.01	0.005	0.002	0.001
N $(1-\alpha)(1)$:	0.25	0.10	0.05	0.025	0.01	0.005	0.00025	0.001	0.0005
4	0.600	1.000	1.000						
5	0.500	0.800	0.900	1.000	1.000				
6	0.371	0.657	0.829	0.886	0.943	1.000	1.000		
7	0.321	0.571	0.714	0.786	0.893	0.929	0.964	1.000	1.000
8	0.310	0.524	0.643	0.738	0.833	0.881	0.905	0.952	0.976
9	0.267	0.483	0.600	0.700	0.783	0.833	0.867	0.917	0.933
10	0.248	0.455	0.464	0.648	0.745	0.794	0.830	0.879	0.903
11	0.236	0.427	0.536	0.618	0.709	0.755	0.800	0.845	0.873
12	0.217	0.406	0.503	0.587	0.678	0.727	0.769	0.818	0.846
13	0.209	0.385	0.484	0.560	0.648	0.703	0.747	0.791	0.824
14	0.200	0.367	0.464	0.538	0.626	0.679	0.723	0.771	0.802
15	0.189	0.354	0.446	0.521	0.604	0.654	0.700	0.750	0.779
16	0.182	0.341	0.429	0.503	0.582	0.635	0.679	0.729	0.762
17	0.176	0.328	0.414	0.485	0.566	0.615	0.662	0.713	0.748
18	0.170	0.317	0.401	0.472	0.550	0.600	0.643	0.695	0.728
19	0.165	0.309	0.391	0.460	0.535	0.584	0.628	0.677	0.712
20	0.161	0.299	0.380	0.447	0.520	0.570	0.612	0.662	0.696
21	0.156	0.292	0.370	0.435	0.508	0.556	0.599	0.648	0.681
22	0.152	0.284	0.361	0.425	0.496	0.544	0.586	0.634	0.667
23	0.148	0.278	0.353	0.415	0.486	0.532	0.573	0.622	0.654

[a]Reproduced from Zar, Jerrold H., *Biostatistical Analysis*, Prentice-Hall, Englewood Cliffs, N.J., © 1974 pp. 498–499. Reprinted by permission of Prentice-Hall Inc.

Table 7. *(continued)*

$(1-\alpha)(2)$:	0.50	0.20	0.10	0.05	0.02	0.01	0.005	0.002	0.001
N $(1-\alpha)(1)$:	0.25	0.10	0.05	0.025	0.01	0.005	0.00025	0.001	0.0005
24	0.144	0.271	0.344	0.406	0.476	0.521	0.562	0.610	0.642
25	0.142	0.265	0.337	0.398	0.466	0.511	0.551	0.598	0.630
26	0.138	0.259	0.331	0.390	0.457	0.501	0.541	0.587	0.619
27	0.136	0.255	0.324	0.382	0.448	0.491	0.531	0.577	0.608
28	0.133	0.250	0.317	0.375	0.440	0.483	0.522	0.567	0.598
29	0.130	0.245	0.312	0.368	0.433	0.475	0.513	0.558	0.589
30	0.128	0.240	0.306	0.362	0.425	0.467	0.504	0.549	0.580
31	0.126	0.236	0.301	0.356	0.418	0.459	0.496	0.541	0.571
32	0.124	0.232	0.296	0.350	0.412	0.452	0.489	0.533	0.563
33	0.121	0.229	0.291	0.345	0.405	0.446	0.482	0.525	0.554
34	0.120	0.225	0.287	0.340	0.399	0.439	0.475	0.517	0.547
35	0.118	0.222	0.283	0.335	0.394	0.433	0.468	0.510	0.539
36	0.116	0.219	0.279	0.330	0.388	0.427	0.462	0.504	0.533
37	0.114	0.216	0.275	0.325	0.383	0.421	0.456	0.497	0.526
38	0.113	0.212	0.271	0.321	0.378	0.415	0.450	0.491	0.519
39	0.111	0.210	0.267	0.317	0.373	0.410	0.444	0.485	0.513
40	0.110	0.207	0.264	0.313	0.368	0.405	0.439	0.479	0.507
41	0.108	0.204	0.261	0.309	0.364	0.400	0.433	0.473	0.501
42	0.107	0.202	0.257	0.305	0.359	0.395	0.428	0.468	0.495
43	0.105	0.199	0.254	0.301	0.355	0.391	0.423	0.463	0.490
44	0.104	0.197	0.251	0.298	0.351	0.386	0.419	0.458	0.484
45	0.103	0.194	0.248	0.294	0.347	0.382	0.414	0.453	0.479

Table 7. *(continued)*

N $(1-\alpha)(2)$: $(1-\alpha)(1)$:	0.50 0.25	0.20 0.10	0.10 0.05	0.05 0.025	0.02 0.01	0.01 0.005	0.005 0.00025	0.002 0.001	0.001 0.0005
46	0.102	0.192	0.246	0.291	0.343	0.378	0.410	0.448	0.474
47	0.101	0.190	0.243	0.288	0.340	0.374	0.405	0.443	0.469
48	0.100	0.188	0.240	0.285	0.336	0.370	0.401	0.439	0.465
49	0.098	0.186	0.238	0.282	0.333	0.366	0.397	0.434	0.460
50	0.097	0.184	0.235	0.279	0.329	0.363	0.393	0.430	0.456
51	0.096	0.182	0.233	0.276	0.326	0.359	0.390	0.426	0.451
52	0.095	0.180	0.231	0.274	0.323	0.356	0.386	0.422	0.447
53	0.095	0.179	0.228	0.271	0.320	0.352	0.382	0.418	0.443
54	0.094	0.177	0.226	0.268	0.317	0.349	0.379	0.414	0.439
55	0.093	0.175	0.224	0.266	0.314	0.346	0.375	0.411	0.435
56	0.092	0.174	0.222	0.264	0.311	0.343	0.372	0.407	0.432
57	0.091	0.172	0.220	0.261	0.308	0.340	0.369	0.404	0.428
58	0.090	0.171	0.218	0.259	0.306	0.337	0.366	0.400	0.424
59	0.089	0.169	0.216	0.257	0.303	0.334	0.363	0.397	0.421
60	0.089	0.168	0.214	0.255	0.300	0.331	0.360	0.394	0.418
61	0.088	0.166	0.213	0.252	0.298	0.329	0.357	0.391	0.414
62	0.087	0.165	0.211	0.250	0.296	0.326	0.354	0.388	0.411
63	0.086	0.163	0.209	0.248	0.293	0.323	0.351	0.385	0.408
64	0.086	0.162	0.207	0.246	0.291	0.321	0.348	0.382	0.405
65	0.085	0.161	0.206	0.244	0.289	0.318	0.346	0.379	0.402
66	0.084	0.160	0.204	0.243	0.287	0.316	0.343	0.376	0.399
67	0.084	0.158	0.203	0.241	0.284	0.314	0.341	0.373	0.396

Table 7. *(continued)*

N \ $(1-\alpha)(2)$: $(1-\alpha)(1)$:	0.50 0.25	0.20 0.10	0.10 0.05	0.05 0.025	0.02 0.01	0.01 0.005	0.005 0.00025	0.002 0.001	0.001 0.0005
68	0.083	0.157	0.201	0.239	0.282	0.311	0.338	0.370	0.393
69	0.082	0.156	0.200	0.237	0.280	0.309	0.336	0.368	0.390
70	0.082	0.155	0.198	0.235	0.278	0.307	0.333	0.365	0.388
71	0.081	0.154	0.197	0.234	0.276	0.305	0.331	0.363	0.385
72	0.081	0.153	0.195	0.232	0.274	0.303	0.329	0.360	0.382
73	0.080	0.152	0.194	0.230	0.272	0.301	0.327	0.358	0.380
74	0.080	0.151	0.193	0.229	0.271	0.299	0.324	0.355	0.377
75	0.079	0.150	0.191	0.227	0.269	0.297	0.322	0.353	0.375
76	0.078	0.149	0.190	0.226	0.267	0.295	0.320	0.351	0.372
77	0.078	0.148	0.189	0.224	0.265	0.293	0.318	0.349	0.370
78	0.077	0.147	0.188	0.223	0.264	0.291	0.316	0.346	0.368
79	0.077	0.146	0.186	0.221	0.262	0.289	0.314	0.344	0.365
80	0.076	0.145	0.185	0.220	0.260	0.287	0.312	0.342	0.363
81	0.076	0.144	0.184	0.219	0.259	0.285	0.310	0.340	0.361
82	0.075	0.143	0.183	0.217	0.257	0.284	0.308	0.338	0.359
83	0.075	0.142	0.182	0.216	0.255	0.282	0.306	0.336	0.357
84	0.074	0.141	0.181	0.215	0.254	0.280	0.305	0.334	0.355
85	0.074	0.140	0.180	0.213	0.252	0.279	0.303	0.332	0.353
86	0.074	0.139	0.179	0.212	0.251	0.277	0.301	0.330	0.351
87	0.073	0.139	0.177	0.211	0.250	0.276	0.299	0.328	0.349
88	0.073	0.158	0.176	0.210	0.248	0.274	0.298	0.327	0.347
89	0.072	0.137	0.175	0.209	0.247	0.272	0.296	0.324	0.345
90	0.072	0.136	0.174	0.207	0.245	0.271	0.294	0.323	0.345

Table 7. *(continued)*

N	$(1-\alpha)(2)$: 0.50 $(1-\alpha)(1)$: 0.25	0.20 0.10	0.10 0.05	0.05 0.025	0.02 0.01	0.01 0.005	0.005 0.00025	0.002 0.001	0.001 0.0005
91	0.072	0.135	0.173	0.206	0.244	0.269	0.293	0.321	0.341
92	0.071	0.135	0.173	0.205	0.243	0.268	0.291	0.319	0.339
93	0.071	0.134	0.172	0.204	0.241	0.267	0.290	0.318	0.338
94	0.070	0.133	0.171	0.203	0.240	0.265	0.288	0.316	0.336
95	0.070	0.133	0.170	0.202	0.239	0.264	0.287	0.314	0.334
96	0.070	0.132	0.169	0.201	0.238	0.262	0.285	0.313	0.332
97	0.069	0.131	0.168	0.200	0.236	0.261	0.284	0.311	0.331
98	0.069	0.130	0.167	0.199	0.235	0.260	0.282	0.310	0.329
99	0.068	0.130	0.166	0.198	0.234	0.258	0.281	0.308	0.327
100	0.068	0.129	0.165	0.197	0.233	0.257	0.279	0.307	0.326

Table 8. Binomial Distribution—Individual Terms[a]

		p																				
N	*K*	.01	.02	.04	.05	.06	.08	.10	.12	.14	.15	.16	.18	.20	.22	.24	.25	.30	.35	.40	.45	.50	*K*
2	0	980	960	922	902	884	846	810	774	740	722	706	672	640	608	578	562	490	422	360	302	250	0
	1	020	039	077	095	113	147	180	211	241	255	269	295	320	343	365	375	420	455	480	495	500	1
	2	0+	0+	002	002	004	006	010	014	020	022	026	032	040	048	058	062	090	122	160	202	250	2
3	0	970	941	885	857	831	779	729	681	636	614	593	551	512	475	439	422	343	275	216	166	125	0
	1	029	058	111	135	159	203	243	279	311	325	339	363	384	402	416	422	441	444	432	408	375	1
	2	0+	001	005	007	010	018	027	038	051	057	065	080	096	113	131	141	189	239	288	334	375	2
	3	0+	0+	0+	0+	0+	001	001	002	003	003	004	006	008	011	014	016	027	043	064	091	125	3
4	0	961	922	849	815	781	716	656	600	547	522	498	452	410	370	334	316	240	179	130	092	063	0
	1	039	075	142	171	199	249	292	327	356	368	379	397	410	418	421	422	412	384	346	299	250	1
	2	001	002	009	014	019	033	049	067	087	098	108	131	154	177	200	211	265	311	346	368	375	2
	3	0+	0+	0+	0+	001	002	004	006	009	011	014	019	026	033	042	047	076	111	154	200	250	3
	4	0+	0+	0+	0+	0+	0+	0+	0+	0+	001	001	001	002	002	003	004	008	015	026	041	062	4
5	0	951	904	815	774	734	659	590	528	470	444	418	371	328	289	254	237	168	116	078	050	031	0
	1	048	092	170	204	234	287	328	360	383	392	398	407	410	407	400	396	360	312	259	206	156	1
	2	001	004	014	021	030	050	073	098	125	138	152	179	205	230	253	264	309	336	346	337	312	2
	3	0+	0+	001	001	002	004	008	013	020	024	029	039	051	065	080	088	132	181	230	276	312	3
	4	0+	0+	0+	0+	0+	0+	0+	001	002	002	003	004	006	009	013	015	028	049	077	113	156	4
	5	0+	0+	0+	0+	0+	0+	0+	0+	0+	0+	0+	0+	0+	001	001	001	002	005	010	018	031	5

[a]From Croxton, Frederick E., and Cowden, Dudley J., *Practical Business Statistics,* Prentice-Hall, New York, 1948, p. 511. Reprinted by permission of the publisher.

Table 8. (*continued*)

N	K	.01	.02	.04	.05	.06	.08	.10	.12	.14	.15	.16	.18	.20	.22	.24	.25	.30	.35	.40	.45	.50	K
6	0	941	886	783	735	690	606	531	464	405	377	351	304	262	225	193	178	118	075	047	028	016	0
	1	057	108	196	232	264	316	354	380	395	399	401	400	393	381	365	356	303	244	187	136	094	1
	2	001	006	020	031	042	069	098	130	161	176	191	220	246	269	288	297	324	328	311	278	234	2
	3	0+	0+	001	002	004	008	015	024	035	041	049	064	082	101	121	132	185	235	276	303	312	3
	4	0+	0+	0+	0+	0+	001	001	002	004	005	007	011	015	021	029	033	060	095	138	186	234	4
	5	0+	0+	0+	0+	0+	0+	0+	0+	0+	0+	001	001	002	002	004	004	010	020	037	061	094	5
	6	0+	0+	0+	0+	0+	0+	0+	0+	0+	0+	0+	0+	0+	0+	0+	0+	001	002	004	008	016	6
7	0	932	868	751	698	648	558	478	409	348	321	295	249	210	176	146	133	082	049	028	015	008	0
	1	066	124	219	257	290	340	372	390	396	396	393	383	367	347	324	311	247	185	131	087	055	1
	2	002	008	027	041	055	089	124	160	194	210	225	252	275	293	307	311	318	298	261	214	164	2
	3	0+	0+	002	004	006	013	023	036	053	062	071	092	115	138	161	173	227	268	290	292	273	3
	4	0+	0+	0+	0+	0+	001	003	005	009	011	014	020	029	039	051	058	097	144	194	239	273	4
	5	0+	0+	0+	0+	0+	0+	0+	0+	001	001	002	003	004	007	010	012	025	047	077	117	164	5
	6	0+	0+	0+	0+	0+	0+	0+	0+	0+	0+	0+	0+	0+	001	001	001	004	008	017	032	055	6
	7	0+	0+	0+	0+	0+	0+	0+	0+	0+	0+	0+	0+	0+	0+	0+	0+	0+	001	002	004	008	7
8	0	923	851	721	663	610	513	430	360	299	272	248	204	168	137	111	100	058	032	017	008	004	
	1	075	139	240	279	311	357	383	392	390	385	378	359	336	309	281	267	198	137	090	055	031	1
	2	003	010	035	051	070	109	149	187	222	238	252	276	294	305	311	311	296	259	209	157	109	2
	3	0+	0+	003	005	009	019	033	051	072	084	096	121	147	172	196	208	254	279	279	257	219	3
	4	0+	0+	0+	0+	001	002	005	009	015	018	023	033	046	061	077	087	136	188	232	263	273	4
	5	0+	0+	0+	0+	0+	0+	0+	001	002	003	003	006	009	014	020	023	047	081	124	172	219	5
	6	0+	0+	0+	0+	0+	0+	0+	0+	0+	0+	0+	001	001	002	003	004	010	022	041	070	109	6

Table 8. *(continued)*

N	K	.01	.02	.04	.05	.06	.08	.10	.12	.14	.15	.16	.18	.20	.22	.24	.25	.30	.35	.40	.45	.50	K
	7	0+	0+	0+	0+	0+	0+	0+	0+	0+	0+	0+	0+	0+	0+	0+	0+	001	003	008	016	031	7
	8	0+	0+	0+	0+	0+	0+	0+	0+	0+	0+	0+	0+	0+	0+	0+	0+	0+	0+	001	002	004	8
9	0	914	834	693	630	573	472	387	316	257	232	208	168	134	107	085	075	040	021	010	005	002	0
	1	083	153	260	299	329	370	387	388	377	368	357	331	302	271	240	225	156	100	060	034	018	1
	2	003	013	043	063	084	129	172	212	245	260	272	291	302	306	304	300	267	216	161	111	070	2
	3	0+	001	004	008	013	026	045	067	093	107	121	149	176	201	224	234	267	272	251	212	164	3
	4	0+	0+	0+	001	001	003	007	014	023	028	035	049	066	085	106	117	172	219	251	260	246	4
	5	0+	0+	0+	0+	0+	0+	001	002	004	005	007	011	017	024	033	039	074	118	167	213	246	5
	6	0+	0+	0+	0+	0+	0+	0+	0+	0+	001	001	002	003	005	007	009	021	042	074	116	164	6
	7	0+	0+	0+	0+	0+	0+	0+	0+	0+	0+	0+	0+	0+	001	001	001	004	010	021	041	070	7
	8	0+	0+	0+	0+	0+	0+	0+	0+	0+	0+	0+	0+	0+	0+	0+	0+	0+	001	004	009	018	8
	9	0+	0+	0+	0+	0+	0+	0+	0+	0+	0+	0+	0+	0+	0+	0+	0+	0+	0+	0+	001	002	9
10	0	904	817	665	599	539	434	349	279	221	197	175	137	107	083	064	056	028	013	006	003	001	0
	1	091	167	277	315	344	378	387	380	360	347	333	302	268	235	203	188	121	072	040	021	010	1
	2	004	015	052	075	099	148	194	233	264	276	286	298	302	298	288	282	233	176	121	076	044	2
	3	0+	001	006	010	017	034	057	085	115	130	145	174	201	224	243	250	267	252	215	166	117	3
	4	0+	0+	0+	001	002	005	011	020	033	040	048	067	088	111	134	146	200	238	251	238	205	4
	5	0+	0+	0+	0+	0+	001	001	003	006	008	011	018	026	037	051	058	103	154	201	234	246	5
	6	0+	0+	0+	0+	0+	0+	0+	0+	001	001	002	003	006	009	013	016	037	069	111	160	205	6
	7	0+	0+	0+	0+	0+	0+	0+	0+	0+	0+	0+	0+	001	001	002	003	009	021	042	075	117	7
	8	0+	0+	0+	0+	0+	0+	0+	0+	0+	0+	0+	0+	0+	0+	0+	0+	001	004	011	023	044	8
	9	0+	0+	0+	0+	0+	0+	0+	0+	0+	0+	0+	0+	0+	0+	0+	0+	0+	001	002	004	010	9
	10	0+	0+	0+	0+	C+	0+	0+	0+	0+	0+	0+	0+	0+	0+	0+	0+	0+	0+	0+	0+	001	0

Table 8. *(continued)*

N	K	.01	.02	.04	.05	.06	.08	.10	.12	.14	.15	.16	.18	.20	.22	.24	.25	.30	.35	.40	.45	.50	K
11	0	895	801	638	569	506	400	314	245	190	167	147	113	086	065	049	042	020	009	004	001	0+	0
	1	099	180	293	329	355	382	384	368	341	325	308	272	236	202	170	155	093	052	027	013	005	1
	2	005	018	061	087	113	166	213	251	277	287	293	299	295	284	268	258	200	140	089	051	027	2
	3	0+	001	008	014	022	043	071	103	135	152	168	197	221	241	254	258	257	225	177	126	081	3
	4	0+	0+	001	001	003	008	016	028	044	054	064	086	111	136	160	172	220	243	236	206	161	4
	5	0+	0+	0+	0+	0+	001	002	005	010	013	017	027	039	054	071	080	132	183	221	236	226	5
	6	0+	0+	0+	0+	0+	0+	0+	001	002	002	003	006	010	015	022	027	057	099	147	193	226	6
	7	0+	0+	0+	0+	0+	0+	0+	0+	0+	0+	0+	001	002	003	005	006	017	038	070	113	161	7
	8	0+	0+	0+	0+	0+	0+	0+	0+	0+	0+	0+	0+	0+	0+	001	001	004	010	023	046	081	8
	9	0+	0+	0+	0+	0+	0+	0+	0+	0+	0+	0+	0+	0+	0+	0+	0+	001	002	005	013	027	9
	10	0+	0+	0+	0+	0+	0+	0+	0+	0+	0+	0+	0+	0+	0+	0+	0+	0+	0+	001	002	005	10
	11	0+	0+	0+	0+	0+	0+	0+	0+	0+	0+	0+	0+	0+	0+	0+	0+	0+	0+	0+	0+	0+	11
12	0	886	785	613	540	476	368	282	216	164	142	123	092	069	051	037	032	014	006	002	001	0+	0
	1	107	192	306	341	365	384	377	353	320	301	282	243	206	172	141	127	071	037	017	008	003	1
	2	006	022	070	099	128	183	230	265	286	292	296	294	283	266	244	232	168	109	064	034	016	2
	3	0+	001	010	017	027	053	085	120	155	172	188	215	236	250	257	258	240	195	142	092	054	3
	4	0+	0+	001	002	004	010	021	037	057	068	080	106	133	159	183	194	231	237	213	170	121	4
	5	0+	0+	0+	0+	0+	001	004	008	015	019	025	037	053	072	092	103	158	204	227	222	193	5
	6	0+	0+	0+	0+	0+	0+	0+	001	003	004	005	010	016	024	034	040	079	128	177	212	226	6
	7	0+	0+	0+	0+	0+	0+	0+	0+	0+	001	001	002	003	006	009	011	029	059	101	149	193	7
	8	0+	0+	0+	0+	0+	0+	0+	0+	0+	0+	0+	0+	001	001	002	002	008	020	042	076	121	8
	9	0+	0+	0+	0+	0+	0+	0+	0+	0+	0+	0+	0+	0+	0+	0+	0+	001	005	012	028	054	9

Table 8. *(continued)*

N	K	.01	.02	.04	.05	.06	.08	.10	.12	.14	.15	.16	.18	.20	.22	.24	.25	.30	.35	.40	.45	.50	K
	10	0+	0+	0+	0+	0+	0+	0+	0+	0+	0+	0+	0+	0+	0+	0+	0+	0+	001	002	007	016	10
	11	0+	0+	0+	0+	0+	0+	0+	0+	0+	0+	0+	0+	0+	0+	0+	0+	0+	0+	0+	001	003	11
	12	0+	0+	0+	0+	0+	0+	0+	0+	0+	0+	0+	0+	0+	0+	0+	0+	0+	0+	0+	0+	0+	12
13	0	878	769	588	513	447	338	254	190	141	121	104	076	055	040	028	024	010	004	001	0+	0+	0
	1	115	204	319	351	371	382	367	336	298	277	257	216	179	145	116	103	054	026	011	004	002	1
	2	007	025	080	111	142	199	245	275	291	294	293	285	268	245	220	206	139	084	045	022	010	2
	3	0+	002	012	021	033	064	100	138	174	190	205	229	246	254	254	252	218	165	111	066	035	3
	4	0+	0+	001	003	005	014	028	047	071	084	098	126	154	179	201	210	234	222	184	135	087	4
	5	0+	0+	0+	0+	001	002	006	012	021	027	033	050	069	091	114	126	180	215	221	199	157	5
	6	0+	0+	0+	0+	0+	0+	001	002	004	006	008	015	023	034	048	056	103	155	197	217	209	6
	7	0+	0+	0+	0+	0+	0+	0+	0+	001	001	002	003	006	010	015	019	044	083	131	177	209	7
	8	0+	0+	0+	0+	0+	0+	0+	0+	0+	0+	0+	001	001	002	004	005	014	034	066	109	157	8
	9	0+	0+	0+	0+	0+	0+	0+	0+	0+	0+	0+	0+	0+	0+	001	001	003	010	024	050	087	9
	10	0+	0+	0+	0+	0+	0+	0+	0+	0+	0+	0+	0+	0+	0+	0+	0+	001	002	006	016	035	10
	11	0+	0+	0+	0+	0+	0+	0+	0+	0+	0+	0+	0+	0+	0+	0+	0+	0+	0+	001	004	010	11
	12	0+	0+	0+	0+	0+	0+	0+	0+	0+	0+	0+	0+	0+	0+	0+	0+	0+	0+	0+	0+	002	12
	13	0+	0+	0+	0+	0+	0+	0+	0+	0+	0+	0+	0+	0+	0+	0+	0+	0+	0+	0+	0+	0+	13
14		869	754	565	488	421	311	229	167	121	103	087	062	044	031	021	018	007	002	001	0+	0+	0
	1	123	215	329	359	376	379	356	319	276	254	232	191	154	122	095	083	041	018	007	003	001	1
	2	008	029	089	123	156	214	257	283	292	291	287	272	250	223	195	180	113	063	032	014	006	2
	3	0+	002	015	026	040	074	114	154	190	206	219	239	250	252	246	240	194	137	085	046	022	3
	4	0+	0+	002	004	007	018	035	058	085	100	115	144	172	195	214	220	229	202	155	104	061	4

Table 8. *(continued)*

N	K	.01	.02	.04	.05	.06	.08	.10	.12	.14	.15	.16	.18	.20	.22	.24	.25	.30	.35	.40	.45	.50	K
	5	0+	0+	0+	0+	001	003	008	016	028	035	044	063	086	110	135	147	196	218	207	170	122	5
	6	0+	0+	0+	0+	0+	0+	001	003	007	009	012	021	032	047	064	073	126	176	207	209	183	6
	7	0+	0+	0+	0+	0+	0+	0+	001	001	002	003	005	009	015	023	028	062	108	157	195	209	7
	8	0+	0+	0+	0+	0+	0+	0+	0+	0+	0+	0+	001	002	004	006	008	023	051	092	140	183	8
	9	0+	0+	0+	0+	0+	0+	0+	0+	0+	0+	0+	0+	0+	001	001	002	007	018	041	076	122	9
	10	0+	0+	0+	0+	0+	0+	0+	0+	0+	0+	0+	0+	0+	0+	0+	0+	001	005	014	031	061	10
	11	0+	0+	0+	0+	0+	0+	0+	0+	0+	0+	0+	0+	0+	0+	0+	0+	0+	001	003	009	022	11
	12	0+	0+	0+	0+	0+	0+	0+	0+	0+	0+	0+	0+	0+	0+	0+	0+	0+	0+	001	002	006	12
	13	0+	0+	0+	0+	0+	0+	0+	0+	0+	0+	0+	0+	0+	0+	0+	0+	0+	0+	0+	0+	001	13
	14	0+	0+	0+	0+	0+	0+	0+	0+	0+	0+	0+	0+	0+	0+	0+	0+	0+	0+	0+	0+	0+	14
15	0	860	739	542	463	395	286	206	147	104	087	073	051	035	024	016	013	005	002	0+	0+	0+	0
	1	130	226	339	366	378	373	343	301	254	231	209	168	132	102	077	067	031	013	005	002	0+	1
	2	009	032	099	135	169	227	267	287	290	286	279	258	231	201	171	156	092	048	022	009	003	2
	3	0+	003	018	031	047	086	129	170	204	218	230	245	250	246	234	225	170	111	063	032	014	3
	4	0+	0+	002	005	009	022	043	069	100	116	131	162	188	208	221	225	219	179	127	078	042	4
	5	0+	0+	0+	001	001	004	010	021	036	045	055	078	103	129	154	165	206	212	186	140	092	5
	6	0+	0+	0+	0+	0+	001	002	005	010	013	017	029	043	061	081	092	147	191	207	191	153	6
	7	0+	0+	0+	0+	0+	0+	0+	001	002	003	004	008	014	022	033	039	081	132	177	201	196	7
	8	0+	0+	0+	0+	0+	0+	0+	0+	0+	001	001	002	003	006	010	013	035	071	118	165	196	8
	9	0+	0+	0+	0+	0+	0+	0+	0+	0+	0+	0+	0+	001	001	003	003	012	030	061	105	153	9
	10	0+	0+	0+	0+	0+	0+	0+	0+	0+	0+	0+	0+	0+	0+	0+	001	003	010	024	051	092	10
	11	0+	0+	0+	0+	0+	0+	0+	0+	0+	0+	0+	0+	0+	0+	0+	0+	001	002	007	019	042	11

Table 8. (*continued*)

N	K	.01	.02	.04	.05	.06	.08	.10	.12	.14	.15	.16	.18	.20	.22	.24	.25	.30	.35	.40	.45	.50	K
	12	0+	0+	0+	0+	0+	0+	0+	0+	0+	0+	0+	0+	0+	0+	0+	0+	0+	0+	002	005	014	12
	13	0+	0+	0+	0+	0+	0+	0+	0+	0+	0+	0+	0+	0+	0+	0+	0+	0+	0+	0+	001	003	13
	14	0+	0+	0+	0+	0+	0+	0+	0+	0+	0+	0+	0+	0+	0+	0+	0+	0+	0+	0+	0+	0+	14
	15	0+	0+	0+	0+	0+	0+	0+	0+	0+	0+	0+	0+	0+	0+	0+	0+	0+	0+	0+	0+	0+	15
16	0	851	724	520	440	372	263	385	129	090	074	061	042	028	019	012	010	003	001	0+	0+	0+	16
	1	138	236	347	371	379	366	329	282	233	210	187	147	113	085	063	053	023	009	003	001	0+	1
	2	010	036	108	146	182	239	275	289	285	277	268	242	211	179	1480	134	073	035	015	006	002	2
	3	0+	003	021	036	054	097	142	184	216	229	238	248	246	236	218	208	146	089	047	022	009	3
	4	0+	0+	003	006	011	027	051	081	114	131	147	177	200	216	224	225	204	155	101	057	028	4
	5	0+	0+	0+	001	002	006	014	027	045	056	067	093	120	146	170	180	210	201	162	112	067	5
	6	0+	0+	0+	0+	0+	001	003	007	013	018	023	037	055	076	098	110	165	198	198	168	122	6
	7	0+	0+	0+	0+	0+	0+	0+	001	003	005	006	012	020	030	044	052	101	152	189	197	175	7
	8	0+	0+	0+	0+	0+	0+	0+	0+	001	001	001	003	006	010	016	020	049	092	142	181	196	8
	9	0+	0+	0+	0+	0+	0+	0+	0+	0+	0+	0+	001	001	002	004	006	019	044	084	132	175	9
	10	0+	0+	0+	0+	0+	0+	0+	0+	0+	0+	0+	0+	0+	0+	001	001	006	017	039	075	122	10
	11	0+	0+	0+	0+	0+	0+	0+	0+	0+	0+	0+	0+	0+	0+	0+	0+	001	005	014	034	067	11
	12	0+	0+	0+	0+	0+	0+	0+	0+	0+	0+	0+	0+	0+	0+	0+	0+	0+	001	004	011	028	12
	13	0+	0+	0+	0+	0+	0+	0+	0+	0+	0+	0+	0+	0+	0+	0+	0+	0+	0+	001	003	009	13
	14	0+	0+	0+	0+	0+	0+	0+	0+	0+	0+	0+	0+	0+	0+	0+	0+	0+	0+	0+	001	002	14
	15	0+	0+	0+	0+	0+	0+	0+	0+	0+	0+	0+	0+	0+	0+	0+	0+	0+	0+	0+	0+	0+	15
	16	0+	0+	0+	0+	0+	0+	0+	0+	0+	0+	0+	0+	0+	0+	0+	0+	0+	0+	0+	0+	0+	16

Table 8. *(continued)*

N	K	.01	.02	.04	.05	.06	.08	.10	.12	.14	.15	.16	.18	.20	.22	.24	.25	.30	.35	.40	.45	.50	K
17	0	843	709	500	418	349	242	167	114	077	063	052	034	023	015	009	008	002	001	0+	0+	0+	0
	1	145	246	354	374	379	358	315	264	213	189	167	128	096	070	051	043	017	006	002	001	0+	1
	2	012	040	118	158	194	249	280	288	279	267	255	225	191	158	128	114	058	026	010	004	001	2
	3	001	004	025	041	062	108	156	196	226	236	243	246	239	223	202	189	125	070	034	014	005	3
	4	0+	0+	004	008	014	033	060	094	129	146	162	189	209	221	223	221	187	132	080	041	018	4
	5	0+	0+	0+	001	002	007	017	033	054	067	080	108	136	162	183	191	208	185	138	087	047	5
	6	0+	0+	0+	0+	0+	001	004	009	018	024	031	047	068	091	116	128	178	199	184	143	094	6
	7	0+	0+	0+	0+	0+	0+	001	002	005	007	009	016	027	040	057	067	120	168	193	184	148	7
	8	0+	0+	0+	0+	0+	0+	0+	0+	001	001	002	004	008	014	023	028	064	113	161	188	185	8
	9	0+	0+	0+	0+	0+	0+	0+	0+	0+	0+	0+	001	002	004	007	009	028	061	107	154	185	9
	10	0+	0+	0+	0+	0+	0+	0+	0+	0+	0+	0+	0+	0+	001	002	002	009	026	057	101	148	10
	11	0+	0+	0+	0+	0+	0+	0+	0+	0+	0+	0+	0+	0+	0+	0+	001	003	009	024	052	094	11
	12	0+	0+	0+	0+	0+	0+	0+	0+	0+	0+	0+	0+	0+	0+	0+	0+	001	002	008	021	047	12
	13	0+	0+	0+	0+	0+	0+	0+	0+	0+	0+	0+	0+	0+	0+	0+	0+	0+	001	002	007	018	13
	14	0+	0+	0+	0+	0+	0+	0+	0+	0+	0+	0+	0+	0+	0+	0+	0+	0+	0+	0+	002	005	14
	15	0+	0+	0+	0+	0+	0+	0+	0+	0+	0+	0+	0+	0+	0+	0+	0+	0+	0+	0+	001	001	15
	16	0+	0+	0+	0+	0+	0+	0+	0+	0+	0+	0+	0+	0+	0+	0+	0+	0+	0+	0+	0+	0+	16
	17	0+	0+	0+	0+	0+	0+	0+	0+	0+	0+	0+	0+	0+	0+	0+	0+	0+	0+	0+	0+	0+	17
18	0	835	695	480	397	328	223	150	100	066	054	043	028	018	011	007	006	002	0+	0+	0+	0+	0
	1	152	255	360	376	377	349	300	246	194	170	149	111	081	058	041	034	013	004	001	0+	0+	1
	2	013	044	127	168	205	258	284	285	268	256	241	207	172	139	109	096	046	019	007	002	001	2
	3	001	005	028	047	070	120	168	207	233	241	244	243	230	209	184	170	105	055	025	009	003	3
	4	0+	0+	004	009	017	039	070	106	142	159	175	200	215	221	218	213	168	110	061	029	012	4

Table 8. *(continued)*

N	K	.01	.02	.04	.05	.06	.08	.10	.12	.14	.15	.16	.18	.20	.22	.24	.25	.30	.35	.40	.45	.50	K
	5	0+	0+	001	001	003	009	022	040	065	079	093	123	151	175	193	199	202	166	115	067	033	5
	6	0+	0+	0+	0+	0+	002	005	012	023	030	038	058	082	107	132	144	187	194	166	118	071	6
	7	0+	0+	0+	0+	0+	0+	001	003	006	009	013	022	035	052	071	082	138	179	189	166	121	7
	8	0+	0+	0+	0+	0+	0+	0+	001	001	002	003	007	012	020	031	038	081	133	173	186	167	8
	9	0+	0+	0+	0+	0+	0+	0+	0+	0+	0+	001	002	003	006	011	014	039	079	128	169	185	9
	10	0+	0+	0+	0+	0+	0+	0+	0+	0+	0+	0+	0+	001	002	003	004	015	038	077	125	167	10
	11	0+	0+	0+	0+	0+	0+	0+	0+	0+	0+	0+	0+	0+	0+	001	001	005	015	037	074	121	11
	12	0+	0+	0+	0+	0+	0+	0+	0+	0+	0+	0+	0+	0+	0+	0+	0+	001	005	015	035	071	12
	13	0+	0+	0+	0+	0+	0+	0+	0+	0+	0+	0+	0+	0+	0+	0+	0+	0+	001	004	013	033	13
	14	0+	0+	0+	0+	0+	0+	0+	0+	0+	0+	0+	0+	0+	0+	0+	0+	0+	0+	001	004	012	14
	15	0+	0+	0+	0+	0+	0+	0+	0+	0+	0+	0+	0+	0+	0+	0+	0+	0+	0+	0+	001	003	15
	16	0+	0+	0+	0+	0+	0+	0+	0+	0+	0+	0+	0+	0+	0+	0+	0+	0+	0+	0+	0+	001	16
	17	0+	0+	0+	0+	0+	0+	0+	0+	0+	0+	0+	0+	0+	0+	0+	0+	0+	0+	0+	0+	0+	17
	18	0+	0+	0+	0+	0+	0+	0+	0+	0+	0+	0+	0+	0+	0+	0+	0+	0+	0+	0+	0+	0+	18
19	0	826	681	460	377	309	205	135	088	057	046	036	023	014	009	005	004	001	0+	0+	0+	0+	0
	1	159	264	364	377	374	339	285	228	176	153	132	096	068	048	033	027	009	003	001	0+	0+	1
	2	014	049	137	179	215	265	285	280	258	243	226	190	154	121	093	080	036	014	005	001	0+	2
	3	001	006	032	053	078	131	180	217	238	243	244	236	218	194	166	152	087	042	017	006	002	3
	4	0+	0+	005	011	020	045	080	118	155	171	186	207	218	219	210	202	149	091	047	020	007	4
	5	0+	0+	001	002	004	012	027	048	076	091	106	137	164	185	199	202	192	147	093	050	022	5
	6	0+	0+	0+	0+	001	002	007	015	029	037	047	070	095	122	146	157	192	184	145	095	052	6
	7	0+	0+	0+	0+	0+	0+	001	004	009	012	017	029	044	064	086	097	153	184	180	144	096	7

Table 8. *(continued)*

		P																				
N	K	.01	.02	.04	.05	.06	.08	.10	.12	.14	.15	.16	.18	.20	.22	.24	.25	.30	.35	.40	.45	.50	K
	8	0+	0+	0+	0+	0+	0+	0+	001	002	003	005	009	017	027	041	049	098	149	180	177	144	8
	9	0+	0+	0+	0+	0+	0+	0+	0+	0+	001	001	003	005	009	016	020	051	098	146	177	176	9
	10	0+	0+	0+	0+	0+	0+	0+	0+	0+	0+	0+	001	001	003	005	007	022	053	098	145	176	10
	11	0+	0+	0+	0+	0+	0+	0+	0+	0+	0+	0+	0+	0+	001	001	002	008	023	053	097	144	11
	12	0+	0+	0+	0+	0+	0+	0+	0+	0+	0+	0+	0+	0+	0+	0+	0+	002	008	024	053	096	12
	13	0+	0+	0+	0+	0+	0+	0+	0+	0+	0+	0+	0+	0+	0+	0+	0+	001	002	008	023	052	13
	14	0+	0+	0+	0+	0+	0+	0+	0+	0+	0+	0+	0+	0+	0+	0+	0+	0+	001	002	008	022	14
	15	0+	0+	0+	0+	0+	0+	0+	0+	0+	0+	0+	0+	0+	0+	0+	0+	0+	0+	001	002	007	15
	16	0+	0+	0+	0+	0+	0+	0+	0+	0+	0+	0+	0+	0+	0+	0+	0+	0+	0+	0+	0+	002	16
	17	0+	0+	0+	0+	0+	0+	0+	0+	0+	0+	0+	0+	0+	0+	0+	0+	0+	0+	0+	0+	0+	17
	18	0+	0+	0+	0+	0+	0+	0+	0+	0+	0+	0+	0+	0+	0+	0+	0+	0+	0+	0+	0+	0+	18
	19	0+	0+	0+	0+	0+	0+	0+	0+	0+	0+	0+	0+	0+	0+	0+	0+	0+	0+	0+	0+	0+	19
20		818	668	442	358	290	189	122	078	049	039	031	019	012	007	004	003	001	0+	0+	0+	0+	0
	1	165	272	368	377	370	328	270	212	159	137	117	083	058	039	026	021	007	002	0+	0+	0+	1
	2	016	053	146	189	225	271	285	274	247	229	211	173	137	105	078	067	028	010	003	001	0+	2
	3	001	006	036	060	086	141	190	224	241	243	241	228	205	178	148	134	072	032	012	004	001	3
	4	0+	001	006	013	023	052	090	130	167	182	195	213	218	213	199	190	130	074	035	014	005	4
	5	0+	0+	001	002	005	015	032	057	087	103	119	149	175	192	201	202	179	127	075	036	015	5
	6	0+	0+	0+	0+	001	003	009	019	035	045	057	082	109	136	159	169	192	171	124	075	037	6
	7	0+	0+	0+	0+	0+	001	002	005	012	016	022	036	055	076	100	112	164	184	166	122	074	7
	8	0+	0+	0+	0+	0+	0+	0+	001	003	005	007	013	022	035	051	061	114	161	180	162	120	8
	9	0+	0+	0+	0+	0+	0+	0+	0+	001	001	002	004	007	013	022	027	065	116	160	177	160	9

Table 8. *(continued)*

N	K	P																					K
		.01	.02	.04	.05	.06	.08	.10	.12	.14	.15	.16	.18	.20	.22	.24	.25	.30	.35	.40	.45	.50	
	10	0+	0+	0+	0+	0+	0+	0+	0+	0+	0+	0+	001	002	004	008	010	031	069	117	159	176	10
	11	0+	0+	0+	0+	0+	0+	0+	0+	0+	0+	0+	0+	0+	001	002	003	012	034	071	119	160	11
	12	0+	0+	0+	0+	0+	0+	0+	0+	0+	0+	0+	0+	0+	0+	001	001	004	014	035	073	120	12
	13	0+	0+	0+	0+	0+	0+	0+	0+	0+	0+	0+	0+	0+	0+	0+	0+	001	004	015	037	074	13
	14	0+	0+	0+	0+	0+	0+	0+	0+	0+	0+	0+	0+	0+	0+	0+	0+	0+	001	005	015	037	14
	15	0+	0+	0+	0+	0+	0+	0+	0+	0+	0+	0+	0+	0+	0+	0+	0+	0+	0+	001	005	015	15
	16	0+	0+	0+	0+	0+	0+	0+	0+	0+	0+	0+	0+	0+	0+	0+	0+	0+	0+	0+	001	005	15
	17	0+	0+	0+	0+	0+	0+	0+	0+	0+	0+	0+	0+	0+	0+	0+	0+	0+	0+	0+	0+	001	16
	18	0+	0+	0+	0+	0+	0+	0+	0+	0+	0+	0+	0+	0+	0+	0+	0+	0+	0+	0+	0+	0+	17
	19	0+	0+	0+	0+	0+	0+	0+	0+	0+	0+	0+	0+	0+	0+	0+	0+	0+	0+	0+	0+	0+	19
	20	0+	0+	0+	0+	0+	0+	0+	0+	0+	0+	0+	0+	0+	0+	0+	0+	0+	0+	0+	0+	0+	20
21	0	810	654	424	341	273	174	109	068	042	033	026	015	010	005	003	002	001	0+	0+	0+	0+	0
	1	172	280	371	376	366	317	255	195	144	122	103	071	048	032	021	017	005	001	0+	0+	0+	1
	2	017	057	155	198	233	276	284	267	234	215	196	157	121	091	066	055	022	007	002	0+	0+	2
	3	001	007	041	066	094	152	200	230	242	241	236	218	192	162	132	117	058	024	009	003	001	3
	4	0+	001	008	016	027	059	100	141	177	191	202	215	216	205	187	176	113	059	026	009	003	4
	5	0+	0+	001	003	006	018	038	065	098	115	131	161	183	197	201	199	164	109	059	026	010	5
	6	0+	0+	0+	0+	001	004	011	024	043	054	067	094	122	148	169	177	188	156	105	057	026	6
	7	0+	0+	0+	0+	0+	001	003	007	015	020	027	044	065	089	114	126	172	180	149	101	055	7
	8	0+	0+	0+	0+	0+	0+	001	002	004	006	009	017	029	044	063	074	129	169	174	144	097	8
	9	0+	0+	0+	0+	0+	0+	0+	0+	001	002	002	005	010	018	029	036	080	132	168	170	140	9

Table 8. *(continued)*

N	K	.01	.02	.04	.05	.06	.08	.10	.12	.14	.15	.16	.18	.20	.22	.24	.25	.30	.35	.40	.45	.50	K
	10	0+	0+	0+	0+	0+	0+	0+	0+	0+	0+	001	001	003	006	011	014	041	085	134	167	168	10
	11	0+	0+	0+	0+	0+	0+	0+	0+	0+	0+	0+	0+	001	002	003	005	018	046	089	137	168	11
	12	0+	0+	0+	0+	0+	0+	0+	0+	0+	0+	0+	0+	0+	0+	001	001	006	021	050	093	140	12
	13	0+	0+	0+	0+	0+	0+	0+	0+	0+	0+	0+	0+	0+	0+	0+	0+	002	008	023	053	097	13
	14	0+	0+	0+	0+	0+	0+	0+	0+	0+	0+	0+	0+	0+	0+	0+	0+	0+	002	009	025	055	14
	15	0+	0+	0+	0+	0+	0+	0+	0+	0+	0+	0+	0+	0+	0+	0+	0+	0+	001	003	009	026	15
	16	0+	0+	0+	0+	0+	0+	0+	0+	0+	0+	0+	0+	0+	0+	0+	0+	0+	0+	001	003	010	16
	17	0+	0+	0+	0+	0+	0+	0+	0+	0+	0+	0+	0+	0+	0+	0+	0+	0+	0+	0+	001	003	17
	18	0+	0+	0+	0+	0+	0+	0+	0+	0+	0+	0+	0+	0+	0+	0+	0+	0+	0+	0+	0+	001	18
	19	0+	0+	0+	0+	0+	0+	0+	0+	0+	0+	0+	0+	0+	0+	0+	0+	0+	0+	0+	0+	0+	19
	20	0+	0+	0+	0+	0+	0+	0+	0+	0+	0+	0+	0+	0+	0+	0+	0+	0+	0+	0+	0+	0+	20
	21	0+	0+	0+	0+	0+	0+	0+	0+	0+	0+	0+	0+	0+	0+	0+	0+	0+	0+	0+	0+	0+	21
22	0	802	641	407	324	256	160	098	060	036	028	022	013	007	004	002	002	0+	0+	0+	0+	0+	0
	1	178	288	373	375	360	306	241	180	130	109	090	061	041	026	017	013	004	001	0+	0+	0+	1
	2	019	062	163	207	241	279	281	258	222	201	181	141	107	078	055	046	017	005	001	0+	0+	2
	3	001	008	045	073	103	162	208	235	241	237	230	207	178	146	116	102	047	018	006	002	0+	3
	4	0+	001	009	018	031	067	110	152	186	199	208	216	211	196	174	161	096	047	019	006	002	4
	5	0+	0+	001	003	007	021	044	075	109	126	143	170	190	199	197	193	149	091	046	019	006	5
	6	0+	0+	0+	001	001	005	014	029	050	063	077	106	134	159	177	183	181	139	086	043	018	6
	7	0+	0+	0+	0+	0+	001	004	009	019	025	033	053	077	102	128	139	177	171	131	081	041	7
	8	0+	0+	0+	0+	0+	0+	001	002	006	008	012	022	036	054	075	087	142	173	164	125	076	8
	9	0+	0+	0+	0+	0+	0+	0+	0+	001	002	004	007	014	024	037	045	095	145	170	164	119	9

Table 8. *(continued)*

N	K	.01	.02	.04	.05	.06	.08	.10	.12	.14	.15	.16	.18	.20	.22	.24	.25	.30	.35	.40	.45	.50	K
	10	0+	0+	0+	0+	0+	0+	0+	0+	0+	001	001	002	005	009	015	020	053	101	148	169	154	10
	11	0+	0+	0+	0+	0+	0+	0+	0+	0+	0+	0+	001	001	003	005	007	025	060	107	151	168	11
	12	0+	0+	0+	0+	0+	0+	0+	0+	0+	0+	0+	0+	0+	001	002	002	010	029	066	113	154	12
	13	0+	0+	0+	0+	0+	0+	0+	0+	0+	0+	0+	0+	0+	0+	0+	001	003	012	034	071	119	13
	14	0+	0+	0+	0+	0+	0+	0+	0+	0+	0+	0+	0+	0+	0+	0+	0+	001	004	014	037	076	14
	15	0+	0+	0+	0+	0+	0+	0+	0+	0+	0+	0+	0+	0+	0+	0+	0+	0+	001	001	016	041	15
	16	0+	0+	0+	0+	0+	0+	0+	0+	0+	0+	0+	0+	0+	0+	0+	0+	0+	0+	001	006	018	16
	17	0+	0+	0+	0+	0+	0+	0+	0+	0+	0+	0+	0+	0+	0+	0+	0+	0+	0+	0+	002	007	17
	18	0+	0+	0+	0+	0+	0+	0+	0+	0+	0+	0+	0+	0+	0+	0+	0+	0+	0+	0+	0+	002	18
	19	0+	0+	0+	0+	0+	0+	0+	0+	0+	0+	0+	0+	0+	0+	0+	0+	0+	0+	0+	0+	0+	19
	20	0+	0+	0+	0+	0+	0+	0+	0+	0+	0+	0+	0+	0+	0+	0+	0+	0+	0+	0+	0+	0+	20
	21	0+	0+	0+	0+	0+	0+	0+	0+	0+	0+	0+	0+	0+	0+	0+	0+	0+	0+	0+	0+	0+	21
	22	0+	0+	0+	0+	0+	0+	0+	0+	0+	0+	0+	0+	0+	0+	0+	0+	0+	0+	0+	0+	0+	22
23	0	794	628	391	307	241	147	089	053	031	024	018	010	006	003	002	001	0+	0+	0+	0+	0+	0
	1	184	295	375	372	354	294	226	166	117	097	079	053	034	021	013	010	003	001	0+	0+	0+	1
	2	020	066	172	215	248	281	277	249	209	188	166	127	093	066	046	038	013	004	001	0+	0+	2
	3	001	009	050	079	111	171	215	237	238	232	222	195	163	131	101	088	038	014	004	001	0+	3
	4	0+	001	010	021	035	074	120	162	194	204	211	214	204	185	160	146	082	037	014	004	001	4
	5	0+	0+	002	004	009	025	051	084	120	137	153	179	194	198	192	185	133	076	035	013	004	5
	6	0+	0+	0+	001	002	006	017	034	059	073	087	118	145	168	182	185	171	122	070	032	012	6
	7	0+	0+	0+	0+	0+	001	005	011	023	031	040	063	088	115	139	150	178	160	113	064	029	7
	8	0+	0+	0+	0+	0+	0+	001	003	008	011	015	028	044	065	088	100	153	172	151	105	058	8
	9	0+	0+	0+	0+	0+	0+	0+	001	002	003	005	010	018	030	046	056	109	155	168	143	097	9

Table 8. *(continued)*

N	K	.01	.02	.04	.05	.06	.08	.10	.12	.14	.15	.16	.18	.20	.22	.24	.25	.30	.35	.40	.45	.50	K
	10	0+	0+	0+	0+	0+	0+	0+	0+	0+	001	001	003	006	012	020	026	065	117	157	164	136	10
	11	0+	0+	0+	0+	0+	0+	0+	0+	0+	0+	0+	001	002	004	008	010	033	074	123	159	161	11
	12	0+	0+	0+	0+	0+	0+	0+	0+	0+	0+	0+	0+	0+	001	002	003	014	040	082	130	161	12
	13	0+	0+	0+	0+	0+	0+	0+	0+	0+	0+	0+	0+	0+	0+	001	001	005	018	046	090	136	13
	14	0+	0+	0+	0+	0+	0+	0+	0+	0+	0+	0+	0+	0+	0+	0+	0+	002	007	022	053	097	14
	15	0+	0+	0+	0+	0+	0+	0+	0+	0+	0+	0+	0+	0+	0+	0+	0+	0+	002	009	026	058	15
	16	0+	0+	0+	0+	0+	0+	0+	0+	0+	0+	0+	0+	0+	0+	0+	0+	0+	001	003	011	029	16
	17	0+	0+	0+	0+	0+	0+	0+	0+	0+	0+	0+	0+	0+	0+	0+	0+	0+	0+	001	004	012	17
	18	0+	0+	0+	0+	0+	0+	0+	0+	0+	0+	0+	0+	0+	0+	0+	0+	0+	0+	0+	001	004	18
	19	0+	0+	0+	0+	0+	0+	0+	0+	0+	0+	0+	0+	0+	0+	0+	0+	0+	0+	0+	0+	001	19
	20	0+	0+	0+	0+	0+	0+	0+	0+	0+	0+	0+	0+	0+	0+	0+	0+	0+	0+	0+	0+	0+	20
	21	0+	0+	0+	0+	0+	0+	0+	0+	0+	0+	0+	0+	0+	0+	0+	0+	0+	0+	0+	0+	0+	21
	22	0+	0+	0+	0+	0+	0+	0+	0+	0+	0+	0+	0+	0+	0+	0+	0+	0+	0+	0+	0+	0+	22
	23	0+	0+	0+	0+	0+	0+	0+	0+	0+	0+	0+	0+	0+	0+	0+	0+	0+	0+	0+	0+	0+	23
24	0	786	616	375	292	227	135	080	047	027	020	015	009	005	003	001	001	0+	0+	0+	0+	0+	0
	1	190	302	375	369	347	282	213	152	105	086	070	045	028	017	010	008	002	0+	0+	0+	0+	1
	2	022	071	180	223	255	282	272	239	196	174	153	114	081	056	038	031	010	003	001	0+	0+	2
	3	002	011	055	086	119	180	221	239	234	225	213	183	149	117	088	075	031	010	003	001	0+	3
	4	0+	001	012	024	040	082	129	171	200	209	213	211	196	173	146	132	069	029	010	003	001	4
	5	0+	0+	002	005	010	029	057	093	130	147	162	185	196	195	184	176	118	062	027	009	003	5
	6	0+	0+	0+	001	002	008	020	040	067	082	098	129	155	174	184	185	160	106	056	024	008	6
	7	0+	0+	0+	0+	0+	002	006	014	028	037	048	073	100	126	149	159	176	147	096	050	021	7

Table 8. (*continued*)

N	K	.01	.02	.04	.05	.06	.08	.10	.12	.14	.15	.16	.18	.20	.22	.24	.25	.30	.35	.40	.45	.50	K
	8	0+	0+	0+	0+	0+	0+	001	004	010	014	019	034	053	076	100	112	160	168	136	087	044	8
	9	0+	0+	0+	0+	0+	0+	0+	001	003	004	007	013	024	038	056	067	122	161	161	126	078	9
	10	0+	0+	0+	0+	0+	0+	0+	0+	001	001	002	004	009	016	027	033	079	130	161	155	117	10
	11	0+	0+	0+	0+	0+	0+	0+	0+	0+	0+	0+	001	003	006	011	014	043	089	1137	161	149	11
	12	0+	0+	0+	0+	0+	0+	0+	0+	0+	0+	0+	0+	001	002	004	005	020	052	099	143	161	12
	13	0+	0+	0+	0+	0+	0+	0+	0+	0+	0+	0+	0+	0+	0+	001	002	008	026	061	108	149	13
	14	0+	0+	0+	0+	0+	0+	0+	0+	0+	0+	0+	0+	0+	0+	0+	0+	003	011	032	069	117	14
	15	0+	0+	0+	0+	0+	0+	0+	0+	0+	0+	0+	0+	0+	0+	0+	0+	001	004	014	038	078	15
	16	0+	0+	0+	0+	0+	0+	0+	0+	0+	0+	0+	0+	0+	0+	0+	0+	0+	001	005	017	044	16
	17	0+	0+	0+	0+	0+	0+	0+	0+	0+	0+	0+	0+	0+	0+	0+	0+	0+	0+	002	007	021	17
	18	0+	0+	0+	0+	0+	0+	0+	0+	0+	0+	0+	0+	0+	0+	0+	0+	0+	0+	0+	002	008	18
	19	0+	0+	0+	0+	0+	0+	0+	0+	0+	0+	0+	0+	0+	0+	0+	0+	0+	0+	0+	001	003	19
	20	0+	0+	0+	0+	0+	0+	0+	0+	0+	0+	0+	0+	0+	0+	0+	0+	0+	0+	0+	0+	001	20
	21	0+	0+	0+	0+	0+	0+	0+	0+	0+	0+	0+	0+	0+	0+	0+	0+	0+	0+	0+	0+	0+	21
	22	0+	0+	0+	0+	0+	0+	0+	0+	0+	0+	0+	0+	0+	0+	0+	0+	0+	0+	0+	0+	0+	22
	23	0+	0+	0+	0+	0+	0+	0+	0+	0+	0+	0+	0+	0+	0+	0+	0+	0+	0+	0+	0+	0+	23
	24	0+	0+	0+	0+	0+	0+	0+	0+	0+	0+	0+	0+	0+	0+	0+	0+	0+	0+	0+	0+	0+	24
25	0	778	603	360	277	213	124	072	041	023	017	013	007	004	002	001	001	0+	0+	0+	0+	0+	0
	1	196	308	375	365	340	270	199	140	094	076	061	038	024	014	008	006	001	0+	0+	0+	0+	1
	2	024	075	188	231	260	282	266	228	183	161	139	101	071	048	031	025	007	002	0+	0+	0+	2
	3	002	012	060	093	127	188	226	239	229	217	203	170	136	104	076	064	024	008	002	0+	0+	3
	4	0+	001	014	027	045	090	138	179	205	211	213	206	187	161	132	118	057	022	007	002	0+	4

Table 8. *(continued)*

N	K	.01	.02	.04	.05	.06	.08	.10	.12	.14	.15	.16	.18	.20	.22	.24	.25	.30	.35	.40	.45	.50	K
		p																					
	5	0+	0+	002	006	012	033	065	103	140	156	170	190	196	190	175	165	103	051	020	006	002	5
	6	0+	0+	0+	001	003	010	024	047	076	092	108	139	163	179	184	183	147	091	044	017	005	6
	7	0+	0+	0+	0+	0+	002	007	017	034	044	056	083	111	137	158	165	171	133	080	038	014	7
	8	0+	0+	0+	0+	0+	0+	002	005	012	017	024	041	062	087	112	124	165	161	120	070	032	8
	9	0+	0+	0+	0+	0+	0+	0+	001	004	006	009	017	029	046	067	078	134	163	151	108	061	9
	10	0+	0+	0+	0+	0+	0+	0+	0+	001	002	003	006	012	021	034	042	092	141	161	142	097	10
	11	0+	0+	0+	0+	0+	0+	0+	0+	0+	0+	001	002	004	008	015	019	054	103	147	158	133	11
	12	0+	0+	0+	0+	0+	0+	0+	0+	0+	0+	0+	0+	001	003	005	007	027	065	114	151	155	12
	13	0+	0+	0+	0+	0+	0+	0+	0+	0+	0+	0+	0+	0+	001	002	002	011	035	076	124	155	13
	14	0+	0+	0+	0+	0+	0+	0+	0+	0+	0+	0+	0+	0+	0+	0+	001	004	016	043	087	133	14
	15	0+	0+	0+	0+	0+	0+	0+	0+	0+	0+	0+	0+	0+	0+	0+	0+	001	006	021	052	097	15
	16	0+	0+	0+	0+	0+	0+	0+	0+	0+	0+	0+	0+	0+	0+	0+	0+	0+	002	009	027	061	16
	17	0+	0+	0+	0+	0+	0+	0+	0+	0+	0+	0+	0+	0+	0+	0+	0+	0+	001	003	012	032	17
	18	0+	0+	0+	0+	0+	0+	0+	0+	0+	0+	0+	0+	0+	0+	0+	0+	0+	0+	001	004	014	18
	19	0+	0+	0+	0+	0+	0+	0+	0+	0+	0+	0+	0+	0+	0+	0+	0+	0+	0+	0+	001	005	19
	20	0+	0+	0+	0+	0+	0+	0+	0+	0+	0+	0+	0+	0+	0+	0+	0+	0+	0+	0+	0+	002	20
	21	0+	0+	0+	0+	0+	0+	0+	0+	0+	0+	0+	0+	0+	0+	0+	0+	0+	0+	0+	0+	0+	21
	22	0+	0+	0+	0+	0+	0+	0+	0+	0+	0+	0+	0+	0+	0+	0+	0+	0+	0+	0+	0+	0+	22
	23	0+	0+	0+	0+	0+	0+	0+	0+	0+	0+	0+	0+	0+	0+	0+	0+	0+	0+	0+	0+	0+	23
	24	0+	0+	0+	0+	0+	0+	0+	0+	0+	0+	0+	0+	0+	0+	0+	0+	0+	0+	0+	0+	0+	24
	25	0+	0+	0+	0+	0+	0+	0+	0+	0+	0+	0+	0+	0+	0+	0+	0+	0+	0+	0+	0+	0+	25

Table 9. Binomial Distribution—Cumulative Terms[a]

N	K	.01	.02	.04	.05	.06	.08	.10	.12	.14	.15	.16	.18	.20	.22	.24	.25	.30	.35	.40	.45	.50	K
2	0	1	1	1	1	1	1	1	1	1	1	1	1	1	1	1	1	1	1	1	1	1	0
	1	020	040	078	098	116	154	190	226	260	278	294	328	360	391	422	438	510	578	640	698	750	1
	2	0+	0+	002	002	004	006	010	014	020	022	026	032	040	048	058	062	090	122	160	202	250	2
3	0	1	1	1	1	1	1	1	1	1	1	1	1	1	1	1	1	1	1	1	1	1	0
	1	030	059	115	143	169	221	271	319	364	386	407	449	488	525	561	578	657	725	784	834	875	1
	2	0+	001	005	007	010	018	028	040	053	061	069	086	104	124	145	156	216	282	352	425	500	2
	3	0+	0+	0+	0+	0+	001	001	002	003	003	004	006	008	011	014	016	027	043	064	091	125	3
4	0	1	1	1	1	1	1	1	1	1	1	1	1	1	1	1	1	1	1	1	1	1	0
	1	039	078	151	185	219	284	344	400	453	478	502	548	590	630	666	684	760	821	870	908	938	1
	2	001	002	009	014	020	034	052	073	097	110	123	151	181	212	245	262	348	437	525	609	688	2
	3	0+	0+	0+	0+	001	002	004	006	010	012	014	020	027	036	045	051	084	126	179	241	312	3
	4	0+	0+	0+	0+	0+	0+	0+	0+	0+	001	001	001	002	002	003	004	008	015	026	041	062	4
5	0	1	1	1	1	1	1	1	1	1	1	1	1	1	1	1	1	1	1	1	1	1	0
	1	049	096	185	226	266	341	410	472	530	556	582	629	672	711	746	763	832	884	922	950	969	1
	2	001	004	015	023	032	054	081	112	147	165	183	222	263	304	346	367	472	572	663	744	812	2
	3	0+	0+	001	001	002	005	009	014	022	027	032	044	058	074	093	104	1163	235	317	407	500	3
	4	0+	0+	0+	0+	0+	0+	0+	001	002	002	003	004	007	010	013	016	031	054	087	131	188	4
	5	0+	0+	0+	0+	0+	0+	0+	0+	0+	0+	0+	0+	0+	001	001	001	002	005	010	018	031	5

[a]From Croxton, Frederick E., and Cowden, Dudley J., *Practical Business Statistics,* Prentice-Hall, New York, 1948, p. 511. Reprinted by permission of the publisher.

Table 9. (*continued*)

											P											
N	*K*	.01	.02	.04	.05	.06	.08	.10	.12	.14	.15	.16	.18	.20	.22	.24	.25	.30	.35	.40	.45	.50	*K*
6	0	1	1	1	1	1	1	1	1	1	1	1	1	1	1	1	1	1	1	1	1	1	0
	1	059	114	217	265	310	394	469	536	595	623	649	696	738	775	807	822	882	925	953	972	984	1
	2	001	006	022	033	046	077	114	156	200	224	247	296	345	394	442	466	580	681	767	836	891	2
	3	0+	0+	001	002	004	009	016	026	039	047	056	076	099	125	154	169	256	353	456	558	656	3
	4	0+	0+	0+	0+	0+	001	001	003	005	006	007	012	017	024	033	038	070	117	179	255	344	4
	5	0+	0+	0+	0+	0+	0+	0+	0+	0+	0+	001	001	002	003	004	005	011	022	041	069	109	5
	6	0+	0+	0+	0+	0+	0+	0+	0+	0+	0+	0+	0+	0+	0+	0+	0+	001	002	004	008	016	6
7	0	1	1	1	1	1	1	1	1	1	1	1	1	1	1	1	1	1	1	1	1	1	0
	1	068	132	249	302	352	442	522	591	652	679	705	751	790	824	854	867	918	951	972	985	992	1
	2	002	008	029	044	062	103	150	201	256	283	311	368	423	478	530	555	671	766	841	898	938	2
	3	0+	0+	002	004	006	014	026	042	062	074	087	115	148	184	223	244	353	468	580	684	773	3
	4	0+	0+	0+	0+	0+	001	003	005	009	012	015	023	033	046	062	071	126	200	290	392	500	4
	5	0+	0+	0+	0+	0+	0+	0+	0+	001	001	002	003	005	007	011	013	029	056	096	153	227	5
	6	0+	0+	0+	0+	0+	0+	0+	0+	0+	0+	0+	0+	0+	001	001	001	004	009	019	036	062	6
	7	0+	0+	0+	0+	0+	0+	0+	0+	0+	0+	0+	0+	0+	0+	0+	0+	0+	001	002	004	008	7
8	0	1	1	1	1	1	1	1	1	1	1	1	1	1	1	1	1	1	1	1	1	1	0
	1	077	149	279	337	390	487	570	640	701	728	752	796	832	863	889	900	942	968	983	992	996	1
	2	003	010	038	057	079	130	187	248	311	343	374	437	497	554	608	633	745	831	894	937	965	2
	3	0+	0+	003	006	010	021	038	061	089	105	123	161	203	249	297	321	448	572	685	780	855	3
	4	0+	0+	0+	0+	001	002	005	010	017	021	027	040	056	076	100	114	194	294	406	523	637	4

Table 9. (*continued*)

		P																				
N	K	.01	.02	.04	.05	.06	.08	.10	.12	.14	.15	.16	.18	.20	.22	.24	.25	.30	.35	.40	.45	.50	K
	5	0+	0+	0+	0+	0+	0+	0+	001	002	003	004	007	010	016	023	027	058	106	174	260	363	5
	6	0+	0+	0+	0+	0+	0+	0+	0+	0+	0+	0+	001	001	002	003	004	011	025	050	088	145	6
	7	0+	0+	0+	0+	0+	0+	0+	0+	0+	0+	0+	0+	0+	0+	0+	0+	001	004	009	018	035	7
	8	0+	0+	0+	0+	0+	0+	0+	0+	0+	0+	0+	0+	0+	0+	0+	0+	0+	0+	001	002	004	8
9	0	1	1	1	1	1	1	1	1	1	1	1	1	1	1	1	1	1	1	1	1	1	0
	1	086	166	307	370	427	528	613	684	743	768	792	832	866	893	915	925	960	979	990	995	998	1
	2	003	013	048	071	098	158	225	295	366	401	435	501	564	622	675	700	804	879	929	961	980	2
	3	0+	001	004	008	014	030	053	083	120	141	163	210	262	316	371	399	537	663	768	850	910	3
	4	0+	0+	0+	001	001	004	008	016	027	034	042	062	086	114	148	166	270	391	517	639	746	4
	5	0+	0+	0+	0+	0+	0+	001	002	004	006	007	012	020	029	042	049	099	172	267	379	500	5
	6	0+	0+	0+	0+	0+	0+	0+	0+	0+	001	001	002	003	005	008	010	025	054	099	166	254	6
	7	0+	0+	0+	0+	0+	0+	0+	0+	0+	0+	0+	0+	0+	001	001	001	004	011	025	050	090	7
	8	0+	0+	0+	0+	0+	0+	0+	0+	0+	0+	0+	0+	0+	0+	0+	0+	0+	001	004	009	020	8
	9	0+	0+	0+	0+	0+	0+	0+	0+	0+	0+	0+	0+	0+	0+	0+	0+	0+	0+	0+	001	002	9
10	0	1	1	1	1	1	1	1	1	1	1	1	1	1	1	1	1	1	1	1	1	1	0
	1	096	183	335	401	461	566	651	721	779	803	825	863	893	917	936	944	972	987	994	997	999	1
	2	004	016	058	086	118	188	264	342	418	456	492	561	624	682	733	756	851	914	954	977	989	2
	3	0+	001	006	012	019	040	070	109	155	180	206	263	322	383	444	474	617	738	833	900	945	3
	4	0+	0+	0+	001	002	006	013	024	040	050	061	088	121	159	201	224	350	486	618	734	828	4
	5	0+	0+	0+	0+	0+	001	002	004	007	010	013	021	033	048	067	078	150	249	367	496	623	5
	6	0+	0+	0+	0+	0+	0+	0+	0+	001	001	002	004	006	010	016	020	047	095	166	262	377	6
	7	0+	0+	0+	0+	0+	0+	0+	0+	0+	0+	0+	0+	001	002	003	004	011	026	055	102	172	7

Table 9. *(continued)*

N	K	.01	.02	.04	.05	.06	.08	.10	.12	.14	.15	.16	.18	.20	.22	.24	.25	.30	.35	.40	.45	.50	K
											P												
	8	0+	0+	0+	0+	0+	0+	0+	0+	0+	0+	0+	0+	0+	0+	0+	0+	002	005	012	027	055	8
	9	0+	0+	0+	0+	0+	0+	0+	0+	0+	0+	0+	0+	0+	0+	0+	0+	0+	001	002	005	011	9
	10	0+	0+	0+	0+	0+	0+	0+	0+	0+	0+	0+	0+	0+	0+	0+	0+	0+	0+	0+	0+	001	10
11	0	1	1	1	1	1	1	1	1	1	1	1	1	1	1	1	1	1	1	1	1	1	
	1	105	199	362	431	494	600	686	755	810	833	853	887	914	935	951	958	980	991	996	999	1–	1
	2	005	020	069	102	138	218	303	387	469	508	545	615	678	733	781	803	887	939	970	986	994	2
	3	0+	001	008	015	025	052	090	137	191	221	252	316	383	449	513	545	687	800	881	935	967	3
	4	0+	0+	001	002	003	009	019	034	056	069	085	120	161	208	260	287	430	574	704	809	887	4
	5	0+	0+	0+	0+	0+	001	003	006	012	016	021	033	050	072	099	115	210	332	467	603	726	5
	6	0+	0+	0+	0+	0+	0+	0+	001	002	003	004	007	012	019	028	034	078	149	247	367	500	6
	7	0+	0+	0+	0+	0+	0+	0+	0+	0+	0+	0+	001	002	004	006	008	022	050	099	174	274	7
	8	0+	0+	0+	0+	0+	0+	0+	0+	0+	0+	0+	0+	0+	0+	001	002	004	012	029	061	113	8
	9	0+	0+	0+	0+	0+	0+	0+	0+	0+	0+	0+	0+	0+	0+	0+	0+	001	002	006	015	033	9
	10	0+	0+	0+	0+	0+	0+	0+	0+	0+	0+	0+	0+	0+	0+	0+	0+	0+	0+	001	002	006	10
	11	0+	0+	0+	0+	0+	0+	0+	0+	0+	0+	0+	0+	0+	0+	0+	0+	0+	0+	0+	0+	0+	11
12	0	1	1	1	1	1	1	1	1	1	1	1	1	1	1	1	1	1	1	1	1	1	0
	1	114	215	387	460	524	632	718	784	836	858	877	908	931	949	963	968	986	994	998	999	1–	1
	2	006	023	081	118	160	249	341	432	517	557	595	664	725	778	822	842	915	958	980	992	997	2
	3	0+	002	011	020	032	065	111	167	230	264	299	370	442	511	578	609	747	849	917	958	981	3
	4	0+	0+	001	002	004	012	026	046	075	092	111	155	205	261	320	351	507	653	775	866	927	4
	5	0+	0+	0+	0+	0+	002	004	009	018	024	031	049	073	102	138	158	276	417	562	696	806	5

Table 9. *(continued)*

N	K	.01	.02	.04	.05	.06	.08	.10	.12	.14	.15	.16	.18	.20	.22	.24	.25	.30	.35	.40	.45	.50	K
	6	0+	0+	0+	0+	0+	0+	001	001	003	005	006	012	019	030	045	054	118	213	335	473	613	6
	7	0+	0+	0+	0+	0+	0+	0+	0+	0+	001	001	002	004	007	011	014	039	085	158	261	387	7
	8	0+	0+	0+	0+	0+	0+	0+	0+	0+	0+	0+	0+	001	001	002	003	009	026	057	112	194	8
	9	0+	0+	0+	0+	0+	0+	0+	0+	0+	0+	0+	0+	0+	0+	0+	0+	002	006	015	036	073	9
	10	0+	0+	0+	0+	0+	0+	0+	0+	0+	0+	0+	0+	0+	0+	0+	0+	0+	001	003	008	019	10
	11	0+	0+	0+	0+	0+	0+	0+	0+	0+	0+	0+	0+	0+	0+	0+	0+	0+	0+	0+	001	003	11
	12	0+	0+	0+	0+	0+	0+	0+	0+	0+	0+	0+	0+	0+	0+	0+	0+	0+	0+	0+	0+	0+	12
13	0	1	1	1	1	1	1	1	1	1	1	1	1	1	1	1	1	1	1	1	1	1	0
	1	122	231	412	487	553	662	746	810	859	879	896	924	945	960	972	976	990	996	999	1–	1–	1
	2	007	027	093	135	181	279	379	474	561	602	640	708	766	815	856	873	936	970	987	995	998	2
	3	0+	002	014	025	039	080	134	198	270	308	346	423	498	570	636	667	798	887	942	973	989	3
	4	0+	0+	001	003	006	016	034	061	097	118	141	194	253	316	382	416	579	722	831	907	954	4
	5	0+	0+	0+	0+	001	002	006	014	026	034	044	068	099	137	182	206	346	499	647	772	867	5
	6	0+	0+	0+	0+	0+	0+	001	002	005	008	010	018	030	046	068	080	165	284	426	573	709	6
	7	0+	0+	0+	0+	0+	0+	0+	0+	001	001	002	004	007	012	019	024	062	129	229	356	500	7
	8	0+	0+	0+	0+	0+	0+	0+	0+	0+	0+	0+	001	001	002	004	006	018	046	098	179	291	8
	9	0+	0+	0+	0+	0+	0+	0+	0+	0+	0+	0+	0+	0+	0+	001	001	004	013	032	070	133	9
	10	0+	0+	0+	0+	0+	0+	0+	0+	0+	0+	0+	0+	0+	0+	0+	0+	001	003	008	020	046	10
	11	0+	0+	0+	0+	0+	0+	0+	0+	0+	0+	0+	0+	0+	0+	0+	0+	0+	0+	001	004	011	11
	12	0+	0+	0+	0+	0+	0+	0+	0+	0+	0+	0+	0+	0+	0+	0+	0+	0+	0+	0+	001	002	12
	13	0+	0+	0+	0+	0+	0+	0+	0+	0+	0+	0+	0+	0+	0+	0+	0+	0+	0+	0+	0+	0+	13

Table 9. (*continued*)

		P																				
N	K	.01	.02	.04	.05	.06	.08	.10	.12	.14	.15	.16	.18	.20	.22	.24	.25	.30	.35	.40	.45	.50	K
14	0	1	1	1	1	1	1	1	1	1	1	1	1	1	1	1	1	1	1	1	1	1	0
	1	131	246	435	512	579	689	771	833	879	897	913	938	956	969	979	982	993	998	999	1–	1–	1
	2	008	031	106	153	204	310	415	514	603	643	681	747	802	847	884	899	953	979	992	997	999	2
	3	0+	002	017	030	048	096	158	232	311	352	393	474	552	624	689	719	839	916	960	981	994	3
	4	0+	0+	002	004	008	021	044	077	121	147	174	235	302	372	443	479	645	779	876	937	971	4
	5	0+	0+	0+	0+	001	004	009	020	036	047	059	091	130	176	230	258	416	577	721	833	910	5
	6	0+	0+	0+	0+	0+	0+	001	004	008	012	016	027	044	066	095	112	219	359	514	663	788	6
	7	0+	0+	0+	0+	0+	0+	0+	001	001	002	003	006	012	020	031	038	093	184	308	454	605	7
	8	0+	0+	0+	0+	0+	0+	0+	0+	0+	0+	001	001	002	005	008	010	031	075	150	259	395	8
	9	0+	0+	0+	0+	0+	0+	0+	0+	0+	0+	0+	0+	0+	001	002	002	008	024	058	119	212	9
	10	0+	0+	0+	0+	0+	0+	0+	0+	0+	0+	0+	0+	0+	0+	0+	0+	008	006	018	043	090	10
	11	0+	0+	0+	0+	0+	0+	0+	0+	0+	0+	0+	0+	0+	0+	0+	0+	0+	001	004	011	029	11
	12	0+	0+	0+	0+	0+	0+	0+	0+	0+	0+	0+	0+	0+	0+	0+	0+	0+	0+	001	002	006	12
	13	0+	0+	0+	0+	0+	0+	0+	0+	0+	0+	0+	0+	0+	0+	0+	0+	0+	0+	0+	0+	001	13
	14	0+	0+	0+	0+	0+	0+	0+	0+	0+	0+	0+	0+	0+	0+	0+	0+	0+	0+	0+	0+	0+	14
15	0	1	1	1	1	1	1	1	1	1	1	1	1	1	1	1	1	1	1	1	1	1	0
	1	140	261	458	537	605	714	794	853	896	913	927	949	965	976	984	987	995	998	1–	1–	1–	1
	2	010	035	119	171	226	340	451	552	642	681	718	781	833	874	906	920	965	986	995	998	1–	2
	3	0+	003	020	036	057	113	184	265	352	396	439	523	602	673	736	764	873	938	973	989	996	3
	4	0+	0+	002	005	010	027	056	096	148	177	209	278	352	427	502	539	703	827	909	958	982	4
	5	0+	0+	0+	001	001	005	013	026	048	062	078	117	164	219	281	314	485	648	783	880	941	5
	6	0+	0+	0+	0+	0+	001	002	006	012	017	023	039	061	090	127	148	278	436	597	739	849	6

Table 9. *(continued)*

N	K	.01	.02	.04	.05	.06	.08	.10	.12	.14	.15	.16	.18	.20	.22	.24	.25	.30	.35	.40	.45	.50	K
	7	0+	0+	0+	0+	0+	0+	0+	001	002	004	005	010	018	030	046	057	131	245	390	548	696	7
	8	0+	0+	0+	0+	0+	0+	0+	0+	0+	001	001	002	004	008	013	017	050	113	213	346	500	8
	9	0+	0+	0+	0+	0+	0+	0+	0+	0+	0+	0+	0+	001	002	003	004	015	042	095	182	304	9
	10	0+	0+	0+	0+	0+	0+	0+	0+	0+	0+	0+	0+	0+	0+	001	001	004	012	034	077	151	10
	11	0+	0+	0+	0+	0+	0+	0+	0+	0+	0+	0+	0+	0+	0+	0+	0+	001	003	009	025	059	11
	12	0+	0+	0+	0+	0+	0+	0+	0+	0+	0+	0+	0+	0+	0+	0+	0+	0+	0+	002	006	018	12
	13	0+	0+	0+	0+	0+	0+	0+	0+	0+	0+	0+	0+	0+	0+	0+	0+	0+	0+	0+	001	004	13
	14	0+	0+	0+	0+	0+	0+	0+	0+	0+	0+	0+	0+	0+	0+	0+	0+	0+	0+	0+	0+	0+	14
	15	0+	0+	0+	0+	0+	0+	0+	0+	0+	0+	0+	0+	0+	0+	0+	0+	0+	0+	0+	0+	0+	15
16	0	1	1	1	1	1	1	1	1	1	1	1	1	1	1	1	1	1	1	1	1	1	0
	1	149	276	480	560	628	737	815	871	910	926	939	958	972	981	988	990	997	999	1–	1–	1–	1
	2	011	040	133	189	249	370	485	588	677	716	751	811	859	897	925	937	974	990	997	999	1–	2
	3	001	004	024	043	067	131	211	300	393	439	484	570	648	717	777	803	901	955	982	993	998	3
	4	0+	0+	003	007	013	034	068	116	176	210	246	322	402	481	558	595	754	866	935	972	989	4
	5	0+	0+	0+	001	002	007	017	035	062	079	099	146	202	265	334	370	550	711	833	915	962	5
	6	0+	0+	0+	0+	0+	001	003	008	017	024	032	053	082	119	164	190	340	510	671	802	895	6
	7	0+	0+	0+	0+	0+	0+	001	002	004	006	008	015	027	043	066	080	175	312	473	634	773	7
	8	0+	0+	0+	0+	0+	0+	0+	0+	001	001	002	004	007	013	021	027	074	159	284	437	598	8
	9	0+	0+	0+	0+	0+	0+	0+	0+	0+	0+	0+	001	001	003	006	007	026	067	142	256	402	9
	10	0+	0+	0+	0+	0+	0+	0+	0+	0+	0+	0+	0+	0+	001	001	002	007	023	058	124	227	10
	11	0+	0+	0+	0+	0+	0+	0+	0+	0+	0+	0+	0+	0+	0+	0+	0+	002	006	019	049	105	11

Table 9. (*continued*)

		P																				
N	K	.01	.02	.04	.05	.06	.08	.10	.12	.14	.15	.16	.18	.20	.22	.24	.25	.30	.35	.40	.45	.50	K
	12	0+	0+	0+	0+	0+	0+	0+	0+	0+	0+	0+	0+	0+	0+	0+	0+	0+	001	005	015	038	12
	13	0+	0+	0+	0+	0+	0+	0+	0+	0+	0+	0+	0+	0+	0+	0+	0+	0+	0+	001	003	011	13
	14	0+	0+	0+	0+	0+	0+	0+	0+	0+	0+	0+	0+	0+	0+	0+	0+	0+	0+	0+	001	002	14
	15	0+	0+	0+	0+	0+	0+	0+	0+	0+	0+	0+	0+	0+	0+	0+	0+	0+	0+	0+	0+	0+	15
	16	0+	0+	0+	0+	0+	0+	0+	0+	0+	0+	0+	0+	0+	0+	0+	0+	0+	0+	0+	0+	0+	16
17	0	1	1	1	1	1	1	1	1	1	1	1	1	1	1	1	1	1	1	1	1	1	0
	1	157	291	500	582	651	758	833	886	923	937	948	966	977	985	991	992	998	999	1–	1–	1–	1
	2	012	045	147	208	272	399	518	622	710	748	781	838	882	915	940	950	981	993	998	999	1–	2
	3	001	004	029	050	078	150	238	335	432	480	527	613	690	758	812	836	923	967	988	996	999	3
	4	0+	0+	004	009	016	042	083	138	207	244	284	367	451	533	611	647	798	897	954	982	994	4
	5	0+	0+	0+	001	003	009	022	045	078	099	122	178	242	313	388	426	611	765	874	940	975	5
	6	0+	0+	0+	0+	0+	001	005	011	023	032	042	069	106	151	205	235	403	580	736	853	928	6
	7	0+	0+	0+	0+	0+	0+	001	002	006	008	012	022	038	060	089	107	225	381	552	710	834	7
	8	0+	0+	0+	0+	0+	0+	0+	0+	001	002	003	006	011	019	032	040	105	213	359	526	685	8
	9	0+	0+	0+	0+	0+	0+	0+	0+	0+	0+	0+	001	003	005	009	012	040	099	199	337	500	9
	10	0+	0+	0+	0+	0+	0+	0+	0+	0+	0+	0+	0+	0+	001	002	003	013	038	092	183	315	10
	11	0+	0+	0+	0+	0+	0+	0+	0+	0+	0+	0+	0+	0+	0+	0+	001	003	012	035	083	166	11
	12	0+	0+	0+	0+	0+	0+	0+	0+	0+	0+	0+	0+	0+	0+	0+	0+	001	003	011	030	072	12
	13	0+	0+	0+	0+	0+	0+	0+	0+	0+	0+	0+	0+	0+	0+	0+	0+	0+	001	003	009	025	13
	14	0+	0+	0+	0+	0+	0+	0+	0+	0+	0+	0+	0+	0+	0+	0+	0+	0+	0+	0+	002	006	14
	15	0+	0+	0+	0+	0+	0+	0+	0+	0+	0+	0+	0+	0+	0+	0+	0+	0+	0+	0+	0+	001	15

Table 9. *(continued)*

		P																				
N	K	.01	.02	.04	.05	.06	.08	.10	.12	.14	.15	.16	.18	.20	.22	.24	.25	.30	.35	.40	.45	.50	K
	16	0+	0+	0+	0+	0+	0+	0+	0+	0+	0+	0+	0+	0+	0+	0+	0+	0+	0+	0+	0+	0+	16
	17	0+	0+	0+	0+	0+	0+	0+	0+	0+	0+	0+	0+	0+	0+	0+	0+	0+	0+	0+	0+	0+	17
18	0	1	1	1	1	1	1	1	1	1	1	1	1	1	1	1	1	1	1	1	1	1	0
	1	165	305	520	603	672	777	850	900	934	946	957	972	982	989	993	994	998	1–	1–	1–	1–	1
	2	014	050	161	226	294	428	550	654	740	776	808	861	901	931	952	961	986	995	999	1–	1–	2
	3	001	005	033	058	090	170	266	369	471	520	567	654	729	792	843	865	940	976	992	997	999	3
	4	0+	0+	005	011	020	051	098	162	238	280	323	411	499	582	659	694	835	922	967	988	996	4
	5	0+	0+	001	002	003	012	028	056	096	121	148	212	284	361	441	481	667	811	906	959	985	5
	6	0+	0+	0+	0+	0+	002	006	015	031	042	055	089	133	187	249	283	466	645	791	892	952	6
	7	0+	0+	0+	0+	0+	0+	001	003	008	012	017	031	051	080	117	139	278	451	626	774	881	7
	8	0+	0+	0+	0+	0+	0+	0+	001	002	003	004	009	016	028	046	057	141	272	437	609	760	8
	9	0+	0+	0+	0+	0+	0+	0+	0+	0+	001	001	002	004	008	015	019	060	139	263	422	593	9
	10	0+	0+	0+	0+	0+	0+	0+	0+	0+	0+	0+	0+	001	002	004	005	021	060	135	253	407	10
	11	0+	0+	0+	0+	0+	0+	0+	0+	0+	0+	0+	0+	0+	0+	001	001	006	021	058	128	240	11
	12	0+	0+	0+	0+	0+	0+	0+	0+	0+	0+	0+	0+	0+	0+	0+	0+	001	006	020	054	119	12
	13	0+	0+	0+	0+	0+	0+	0+	0+	0+	0+	0+	0+	0+	0+	0+	0+	0+	001	006	018	048	13
	14	0+	0+	0+	0+	0+	0+	0+	0+	0+	0+	0+	0+	0+	0+	0+	0+	0+	0+	001	005	015	14
	15	0+	0+	0+	0+	0+	0+	0+	0+	0+	0+	0+	0+	0+	0+	0+	0+	0+	0+	0+	001	004	15
	16	0+	0+	0+	0+	0+	0+	0+	0+	0+	0+	0+	0+	0+	0+	0+	0+	0+	0+	0+	0+	001	16
	17	0+	0+	0+	0+	0+	0+	0+	0+	0+	0+	0+	0+	0+	0+	0+	0+	0+	0+	0+	0+	0+	17
	18	0+	0+	0+	0+	0+	0+	0+	0+	0+	0+	0+	0+	0+	0+	0+	0+	0+	0+	0+	0+	0+	18

Table 9. (*continued*) Binom

		P																				
N	*K*	.01	.02	.04	.05	.06	.08	.10	.12	.14	.15	.16	.18	.20	.22	.24	.25	.30	.35	.40	.45	.50	*K*
19	0	1	1	1	1	1	1	1	1	1	1	1	1	1	1	1	1	1	1	1	1	1	0
	1	174	319	540	623	691	795	865	912	943	954	964	977	986	991	995	996	999	1−	1−	1−	1−	1
	2	015	055	175	245	317	456	580	683	767	802	832	881	917	943	962	969	990	997	999	1−	1−	2
	3	001	006	038	067	102	191	295	403	509	559	606	691	763	822	869	889	954	983	995	998	1−	3
	4	0+	0+	006	013	024	060	115	187	271	316	362	455	545	628	703	737	867	941	977	992	998	4
	5	0+	0+	001	002	004	015	035	069	116	144	176	248	327	410	494	535	718	850	930	972	990	5
	6	0+	0+	0+	0+	001	003	009	020	040	054	070	111	163	225	295	332	526	703	837	922	968	6
	7	0+	0+	0+	0+	0+	0+	002	005	011	016	023	041	068	103	149	175	334	519	692	827	916	7
	8	0+	0+	0+	0+	0+	0+	0+	001	003	004	006	013	023	040	063	077	182	334	512	683	820	8
	9	0+	0+	0+	0+	0+	0+	0+	0+	001	001	001	003	007	013	022	029	084	185	333	506	676	9
	10	0+	0+	0+	0+	0+	0+	0+	0+	0+	0+	0+	001	002	003	007	009	033	087	186	329	500	10
	11	0+	0+	0+	0+	0+	0+	0+	0+	0+	0+	0+	0+	0+	001	002	002	011	035	088	184	324	11
	12	0+	0+	0+	0+	0+	0+	0+	0+	0+	0+	0+	0+	0+	0+	0+	0+	003	011	035	087	180	12
	13	0+	0+	0+	0+	0+	0+	0+	0+	0+	0+	0+	0+	0+	0+	0+	0+	001	003	012	034	084	13
	14	0+	0+	0+	0+	0+	0+	0+	0+	0+	0+	0+	0+	0+	0+	0+	0+	0+	001	003	011	032	14
	15	0+	0+	0+	0+	0+	0+	0+	0+	0+	0+	0+	0+	0+	0+	0+	0+	0+	0+	001	003	010	15
	16	0+	0+	0+	0+	0+	0+	0+	0+	0+	0+	0+	0+	0+	0+	0+	0+	0+	0+	0+	001	002	16
	17	0+	0+	0+	0+	0+	0+	0+	0+	0+	0+	0+	0+	0+	0+	0+	0+	0+	0+	0+	0+	0+	17
	18	0+	0+	0+	0+	0+	0+	0+	0+	0+	0+	0+	0+	0+	0+	0+	0+	0+	0+	0+	0+	0+	18
	19	0+	0+	0+	0+	0+	0+	0+	0+	0+	0+	0+	0+	0+	0+	0+	0+	0+	0+	0+	0+	0+	19
20	0	1	1	1	1	1	1	1	1	1	1	1	1	1	1	1	1	1	1	1	1	1	0
	1	182	332	558	642	710	811	878	922	951	961	969	981	988	993	996	997	999	1−	1−	1−	1−	1

Table 9. *(continued)*

		P																					
N	K	.01	.02	.04	.05	.06	.08	.10	.12	.14	.15	.16	.18	.20	.22	.24	.25	.30	.35	.40	.45	.50	K
	2	017	060	190	264	340	483	608	711	792	824	853	898	931	954	970	976	992	998	999	1–	1–	2
	3	001	007	044	075	115	212	323	437	545	595	642	725	794	849	891	909	965	988	996	999	1–	3
	4	0+	001	007	016	029	071	133	213	304	352	401	497	589	671	743	775	893	956	984	995	999	4
	5	0+	0+	001	003	006	018	043	083	137	170	206	285	370	458	544	585	762	882	949	981	994	5
	6	0+	0+	0+	0+	001	004	011	026	051	067	087	136	196	266	343	383	584	755	874	945	979	6
	7	0+	0+	0+	0+	0+	001	002	007	015	022	030	054	087	130	184	214	392	583	750	870	942	7
	8	0+	0+	0+	0+	0+	0+	0+	001	004	006	009	018	032	054	083	102	228	399	584	748	868	8
	9	0+	0+	0+	0+	0+	0+	0+	0+	001	001	002	005	010	019	032	041	113	238	404	586	748	9
	10	0+	0+	0+	0+	0+	0+	0+	0+	0+	0+	0+	001	003	005	010	014	048	122	245	409	588	10
	11	0+	0+	0+	0+	0+	0+	0+	0+	0+	0+	0+	0+	001	001	003	004	017	053	128	249	412	11
	12	0+	0+	0+	0+	0+	0+	0+	0+	0+	0+	0+	0+	0+	0+	001	001	005	020	057	131	252	12
	13	0+	0+	0+	0+	0+	0+	0+	0+	0+	0+	0+	0+	0+	0+	0+	0+	001	006	021	058	132	13
	14	0+	0+	0+	0+	0+	0+	0+	0+	0+	0+	0+	0+	0+	0+	0+	0+	0+	002	006	021	058	14
	15	0+	0+	0+	0+	0+	0+	0+	0+	0+	0+	0+	0+	0+	0+	0+	0+	0+	0+	002	006	021	15
	16	0+	0+	0+	0+	0+	0+	0+	0+	0+	0+	0+	0+	0+	0+	0+	0+	0+	0+	0+	002	006	16
	17	0+	0+	0+	0+	0+	0+	0+	0+	0+	0+	0+	0+	0+	0+	0+	0+	0+	0+	0+	0+	001	17
	18	0+	0+	0+	0+	0+	0+	0+	0+	0+	0+	0+	0+	0+	0+	0+	0+	0+	0+	0+	0+	0+	18
	19	0+	0+	0+	0+	0+	0+	0+	0+	0+	0+	0+	0+	0+	0+	0+	0+	0+	0+	0+	0+	0+	19
	20	0+	0+	0+	0+	0+	0+	0+	0+	0+	0+	0+	0+	0+	0+	0+	0+	0+	0+	0+	0+	0+	20
21	0	1	1	1	1	1	1	1	1	1	1	1	1	1	1	1	1	1	1	1	1	1	0
	1	190	346	576	659	727	826	891	932	958	967	974	985	991	995	997	998	999	1–	1–	1–	1–	1

Table 9. *(continued)*

N	K	.01	.02	.04	.05	.06	.08	.10	.12	.14	.15	.16	.18	.20	.22	.24	.25	.30	.35	.40	.45	.50	K
	2	019	065	204	283	362	509	635	736	814	845	872	913	943	962	976	981	994	999	1–	1–	1–	2
	3	001	008	050	085	128	234	352	470	580	630	676	756	831	872	910	925	973	999	998	999	1–	3
	4	0+	001	009	019	034	082	152	240	338	389	440	538	630	710	779	808	914	967	989	997	999	4
	5	0+	0+	001	003	007	023	052	098	161	197	237	323	414	505	592	633	802	908	963	987	996	5
	6	0+	0+	0+	0+	001	005	014	033	063	083	106	162	231	308	391	433	637	799	904	961	987	6
	7	0+	0+	0+	0+	0+	001	003	009	020	029	039	068	109	160	222	256	449	643	800	904	961	7
	8	0+	0+	0+	0+	0+	0+	001	002	005	008	012	024	043	070	108	130	277	464	650	803	905	8
	9	0+	0+	0+	0+	0+	0+	0+	0+	001	002	003	007	014	026	044	056	148	294	476	659	808	9
	10	0+	0+	0+	0+	0+	0+	0+	0+	0+	0+	001	002	004	008	016	021	068	162	309	488	669	10
	11	0+	0+	0+	0+	0+	0+	0+	0+	0+	0+	0+	0+	001	002	005	006	026	077	174	321	500	11
	12	0+	0+	0+	0+	0+	0+	0+	0+	0+	0+	0+	0+	0+	001	001	002	009	031	085	184	332	12
	13	0+	0+	0+	0+	0+	0+	0+	0+	0+	0+	0+	0+	0+	0+	0+	0+	002	011	035	091	192	13
	14	0+	0+	0+	0+	0+	0+	0+	0+	0+	0+	0+	0+	0+	0+	0+	0+	001	003	012	038	095	14
	15	0+	0+	0+	0+	0+	0+	0+	0+	0+	0+	0+	0+	0+	0+	0+	0+	0+	001	004	013	039	15
	16	0+	0+	0+	0+	0+	0+	0+	0+	0+	0+	0+	0+	0+	0+	0+	0+	0+	0+	001	004	013	16
	17	0+	0+	0+	0+	0+	0+	0+	0+	0+	0+	0+	0+	0+	0+	0+	0+	0+	0+	0+	001	004	17
	18	0+	0+	0+	0+	0+	0+	0+	0+	0+	0+	0+	0+	0+	0+	0+	0+	0+	0+	0+	0+	001	18
	19	0+	0+	0+	0+	0+	0+	0+	0+	0+	0+	0+	0+	0+	0+	0+	0+	0+	0+	0+	0+	0+	19
	20	0+	0+	0+	0+	0+	0+	0+	0+	0+	0+	0+	0+	0+	0+	0+	0+	0+	0+	0+	0+	0+	20
	21	0+	0+	0+	0+	0+	0+	0+	0+	0+	0+	0+	0+	0+	0+	0+	0+	0+	0+	0+	0+	0+	21

Table 9. *(continued)*

N	K	.01	.02	.04	.05	.06	.08	.10	.12	.14	.15	.16	.18	.20	.22	.24	.25	.30	.35	.40	.45	.50	K
22	0	1	1	1	1	1	1	1	1	1	1	1	1	1	1	1	1	1	1	1	1	1	0
	1	198	359	593	676	744	840	902	940	964	972	978	987	993	996	998	998	1–	1–	11–	1–	1–	1
	2	020	071	219	302	384	535	661	760	834	863	888	926	952	970	981	985	996	999	1–	1–	1–	2
	3	001	009	056	095	142	256	380	502	612	662	707	785	846	892	926	939	979	994	998	1–	1–	3
	4	0+	001	011	022	040	094	172	267	372	425	477	578	668	746	810	838	932	975	992	998	1–	4
	5	0+	0+	002	004	009	027	062	115	186	226	270	363	457	550	637	677	835	928	973	992	998	5
	6	0+	0+	0+	001	002	006	018	041	077	100	227	191	267	351	439	483	687	837	928	973	992	6
	7	0+	0+	0+	0+	0+	001	004	012	026	037	050	085	133	193	263	301	506	698	842	929	974	7
	8	0+	0+	0+	0+	0+	0+	001	003	008	011	017	032	056	090	135	162	329	526	710	848	933	8
	9	0+	0+	0+	0+	0+	0+	0+	001	002	003	005	010	020	036	060	075	186	353	546	724	857	9
	10	0+	0+	0+	0+	0+	0+	0+	0+	0+	001	001	003	006	012	022	030	092	208	376	565	738	10
	11	0+	0+	0+	0+	0+	0+	0+	0+	0+	0+	0+	001	002	004	007	010	039	107	228	396	584	11
	12	0+	0+	0+	0+	0+	0+	0+	0+	0+	0+	0+	0+	0+	001	002	003	014	047	121	246	416	12
	13	0+	0+	0+	0+	0+	0+	0+	0+	0+	0+	0+	0+	0+	0+	0+	001	004	018	055	133	262	13
	14	0+	0+	0+	0+	0+	0+	0+	0+	0+	0+	0+	0+	0+	0+	0+	0+	001	006	021	062	143	14
	15	0+	0+	0+	0+	0+	0+	0+	0+	0+	0+	0+	0+	0+	0+	0+	0+	0+	002	007	024	067	15
	16	0+	0+	0+	0+	0+	0+	0+	0+	0+	0+	0+	0+	0+	0+	0+	0+	0+	0+	002	008	026	16
	17	0+	0+	0+	0+	0+	0+	0+	0+	0+	0+	0+	0+	0+	0+	0+	0+	0+	0+	0+	002	008	17
	18	0+	0+	0+	0+	0+	0+	0+	0+	0+	0+	0+	0+	0+	0+	0+	0+	0+	0+	0+	0+	002	18
	19	0+	0+	0+	0+	0+	0+	0+	0+	0+	0+	0+	0+	0+	0+	0+	0+	0+	0+	0+	0+	0+	19
	20	0+	0+	0+	0+	0+	0+	0+	0+	0+	0+	0+	0+	0+	0+	0+	0+	0+	0+	0+	0+	0+	20

Table 9. *(continued)*

N	K	.01	.02	.04	.05	.06	.08	.10	.12	.14	.15	.16	.18	.20	.22	.24	.25	.30	.35	.40	.45	.50	K
	21	0+	0+	0+	0+	0+	0+	0+	0+	0+	0+	0+	0+	0+	0+	0+	0+	0+	0+	0+	0+	0+	21
	22	0+	0+	0+	0+	0+	0+	0+	0+	0+	0+	0+	0+	0+	0+	0+	0+	0+	0+	0+	0+	0+	22
23	0	1	1	1	1	1	1	1	1	1	1	1	1	1	1	1	1	1	1	1	1	1	0
	1	206	372	609	693	759	853	911	947	969	976	982	990	994	997	998	999	1–	1–	1–	1–	1–	1
	2	022	077	234	321	405	559	685	781	852	880	902	937	960	975	985	988	997	999	1–	1–	1–	2
	3	002	011	062	105	157	278	408	533	643	692	736	810	867	909	939	951	984	996	999	1–	1–	3
	4	0+	001	012	026	046	107	193	295	405	460	514	615	703	778	838	863	946	982	995	999	1–	4
	5	0+	0+	002	005	011	033	073	133	212	256	303	401	499	593	678	717	864	945	981	995	999	5
	6	0+	0+	0+	001	002	008	023	050	092	119	150	222	305	395	487	532	731	869	946	981	995	6
	7	0+	0+	0+	0+	0+	002	006	015	033	046	062	104	160	227	305	346	560	747	876	949	983	7
	8	0+	0+	0+	0+	0+	0+	001	004	010	015	022	042	072	113	166	196	382	586	763	885	953	8
	9	0+	0+	0+	0+	0+	0+	0+	001	003	004	007	014	027	048	078	096	229	444	612	780	895	9
	10	0+	0+	0+	0+	0+	0+	0+	0+	001	001	002	004	009	017	031	041	120	259	444	636	798	10
	11	0+	0+	0+	0+	0+	0+	0+	0+	0+	0+	0+	001	003	005	011	015	055	142	287	472	661	11
	12	0+	0+	0+	0+	0+	0+	0+	0+	0+	0+	0+	0+	001	001	003	005	021	068	164	313	500	12
	13	0+	0+	0+	0+	0+	0+	0+	0+	0+	0+	0+	0+	0+	0+	001	001	007	028	081	184	339	13
	14	0+	0+	0+	0+	0+	0+	0+	0+	0+	0+	0+	0+	0+	0+	0+	0+	002	010	035	094	202	14
	15	0+	0+	0+	0+	0+	0+	0+	0+	0+	0+	0+	0+	0+	0+	0+	0+	001	003	013	041	105	15
	16	0+	0+	0+	0+	0+	0+	0+	0+	0+	0+	0+	0+	0+	0+	0+	0+	0+	001	004	015	047	16
	17	0+	0+	0+	0+	0+	0+	0+	0+	0+	0+	0+	0+	0+	0+	0+	0+	0+	0+	001	005	017	17
	18	0+	0+	0+	0+	0+	0+	0+	0+	0+	0+	0+	0+	0+	0+	0+	0+	0+	0+	0+	001	005	18
	19	0+	0+	0+	0+	0+	0+	0+	0+	0+	0+	0+	0+	0+	0+	0+	0+	0+	0+	0+	0+	001	19

Table 9. *(continued)*

N	K	.01	.02	.04	.05	.06	.08	.10	.12	.14	.15	.16	.18	.20	.22	.24	.25	.30	.35	.40	.45	.50	K
	20	0+	0+	0+	0+	0+	0+	0+	0+	0+	0+	0+	0+	0+	0+	0+	0+	0+	0+	0+	0+	0+	20
	21	0+	0+	0+	0+	0+	0+	0+	0+	0+	0+	0+	0+	0+	0+	0+	0+	0+	0+	0+	0+	0+	21
	22	0+	0+	0+	0+	0+	0+	0+	0+	0+	0+	0+	0+	0+	0+	0+	0+	0+	0+	0+	0+	0+	22
	23	0+	0+	0+	0+	0+	0+	0+	0+	0+	0+	0+	0+	0+	0+	0+	0+	0+	0+	0+	0+	0+	23
24	0	1	1	1	1	1	1	1	1	1	1	1	1	1	1	1	1	1	1	1	1	1	0
	1	214	384	625	708	773	865	920	953	973	980	985	991	995	997	999	999	1−	1−	1−	1−	1−	1
	2	024	083	249	339	427	583	708	801	869	894	915	946	967	980	988	991	998	1−	1−	1−	1−	2
	3	002	012	069	116	172	301	436	563	673	720	763	833	885	924	950	960	988	997	999	1−	1−	3
	4	0+	001	014	030	053	121	214	324	439	495	550	650	736	807	862	885	958	987	996	999	1−	4
	5	0+	0+	002	006	013	039	085	153	239	287	337	439	540	634	717	753	889	958	987	996	999	5
	6	0+	0+	0+	001	002	010	028	060	109	139	174	254	344	439	533	578	771	896	960	987	999	6
	7	0+	0+	0+	0+	0+	002	007	019	041	057	076	126	189	264	349	393	611	789	904	964	989	7
	8	0+	0+	0+	0+	0+	0+	002	005	013	020	028	053	089	138	199	234	435	642	808	914	968	8
	9	0+	0+	0+	0+	0+	0+	0+	001	004	006	009	019	036	062	099	121	275	474	672	827	924	9
	10	0+	0+	0+	0+	0+	0+	0+	0+	001	002	002	006	013	024	042	055	153	313	511	701	846	10
	11	0+	0+	0+	0+	0+	0+	0+	0+	0+	0+	001	002	004	008	016	021	074	183	350	546	729	11
	12	0+	0+	0+	0+	0+	0+	0+	0+	0+	0+	0+	0+	001	002	005	007	031	094	213	385	581	12
	13	0+	0+	0+	0+	0+	0+	0+	0+	0+	0+	0+	0+	0+	001	001	002	012	042	114	242	419	13
	14	0+	0+	0+	0+	0+	0+	0+	0+	0+	0+	0+	0+	0+	0+	0+	001	004	016	053	134	271	14
	15	0+	0+	0+	0+	0+	0+	0+	0+	0+	0+	0+	0+	0+	0+	0+	0+	001	005	022	065	154	15
	16	0+	0+	0+	0+	0+	0+	0+	0+	0+	0+	0+	0+	0+	0+	0+	0+	0+	002	008	027	076	16
	17	0+	0+	0+	0+	0+	0+	0+	0+	0+	0+	0+	0+	0+	0+	0+	0+	0+	0+	002	010	032	17

Table 9. (*continued*)

		P																				
N	K	.01	.02	.04	.05	.06	.08	.10	.12	.14	.15	.16	.18	.20	.22	.24	.25	.30	.35	.40	.45	.50	K
	18	0+	0+	0+	0+	0+	0+	0+	0+	0+	0+	0+	0+	0+	0+	0+	0+	0+	0+	001	003	011	18
	19	0+	0+	0+	0+	0+	0+	0+	0+	0+	0+	0+	0+	0+	0+	0+	0+	0+	0+	0+	001	003	19
	20	0+	0+	0+	0+	0+	0+	0+	0+	0+	0+	0+	0+	0+	0+	0+	0+	0+	0+	0+	0+	001	20
	21	0+	0+	0+	0+	0+	0+	0+	0+	0+	0+	0+	0+	0+	0+	0+	0+	0+	0+	0+	0+	0+	21
	22	0+	0+	0+	0+	0+	0+	0+	0+	0+	0+	0+	0+	0+	0+	0+	0+	0+	0+	0+	0+	0+	22
	23	0+	0+	0+	0+	0+	0+	0+	0+	0+	0+	0+	0+	0+	0+	0+	0+	0+	0+	0+	0+	0+	23
	24	0+	0+	0+	0+	0+	0+	0+	0+	0+	0+	0+	0+	0+	0+	0+	0+	0+	0+	0+	0+	0+	24
25	0	1	1	1	1	1	1	1	1	1	1	1	1	1	1	1	1	1	1	1	1	1	0
	1	222	397	640	723	787	876	928	959	977	983	987	993	996	998	999	999	1−	1−	1−	1−	1−	1
	2	026	089	264	358	447	605	729	820	883	907	926	955	973	984	991	993	998	1−	1−	1−	1−	2
	3	002	013	076	127	187	323	463	591	700	746	787	853	902	936	959	968	991	998	1−	1−	1−	3
	4	0+	001	017	034	060	135	236	352	471	529	584	683	766	832	883	904	967	990	998	1−	1−	4
	5	0+	0+	003	007	015	045	098	173	267	318	371	477	579	672	752	786	910	968	991	998	1−	5
	6	0+	0+	0+	001	003	012	033	071	127	162	200	288	383	482	577	622	807	917	971	991	998	6
	7	0+	0+	0+	0+	001	003	009	024	051	070	092	149	220	303	393	439	659	827	926	974	993	7
	8	0+	0+	0+	0+	0+	001	002	007	017	025	036	066	109	166	235	273	488	694	846	936	978	8
	9	0+	0+	0+	0+	0+	0+	0+	002	005	008	012	025	047	079	123	149	323	533	726	866	946	9
	10	0+	0+	0+	0+	0+	0+	0+	0+	001	002	003	008	017	033	056	071	189	370	575	758	885	10
	11	0+	0+	0+	0+	0+	0+	0+	0+	0+	0+	001	002	006	012	022	030	098	229	414	616	788	11
	12	0+	0+	0+	0+	0+	0+	0+	0+	0+	0+	0+	001	002	004	008	011	044	125	268	457	655	12
	13	0+	0+	0+	0+	0+	0+	0+	0+	0+	0+	0+	0+	0+	001	002	003	017	060	154	306	500	13
	14	0+	0+	0+	0+	0+	0+	0+	0+	0+	0+	0+	0+	0+	0+	001	001	006	025	078	183	345	14

15	0+	0+	0+	0+	0+	0+	0+	0+	0+	0+	0+	0+	0+	0+	0+	0+	002	009	034	096	212	15
16	0+	0+	0+	0+	0+	0+	0+	0+	0+	0+	0+	0+	0+	0+	0+	0+	0+	003	013	044	115	16
17	0+	0+	0+	0+	0+	0+	0+	0+	0+	0+	0+	0+	0+	0+	0+	0+	0+	001	004	017	054	17
18	0+	0+	0+	0+	0+	0+	0+	0+	0+	0+	0+	0+	0+	0+	0+	0+	0+	0+	001	006	022	18
19	0+	0+	0+	0+	0+	0+	0+	0+	0+	0+	0+	0+	0+	0+	0+	0+	0+	0+	0+	002	007	19
20	0+	0+	0+	0+	0+	0+	0+	0+	0+	0+	0+	0+	0+	0+	0+	0+	0+	0+	0+	0+	002	20
21	0+	0+	0+	0+	0+	0+	0+	0+	0+	0+	0+	0+	0+	0+	0+	0+	0+	0+	0+	0+	0+	21
22	0+	0+	0+	0+	0+	0+	0+	0+	0+	0+	0+	0+	0+	0+	0+	0+	0+	0+	0+	0+	0+	22
23	0+	0+	0+	0+	0+	0+	0+	0+	0+	0+	0+	0+	0+	0+	0+	0+	0+	0+	0+	0+	0+	23
24	0+	0+	0+	0+	0+	0+	0+	0+	0+	0+	0+	0+	0+	0+	0+	0+	0+	0+	0+	0+	0+	24
25	0+	0+	0+	0+	0+	0+	0+	0+	0+	0+	0+	0+	0+	0+	0+	0+	0+	0+	0+	0+	0+	25

Table 10. Selected Range Adjustment Factors for Unit Normal Distribution[a]

N	$D(N)$
2	1.1284
3	1.6926
4	2.0588
5	2.3259
6	2.5344
7	2.7044
8	2.8472
9	2.9700
10	3.0775
11	3.1729
12	3.2585
13	3.3360
14	3.4068
15	3.4718
16	3.5320
17	3.5879
18	3.6401
19	3.6890
20	3.7350

[a]Adapted from Forman Acton, *Analysis of Straight-Line Data,* Dover Press, New York, 1967, p. 258.

Table 11. Selected Values for the Exponential Distribution

P	Δ	P	Δ	P	Δ
0.01	0.010050	0.34	0.415515	0.67	1.108662
0.02	0.020203	0.35	0.430783	0.68	1.139434
0.03	0.030459	0.36	0.446287	0.69	1.171183
0.04	0.040822	0.37	0.462035	0.70	1.203973
0.05	0.051293	0.38	0.478036	0.71	1.237874
0.06	0.061875	0.39	0.494296	0.72	1.272966
0.07	0.072571	0.40	0.510826	0.73	1.309333
0.08	0.083382	0.41	0.527633	0.74	1.347073
0.09	0.094311	0.42	0.544727	0.75	1.386294
0.10	0.105360	0.43	0.562119	0.76	1.427116
0.11	0.116534	0.44	0.579818	0.77	1.469676
0.12	0.127833	0.45	0.597837	0.78	1.514128
0.13	0.139262	0.46	0.616186	0.79	1.560648
0.14	0.150823	0.47	0.634878	0.80	1.609438
0.15	0.162519	0.48	0.653926	0.81	1.660731
0.16	0.174353	0.49	0.673344	0.82	1.714798
0.17	0.186330	0.50	0.693147	0.83	1.771957
0.18	0.198451	0.51	0.713350	0.84	1.832581
0.19	0.210721	0.52	0.733969	0.85	1.897120
0.20	0.223144	0.53	0.755023	0.86	1.966113
0.21	0.235722	0.54	0.776529	0.87	2.040220
0.22	0.248461	0.55	0.798508	0.88	2.120263
0.23	0.261365	0.56	0.820980	0.89	2.207275
0.24	0.274437	0.57	0.843970	0.90	2.302585
0.25	0.287682	0.58	0.867501	0.91	2.407945
0.26	0.301105	0.59	0.891598	0.92	2.525728
0.27	0.314711	0.60	0.916291	0.93	2.659259
0.28	0.328504	0.61	0.941608	0.94	2.813411
0.29	0.342490	0.62	0.967584	0.95	2.995732
0.30	0.356675	0.63	0.994252	0.96	3.218875
0.31	0.371064	0.64	1.021651	0.97	3.506557
0.32	0.385662	0.65	1.049822	0.98	3.912021
0.33	0.400478	0.66	1.078810	0.99	4.605165

Table 12. Table of Common Logarithms—Five Place[a]

N	L0	1	2	3	4	5	6	7	8	9
0	$-\infty$	00 000	30 103	47 712	60 206	69 897	77 815	84 510	90 309	95 424
1	00 000	04 139	07 918	11 394	14 613	17 609	20 412	23 04$\bar{5}$	25 527	27 875
2	30 103	32 222	34 242	36 173	38 021	39 794	41 497	43 136	44 716	46 240
3	47 712	49 136	50 515	51 851	53 148	54 407	55 630	56 820	57 978	59 106
4	60 206	61 278	62 32$\bar{5}$	63 347	64 345	65 321	66 276	67 210	68 124	69 020
5	69 897	70 757	71 600	72 428	73 239	74 036	74 819	75 587	76 343	77 085
6	77 815	78 533	79 239	79 934	80 618	81 291	81 954	82 607	83 251	83 885
7	84 510	85 126	85 733	86 332	86 923	87 506	88 081	88 649	89 209	89 763
8	90 309	90 849	91 381	91 908	92 428	92 942	93 4$\bar{5}$0	93 952	94 448	94 939
9	95 424	95 904	96 379	96 848	97 313	97 772	98 227	98 677	99 123	99 564
10	00 000	00 432	00 860	01 284	01 703	02 119	02 531	02 938	03 342	03 743
11	04 139	04 532	04 922	05 308	05 690	06 070	06 446	06 819	07 188	07 55$\bar{5}$
12	07 918	08 279	08 636	08 991	09 342	09 691	10 037	10 380	10 721	11 059
13	11 394	11 727	12 057	12 385	12 710	13 033	13 354	13 672	13 988	14 301
14	14 613	14 922	15 229	15 534	15 836	16 137	16 435	16 732	17 026	17 319
15	17 609	17 898	18 184	18 469	18 752	19 033	19 312	19 590	19 866	20 140
16	20 412	20 683	20 952	21 219	21 484	21 748	22 011	22 272	22 531	22 789
17	23 04$\bar{5}$	23 300	23 553	23 80$\bar{5}$	24 05$\bar{5}$	24 304	24 551	24 797	25 042	25 285
18	25 527	25 768	26 007	26 245	26 482	26 717	26 951	27 184	27 416	27 646
19	27 875	28 103	28 330	28 556	28 780	29 003	29 226	29 447	29 667	29 885

[a]Tables on pp. 2 and 3 in LOGARITHMIC AND TRIGONOMETRIC TABLES TO FIVE PLACES by Kai L. Nielsen (Barnes & Noble).

Table 12. (*continued*)

N	L0	1	2	3	4	5	6	7	8	9
20	30 103	30 320	30 535	30 75̄0	30 963	31 175	31 387	31 597	31 806	32 015̄
21	32 222	32 428	32 634	32 838	33 041	33 244	33 445	33 646	33 846	34 044
22	34 242	34 439	34 635	34 830	35 025̄	35 218	35 411	35 603	35 793	35 984
23	36 173	36 361	36 549	36 736	36 922	37 107	37 291	37 475̄	37 658	37 840
24	38 021	38 202	38 382	38 561	38 739	38 917	39 094	39 270	39 445	39 620
25	39 794	39 907	40 140	40 312	40 483	40 654	40 824	40 993	41 162	41 330
26	41 497	41 664	41 830	41 996	42 160	42 325̄	42 488	42 651	42 813	42 975
27	43 136	43 297	43 457	43 616	43 775	43 933	44 091	44 248	44 404	44 560
28	44 716	44 871	45 025̄	45 179	45 332	45 484	45 637	45 788	45 939	46 090
29	46 240	46 389	46 538	46 687	46 835̄	46 982	47 129	47 276	47 422	47 567
30	47 712	47 857	48 001	48 144	48 287	48 430	48 572	48 714	48 855	48 996
31	49 136	49 276	49 415	49 554	49 693	49 831	49 969	50 106	50 243	50 379
32	50 515̄	50 651	50 786	50 920	51 055̄	51 188	51 322	51 455̄	51 587	51 720
33	51 851	51 983	52 114	52 244	52375̄	52 504	52 634	52 763	52 892	53 020
34	53 148	53 275	53 493	53 529	53 656	53 782	53 908	54 033	54 158	54 283
35	54 407	54 531	54 654	54 777	54900	55 023	55 145̄	55 267	55 388	55 509
36	55 630	55 751	55 871	55 991	56 110	56 229	56 348	56 467	56 585̄	56 703
37	56 820	56 937	57 054	57 171	57 287	57 403	57 519	57 634	57 749	57 864
38	57 928	58 092	58 206	58 320	58 433	58 546	58 659	58 771	58 883	58 995̄
39	59 106	59 218	59 329	59 439	59 55̄0	59 660	59 770	59 879	59 988	60 097

Table 12. (*continued*)

N	L0	1	2	3	4	5	6	7	8	9
40	60 206	60 314	60 423	60 531	60 638	60 746	60 853	60 959	61 066	61 172
41	61 278	61 384	61 490	61 595	61 700	61 80$\bar{5}$	61 909	62 014	62 118	62 271
42	62 32$\bar{5}$	62 428	62 531	62 634	62 737	62 839	62 941	63 043	63 144	63 246
43	63 347	63 448	63 548	63 649	63 749	63 849	63 949	64 048	64 147	64 246
44	64 345	64 444	64 542	64 640	64 738	64 836	64 933	65 031	65 128	65 22$\bar{5}$
45	65 321	05 418	65 514	65 610	65 706	65 801	65 896	65 992	66 087	66 181
46	66 276	66 370	66 464	66 558	66 652	66 745	66 839	66 932	67 02$\bar{5}$	67 117
47	67 210	67 302	67 394	67 486	67 578	67 669	67 761	67 852	67 943	68 034
48	68 124	68 21$\bar{5}$	68 30$\bar{5}$	68 39$\bar{5}$	68 48$\bar{5}$	68 574	68 664	68 753	68 842	68 931
49	69 020	69 108	69 197	69 28$\bar{5}$	69 373	69 461	69 548	69 636	69 723	69 810
50	69 897	69 984	70 070	70 157	70 243	70 329	70 415	70 501	70 586	70 672
51	70 757	70 842	70 927	71 012	71 096	71 181	71 26$\bar{5}$	71 349	71 433	71 517
52	71 600	71 684	71 767	71 850	71 933	72 016	72 009	72 181	72 263	72 346
53	72 428	72 509	72 591	72 673	72 754	72 835	72 916	72 997	73 078	73 159
54	73 239	73 320	73 400	73 480	73 560	73 640	73 719	73 799	73 878	73 957
55	74 036	74 115	74 194	74 273	74 351	74 429	74 507	74 586	74 663	74 741
56	74 819	74 896	74 974	75 051	75 128	75 20$\bar{5}$	75 282	75 358	75 43$\bar{5}$	75 511
57	75 587	75 664	75 740	75 815	75 891	75 967	76 042	76 118	76 193	76 268
58	76 345	76 418	76 492	76 567	76 641	76 716	76 790	76 864	76 938	77 012
59	77 085	77 159	77 232	77 395	77 379	77 452	77 52$\bar{5}$	77 597	77 670	77 743

Table 12. *(continued)*

N	L0	1	2	3	4	5	6	7	8	9
60	77 815	77 887	77 960	78 032	78 104	78 176	78 247	78 319	78 390	78 462
61	78 533	78 604	78 675	78 746	78 817	78 888	78 958	79 029	79 009	79 169
62	79 239	79 309	79 379	79 449	79 518	79 588	79 657	79 727	79 796	79 865
63	79 934	80 003	80 072	80 140	80 209	80 277	80 346	80 414	80 482	80 550
64	80 618	80 686	80 754	80 821	80 889	80 956	81 023	81 090	81 158	81 224
65	81 291	81 358	81 42$\bar{5}$	81 491	81 558	81 624	81 690	81 757	81 823	81 889
66	81 954	82 020	82 086	82 151	82 217	82 282	82 347	82 413	82 478	82 543
67	82 607	82 672	82 737	82 808	82 866	82 930	82 99$\bar{5}$	83 059	83 123	83 187
68	83 251	83 31$\bar{5}$	83 378	83 442	83 506	83 569	83 632	83 696	83 759	83 822
69	83 88$\bar{5}$	83 948	84 011	84 073	84 136	84 198	84 261	84 323	84 386	84 448
70	84 510	84 572	84 634	84 696	84 757	84 819	84 880	84 942	85 003	85 06$\bar{5}$
71	85 126	85 187	85 248	85 309	85 370	85 431	85 491	85 552	85 612	85 673
72	85 733	85 794	85 854	85 914	85 974	86 034	86 094	86 153	86 213	86 273
73	86 332	86 392	86 451	86 510	86 570	86 629	86 688	86 747	86 806	86 864
74	86 923	86 982	87 040	87 099	87 157	87 216	87 274	87 332	87 390	87 448
75	87 506	87 564	87 622	87 679	87 737	87 79$\bar{5}$	88 423	88 480	88 536	88 593
76	88 081	88 138	88 195	88 252	88 309	88 366	88 423	88 480	88 536	88 593
77	88 649	88 705	88 762	88 818	88 874	88 930	88 986	89 042	89 098	89 154
78	89 209	89 265	89 321	89 376	89 432	89 487	89 542	89 597	89 653	89 708
79	89 763	89 818	89 873	89 927	89 982	90 037	90 091	90 146	90 200	90 25$\bar{5}$

Table 12. *(continued)*

N	L0	1	2	3	4	5	6	7	8	9
80	90 309	90 363	90 417	90 472	90 526	90 580	90 634	90 687	90 741	90 79$\bar{5}$
81	90 849	90 902	90 956	91 009	91 062	91 116	91 169	91 222	91 275	91 328
82	91 381	91 434	91 487	91 540	91 593	91 645	91 698	91 751	91 803	91 855
83	91 908	91 960	92 012	92 06$\bar{5}$	92 117	92 169	92 221	92 273	92 324	92 376
84	92 428	92 480	92 531	92 583	92 634	92 686	92 737	92 788	92 840	92 891
85	92 942	92 993	93 044	93 09$\bar{5}$	93 146	93 197	93 247	93 298	93 349	93 399
86	93 4$\bar{5}$0	93 500	93 551	93 601	93 651	93 702	93 752	93 802	93 852	93 902
87	93 952	94 002	94 052	94 101	94 151	94 201	94 250	94 300	94 349	94 399
88	94 448	94 498	94 547	94 506	94 645	94 694	94 743	94 792	94 841	94 890
89	94 939	94 988	95 036	95 086	95 134	95 182	95 231	95 279	95 328	95 376
90	95 424	95 472	95 521	95 569	95 617	95 66$\bar{5}$	95 713	95 761	95 809	95 856
91	95 904	95 952	95 999	96 047	96 09$\bar{5}$	96 142	96 100	96 237	96 284	96 332
92	96 379	96 426	96 473	96 520	96 567	96 614	96 661	96 708	96 75$\bar{5}$	96 802
93	96 848	96 89$\bar{5}$	96 942	96 988	97 03$\bar{5}$	97 081	97 128	97 174	97 220	97 267
94	97 313	97 359	97 405	97 451	97 497	97 543	97 589	97 63$\bar{5}$	97 681	97 727
95	97 772	97 818	97 864	97 909	97 95$\bar{5}$	98 000	98 046	98 091	98 137	98 182
96	98 227	98 272	98 318	98 363	98 408	98 453	98 498	98 543	98 588	98 632
97	93 677	98 722	98 767	98 811	98 856	98 900	98 94$\bar{5}$	98 989	99 034	99 078
98	99 123	99 167	99 211	99 255	99 300	99 344	99 388	99 432	99 476	99 520
99	99 564	99 607	99 651	99 69$\bar{5}$	99 739	99 782	99 826	99 870	99 913	99 957
100	00 000	00 043	00 087	00 130	00 173	00 217	00 260	00 303	00 346	00 389

Table 13. Table of Natural or Naperian Logarithms, .01–11.09[a, b]

A. 0.00–0.99[b]

N	.00	.01	.02	.03	.04	.05	.06	.07	.08	.09
0.0		5.395	6.088	6.493	6.781	7.004	7.187	7.341	7.474	7.592
0.1	7.697	7.793	7.880	7.960	8.034	8.103	8.167	8.228	8.285	8.339
0.2	8.391	8.439	8.486	8.530	8.573	8.614	8.653	8.691	8.727	8.762
0.3	8.796	8.829	8.861	8.891	8.921	8.950	8.978	9.006	9.032	9.058
0.4	9.084	9.108	9.132	9.156	9.179	9.201	9.223	9.245	9.266	9.287
0.5	9.307	9.327	9.346	9.365	9.384	9.402	9.420	9.438	9.455	9.472
0.6	9.489	9.506	9.522	9.538	9.554	9.569	9.584	9.600	9.614	9.629
0.7	9.643	9.658	9.671	9.685	9.699	9.712	9.726	9.739	9.752	9.764
0.8	9.777	9.789	9.802	9.814	9.826	9.837	9.849	9.861	9.872	9.883
0.9	9.805	9.906	9.917	9.927	9.938	9.949	9.959	9.970	9.980	9.990

B. 1.00–10.09

$–N$	.00	.00	.01	.02	.03	.04	.05	.06	.07	.08	.09
1.0	0.0	0000	0995	1980	2956	3922	4879	5827	6766	7696	8618
1.1		9531	*0436	*1333	*2222	*3103	*3976	*4842	*4700	*6551	*7395
1.2	0.1	8232	9062	9885	*0701	*1511	*2314	*3111	*2902	*4686	*5464

[a]Reprinted with permission from *Mathematical Tables*, copyright Chemical Rubber Publishing Co., CRC Press, Inc., 2000 Corporate Blvd, NW, Boca Raton, FL 33431, 1941, pp. 139–142.

[b]To find the natural logarithm of a number which is 1/10 or 10 times a number whose logarithm is given, subtract from or add to the given logarithm is given, subtract from or add to the given logarithm the logarithm of 10.

[t]–10 should be appended to each logarithm.

Table 13. *(continued)*

B. 1.00–10.09										
N	.00		.01	.02	.03	.04	.05	.06	.07	.08	.09
1.3	0.2	6236	7003	7763	8518	9267	*0010	*0748	*1481	*2208	*2930
1.4	0.3	3647	4359	5066	5767	6464	7156	7844	8526	9204	9878
1.5	0.4	0547	1211	1871	2527	3176	3825	4469	5108	5742	6373
1.6		7000	7623	8243	8858	9470	*0078	*0682	*1282	*1879	*2473
1.7	0.5	3063	3649	4232	4812	5389	5962	6531	7098	7661	8222
1.8		8779	9333	9884	*0432	*0977	*1519	*2058	*2594	*3127	*3658
1.9	0.6	4185	4710	5233	5752	6269	6783	7294	7803	8310	8813
2.0		9315	9813	*0310	*0804	*1295	*1784	*2271	*2755	*3237	*3716
2.1	0.7	4194	4669	5142	5612	6081	6547	7011	7473	7932	8390
2.2		8846	9299	9751	*0200	*0648	*1093	*1536	*1978	*2418	*2855
2.3	0.8	3291	3725	4157	4587	5015	5442	5866	6289	6710	7129
2.4		7547	7963	8377	8789	9200	9609	*0016	*0422	*0826	*1228
2.5	0.9	1629	2028	2426	2822	3216	3609	4001	4391	4779	5166
2.6		5551	5935	6317	6698	7078	7456	7833	8208	8582	8954
2.7		9325	9695	*0063	*0430	*0796	*1160	*1523	*1885	*2245	*2604
2.8	1.0	2962	3318	3674	4028	4380	4732	5082	5431	5779	6126
2.9		6471	6815	7158	7500	7841	8181	8519	8856	9192	9527
3.0		9861	*0194	*0526	*0856	*1186	*1514	*1841	*2168	*2493	*2817
3.1	1.1	3140	3462	3783	4103	4422	4740	5057	5373	5688	6002
3.2		6315	6627	6938	7248	7557	7865	8173	8479	8784	9089
3.3		9392	9695	9996	*0297	*0597	*0896	*1194	*1491	*1788	*2083
3.4	1.2	2378	2671	2964	3256	3547	3837	4127	4415	4703	4990
3.5		5276	5562	5846	6130	6413	6695	6976	7257	7536	7815
3.6		8093	8371	8647	8923	9198	9473	9746	*0019	*0291	*0563

Table 13. (*continued*)

B. 1.00–10.09										
N	.00	.01	.02	.03	.04	.05	.06	.07	.08	.09
3.7	1.3 0833	1103	1372	1641	1909	2176	2442	2708	2972	3237
3.8	3500	3763	4025	4286	4547	4807	5067	5325	5584	5841
3.9	6098	6354	6609	6864	7118	7372	7624	7877	8128	8379
4.0	8629	8879	9128	9377	9624	9872	*0118	*0364	*0610	*0854
4.1	1.4 1099	1342	1585	1828	2070	2311	2552	2792	3031	3270
4.2	3508	3746	3984	4220	4456	4692	4927	5161	5395	5629
4.3	5862	6094	6326	6557	6787	7018	7247	7476	7705	7933
4.4	8160	8387	8614	8840	9065	9290	9515	9739	9962	0185
4.5	1.5 0408	0630	0851	1072	1293	1513	1732	1951	2170	2388
4.6	2606	2823	3039	3256	3471	3687	3902	4116	4330	4543
4.7	4756	4969	5181	5393	5604	5814	6025	6235	6444	6653
4.8	6862	7070	7277	7485	7691	7898	8104	8309	8515	8719
4.9	8924	9127	9331	9534	9737	9939	*0141	*0342	*0543	*0744
5.0	1.6 0944	1144	1343	1542	1741	1939	2137	2334	2531	2728
5.1	2924	3120	3315	3511	3705	3900	4094	4287	4481	4673
5.2	4866	5058	5250	5441	5632	5823	6013	6203	6393	6582
5.3	6771	6959	7147	7335	7523	7710	7896	8083	8269	8455
5.4	8640	8825	9010	9194	9378	9562	9745	9928	*0111	*0293
5.5	1.7 0475	0656	0838	1019	1199	1380	1560	1740	1919	2098
5.6	2277	2455	2633	2811	2988	3166	3342	3519	3695	3871
5.7	4047	4222	4397	4572	4746	4920	5094	5267	5440	5613
5.8	5786	5958	6130	6302	6473	6644	6815	6985	7156	7326
5.9	7495	7665	7834	8002	8171	8339	8507	8675	8842	9009
6.0	9176	9342	9509	9675	9840	*0006	*0171	*0336	*0500	*0665

Table 13. *(continued)*

B. 1.00–10.09

N	.00	.01	.02	.03	.04	.05	.06	.07	.08	.09
6.1	1.8 0829	0993	1156	1319	1482	1645	1808	1970	2132	2294
6.2	2455	2616	2777	2938	3098	3258	3418	3578	3737	3896
6.3	4055	4214	4372	4530	4688	4845	5003	5160	5317	5473
6.4	5630	5786	5942	6097	6253	6408	6563	6718	6872	7026
6.5	7180	7334	7487	7641	7794	7947	8099	8251	8403	8555
6.6	8707	8858	9010	9160	9311	9462	9612	9762	9912	*0061
6.7	1.9 0211	0360	0509	0658	0806	0954	1102	1250	1398	1545
6.8	1692	1839	1986	2132	2279	2425	2571	2716	2862	3007
6.9	3152	3297	3442	3586	3730	3874	4018	4162	4305	4448
7.0	4591	4734	4876	5019	5161	5303	5445	5586	5727	5869
7.1	6009	6150	6291	6431	6571	6711	6851	6991	7130	7269
7.2	7408	7547	7685	7824	7962	8100	8238	8376	8513	8650
7.3	8787	8924	9061	9198	9334	9470	9606	9742	9877	*0013
7.4	2.0 0148	0283	0418	0553	0687	0821	0956	1089	1223	1357
7.5	1490	1624	1757	1890	2022	2155	2287	2419	2551	2683
7.6	2815	2946	3078	3209	3340	3471	3601	3732	3862	3992
7.7	4122	4252	4381	4511	4640	4769	4898	5027	5156	5284
7.8	5 5412	5540	5668	5796	5924	6051	6179	6306	6433	6560
7.9	6686	6813	6939	7065	7191	7317	7443	7568	7694	7819
8.0	7944	8069	8194	8318	8443	8567	8691	8815	8939	9063
8.1	9186	9310	9433	9556	9679	9802	9924	*0047	*0169	*0291
8.2	2.1 0413	0535	0657	0779	0900	1021	1142	1263	1384	1505
8.3	1626	1746	1866	1986	2106	2226	2346	2465	2585	2704
8.4	2823	2942	3061	3180	3298	3417	3535	3653	3771	3889
8.5	4007	4124	4242	4359	4476	4593	4710	4827	4943	5060
8.6	5176	5292	5409	5524	5640	5756	5871	5987	6102	6217
8.7	6332	6447	6562	6677	6791	6905	7020	7134	7248	7361

Table 13. *(continued)*

B. 1.00–10.09 (Concluded)

N	0	1	2	3	4	5	6	7	8	9
8.8	7475	7589	7702	7816	7929	8042	8155	8267	8380	8493
8.9	8605	8717	8830	8942	9054	9165	9277	9389	9500	9611
9.0	9722	9834	9944	*0055	*0166	*0276	*0387	*0497	*0607	*0717
9.1	2.2 0827	0937	1047	1157	1266	1375	1485	1594	1703	1812
9.2	1920	2029	2138	2246	2354	2462	2570	2678	2786	2894
9.3	3001	3109	3216	3324	3431	3538	3645	3751	3858	3965
9.4	4071	4177	4284	4390	4496	4601	4707	4813	4918	5024
9.5	5129	5234	5339	5444	5549	5654	5759	5863	5968	6072
9.6	6176	6280	6384	6488	6592	6696	6799	6903	7006	7109
9.7	7213	7316	7419	7521	7624	7727	7829	7932	8034	8136
9.8	8238	8340	8442	8544	8646	8747	8849	8950	9051	9152
9.9	9253	9354	9455	9556	9657	9757	9858	9958	*0058	*0158
10.0	2.3 0259	0358	0458	0558	0658	0757	0857	0956	1055	1154
1	2.30259	39790	48491	56495	63906	70805	77259	83321	89037	94444
2	99573	*04452	*09104	*13549	*17805	*21888	*25810	*29584	*33220	*36730
3	3.40120	43399	46574	49651	52636	55535	58352	61092	63759	66356
4	68888	71357	73767	76120	78419	80666	82864	85015	87120	89182
5	91202	93183	95124	97029	98898	*00733	*02535	*04305	*06044	*07754
6	4.09434	11087	12713	14313	15888	17439	18965	20469	21951	23411
7	24850	26268	27667	29046	30407	31749	33073	34381	35671	36945
8	38203	39445	40672	41884	43082	44265	45435	46591	47734	48864
9	49981	51086	52179	53260	54329	55388	56435	57471	58497	59512

Appendix Four

Erosion Detection Techniques

In *Taming the Pits: A Technical Approach to Commodity Trading,*[1] Robert M. Barnes describes the use of an "erosion detection technique" for estimating how large the losses of a *successful* managed account might be. Notice in Exhibit 85 that despite the upward trend in the account equity value, there are numerous losing periods. During these periods, money managers would say the account equity is "eroding;" clients often use more colorful phrases.

Be that as it may, if erosions can be measured and anticipated, both the manager and client are likely to gain valuable peace of mind. Barnes' technique essentially allows the trader to budget for this type of disaster. If, for example, the trader budgets for a 0.30 equity erosion and a 0.25 erosion takes place, the trader need neither worry nor close the account. On the other hand, an erosion larger than 0.30 is evidence that the account is not being managed as it should be. The manager or method currently being used should at least be examined, and possibly abandoned.

Of course, a large loss may simply be a fluke. Barnes' technique does not estimate the largest possible erosion; it estimates the largest probable erosion if the erosions are a function of the account size, if the erosions are exponentially distributed, and if the average erosion is a known value **AE**. Larger values than the one calculated are not impossible, merely improbable. In other words, large values happen. A trader who abandons an account because of a large equity erosion may well be abandoning a valuable manager or method.

There is clearly a tradeoff here. If the trader is willing to take large financial risks, he will have to accept very little risk of abandoning a successful manager or method. On the other hand, if the trader is willing to accept only small financial risks, he will have to accept a large risk of abandoning a successful manager or method. There is no way to avoid the tradeoff. The trader can only choose the mixture of risks to accept.

This mixture is chosen by selecting a value P from zero to one inclusive. This value P is the probability that if the erosions are exponentially distributed and if the average erosion is a known value **AE**, then in any given case the account value will not erode beyond a calculated amount.

If a value of zero is chosen, the trader must abandon the account if any loss whatever is shown. If a value of one is chosen, the trader cannot abandon the account if any money whatever remains. If any other value is chosen, the trader must abandon the account when a given portion of the account is lost, but not before.

---

[1] Barnes, Robert M., *Taming The Pits: A Technical Approach to Commodity Trading,* Wiley, New York, 1979, pp. 222–227.

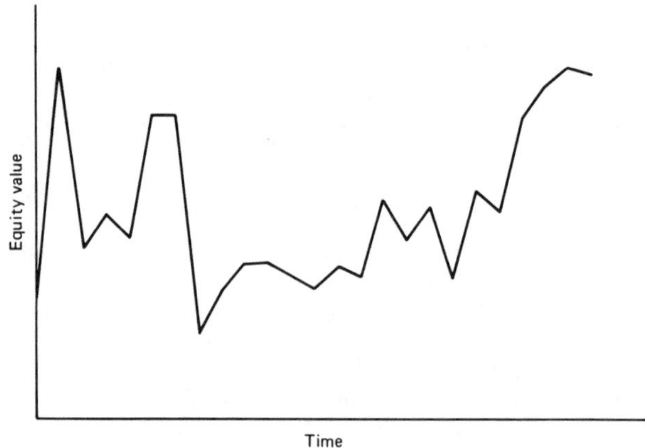

Exhibit 85. Equity value of a successfully managed account. Notice the numerous unprofitable periods. Source: David R. Aronson, Advocom (personal communication).

Whereas the trader is free to choose whatever value of P he finds appealing, he is not free not to choose a value. A trader who does not explicitly choose implicitly chooses. In other words, he will have to choose whether or not to abandon the account while the equity is eroding. For reasons explained in Chapter 7, these choices are almost always wrong.

If a trader will not abandon an account on the basis of erosion, he has implictly or explicitly chosen a value of one. In this case, the trader must use another technique for determining when the account should be abandoned. Other, more interesting and sophisticated techniques are discussed in Chapter 8. The trader should consider them carefully.

However, even if the trader would like to use Barnes' technique, he cannot do so if the distribution of erosion is not exponential (see Exhibit 86). Barnes assumed an exponential distribution, but like all assumptions, it need not be true.

It is nevertheless a reasonable assumption. The exponential distribution has properties that the distribution of erosions *should* have, the most important of these being that the distribution is *memoryless.* In other words, the conditional

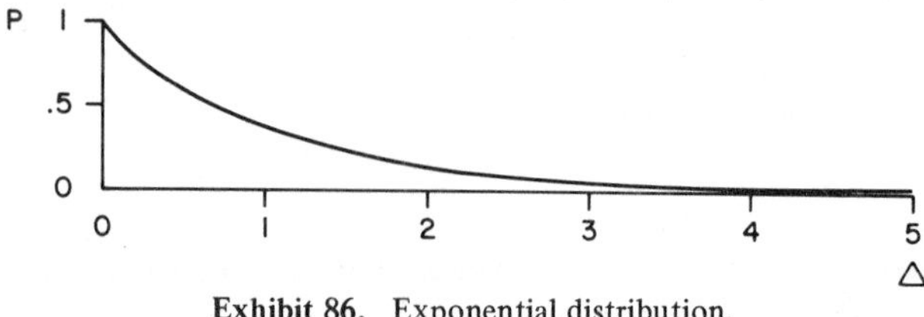

Exhibit 86. Exponential distribution.

probability of an account decline of 0.01 is the same after a decline of 0.01 as it was before. This may not be true in any given case, but if it is not, the account is not being traded as it should be.

In other words, in a properly traded account, the equity will behave like a random walk (see Exhibit 87) with a positive drift. Random walks with negative and zero drifts are also possible (see Exhibits 88 and 89). Although trading should be profitable, on average, the fact that the previous day's trading was profitable should give no information whatsoever about today's trading.

Clearly, if today's profits or losses give any information about tomorrow's, that information should be incorporated in the trading plan. For example, a trader who found his profits equaling or exceeding his losses and found his profits and losses grouped as follows (+ indicate profitable trades; -, unprofitable ones):

---+++--+--++----+-+-++---+++-++

could improve his return by restricting himself to trades that were preceded either by profitable trades or paper trades that would have been profitable if they had been taken. In this case, the results would be:

++--+-+---+-++-+

Notice that although the second series is shorter than the first, it has a higher proportion of winning trades. All other things being equal, it would be more profitable to use the second trading method than it would be to use the original

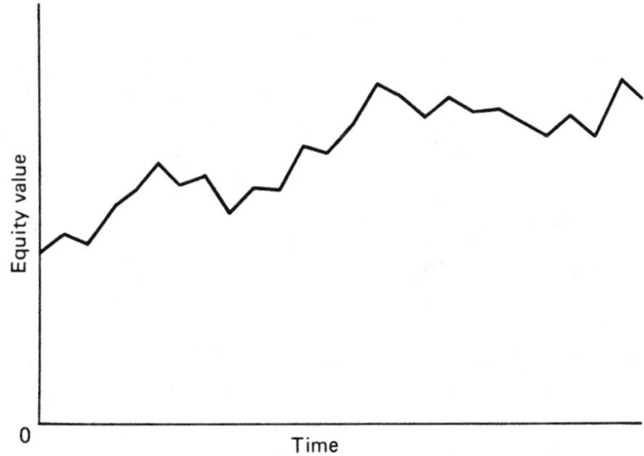

Exhibit 87. Random walk with positive drift.

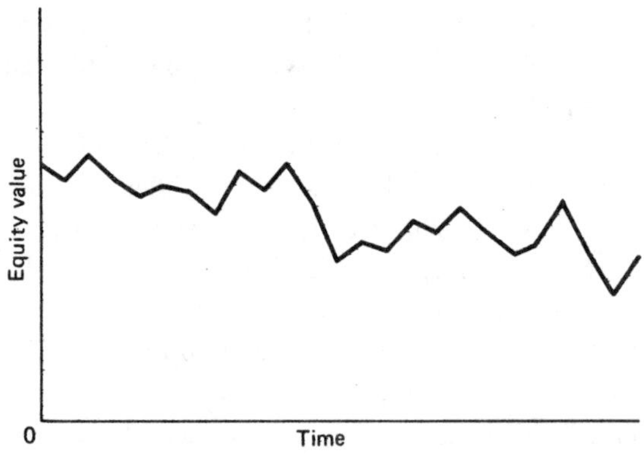

Exhibit 88. Random walk with negative drift.

method. However, and this is critical, the second series is random, whereas the original series is not.

Clearly, if profits and losses are not random, the account is not being managed as it should be. The trader would therefore be well advised to use the tools presented in Chapter 5 to test for randomness. If profits and losses are not random, trading can probably be made more profitable.[2] If profits and losses are random, Barnes' technique can be used.

Unfortunately, Barnes' technique cannot be used as he presented it. The first step in the correct procedure is to determine whether erosion is a function of account size. Erosion will be a function of account size when the number of contracts traded is a function of account size.

When erosion is a function of account size:

A. Calculate the individual erosion factors. These values are calculated by locating cumulative account value tops (TOP) and cumulative account value bottoms (BOT). A top is a value that is both higher than the preceding and following values and does not fall between another top and the point where that top is next equaled or exceeded. A bottom is the lowest value between a top and the point where that top is next equaled or exceeded (see Exhibit 90). When erosion is a function of account size, the erosion factor (EF′) is:

[2] Strictly speaking, it's possible that the trader might not be able to exploit nonrandomness in the profit stream; for example, the nonrandomness might be so weak that it would not be worth exploiting. If this is the case, Barnes' technique cannot be used. It is difficult to say how rare such cases are, unfortunately.

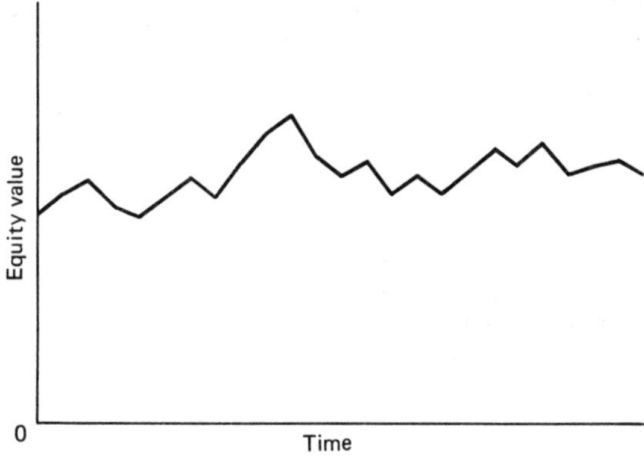

Exhibit 89. Random walk with no drift.

$$EF' = (TOP - BOT)/TOP$$

B. Calculate the sample erosion value AE′ as a measure of **AE**. AE′ is the arithmetic average of EF′. Naturally, the larger the sample size, the more reasonable the sample.

C. Select a value of *P*. *P* represents the probability that any given account erosion will *not* exceed a calculated value. If *P* equals zero, the calculated value will be zero. If *P* equals one, the calculated value will equal the account value.

D. Find the value of Δ in Table 11 in Appendix 3 that corresponds to the value of *P* selected.

E. Calculate the unacceptable erosion proportion (UE′). The formula is:

$$UE' = \Delta AE'$$

When erosion is not a function of account size:

A. Calculate the individual erosion factors. These values are calculated by locating cumulative account value tops (TOP) and cumulative account value bottoms (BOT). A top is a value that is both higher than the preceding and following values and does not fall between another top and the point where that top is next equaled or exceeded. A bottom is the lowest value between a top and the point where that top is next equaled or exceeded (see Exhibit 90). When erosion is not a function of account size, the erosion factor (EF″) is:

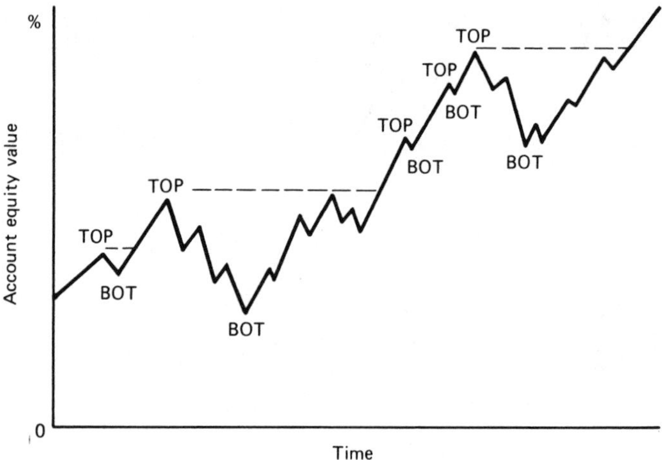

Exhibit 90. Adapted from Barnes, Robert M., *Taming the Pits: A Technical Approach to Commodity Trading,* Wiley, New York, 1979, p. 223.

$$EF'' = TOP - BOT$$

B. Calculate the sample average erosion value (AE″) as a measure of **AE.** AE″ is the arithmetic average of EF″. Naturally, the larger the sample size, the more reasonable the sample.

C. Select a value of *P*. *P* represents the probability that any given account erosion will *not* exceed a calculated value. If *P* equals zero the calculated value will be zero. If *P* equals one the calculated value will be infinite.

D. Find the value of Δ in Table 11 in Appendix 3 that corresponds to the value of *P* selected above.

E. Calculate the unacceptable erosion (UE″). The formula is:

$$UE'' = \Delta AE''$$

For example, there are four tops (which are underlined twice) and three bottoms (which are underlined once) in the series below:

100, 110, 95, 97, 90, 100, 115, 120, 118, 122, 119, 105, 107, 98,
106, 117, 113, 120, 125, 123, 120, 124, 118

The last value in the series (e.g., 118) may or may not be a bottom. Until the previous top (e.g., 125) is exceeded, it is impossible to tell.

For that reason only the first three tops and bottoms will be considered. When erosion is assumed to be a function of account size, the calculations are as follows:

A. $EF' = (110 - 90)/110 = 0.1818$
$EF' = (120 - 118)/120 = 0.0167$
$EF' = (122 - 98)/122 = 0.1967$

B.
$$\begin{array}{r} 0.1818 \\ 0.0167 \\ \underline{+0.1967} \\ 0.3952 \end{array}$$

$AE' = 0.3952/3 = \underline{\underline{0.1317}}$

C. Assume that the trader wishes to be 0.90 certain that the account size does not fall below the value calculated.

D. The value of Δ that corresponds to P in Table 11 in Appendix 3 is 2.302585.

E. $UE' = 2.302585 \cdot 0.1317$
$= 0.30325$

When erosion is assumed not to be a function of account size:

A. $EF'' = 100 - 90 = 20$
$EF'' = 120 - 118 = 2$
$EF'' = 122 - 98 = 24$

B.
$$\begin{array}{r} 20 \\ 2 \\ \underline{+\,24} \\ 46 \end{array}$$

$AE'' = 46/3 = \underline{\underline{15.3333}}$

C. Assume that the trader wishes to be 0.95 certain that the account size does not fall below the value calculated.

D. The value of Δ that corresponds to P in Table 11 in Appendix 3 is 2.995732.

E. $UE'' = 2.995732 \cdot 15.3333$
$= 45.9344$

Alternatively, the technique can be modified to estimate how long an erosion period a successfully managed account might have.

When the erosion period is of interest:

A. Calculate the individual erosion factors. These values are calculated by locating cumulative account value tops (TOP) and cumulative account bottoms (BOT). A top is a value that is both higher than the preceding and following values and does not fall between another top and the point where that top is next equaled or exceeded. A bottom is the lowest value between a top and the point where that top is next equaled or exceeded. In this case, it is the erosion period, not the dollar value, that is of interest. The erosion period is indicated by the subscript t which indicates how many market days have passed from an arbitrary starting point. In this case, the erosion factor (EF‴) is:

$$EF''' = BOT(t) - TOP(t)$$

B. Calculate the average erosion period (AE‴) as a measure of AE. AE‴ is the arithmetic average of EF‴. Naturally, the larger the sample size, the more reasonable the sample.

C. Select a value of P. P represents the probability that any given erosion value will *not* exceed a calculated value. If P equals zero, the calculated value will be zero. If P equals one, the calculated value will be infinite.

D. Find the value of Δ in Table 11 in Appendix 3 that corresponds to the value of P selected above.

E. Calculate the unacceptable erosion period (UE″′). The formula is:

$$UE''' = \Delta AE'''$$

For example, using the data above and numbering the days 1, 2, 3, and so forth:

A. $EF''' = 5 - 2 = 3$
$EF''' = 9 - 8 = 1$
$EF''' = 14 - 10 = 4$

B. 3
1
+4
———
8

$AE''' = 8/3 = 2.6667$

C. Assume that the trader wishes to be 0.90 certain that the erosion period does not exceed the time period calculated.

D. The value of Δ that corresponds to P in Table 11 in Appendix 3 is 2.302585.

E. $\text{UE}''' = 2.302585 \cdot 2.6667$
$= 6.1403$

Unfortunately, because the probabilities involved are not independent, the largest probable dollar erosion and the largest probable erosion period cannot be calculated simultaneously. Nor can the techniques above be used with the techniques in Chapter 8. There are, of course, more sophisticated measures, measures that allow for the dependencies involved, but they are too complex to discuss here.

Appendix Five

Growth and Deflation Estimation

Almost all traders measure their trading success by their account growth. Unfortunately, almost all traders use the wrong measure.

Most traders measure growth by calculating an unweighted *arithmetic* average of their account's growths and erosions. The arithmetic average is one of an infinite number of averages of which twenty or so are reasonably useful. It is the most widely used and most widely useful average. When the data are all of equal importance, an unweighted average is calculated; this is done, of course, by summing the data and dividing the resulting sum by the number in the sample.

This approach is correct if the growth rate does not vary, which is sometimes the case (e.g., savings accounts). Unfortunately, whenever there is any variability at all in the growth rate, this approach will overestimate the average growth. Consider, for example, an investment that doubled in value one year and then fell to half its value the next. The arithmetic average indicates that the investment grew by 1.25 a year. Thus:

$$\begin{array}{r} 2.0 \\ \underline{+0.5} \\ 2.5 \\ \underline{\div\ 2} \\ \underline{\underline{1.25}} \end{array}$$

But clearly the investment's value is unchanged two years later. There is no paradox here. An investment's growth rate must be measured by a *geometric* average. The geometric average is calculated by taking the product of the data, that is, by multiplying together all of the numbers in the sample and then taking the *N*th root of the resulting data, where *N* is equal to the sample size. Using the example above:

$$\begin{array}{r} 2.0 \\ \underline{\times 0.5} \\ \sqrt[2]{1.0} \\ \underline{\underline{1.0}} \end{array}$$

An easier approach is:

$$GA = \sqrt[t]{V(t)/V(0)}$$

where

$$\text{GA} = \text{the geometric average}$$

$$V(t) = \text{the value at the end of } t \text{ periods}$$

$$V(0) = \text{the value at time 0}$$

$$t = \text{the number of periods}$$

For example, if $V(t)$ = \$10,000, $V(0)$ = \$4000, and $t = 5$, then:

$$\text{GA} = \sqrt[5]{10{,}000/4000}$$

$$= \sqrt[5]{2.5}$$

$$= 1.2011$$

The importance of the geometric average depends on the variability of the growth rate. In fact, the larger the variability, the smaller the real growth rate will be as a proportion of the arithmetic growth rate (see Exhibit 47). This phenomena is known as variance slippage. The variance of a distribution is a measure of its dispersion; indeed, it is the distribution's standard deviation squared. The relationship between the geometric average, the arithmetic average, and the standard deviation can be found in the following approximation (where $\simeq$ indicates approximate equality):

$$\text{GA} \simeq \sqrt{\text{EX}^2 - \text{SD}^2}$$

For example,
if EX = 1.5 and SD = 1.05

$$\text{GA} \simeq \sqrt{1.5^2 - 1.05^2}$$

$$\simeq \sqrt{2.25 - 1.1025}$$

$$\simeq \sqrt{1.1475}$$

$$\simeq 1.0712$$

Unlike the arithmetic average, the geometric average cannot be used to average negative values. Theoretically, therefore, profits and losses should be proportional to the trader's trading capital. A value of zero would indicate that the trader has been ruined. Values below zero are theoretically impossible.

In fact, a trader can lose more than he or she commits to the market, but this is rare enough that the technique above will generally suffice. However, if the trader's profits are dependent on accepting extraordinary risks, the average should be proportional to the trader's total wealth. In this case, a value of zero indicates bankruptcy. Negative values are theoretically and legally impossible.

For budgeting purposes, it is occasionally necessary to know how quickly a given amount will grow or diminish, at a given growth or deflation rate, to another given amount. The number of time periods of growth or deflation can be calculated as follows:

$$t = \log\,[V(t)/V(0)]\,/\log\,(1 + \iota)$$

where ι = the interest or deflation rate; "log," of course, is the natural logarithm.

For example, if the trader wished to know how quickly \$5000 would grow into \$10,000 at a growth rate of 0.2 per time period, the calculations would be as follows:

$$t = \log\,(10{,}000/5000)/\log\,(1 + 0.2)$$

$$= \log\,(2)/\log\,(1.2)$$

$$= 0.3010/0.0792$$

$$= 3.8$$

On the other hand, if the trader wished to know how quickly \$10,000 would diminish to \$2000 at a 0.25 deflation rate, the calculations would be:

$$t = \log\,(2000/10{,}000)/\log\,[1 + (-0.25)]$$

$$t = \log\,(0.2)/\log\,(0.75)$$

$$t = 0.699/-0.1254$$

$$t = 5.3563$$

These techniques can and should be used instead of the popular rule of thumb that capital will double in the number of time periods equal to 72 divided by the interest rate expressed in percent form. When the rate is low, this popular technique will give reasonable answers. For example, according to this technique, capital invested at 0.09 will double in $\frac{72}{9} = 8.0$ time periods; the correct answer is 8.048.

Unfortunately, the technique in unusable during deflation or when the growth involves something other than one or more doublings. In addition, when the growth rates are high, the popular technique will seriously overestimate the time periods involved. The techniques presented here, which are scarcely more difficult, do not have these problems.

Index